COMING APART AT THE SEAMS

BIBLICALLY UNRAVELLING

THE EVILS OF

GREEK FRATERNITIES AND SORORITIES

BY

MINISTER FRED HATCHETT

© 1999, 2001, 2002 by
Frederic L. Hatchett.
All rights reserved.

No part of this book may be reproduced, stored in a retrieval system, or transmitted by any means, electronic, mechanical, photocopying, recording, or otherwise, without written permission from the author.

ISBN: 1-4033-1629-5 (E-book)
ISBN: 1-4033-1630-9 (Paperback)

This book is printed on acid free paper.

1stBooks – rev. 09/06/02

Unless otherwise noted, scripture quotations are from the King James Version of the Bible.

Scriptures taken from The Amplified Bible are designated by **(amp)**.

"Scripture taken from THE AMPLIFIED BIBLE, Old Testament copyright © 1965, 1987 by Zondervan Corporation. The Amplified New Testament copyright © 1958, 1987 by the Lockman Foundation. Used by permission."

A publication of Reprove, Rebuke and Restore Ministries
328 Summit Avenue
Raleigh, North Carolina 27603-2352
919/829-3513

DEDICATION

TO MY LORD AND SAVIOR JESUS CHRIST.

ACKNOWLEDGEMENTS

TO MY LOVING WIFE, AND THREE BOYS. APOSTLE DONALD Q. FOZARD, SR. SPECIAL THANKS TO R. DOWNS, T. MARKS, L. FLUONOY SR., MINISTER J. DAVIS, MINISTER L. WILLIAMS, DEACON M. NEWELL, T. BELL, MAX, AND ALL OTHER PROVIDERS OF INSPIRATION, GODLY WISDOM AND KNOWLEDGE, AND INTERCESSION BEFORE GOD.

COVER DRAWN BY: TERROD DAWKINS

TABLE OF CONTENTS

PREFACE xiii

PURPOSE xvii

CHAPTER 1 1
INTRODUCTION

CHAPTER 2 19
SECRECY

CHAPTER 3 50
PART 1
ORIGIN OF GREEK-LETTERED ORGANIZATIONS

PART 2 120
ORIGIN OF HAZING

PART 3 142
IDOLATRY

CHAPTER 4 156
PART 1
ARE YOU RELIGIOUS OR A CHRISTIAN?

PART 2 171
SCRIPTURAL ASSAULT OF
GREEK-LETTERED
ORGANIZATIONS

PART 3 292
THEOLOGICAL CONTRAST AND
COMPARISON

CHAPTER 5 346
THE CHURCH vs. FRATERNITIES
AND SORORITIES

CHAPTER 6 369
BEWARE OF FALSE PROPHETS
AND TEACHERS

CHAPTER 7 383
THE SPIRIT OF PREJUDICE

CHAPTER 8 392
THE TRUE ROLE OF
FRATERNITIES
AND SORORITIES IN THE
BLACK COMMUNITY:
WHAT ARE BLACK GREEK-
LETTERED ORGANIZATIONS
WORTH TO THEIR COMMUNITY
AND THEIR CULTURE?

CHAPTER 9 398
TESTIMONIES

CHAPTER 10 405
PART 1
WORDS OF ADVICE

PART 2 410
DENOUNCING YOUR
GREEK-LETTERED
ORGANIZATION

PART 3 423
WITNESSING

PART 4 448
CONCLUSION

PART 5 452
INVITATION

PART 6 454
THE CHALLENGE AND FINAL
COMMENTS

GLOSSARY 458

ENDNOTES 463

PREFACE

GREEK-LETTERED ORGANIZATIONS OR GLO'S HAVE BEEN IN THE U.S.A. FOR ABOUT 220 YEARS. THEY MAY HAVE DONE MANY GREAT DEEDS, BUT AT WHOSE EXPENSE? GREEK CHRISTIANS AND THEIR SUPPORTERS LOOK AT THEM IN TERMS OF THEIR BENEFITS TOWARD SOCIETY. UNFORTUNATELY, THEY IGNORE THE DESTRUCTION OF THEIR SOULS IN THEM INCLUDING THEIR OWN. GREEK-LETTERED ORGANIZATIONS NEGLECT THE SPIRITUALLY RIGHTEOUS THINGS ONLY TO INVITE AND OPEN DOORS TO SIN, ALLOWING SATAN TO COME AND GO AS HE PLEASES. THERE IS NO PRFIT IN SIN. ITS ONLY REWARD IS DEATH. GOOD WORKS AND A FORM OF GODLINESS (RELIGION) WERE USED BY GREEK-LETTERED ORGANIZATIONS AS AN APPEAL TO THE CHURCH AND SOCIETY TO SAY THAT, "LOOK, WE'RE NOT ALL THAT BAD." ONCE ACCEPTED BY THE CHURCH, GLO'S HAVE GAINED WIDESPREAD ACCEPTANCE WITHOUT EVER STOPPING THEIR OTHER UNGODLY ACTIVITIES. APOSTLES, PROPHETS, PASTORS, EVANGELISTS, TEACHERS, MINISTRIES, ELDERS, BISHOPS, DEACONS, AND MANY CHRISTIANS HAVE BEEN SUCKED UP INTO THE HIGH IDEAL, PHILANTHROPIC GLO'S. THE REVELATION OF GOD'S TRUTH THAT WILL BE GIVEN IN THIS BOOK IS GOING TO SHOCK MEMBERS, THOSE INTERESTED, CHURCH LEADERSHIP, AND THE GENERAL PUBLIC WHO REALLY HAVE NO FACTS ON THE SUBJECT OF GREEK-LETTERED ORGANIZATIONS (GLO'S). THE TRUTH WILL SET MANY FREE.

John 8:32- And ye shall know the truth, and the truth shall make you free.

JESUS WOULD HAVE NEVER JOINED A GLO, BEACAUSE HE NEVER KNEW SIN, OR COMITTED SIN.

I Peter 2:22 Who did no sin, neither was guile found in his mouth:

II Corinthians 5:21 For he hath made him to be sin for us, who knew no sin; that we might be made the righteousness of God in him.

The word "NO" means "NO" in these scriptures.

GREEK-LETTERED ORGANIZATIONS ARE FULL OF SINS THAT THEY CAN'T GET RID OF WITHOUT LOSING THEIR IDENTITY. GREEK-LETTERED ORGANIZATIONS WOULDN'T BE TRUE GREEK-LETTERED ORGANIZATIONS IF THEY DROPPED SOME OF THE SINFUL THINGS THEY DO. THEREFORE, GREEK-LETTERED ORGANIZATIONS WILL ALWAYS BE UNGODLY ORGANIZATIONS IN ONE WAY OR ANOTHER.

FRATERNIITIES AND SORORITIES TODAY ARE DESTROYING THE TRUE CHRISTIAN'S RELATIONSHIP WITH CHRIST. WITH THEIR FALSE DOCTRINES, FALSE gods, SECRECY, DECEPTION, AND FORM OF GODLINESS (i.e. doing good works, going to church, etc.), THEY LEAD MANY INTO PRESENT AND POSSIBLE ETERNAL DESTRUCTION. THE LEADERSHIP IN MANY CHURCHES HAVE NOT

STOOD UP TO THEM, EVEN AGREE WITH THEM, AND REALLY DON'T CARE ABOUT THE LOST SOULS THEY WERE CALLED TO OVERSEE. GREEK CHRISTIANS' ACCEPTANCE AS BEING TRUE CHRISTIANS MUST BE REPROVED AND REBUKED, SO THAT THEY CAN BE RESTORED TO FELLOWSHIP WITH CHRIST. TO THE SINNER, A DENUNCIATION WITHOUT A DECISION TO ACCEPT CHRIST AS LORD AND SAVIOR IS WORTHLESS CONCERNING YOUR ETERNAL LIFE. IT MAY SOOTHE YOUR CONSCIENCE IN THIS LIFE, BUT IT WON'T STOP THE JUDGMENT OF GOD CONCERNING YOUR ETERNAL LIFE.

PURPOSE

THE PURPOSE OF THIS BOOK IS **1.) TO PROVE** THAT **GREEK-LETTERED ORGANIZATIONS (GLO's)** ARE NOT OF GOD BASED ON BIBLICAL TRUTH, AND THAT TRUE CHRISTIANS SHOULD WILLFULLY SEPARATE FROM THEM. **2.) TO PROVIDE** A WITNESSING TOOL TO ALL CHRISTIANS THAT KNOW OTHERS, ESPECIALLY "PROFESSING" BROTHERS AND SISTERS IN CHRIST, WHO DESIRE TO BE OR ARE IN GLO's, BUT DON'T KNOW HOW TO EFFECTIVELY MINISTER TO THEM; **3.) TO WIN** SOULS TO CHRIST BY **RESTORATION OR SALVATION.**

GALATIANS 6:1 Brethren, if a man be overtaken in a fault, ye which are spiritual, **restore** such an one in the spirit of meekness; considering thyself, lest thou be tempted.

JOHN 3:3 Jesus said, verily, verily I say unto thee, except a man be **born again**, he cannot see the kingdom of God.

THESE 4 FOLLOWING SCRIPTURES SET THE TONE OF THE BOOK AS WELL AS ADD TO AND CONFIRM MY PURPOSE.

1.) **EPHESIANS 5:11(amp)** Take no part and have no fellowship with the fruitless deeds and enterprises of darkness, but instead [**let your lives** be so in contrast as to] **expose** and **reprove** and **convict** them.

2.) **II TIMOTHY 4:2(amp)** Herald and preach the Word! Keep your sense of urgency [stand by, be at hand and ready], whether the opportunity seems to be favorable or unfavorable. [Whether it is convenient or inconvenient, whether it is welcome or unwelcome, you as a preacher of the Word are to **show people in what way their lives are wrong**.] And convince them, **rebuking** and **correcting**, **warning** and **urging** and **encouraging them**, being unflagging and inexhaustible in patience and teaching.

3.) **GALATIANS 4:16(amp)** Have I then become your enemy for telling the truth to you and dealing with you plainly?

4.) **ACTS 19:11-20** And God wrought special miracles by the hand of Paul: So that from his body were brought unto the sick handkerchiefs or aprons, and the diseases departed from them, and the evil spirits went out of them. Then certain of the vagabond Jews, exorcists, took upon them to call over them which had evil spirits the name of the Lord Jesus, saying, We adjure you by Jesus whom Paul preacheth. And there were seven sons of ones Sce'va, a Jew, and chief of the priests, which did so. And the evil spirit answered and said, Jesus I know, and Paul I know, but who are ye? And the man whom the spirit was leaped on them, and overcame them, and prevailed against them, so that they fled out of that house naked and wounded. And this was known to all Jews and Greeks also dwelling at Ephesus; and fear fell on them all, and the name of the Lord Jesus was magnified. And many **believed** came, and **confessed and shewed their deeds**. Many of them also which used curious arts brought their books together, and **burned them** before all men: and they counted the price of them, and found it fifty thousand pieces of silver. So mightily grew the word of GOD and prevailed.

When the devil is defeated in your life, allow God's Word to take his place. At this point, you will be able to grow as a free Christian. You will no longer be in bondage to rituals and the god (**YOUR GLO**) you were serving. Confess and show your deeds. Come out of the secrecy you use to hide your shame, and the shameful things you perform behind close doors.

What I am about to ask of you next is very important. I would like all of those rituals, history books, paraphrenalia, and all other things associated with your GLO sent to me. I will pay for shipping and handling. I plan to do with all of those things what

<u>those in the above scripture did with their belongings. And you know what? You will be invited. It will be a televised event. All those who share my convictions will be invited to watch their bondage that died spiritually, be burned to death physically.</u>

THE FOUNDATION ON WHICH I CAN WRITE THIS BOOK ABOUT GLO's IS **BIBLICAL TRUTH, FIVE YEARS EXPERIENCE IN A GLO, AND TWO YEARS IN THE CLOSELY RELATED MASONIC ORDER. THE SOLE AUTHORITY** OF THIS BOOK **IS THE HOLY GHOST**.

I CAN TRUTHFULLY PROCLAIM THAT THIS BOOK IS FOUNDED UPON THE WORD OF GOD.

BEFORE I GIVE THE INTRODUCTION, I WANT TO GET STRAIGHT TO THE POINT WITH GLO's. I AM SICK AND TIRED OF YOUR CLAIMS OR INTENTION TO CLAIM A FOUNDATION ON CHRISTIAN PRINCIPLES. HERE'S A FEW EXCERPTS FROM SOME SORORITY AND FRATERNITY RITUALS AND HISTORY TO PROVE IT.

1.) "That is why <u>Minerva</u>, the Goddess of Wisdom, is our Sorority mentor." (DELTA SIGMA THETA SORORITY, INC., GRAND CHAPTER, MEMBERSHIP INTAKE PROGRAM, 1990, p.106.)

   Sigma Alpha Epsilon Ritual takes it a step further by clearly claiming <u>Minerva</u> to be the <u>Goddess</u> of their fraternity.

2.) Basileus: "Whence come ye, my friends, clothed as ye be and accompanied by these my true and tried brothers. Neophyte Commandant: 'From the outer chamber of darkness, into the Shekinah of **Light of Omega**.'" (OMEGA PSI PHI

FRATERNITY (Incorporated 1914), THE RITUAL, 1970, p.20.)

The secret motto of Sigma Alpha Epsilon is "Phi Alpha", which in the Greek is "Phonatas Adoxia". It means, **from darkness to light.**

3.) "**Faith** shall have to be manifested **in an unshakable belief in Kappa Alpha Psi, its** ideals, **its** purposes, **its** membership, its programs, and **its** forward movement." (William L. Crump, THE STORY OF KAPPA ALPHA PSI, A History Of The Beginning And Development Of A College Greek Letter Organization, 1911-1983, Third Edition, 1983, p.267.)

4.) Tau Kappa Epsilon states on the Internet that, "the mythological ideal or patron of Tau Kappa Epsilon is **Apollo,** one of the most important **of Olympian divinities.** The Grecian **god of music and culture, of light** and the ideals toward which all Tekes must constantly be striving. Typifying the finest development of manhood, the selection of **Apollo** is most appropriate." (TKEnet: TKE Symbols and Traditions http://ww.tke.org/tkesymb.shtml#Apollo)

Problem with #1 and #4 is **Exodus 20:3(amp)** You shall have no other gods before or **beside** me.

How does the Christian in these organizations justify having a relationship with another god.

Problem with #2 is **JOHN 1:9(amp)** There it was; the **true Light** [was then] coming into the world [the genuine, perfect, steadfast light] **that illuminates every person.**

The light that these two organizations and others claim to offer IS NOT the LIGHT of John 1:9.

Problem with #3 is **HEBREWS 11:6(amp)** But without faith it is impossible to please and be satisfactory to him. For whoever would come near to God must [necessarily] believe that God exists and that he is a rewarder of those who earnestly and diligently seek him [out].

The very means by which we are saved is given to another "savior". Kappa Alpha Psi has grossly spat in God's face.

All Greek-Lettered Organizations share these common characteristics. These are not the characteristics of a Christian foundation. These are their words compared with God's word. Why a fake god, a false light, and a vain faith? Why not Jesus Christ, the true and living God, the true light, and the only One in Whom we must put our faith to have eternal life. He is the only way to go from darkness to light. Any Christian! Right here and right now, whether this is your specific organization or not, should denounce!!!!!!

In all four of these quotes, the foul stench of idolatry can be easily detected.

BEFORE GOING ON, I WOULD LIKE TO DEFINE A FEW COMMON TERMS AND ABBREVIATIONS.

1.) GLO ('s)- GREEK-LETTERED ORGANIZATION(S)

GREEK CHRISTIAN- **ONE WHO CONFESSES JESUS CHRIST AS THEIR LORD AND SAVIOR AND BELONGS TO A GLO,** BUT ARE NOT TRUE CHRISTIANS BASED ON THEIR MEBERSHIP IN A GLO.

Notes- At the end of each chapter, there will be space to put any thoughts, words or specific pages that you want to keep in mind. Notes will be kind of like a personal index.

For very long chapters, the last page has plenty of space.

Notes

CHAPTER 1

Introduction

NOW YOU CAN SEE THAT I AM VERY SERIOUS ABOUT EXPOSING GLO's. LET US BEGIN ON THIS JOURNEY TO YOUR DENUNCIATION, A NEW OR RESTORED LIFE IN CHRIST, AND TO THOSE WHO WANT TO BE A BETTER WITNESS. LET'S START BY DEFINING A SECRET SOCIETY.

"A **secret society** is an association whose existence, membership, purpose, or ritual is not revealed to non-members." (Mark C. Carnes, Secret Societies, Encyclopedia Americana, Grolier, Inc., 1999, p.508.)

THE WAY THIS BOOK IS WRITTEN MAY SEEM UNNECESSARY AND REPETITIOUS, BUT YOU WOULD BE SURPRISED OF ALL THE REPITITIOUS EXCUSES I HEAR FROM "CHRISTIANS" THAT SAY IT'S OKAY TO BE IN A GREEK LETTERED ORGANIZATION WHICH IS A **SECRET SOCIETY**. THEY MAKE THE SAME EXCUSES WHEN PROTECTING THE GOODNESS OF GREEK-LETTERED ORGANIZATIONS. ONE WOULD ALSO BE SURPRISED HOW MANY TRUE CHRISTIANS ARE NOT INFORMED ABOUT THE FACTS ON SECRET SOCIETIES, AND ARE TOTALLY UNABLE TO GIVE ANOTHER CHRISTIAN CONCRETE **BIBLICAL** AND **PRACTICAL** PROOF THAT JOINING OR BEING A MEMBER OF A GLO IS SINFUL. ALL OF THE LIP SERVICE THEY GIVE TO BEING FOUNDED UPON CHRISTIAN PRINCIPLES IS NOT BASED ON THE WORD OF GOD. I WILL PROVE THIS IN CHAPTER 3 WITH THE PROOF COMING FROM THEIR OWN DOCUMENTS. ASK GREEK CHRISTIANS TO PROVE A CHRISTIAN FOUNDATION, NOT BY QUOTING A SINGLE SCRIPTURE,

FREDERIC L. HATCHETT

BUT BY OPENING UP THE WORD AND SHOWING YOU MANY SCRIPTURES. GREEK CHRISTIANS, ASIDE FROM THEMSELVES, ARE LEADING MANY TO BELIEVE THAT MEMBERSHIP WITH THEIR GLO GIVES ETERNAL LIFE WITH THEIR SWELLING WORDS AND **FLATTERY**. WHEN IN REALITY, GREEK CHRISTIANS AND THOSE THEY CONVINCE TO JOIN, ARE IN DANGER OF HELLFIRE.

JUDE 16(amp) These are inveterate murmurers (grumblers) who complain [of their lot in life], going after **their own** desires [controlled by their own passions]; their talk is boastful and arrogant, [and **they claim to**] admire men's persons and pay people flattering compliments to gain advantage.

MATTHEW 23:15 Woe unto you scribes and Pharisees, hypocrites! For ye compass sea and land to make one proselyte, and when he is made, ye make him twofold more the child of hell than yourselves.

IF GLO's COULD GIVE ETERNAL LIFE TO ITS MEMBERS, THEN THERE WOULD BE MORE THAN ONE WAY TO HEAVEN. DECEASED KAPPAS GO TO **DELPHI** WHEN THEY DIE, OMEGAS TO **THE GREAT BEYOND**, DELTAS GO TO THE **HAVEN OF REST**, BUT ONLY TRUE CHRISTIANS GO TO **HEAVEN**. THE BIBLE SAYS THAT JESUS IS THE ONLY WAY TO HEAVEN, AND SINCE NO GLO's PROFESS THIS, THE PLACES THEY MENTION CANNOT BE HEAVEN. THEREFORE, IT IS NOT POSSIBLE FOR THEM TO GO THERE. WHY WOULD A CHRISTIAN WANT TO BE A PART OF SUCH A GROUP? THERE ARE MANY REASONS, BUT SCRIPTURE ACCEPTS NONE. SINCE I AM ABLE TO PROVE THAT BY ORIGIN, GLO's ARE DEMONIC, THIS MEANS THAT THE MEMBERS ARE INCAPABLE OF REDEMPTION UNLESS THEY **REPENT, DENOUNCE, AND TOTALLY DISASSOCIATE** WITH GLO's, AND ALL MEMBERS OF THEM. **GOD DID NOT REDEEM THAT WHICH HE DID NOT DIE FOR. HE SHOWS US IN HIS WORD WHO HE REDEEMED AND DID NOT REDEEM.**

HEBREWS 2:15-18(amp) And also that He might deliver and completely set free those who through the [haunting] fear of death were held in bondage throughout the whole course of their lives. For, as we all know, He [Christ] **did not take hold of angels** [the fallen angels, to give them a helping and delivering hand], but **He did take hold of [the fallen] descendants of Abraham** [to reach out to them a helping and delivering hand]. So it is evident that it was essential that He **made like his brethren** in every respect, in order that He might become a merciful (sympathetic) and faithful High Priest in the things related to God, to make atonement and propitiation for the people's sins. For because He Himself [in His humanity] has suffered in being tempted (tried and tested), He is able [immediately] to run to the cry of (assist, relieve) those who are being tempted and tested and tried [and who therefore are being exposed to suffering].

ALL GLO'S WERE NEVER REDEEMED BY GOD (i.e. GOD DID NOT DIE FOR THEM, HAVE ANYTHING TO DO WITH THEM AND NEVER WILL, EXCEPT TO JUDGE THEM). **ALL MEMBERS WHO DO NOT DENOUNCE HAVE THE SAME PROBLEM.** ONLY A PERSON WHO WISHES TO SEPARATE FROM THEIR GLO CAN BE AMONG THE REDEEMED. ONLY MAN CAN BE REDEEMED. THE WORLD, THE CHURCH OR ANY OTHER ORGANIZATION HAS THE ABILITY IF GONE ASTRAY TO COMEBACK TO GOD THROUGH REPENTANCE OF THE TRUE CHRISTIANS (**II CHRONICLES 7:14**). GLO'S DO NOT FIT THIS CATEGORY, BECAUSE BY CHANGING THEY COULD NOT BE WHAT THEY ARE TODAY. THE DEVIL KNOWS THE **IMPOSSIBILITY** OF THESE GROUPS BEING MADE RIGHT WITH GOD WITHOUT CHANGING THEIR PRACTICES. SO THE DEVIL USES SECRECY, DECEPTION, AND LIES TO COVER UP HIS EVIL PLANS. THE DEVIL DECEIVES THE MEMBERS OF THESE ORGANIZATIONS BY TELLING THEM THEY CAN MAKE THE ORGANIZATION **APPEAR** SUITABLE BEFORE GOD AND MAN.

LUKE 16:13-15(amp) No servant is able to serve two masters; for either he will hate one and serve and love the other, or he will stand and be devoted to the one and despise the other. You cannot serve God and mammon (riches, or anything in which you rely) Now the Pharisees, who were covetous and lovers of money, heard all these things [taken together], and they begin to sneer at and ridicule and scoff at him. But he said to the, you are the ones who declare yourselves just and upright before men, but God knows your hearts. For what is exalted and highly thought of among men is detestable and abhorrent (an abomination) in the sight of God.

THEY USE RELIGION IN THE FORM OF CHRISTIANITY AS THE MAIN TOOL OF DECEPTION, AND IT IS SUCCEEDING AGAINST THE WEAK AND UNINFORMED CHRISTIANS AND SINNERS AS WELL. IF IT IS NECESSARY TO USE REPETITIOUS AND **OUT-OF-PLACE** EXPLANATIONS TO GET MY POINT ACROSS, THEN SO BE IT. THIS IS FOR THE SAKE OF THOSE REBELLIOUS "CHRISTIANS" AND IMPENITENT SINNERS WHO BELIEVE THEY CAN USE GOD'S WORD ANY WAY THEY WANT, NOT EVEN KNOWING THAT IT LEADS TO THEIR OWN DESTRUCTION.

II CORINTHIANS 4:2(amp) We have renounced disgraceful things (secret thoughts, feelings, desires and underhandedness, **the methods and arts that men hide through shame**); We refuse to deal craftily (to practice trickery and cunning) or to **adulterate or handle dishonestly the word of God**, but we state the truth openly (clearly and candidly). And so we commend ourselves in the sight and presence of God to every man's conscience.

II PETER 3:16-18(amp) Speaking of this as he does in all of his letters. There are some things in those [epistles of Paul] that are difficult to understand, which the ignorant and unstable twist and misconstrue to their own utter destruction, just as [they distort and misinterpret] the rest of the scriptures. Let me warn you therefore, beloved, that knowing these things beforehand, you should be on your guard, lest you be carried away by the error of lawless and wicked [persons and] fall from your own [present] firm condition [your own steadfastness or mind]. But grow in grace (undeserved favor, spiritual strength) and recognition and knowledge and understanding of our Lord and Saviour Jesus Christ (The Messiah). To him [be] glory (honor, majesty, and splendor) both now until the day of eternity. Amen (so be it)!

THE BOLD TYPE IN **II CORINTHIANS 4:2** IS SO OBVIOUSLY CHARACTERISTIC OF GLO's. ANY GREEK CHRISTIAN WHO CAN DENY THIS; **I DARE THEM TO PROVE IT BY EXPOSING THEIR SECRET BOOKS AND CEREMONIES. SHOW THE WORLD THE HAZING AND EVERYTHING ELSE THAT YOU ALL DO IN PRIVATE.** TO ALL THE MEMBERS OF GLO's WHO HIDE BEHIND THE TITLES OF MINISTER, DEACON, PASTOR, PROPHET AND OTHERS: FOOL IS ONLY ONE OF THE NAMES THE WORD OF GOD CAN GIVE YOU. ALL WHO LOOK UP TO THE TITLES, DO NOT BE FOOLED BY THEM. LOOK TO JESUS FOR THE TRUTH, NOT MAN. THAT IS WHY THIS BOOK HAS SO MANY SCRIPTURES. IT IS CLEAR TO SEE THAT I AM NOT CLAIMING MY OWN WISDOM AND KNOWLEDGE. I TYPED MOST OF THE SCRIPTURES IN HERE, SO YOU WOULDN'T HAVE TO STOP READING TO FIND THE THEM.

I BELIEVE THAT ANYONE WHO READS THIS BOOK WILL HAVE A DIFFERENT OUTLOOK ON **ALL SECRET SOCIETIES, BUT PRIMARILY GLO's**. ONE WILL **SEE** THAT THEY ARE ACTUALLY WOLVES IN SHEEP'S CLOTHING.

MATTHEW 7:15 Beware of false prophets who come to you dressed as sheep, but inside they are devouring wolves.

FREDERIC L. HATCHETT

THIS BOOK MAINLY CONCENTRATES ON REVEALING THE SEEN AND **UNSEEN** FACTS ABOUT GREEK FRATERNITIES AND SORORITIES; BECAUSE THERE IS SO LITTLE INFORMATION THAT **PUBLIC** CAN SEE OR UNDERSTAND. FOR EXAMPLE, HOW WOULD SOMEONE KNOW THAT AKA'S SWEAR AN OATH TO MAKE THEIR SORORITY, **SUPREME** IN SERVICE, OR THAT THE **god** OF DELTA SIGMA THETA AND SIGMA ALPHA EPSILON IS **Minerva**? IN THIS INTRODUCTION, I WANT ALL THE READERS TO GET A CLEAR UNDERSTANDING THAT GLO's ARE EVIL IN MORE WAYS THAN ONE. THE DEVIL TEMPTS US THROUGH USING THREE METHODS: THE LUST OF THE FLESH, THE LUST OF THE EYES, AND THE PRIDE OF LIFE, AS HE HAS ALWAYS DONE TO US. SATAN, THROUGH GLO'S, USES ALL THREE. IN THESE THREE WAYS, THERE ARE MANY AVENUES. FOR GLO's, THEY ARE FORNICATION, WITCHCRAFT, UNFORGIVENESS, **HATRED**, **PREJUDICE**, **UNEQUAL YOKING**, **IDOLATRY**, GREED, LOVE OF THE WORLD, **HAZING**, WORLDY PARTYING, **PRIDE**, AND COVETOUSNESS JUST TO NAME **A FEW**.

THE BIBLE SAYS IN,

MATTHEW 7:13-14 Enter ye in at the straight gate: for wide is the gate, and broad is the way, that leadeth to **destruction**, and **many** there be which **go in there at**: Because straight is the gate, and narrow is the way, which leadeth unto life, and **few** there be that **find it**.

REMEMBER THAT ALL PEOPLE WILL NOT ACCEPT THE TRUTH OF YOUR WITNESS. DO NOT WORRY; JUST MOVE ON, BECAUSE THERE IS A WILLING SOUL DESIRING TO BE LIKE JESUS EVEN IF IT MEANS DENOUNCING THEIR BELOVED GLO. THERE ARE MANY PEOPLE IN A GLO WHO REALLY WANT TO KNOW, **"CAN I DO BOTH AND HAVE ETERNAL LIFE"**? I ASKED A MAN WHO HAD BEEN IN OMEGA PSI PHI FRATERNITY FOR 21 YEARS, AND FOUNDED THE CHAPTER AT N.C. STATE UNIVERSITY. ON THAT CHAPTER'S 20th YEAR ANNIVERSARY, THE FOUNDER WAS NOWHERE TO BE FOUND. THEIR FOUNDER/SHEPHERD WAS GONE. "WHY DID YOU

DENOUNCE"? I ASKED. HIS ANSWER WAS, "I WANTED ETERNAL LIFE". I COULD ONLY SAY ONE WORD, "AMEN". THIS MAN **KNEW** THAT HE COULD NOT DO BOTH AND DID SOMETHING ABOUT IT. **HE GOT SAVED, DENOUNCED THE FRATERNITY, AND IS WITNESSING TO OTHER BROTHERS.** THIS DISPELLS THE THEORY THAT YOU HAVE TO JOIN A GLO TO BE A LIGHT OR WITNESS TO THE PEOPLE IN THE GLO YOU JOIN. BESIDES, THAT IS BEING A RESPECTOR OF PERSONS. THIS IS JUST A PIOUS EXCUSE TO NUMB AN UNHOLY DESIRE. MY CONCERN ABOUT THIS BOOK IS THE SAME AS GOD'S; THAT THEY SEE THE TRUTH AND REPENT. GOD HAS ALREADY APPROVED IT. ALL I AM AWAITING IS THE ACHIEVEMENT OF WHAT IS WRITTEN IN THE **PURPOSE.** IF A MEMBER OF A GLO IS NOT SAVED, WITNESS THE LORD FIRST TO THEM, THEN WAIT FOR THE HOLY SPIRIT TO WORK ON THEM, AND OPEN A DOOR TO DISCUSS THE EVILS OF GLO's. USE EXTREME CAUTION NOT TO ATTACK THE GLO FIRST, BUT IF YOU DO, **QUOTE THE WORD OF GOD EVERY CHANCE YOU GET.** QUOTE SCRIPTURES THAT DIRECTLY REFUTE THE GREEK CHRISTIAN'S STAND THAT THEY CAN BELONG TO A GLO AND BE A TRUE CHRISTIAN AT THE SAME TIME. THE SCRIPTURES ARE **AMOS 3:3, II CORINTHIANS 6:14-18, PSALM 1:1, I CORINTHIANS 15:33, I KINGS 18:21, JOSHUA 24:1-16, 22-24** AND **EXODUS 20:3.** HAVE THIS BOOK WITH YOU, BECAUSE IN IT THERE IS A DETAILED CHAPTER AND OUTLINE ON WITNESSING. WHEN YOU GIVE THE WORD, THEY CAN ONLY FIGHT GOD. LET THEM ATTACK YOU ALL THEY WANT TO, THE SEED HAS BEEN PLANTED. THEY WILL USE EVERY DEVILISH ATTACK. DON'T FALL FOR IT. TRUE CHRISTIAN!! YOU ALREADY KNOW THE TRUTH. GOD'S WORD AND HIS WISDOM IS ALL YOU CAN OFFER.

FREDERIC L. HATCHETT

PAUL SAYS TO THE COLOSSIANS IN,

COLOSSIANS 2:8, 18, 23(amp) 8 Beware lest any man spoil you through philosophy and vain deceit, after the **traditions of men**, after the rudiments of the world (or the **superiority of faith in the world**) and **not** after Christ (or **faith in Christ**). 18 Let **no man** beguile you of your reward in a **voluntary humility** and worshipping of angels, intruding into those things which he hath not seen, vainly puffed up by his fleshly mind. 23 Such [practices] **have** indeed the **outward appearance [that popularly passes] for wisdom**, in promoting self-rigor of devotion and **delight in self-humiliation** and **severity of discipline of the body**, but they are of **no value** in checking the indulgence of the flesh (the lower nature). [Instead, **they do not honor God** but **serve only to indulge the flesh**.]

This voluntary humility or **self-abasement** gives permission to be paddled, humiliated, mocked, and scorned **just to wear some Greek letters**. Their principles come from the Greek philosophical and religious systems (rudiments of the world), NOT CHRISTIANITY, as you will see later IN CHAPTER 3, principles such as manhood, scholarship, fidelity, friendship, brotherhood and sisterhood, and service are redefined according to the GLO's standard. These are to be revered and followed by all members. I agree that ALL of these are admirable and worthy to do, **but not as they are defined by GLO's**, but **only** according to the Word of God. They use them in dealing with aspects of the **natural (unsaved)** man, not the **spiritual, saved (Christlike)** man. GLO's define their attributes according to the way Ancient Greek, Egyptian, and Babylonian false religious systems defined them. All are **demonic in origin. Without a relationship with Jesus,**

manhood becomes nothing more than your gender. **Scholarship** becomes nothing more than just a piece of paper on the wall and **stuff** in your head. **Fidelity** is nothing more than how well you remain faithful to the devil, and **friendship** is nothing more than a relationship with the world. **Brotherhood and sisterhood** are just the words of an oath, and **service** is nothing more than having only treasures laid upon the earth.

I JOHN 2:15(amp) Do not love or cherish the world or the things that are in the world, if anyone loves the world, love for the Father is not in him.

JAMES 4:4(amp) You [are like] unfaithful wives [having illicit love affairs with the world and breaking your marriage vow to God! Do you not know that being the world's friend is being God's enemy? So whoever chooses to be a friend of the world takes his stand in being an enemy of God.

Where is **salvation**? In **Jesus Christ** ONLY (**ACTS 4:12**). Whose **Blood saves**? It's **Jesus Christ's** Blood (**REVELATION 1:5**). Who gives you **joy unspeakable**? It's in **Jesus Christ** (**I PETER 1:7-8**). Whose **peace** do you have? **Christ's** peace (**PHILIPIANS 4:7**). How you know God **loves** (AGAPÉ) you? **Christ died** on the cross for you (**ROMANS 5:8**), who **justified** you? **Jesus Christ** (**ROMANS 4:24-25**). Who **reconciled** you to GOD? **Christ's** through His Blood (**II CORINTHIANS 5:18-19**).

These terms may be a part of Greek-Lettered Organizations, but not through Jesus Christ, because He is not a part of their **foundation/origin. Therefore, They cannot be Christ-centered, nor are they able to be founded upon Christian principles.**

If founded in Christ, they would have been exhibiting the above attributes from the start, and would have never adopted hazing, secrecy, unequal yoking, etc. Their history books would be full of testimonies of what **God has done** and **not what they have done themselves.** GLO'S have seriously misled people astray from true Christianity with their false rhetoric and hiding behind their cloak of secrecy. The truth of God's Word will say "DENOUNCE", but how you respond is the key to your eternal life.

HEBREWS 4:12 (amp) For the word that God speaks is alive and full of power [making it active]; it is sharper than any two-edged sword, penetrating to dividing line of breath of life (soul) and [the immortal] spirit, and of joints and marrow [of the deepest parts of our nature].

The Word of God is going to strip off their cloak and expose their false rhetoric, so that many innocent souls will not be devoured before their time. There will be no more excuses for the **already saved** that have read to this point to continue in their GLO. Go to the chapter on denouncing your GLO, and do it before you die. God's grace is no good for one who is in hell.

Did you know that GLO's, and all secret societies are CULTS AND OCCULT organizations? Should Christians really be involved with or members of them? **NO!** Should Christians even be alarmed about their increasing acceptance in the church? **YES!** Should Christians belong to them? **NO!** Should Christians *haze* or allow themselves to be *hazed*? **NO! Why all the secrecy? Because darkness cannot exist in or understand the LIGHT.** If the organizations are **so great as they boast themselves to be**, why not give anyone access to the secrets before initiation so they can come out of darkness? Don't you (GLO's) want everyone to go to heaven? It's **because they know and the devil knows they practice ungodly (non-Christian) things that they would rather keep secret.** What do you have that's worth keeping secret? **YOUR LIES AND DECEPTION!**

Being used by the Holy Spirit, I have done some extensive research and study, used testimonies, and other resources, in order to uncover the evil behind these organizations. May I say that, "my labor was not in vain". I found that their **ORIGINS, SYMBOLISM and TRADITIONS are rooted** in ancient Babylonian, Egyptian and Greek culture. Along with The fact that they **jealously withhold secrets, blasphemously contradict God's Word, purposefully disregard and deny many of Christ's doctrines** proves them to be **CULTS** AND of the **OCCULT**. They claim to be biblically based; yet there is none or very little mention of the six foundational principles of Christ, **AS DEFINED IN SCRIPTURE**, which every Christian needs to grow spiritually.

HEBREWS 6:1-2 THEREFORE leaving the principles of the doctrine of Christ, let us go on unto perfection; not laying again the foundation of repentance from the dead works, and of faith toward God, Of the doctrine of baptisms, and of laying on of hands, and of resurrection from the dead, and of eternal judgment.

This is why so many people in these organizations including Christians are so lost and deceived. Numbers 5 and 6 are mentioned by GLO's, but not according to the Word of God. Since they are not, all that they have built upon is worthless (dead works being the principles of their organizations), because their foundation is worthless. **Now, not because I have decided it, but because God has decreed that it is the time to EXPOSE (SECRETS, WRITTEN AND <u>UNWRITTEN</u>) Greek-lettered organizations for what they really are and not what they seem to be, by hiding behind their veils of secrecy. Dead works** are the man-made rites, customs, beliefs, and good works that we perform believing they will earn us favor of God and an entrance into His Kingdom. They are based on the traditions of the elders rather than on Scripture and are futile attempts to work out our own salvation hoping that God will approve. Young Christians are sucked in by their appearance of righteousness and flattering words. Young Christians need to understand that when they emphasize their works(pride and vainglory), they are trying to make themselves more acceptable and presentable to God. When they flatter you with words, give them the Word of God. When they say they are founded upon Christian principles, make them prove it according to the Word. DO NOT LET THEM OFF THE HOOK. Let them know that the only thing that allows us to come into the presence of God is **the WORK of Jesus** (i.e. **His shed BLOOD).**

MATTHEW 15:3,6,8 But he answered and said unto them, Why do ye also transgress the commandment of God by your tradition? And honour not his father or his mother, he shall be free, Thus have ye made the commandment of God of none effect by your tradition. This people draweth nigh unto me with **their mouth**, and honoureth me with **their lips**: but **their heart** is far from me.

THE TRADITIONS OF THE ELDERS,

COMING APART AT THE SEAMS

MARK 7:7-9 Howbeit **in vain do they worship me**, teachings for doctrines the commandments of men. For laying aside the commandment of God, ye hold the tradition of men, as the washing of pots and cups: and many other such like things ye do. And he said unto them, Full well ye **reject the commandment of God**, that ye may keep your own tradition.

ROMANS 2:29 But he is a Jew, which is one **inwardly**; and circumcision is that of the heart, in the spirit, and not in the letter, whose praise is not of men, but of God.

JOHN 5:44 How can we believe, which receive honour one of another, and seek not the honour that cometh from God only?

Pledges and new members are first pre-brainwashed by the older brainwashed members to keep and uphold their organization's traditions. These are the doctrines and commandments of men found in their rituals and history books which in themselves reject the commandments of God. GLO's and their members are out to please man not God. If they operated by faith, they would succeed in pleasing God. Sadly, faith in God is one of the essentials that Greek Christians do not possess. Without faith, it is impossible to please God. Evil trees bring forth evil fruit. Members are even fooled into thinking that eternal life can be achieved by excellent **service** to their respective group. Only the devil could be the author of such deception, and by this we clearly see that any Christian in this organization is breaking the covenant they made with Jesus according to,

ROMANS 10:9-10(amp) Because if you acknowledge and confess with your lips that Jesus is Lord and in your heart believe (adhere to, trust in, and rely on the truth) that God raised him from the dead, you will be saved.

FREDERIC L. HATCHETT

For with the heart a person believes (adhere to, trust in, and relies on Christ) and so is justified (declared righteous, acceptable to God) and with the mouth he confesses (declares openly and speaks out freely his faith) and confirms [his] salvation.

They confessed by faith that eternal life is in Jesus only.

As I claimed before, these are **occult** organizations, and now I will prove it by definition.

Occult- available only to the initiate, or secret. (Copyright 1997 by Houghton Mifflin Company. Reproduced by permission from *The American Heritage College Dictionary, Third Edition*)

This definition gives anyone, especially a Christian, all the proof they need to see what a GLO is **by nature**. Both characteristics are what GLO's do. Any Christian who honestly reads this definition and remains in or joins a GLO is disobedient to God. To obey or not to obey, determines a life spent in heaven or hell. Secrecy is that element which attracts the man. This attraction is a witchcraft spirit causes this attraction by **manipulation** of the human mind. The outward appearance is for some reason often overlooked, because of the inner desire to know the secret knowledge. Hey Christian!! Why would you, having the mind of Christ, the Word of God, the Holy Spirit, and **free** access to God's throne need some organization's knowledge that keeps it from everyone else? God gives His wisdom freely to all that ask without rebuking them or making them earn it. I asked a sister in Christ why she didn't join a GLO. Her response was, "one day I saw them doing something that I knew was not of God, and left it alone." The something she saw the GLO's doing was a party. CHRISTIANS IT IS TIME TO BE ALERT. STOP FLIRTING WITH THE DANGER OF YOUR

LOSING ETERNAL LIFE. DO NOT ALLOW THE DESIRES OF YOUR HEART CAUSE YOU TO IGNORE THE WILES OF THE DEVIL. **SATAN LOVES TO CONCEAL TRUTH(keep secret) BY USING HIS PERMITTED SUPERNATURAL AUTHORITY**. Satan does this best by revealing much truth with a little error. Read:

PSALM 91:9-12(amp) Because you have made the Lord your refuge, and the Most High your dwelling place, There shall no evil befall you, nor any plague or calamity come your tent. For He will give His angels (especial) charge over you to accompany and defend and preserve you in all your ways **(of obedience and service)**. They shall bear you up on their hands, lest you dash your foot against a stone.

Now read,

MATTHEW 4:5-7(amp) 5 Then the devil took Him into the holy city and placed Him on a turret (pinnacle, gable) of the temple sanctuary. 6 And he said to Him, If you are the Son of God, throw Yourself down; for it is written, He will give His angels charge over you, and they will bear you up on their hands, lest you strike your foot against a stone. 7 Jesus said to him, On the other hand, it is **written** also, You shall not tempt, test thoroughly, or try exceedingly the Lord your God.

The devil purposely leaves out the highlighted scripture in Psalms when talking to Jesus. Jesus did not give His own opinion, He said, it is written!!!.

Here is another example of the devil's trickery.

GENESIS 2:16-17(amp) And the Lord God commanded the man, saying, You may freely eat of every tree of the garden; But of the tree of the knowledge of good and evil and blessing and calamity you shall not eat, for in the day that you eat of it **you shall surely die**.

GENESIS 3:1-5(amp) Now the serpent was more subtle and crafty than any living creature of the field which the Lord God had made. And he (Satan) said to the woman, Can it really be that God has said, You shall not eat from every tree of the garden? And the woman said to the serpent, we may eat the fruit from the trees of the garden, Except the fruit from the tree which is in the middle of the garden. But the serpent said to the woman, **You shall not surely die**, For God knows that in the day you eat of it your eyes will be opened, and you will be like God, knowing the difference between good and evil and blessing and calamity.

Can you see the craftiness of the devil?? Jesus also says in **MATTHEW 22:29** that our problem is a lack of knowledge of the scriptures which will also cause us to have a lack of knowledge of our enemy, Satan. He fooled Adam and Eve, but he couldn't fool Jesus. One drop of poison (lie) or form of godliness is all the GLO needs to deceive initiates. The devil uses the spirit of error to achieve this goal through GLO's.

I JOHN 4:6(amp) We are (children) of God. Whoever is learning to know God (progressively to perceive, recognize, and understand God by observation and experience, and to get an ever-clearer knowledge of Him) listens to us; and he who is not of God does not listen or pay attention to us. By this we know (recognize) the Spirit of Truth and the spirit of error.

Pure water (truth) is no longer pure when 1 drop of poison is in it. Instead it is poisonous water (evil/error)- **No lie is of the truth,**

I JOHN 2:21b. I have not written unto you because ye know not the truth, but because ye know it, and that no lie is of the truth.

Bottom line: There is no middle ground, straddling the fence, or **compromise** with God. **You are either with the GLO's and separated from God or with God and separated from the Greeks.** The occult rituals of GLO's are breaking the rule of NO COMPROMISING with God. Any form of ritual activity signifies worship of a deity. All **except** the ones set down by God and the Lord Jesus are **occult and idolatrous.** So "Greeks," who are you worshipping? It's not God the Father, God the Son, and God the Holy Spirit. **Words** such as cult, occult, secrecy, and works; **characteristics** such as mixing Greek mythology, philosophy, and religion with Christianity; and **practices** such as hazing and idolatry are definitely found in today's Greek-lettered organizations. None of these words, practices, or characteristics meet the approval of Jesus. Anyone desiring to be in a GLO should seriously consider the dangers both **spiritual and physical**. Your life ought to speak for who you are, and it does with GLO's and their members.

What they are (**characteristics**), what they say (**words**), and what they do (**practices**) are ungodly, not just as a group, but individually as well. How and Why would a Christian want to be a part of an organization that does not respect and honor Jesus? They are not true Christians is the answer.

Notes

CHAPTER 2

SECRECY

Secrecy is the most vital weaponry of GLO's (Greek-Lettered Organizations). With it, they can deceive, **manipulate, intimidate, dominate,** coerce, LIE, and hide unrighteousness (physically or spiritually). You see I know that when GLO members see words like domination or intimidation, they will think, physical hazing, but this is not always the case. Secrecy has many bed partners: deception, manipulation, lying, dishonesty, and many other negative words share a friendly relationship with secrecy. Whenever you see these words, and others like them, think ungodly secrecy. Although GLO's do give their secrets to the initiates only, true revelation is when it is free to all. To the Christian witness: many scriptural challenges can be made concerning secrecy. Allow the Holy Ghost to show you how to contradict the gainsayers. A Greek member will plead the fifth in a heartbeat. Remember that a common argument Greek Christians will use is the similarities of themselves to other organizations. <u>You remind them that their eternal life is not based on what others do, but what God's Word says.</u> They believe you are attacking them, because you are attacking what they belong to. The same happened to Jesus, John the Baptist, the Apostles, etc. So you should not expect anything less.

Secrecy is how **cults** and **occult** organizations thrive. In chapter 3 Part 1, I will show that GLO's are descendants of the Babylonian Mystery or Cult system, which used secrecy. The next quote is a witness to this fact.

"their (Babylonian Cults) primary object was to introduce **privately**, by **little and little**, under the **seal of secrecy** and the **sanction of an oath**, what it would not have been **safe** all at once and openly to propound. It was a matter, therefore, of **necessity, if idolatry were to be brought in**, and especially such foul idolatry as the Babylonian system contained in its bosom, that it should be done **stealthily and in secret.**" (THE LATE REV. ALEXANDER HISLOP, THE TWO BABYLONS OR PAPAL WORSHIP: Proved to be THE WORSHIP OF NIMROD AND HIS WIFE, LOIZEUAX BROTHERS, INC., AMERICA, SECOND AMERICAN EDITION, 1959, pp.5&7, Adapted.)

The GLO's **did and still do** these things the same exact way. Knowing they would not be accepted only as a secret group, GLO's adopted their so-called, "Foundation on Christian principles." Being a member of two secret groups enables me to cut through a GLO's deception. I want to look at secrecy from a biblical perspective and see for yourself that operating in secrecy is not scriptural and useless, because God will reveal all that is hidden, even the secret thoughts (**ROMANS 2:16**). Matters of privacy are in no way to be confused with the secrecy that GLO's practice. If matters of privacy were the same as GLO secrecy, then their natures would be the same. Remember, many things are based on being able to see with spiritual eyes. Matters of privacy ALWAYS consider what's best for all parties involved. Question to consider is,

1.) <u>Do I have the **right**</u> to keep something secret?

2.) <u>Should I</u> keep something secret?

COMING APART AT THE SEAMS

3.) Will what I keep secret <u>endanger</u> the spiritual, emotional and/or physical life of **others** or **myself**?

As you will see in this chapter and throughout this book, the secrecy that GLO's practice will endanger one's spiritual, emotional, and physical life. Here is the perfect example of their hypocrisy concerning their secrets. Greeks tell people to research the organization they wish to join to know what they are getting into. This would be great advice if it were sincere. You see Greeks will never give you ALL of what you want to know (i.e. the secrets). So how can one do the complete and thorough research they need to without ALL the information? It's like an abortion clinic showing a woman an ultrasound of her baby minutes before they are going to kill it. It would defeat the purpose of what they are supposed to be doing. So you Greeks who fake, the "know us before you join us" routine, stop lying. You all let them know what you want them to know. Christians! Why would you want to even be associated with a bunch of liars.

Dear Christian,
If you **knew** that a Greek god was the god of the sorority or fraternity you were going to join, would you? If you **knew** that you had to take on the identity of a god or goddess to join, would you?

When you know these things before hand, at least you have all the information. Then the decision is truly yours and not one based on ignorance. This is how they **truly intend** for your decision to be made. Do you want to be ignorant?

FREDERIC L. HATCHETT

"The power of sin is secrecy"

(Roosevelt Hunter at Honor Bound Men's Conference at Brownsville Assembly of God in Pensacola, Florida on June 3, 1999. It was received from Ezekiel318@aol.com on 06/08/99.)

GLO's USE SECRECY TO ACCOMPLISH MANY TASKS. GLO's USE SECRECY TO FEND OFF ITS ACCUSERS. HERE'S HOW THEY DO IT.

QUESTION- I HEARD THAT YOU DELETE JESUS OUT OF SCRIPTURES IN YOUR RITUAL?

REPLIES!
1.) HOW DO YOU KNOW? YOU HAVEN'T READ OUR RITUAL.
2.) IT'S NONE OF YOUR BUSINESS.
3.) WHAT DIFFERENCE DOES IT MAKE?
4.) NO WE DON'T! YES THEY DO. I HAVE MANY RITUALS WHERE JESUS IS NOT MENTIONED. THEY LIE.
5.) THEY EVEN TELL YOU TO GO TO THE LIBRARY OF CONGRESS

TO FIND OUT; ALREADY AWARE THAT THEIR RITUALS ARE NOT THERE TO BE FOUND.

ALL REPLIES WILL BE **EVASIVE**, **DECEPTIVE**, OR **OUTRIGHT LIES**. I HAVE THE E-MAILS TO PROVE IT. <u>E-MAIL ME ANYTIME AND I WILL SEND THEM TO YOU</u>. THEY HAVE SECRECY ON THEIR SIDE ALLOWING THEM TO COMMIT SIN UNAWARES TO THE OUTSIDER.

If you are a Christian witness, expect these types of answers.

A Chosen Generation Campus Ministry (N.C. State University) sponsored the forum, "Biblical Perspectives of Greek Fraternities and Sororities. The speaker, a student in the Advanced Apologetics Class of Hosanna Bible College at Mount Zion Christian Church, Durham, N.C., said that secrecy is not of God, and neither was it his intention. She is right, and has three scriptures to support her claim.

MATTHEW 10:26-27 So have no fear of them; for nothing is concealed that will not be revealed, or kept secret that will not become known. **What I say to you in the dark, tell in the light; and what you here whispered in the ear, proclaim upon the housetops.**

JOHN 18:20(amp) Jesus answered him, I have always taught in a synagogue and in the temple

[area], where the Jews [habitually] congregate (assemble); and **I have spoken nothing secretly.**

ACTS 26:26 For the king knoweth of these things, before whom I also speak freely: for I am persuaded that none of these things are hidden from him; for this thing was not done in a corner.

They all show that Jesus and true Christians do not practice secrecy. It also denounces the **intentional** keeping of secrets, and promises that all things that we try to keep secret will be revealed. The question from the audience (A professing "Christian" and member of Alpha Kappa Alpha Sorority) was the following scripture about what she thought to be **"secrecy",** as practiced by GLO's, was the same as Jesus speaks of in the Bible. She is wrong. This type of secrecy is not intended to be kept a secret, but to be rewarded openly by God.

MATTHEW 6:4-6 And when thou prayest, thou shalt not be as the hypocrites are: for they love to pray standing in the synagogues and the corners of the streets, **that they may be seen of men**. Verily I say unto you, They have their reward. But thou, when thou prayest, enter into thy closet, and when thou hast shut the door, pray to thy Father which is **in secret**; and thy Father which seeth **in secret** shall reward thee **openly**.

The scripture is not even talking about secrecy as it relates to concealment **never to be known**. A bank robber would prefer no cameras and no other security at a robbery. He will do everything he can to conceal his identity. GLO's will do anything to conceal their secrets which would reveal their TRUE identity. Those who twist the scriptures to **support their beliefs**, and **defend their actions** are **unlearned and unstable in the Word.**

COMING APART AT THE SEAMS

II Peter 3:16-18(amp) Speaking of this as he does in all of his letters. There are some things in those [epistles of Paul] that are difficult to understand, which the ignorant and unstable twist and misconstrue to their own utter destruction, just as [they distort and misinterpret] the rest of the Scriptures. Let me warn you therefore, beloved, that knowing these things beforehand, you should be on your guard, lest you be carried away by the error of lawless and wicked (persons and) fall from your own (present) firm condition (your own steadfastness of mind). But grow in grace (undeserved favor, spirit strength) and recognition and knowledge and understanding of our Lord and Savior Jesus Christ (the Messiah). To Him (be) glory (honor, majesty, and splendor) both now and to the day of eternity. Amen (so be it)!

What does God command of True Christians?

II TIMOTHY 2:15(amp) Study and be eager and do your utmost to present yourself to God approved (tested by trial), a workman who has no cause to be ashamed, correctly analyzing and accurately dividing [rightly handling and skillfully teaching] the word of truth.

This was clearly not performed by this member of Alpha Kappa Alpha.

GLO's **purposely adulterate the Word of God** to soothe the initiates as well as their own conscience to the point of not accepting the obvious truth even when they know the truth. They reject the truth willfully.

II CORINTHIANS 4:1-4(amp) Therefore, Since we do hold and engage in this ministry by the mercy of God [granting us favour, benefits, opportunities, and especially salvation], we do not get discouraged (spiritless and despondent with fear) or become faint with weariness and exhaustion. **We have renounced disgraceful ways (secret thoughts,** feelings, desires and underhandedness, **the methods and arts that men hide through shame); we refuse to deal craftily (to practice trickery and cunning) or to adulterate or handle dishonestly the word of God, but we state the truth openly (clearly and candidly).** And so we commend ourselves in the sight and presence of God to every man's **conscience.** But even if our gospel (the glad tidings) also be hidden (obscured and covered up with a veil that hinders the knowledge of God), **it is hidden** [only] to those who are perishing and obscured [only] to **those who are spiritually dying** and veiled [only] to those who are lost.

Unfortunately, many Christians are not able to answer this question about secrecy or many other excuses, but praise God for the answer in His Word. The Greek **translation** of secrecy and **context** of the scripture clearly shows the necessity of inner righteousness. **This righteousness is not secret, for it is manifested by the life of that person before man and that life gives glory to the Father.**

MATTHEW 5:16 Let your light so shine before men, that they may see your good works, and glorify your Father which is in heaven.

The translation for secrecy in the original Greek manuscripts in **MATTHEW 6:4,6** is **(kruptos) which means privately or inwardly.**[1] When you read this scripture, Jesus warns us not to **purposely make a PUBLIC (outwardly unrighteous) display** to get the glory of men or your reward will only be whatever man can give you, and man cannot give ETERNAL LIFE. God wants man to look to Him for approval and reward, because He loves you. Your PRIVATE, SECRET (inwardly righteous) prayer, alms, and fasting will be made known to man by God's open

reward to the one doing it, but to the one that tries to get the approval of man by doing it openly receives his reward from man not from God. Some may notice you giving alms, praying, or fasting without you having to say to people, **"Hey watch me give this money".** The **intent of the heart** is the subject of judgment. **Giving, praying, and fasting just to be seen by man is wrong and unprofitable.** This behavior begins with your insecurity of how man and God see your spiritual life. This **results in pride or self-exaltation (trying to make yourself somebody before men and God). Privacy and inward prayer deals with the DESIRE to be alone spiritually with God as Jesus did at Gethsemane,** and to do things for God that have no need for an audience, although you may have one. The whole meaning behind this type of secrecy is **RELATIONSHIP with CHRIST.** Those with **no relationship** with CHRIST have **no access to the FATHER.** There's no such thing as praying to the Father in secret for the sinner. **Only the believer** has this privilege. Praying in private (away from the distractions of the world such as phone, family, radio, etc.) from the depths of your heart is what is meant by **MATTHEW 6:4,6.** Praying in secret is that quality time you spend with the Father. In prayer, you speak to God. After prayer, you wait on God to answer. Remember: **His answer will never contradict His Word.** So all of you who sought God about joining a GLO, and you said that God said, it was okay, did not hear it from God. You heard it from Satan, who used the desire of your heart, to make you think it was okay. **GLO's do contradict God's Word.** Prayer is not **casually** talking to God. **How can one claim inner righteousness and concentrate on hearing God's voice when looking to man for approval?** When Peter, walking on the water, took His eyes off Jesus, only then did he begin to sink. Jesus is the only Man you better look to for approval.

Finally, the word in the scripture does not say to pray secretly as if you **desire** to keep your prayer a secret to **hide it out of fear or shame, but to pray inwardly or privately (i.e. alone spiritually, and sometimes alone physically).** Secrecy used by GLO's leads to dishonesty, pride, haughtiness, snobbery, and actually an insult of God the Holy Spirit, Whose **nature** is to **reveal TRUTH**. Secrecy is used to cover shame. Secrecy allows GLO's to **appear** righteous on the outside, by not letting you know what's on the inside. Secrecy does not put God first. GLO secrecy plays a major role in who they choose for membership. Your rejection letter more than likely has nothing to do with the real reason. This use of secrecy brings about **elitism. ELITISM is a nasty characteristic that no true Christian should be a part of, because it involves partiality. The woes of elitism can be seen with the rich, the highly educated, and those with great influence. Few to none want Jesus as their Lord, because they believe their answer is in money, education, or fame.**

I CORINTHIANS 1:26(amp) For [simply] consider your own call, brethren; not many [of us were considered to be] wise according to **human estimates and standards**, not many influential and powerful, not many of high and noble birth.

Why pray and supplicate for man to see anyway? Besides, **it is not scriptural**. Praying **for a person** (i.e. intercession), **with a person** (i.e. in agreement), and praying for oneself is scriptural.

Secrecy of GLO's deal with the purposeful desire, and NECESSITY to HIDE FROM THE PUBLIC EYE usually because of fear, shame, brainwashing, or known wrongdoing. GLO's do not want anyone to see or hear their secret practices, because they know it's ungodly, and

COMING APART AT THE SEAMS

are afraid of it being revealed and rebuked by the <u>True Church</u>. Honestly, most Greek Christians, see other Christians as their worst enemies. When you witness to them, you will see. The best scriptural example is when Ananias and Sapphira used secrecy to try and deceive the Apostles. Look at what happened to them, and look at how much common sense the sinners had not to join or associate with the true Christians. Why? Because they knew and were afraid of being revealed just like Ananias and Sapphira.

Acts 5:1-11, 13(amp) But a certain man named Ananias with his wife Sapphira sold a piece of property. And with his wife's knowledge and connivance he kept back and wrongfully appropriated some of the proceeds, bringing only a part and putting it at the feet of the apostles. But Peter said, Ananias, why has Satan filled your heart that you should lie and attempt to deceive the Holy Spirit, and should [in violation of your promise] **withdraw secretly** and appropriate to your own use part of the price from the sale of the land? As long as it remained unsold, was it not still your own? And [even] after it was sold, was not [the money] at your disposal and under your control? Why then, is it that you have proposed and purposed in your heart to do this thing? [How could you have the heart to do such a deed?] You have not [simply] lied to men [playing and showing yourself utterly deceitful] but to God. Upon hearing these words, Ananias fell down and died. And great dread and terror took possession of all who heard of it. And the young men arose and wrapped up [the body] and carried it out and buried it. Now after an interval of about three hours his wife came in, not having learned what had happened. And Peter said to her, Tell me, did you sell the land for so much? Yes, she said, for so much. Then Peter said to her, How could you two have agreed and conspired together to try to deceive the Spirit of the Lord? Listen! The feet of those who have buried your husband are at the door, and they will carry you out [also]. And instantly she fell down at his feet and died; and the young men entering found her dead, and they carried her out and buried her beside her husband. And the whole church and all others who heard of these things were appalled [great awe and strange terror and dread seized them]. And none of those who were <u>not of their number</u> **dared to join and associate with them**, but the people held them in high regard and praised and made much of them.

Here is proof of this desire to purposely keep certain information "**secret**".

Candidate: "I_____ (name), do promise in the presence of the Eternal Spirit of Truth, and these finite witnesses, that I will **never reveal in any manner whatsoever, for any purpose whatsoever, any of the secrets, passwords, signs, grips or other confidences** entrusted to my keeping as a member of Delta Sigma Theta Sorority, Incorporated, now at the time of my initiation into the Sisterhood, or that may hereafter from time to time be so entrusted." (DELTA SIGMA THETA SORORITY, INC., GRAND CHAPTER, RITUAL, 1990, p. 29.)

My only question is, What are you hiding that's so evil? What are those OTHER confidences? They could be ANYTHING. These GLO's even put people at the entrance door where they conduct their secret rituals so that no one may come in and observe. **Revelation of the TRUTH is the enemy of the Devil.** The scripture does not say to pray secretly, it says **in secret** so that the Father who is **in secret, or in The Holy of Holies**, can reward you openly. The Holy of Holies is where only **the true believer** can enter because of Jesus' shed blood. This is where Believers go to meet God.

MATTHEW 6:18 That thou appear **not unto men** to fast, **but unto thy father** which is **in secret**: and thy father, which seeth **in secret**, shall reward thee **openly**.

Jesus prayed in secret (i.e. privately, inwardly, and alone where the Father dwells) to the Father which is in secret. This shows personal relationship, not lip service. Anyone can pray, but **it does not mean they are saved or living holy**. Read Matthew 6:16-18 **in context** to really understand what is meant by the term **"in secret"**. The original translation, which is PRIVACY, is not really necessary to know to understand what Jesus means. **If** this scripture did translate secrecy as that AKA believes it to be, then GLO's would have no reason to keep hazing or any other ungodly practices a secret (i.e. behind closed doors). **In CONTEXT, the inordinate desire of outward religious expression or piety, which is not Christlike, is proof of the lack of inner righteousness and security of your relationship with Christ.** Even historical knowledge from the Bible shows the fruit of practicing ungodly secrecy. The magicians that opposed Moses illustrates the type of secrecy that is ungodly, and overthrown by God's power. It is ungodly because of the divination and magic that was **purposely concealed** (i.e. occult).

Overthrown by God's power, as the magicians were not able to bring forth gnats, so are GLO's principles, practices and doctrines powerless in secret and in the open. They are unable to use or be used by God's power, because they practice ungodly things. **Many members in GLO's harden their hearts, because of love and trust for their GLO, as did Pharaoh and his magicians believe, love, and trust their gods.**

EXODUS 7:11,22 (amp) Then Pharaoh called for the wise men [**skilled in magic and divination**] and the sorcerers (wizards and jugglers). And they also, these magicians of Egypt, did similar things with their **enchantments** and **secret** arts.

EXODUS 8:18-19 (amp) The magicians tried by their **enchantments** and **secret** arts to bring forth gnats or mosquitoes, but they could not; and there were gnats or mosquitoes on man and beast. Then the magicians said to Pharaoh, **this is the finger of God**! But pharaoh's heart was hardened and strong and he would not listen to them, just as the Lord had said.

The word here for secret in the Hebrew is lât which can be found in, Strong's Exhaustive Concordance of the Bible, James Strong, ST.P, L.L.D. MACDONALD PUBLISHING COMPANY, MCLEAN, VIRGINIA 22102, #3909.)

By looking at the scriptures above, it is easy to see that it was ungodly. The words magic, enchantments, and divination are anti-biblical, antichrist, and have nothing to do with Christianity. When one looks at the results of this encounter between Moses and Pharaoh's magicians, **some will admit who the true God is**, and **others will rebel against the true God**, as I witnessed that night at N.C. State, and on many other occasions. The historical context of **MATTHEW 6** reveals the reasons for the hypocritical display of righteousness that Greek Christians practice by works, especially those pertaining to religious and social causes. This is why we must **study to show ourselves approved unto GOD**. That AKA who asked the question had not studied MATTHEW 6 thoroughly. What's worse is that this AKA chapter has a Bible study. It's a case of the blind leading the blind. Privacy and/or SECRECY as written in these scriptures reveal the truth about God that through the actions of the true believer God is glorified. **Inward righteousness is revealed by outward holiness, which is true outward religious expression.**

A true Christian, depending when they got saved (i.e. before, during, or after pledging), needs to know and have all the secrets revealed about GLO's. A true Christian would also want everyone else to know about all ungodly information of any organization. Yet, many who claim to be Christians who are in fraternities and sororities or have denounced, refuse and rebel when it comes to revealing the secrets. Fortunately, this is not always the case. Others should see those who reveal their secrets for the sake of souls as **faithful to God.** The secret rituals, handshakes, challenges, and meanings of symbols of GLO's do not reveal godliness and have no place in God's kingdom, need to be revealed for the sake of SOULS, truth, and honesty. If not, you will allow **the god of this world** the ability to continue to blind the mind of GLO members, and those interested in GLO's by shutting out the Gospel.

II CORINTHIANS 4:1-4(amp) Therefore, since we do hold and engage in this ministry by the mercy of God [granting us favor, benefits, opportunities, and especially salvation], we do not get discouraged (spiritless and despondent with fear) or become faint with weariness and exhaustion. We have renounced disgraceful ways (secret thoughts, feelings, desires and underhandedness, the methods and arts that men hide through shame); **we refuse to deal craftily** (to practice trickery and cunning) or to adulterate or handle dishonestly the word of God, but we state the truth openly (clearly and candidly). (clearly and candidly). And so we commend ourselves in the sight and presence of God to every man's conscience. But even if our gospel (the glad tidings) also be hidden (obscured and covered up with a veil that hinders the knowledge of God), it is hidden [only] to those who are perishing and obscured [only] to those who are spiritually dying and veiled [only] to those who are lost. For the god of this world has blinded the unbelievers' minds [that they should not discern the truth], preventing them from seeing the illuminating light of the gospel of the glory of Christ (the Messiah), who is the image and likeness of God.

Since stubborn, blind, and unwilling members (Greek Christians included) refuse to be completely honest(which is to be totally dishonest) and truthful about their groups, it must be done by those who care for the souls of innocent people. This scripture is saying that once you denounce; the signs, handshakes, hazing, and all secrets are to be revealed openly. This is why I have no problem quoting rituals, even from my former GLO. I gave up discretion when I denounced Omega Psi Phi: A GLO that stresses discretion.

In conclusion, the secrecy that GLO's practice is the Greek (apokruphos), which means to **purposely** hide or

fully conceal. (James Strong, ST.P, L.L.D., Strong's Exhaustive Concordance of the Bible, MACDONALD PUBLISHING COMPANY, MCLEAN, VIRGINIA 22102, p. 14.)

To deceive is in direct rebellion against God's Word. His nature, which is to reveal, are the practices of Christ and true Christians. Don't forget **Acts 5:1-11, 13. This is the type of secrecy that GLO's practice. They use secrecy to deceive, mislead, and distort Biblical Truth. The only thing is they don't fear God enough like those in verse 13 to stop faking like they are Christians.**

MATTHEW 10:26-28 So have no fear of them; for nothing is concealed that will not be revealed, or kept secret that will not become known. What I say to you in the dark, tell in the light; and what you here whispered in the ear, proclaim upon the housetops. **And do not be afraid of those who kill the body but cannot kill the soul; But rather be afraid of him who can kill both the body and soul.**

DON'T WORRY ABOUT GIVING UP THEIR SECRETS WHEN IT REVEALS THE TRUTH. WHEN WITNESSING, USE THEIR SECRET MATERIAL WISELY.

JOHN 18:20(amp) Jesus answered him, I have **spoken openly** to the world, I have always taught in a synagogue and in the temple [area], where the Jews [habitually] congregate (assemble); and I have spoken **nothing secretly.**

They questioned His doctrine and **He responded openly;** Why won't GLO's??? **Because they are not Christ-like**, and have secrecy to protect them. Paul told King Agrippa that God does not practice secrecy. Why? Jesus has nothing to be ashamed of, and neither should Christians. (**Romans 1:17**)

ACTS 26:26(amp) For the king understands about these things well enough, and [therefore] to him I speak with bold frankness and confidence. I am convinced that not one of these things has escaped his notice, **for all this did not take place in a corner [in secret]**.

Jesus is a revealer, not some God dangling you on a string or putting a blindfold on you before you receive more knowledge and wisdom. If God chooses to withhold something from us, it will never be something ungodly as it is with GLO's. Remember that God knows what to reveal and what not to reveal. GLO's have chosen to practice secrecy in demonic form.

JAMES 1:5(amp) If any of you is deficient in wisdom, let him ask of the giving God [who **gives**] **to everyone liberally** and ungrudgingly, **without reproaching or faultfinding**, and it will be given him.

This scripture is key, because it shows the freedom of access to God's wisdom. With GLO's, you have to do this and pay that, learn this song and recite that poem as pre-requisites for initiation. Until then, you receive none of their wisdom or knowledge. Jesus is not a secret holder; rather He is a mystery revealer to those **that believe. Christ Himself and Christians** profess that nothing was done to be kept secret, but that it will be eventually revealed. People in GLO's are obsessed and downright dogmatic about keeping their secrets. **I'm just as dogmatic about revealing their secrets.** This book gives a small amount of their secrets, what they practice, and what they believe.

Another word that causes a stir **to supporters of GLO's is the word** Cult. **By definition,** secrecy plays a major role in

COMING APART AT THE SEAMS

the cult system. Isolation (for the purpose of secrecy) is also another common **practice of cults and GLO's.**

"**A Cult** is a group with an *obsessive* **devotion** to, or **veneration** (deep respect) for a **person** (D.P.-Dean of Pledges, big brothers or big sisters), **principle** (brotherhood, scholarship, wisdom, sisterhood, temperance, zeal, and service), **or thing;** (a dog, sphinx, elephant, goddesses, gods, etc.)"
(Copyright 1997 by Houghton Mifflin Company. Adapted and reproduced by permission from *The American Heritage College Dictionary, Third Edition*)

Members take time to give desirable meanings to these animals and symbols, which of course are not based on God's word, but usually on **Greek legends or myths**. This is taking **profane** things and making them **sacred**. A fact of all cults.

ISAIAH 5:20- Woe unto them in the days when good will be called evil and evil will be called good.

This principle of making evil seem good used by GLO's is another **common** characteristic of cults as well. Delta Sigma Theta/Sigma Alpha Epsilon praise **Minerva**, Tau Kappa Epsilon praises **Apollo**, Iota Phi Theta praises the **Centaur**, and Alpha Phi Alpha's deifies the **Sphinx**. There is **no good** in Minerva, Apollo, a Centaur, or the Sphinx.

"**A cult** is also **an exclusive** group of persons sharing **an esoteric** (understood by **only those belonging to a specific** group/occult), **intellectual** (knowledge) **interest.**" (Copyright 1997 by Houghton Mifflin Company. Adapted and reproduced by permission from *The American Heritage College Dictionary, Third Edition.*)

This **exclusive** **(secret/specific/occult)** knowledge possessed by each group is what they **aggressively hide** from each other's organization and all who do not belong (i.e. GLO's by their choice **exclude certain people**). The true exclusion principle/or segregation says only you can exclude yourself from God or anything else by **your choice.** Greeks will sit there and tell you that there is nothing in their rituals that deny God's Word, but **never produce** one shred of evidence.

That IF thou shalt confess with thy mouth the Lord Jesus, and shalt believe in thine heart that God hath raised him from the dead, thou shalt be saved. For with the heart man believeth unto righteousness; and with the mouth confession is made unto salvation (**ROMANS 10:9-10**).

IF signifies **choice** and the rest are the conditions. Salvation is God's desire for all mankind. God **wants all** to be saved (**not excluded**) and not be entangled with the affairs of this world **which he has not enlisted Christians to be a part of.**

I TIMOTHY 2:4- Who will have **all men to be saved,** and to come unto the knowledge of **the truth.**

II TIMOTHY 2:4- No man that warreth entangleth himself with the affairs **of this life**; that he may please him who hath chosen him to be a soldier.

And yes, God the Father produces evidence for your decision, His Word and His Spirit, using both to draw you to His Son, Jesus Christ the Righteous.

Greek Christians are concerned greatly with the affairs of this life. No thought is given to eternal life, because they are led to believe that it's guaranteed. God says they are not worthy to be His soldiers.

GLO's have a principle where they can and will **exclude you by their choice** while the biblical principle is God will **include everyone based on their choice**, but only because He chose us first. God never turns away from one who repents. Unfortunately it's not everyone's choice to do so. It is also a person's choice **to leave** God, **their fraternity, sorority**, mom, dad, etc. There is no such thing as **"once an ALPHA always an ALPHA"**. Who gave man the right and power to make you a Greek for life? **This is bondage.** If you want your share of this **intellectual interest**, you must meet **their specific guidelines**, but Jesus says to just ask for it. Almost everything GLO's say and do contradict God's Word.

Now that I have proven GLO's to be **cults** and of the **occult**, I can also prove that they can be classified as a **religion**. By definition, religion is 1.)

"a belief and reverence for a supernatural power or powers regarded as creator and governor of the universe."
(Copyright 1997 by Houghton Mifflin Company. Adapted and reproduced by permission from *The American Heritage College Dictionary, Third Edition*)

2.) Ritual is how this belief is expressed (i.e. WORSHIP). 3.) Any idea (Christianity is not an idea) used to **control (i.e. to be deceptively put in bondage) the masses** can be considered as a religion. The religion these groups preach **is not a relationship with Christ**. It is rather an allegiance to **their** rules, standards, constitution, and principles. **Greek Christians (people who have and still confess Christ as their Lord and Savior, but are not and cannot be saved), WORSHIP** and show allegiance to **their** organizations <u>through</u>

ritual, and give **PRAISE, HONOR, THANKSGIVING, and GLORY to their organizations through song, poetry, service, and historical documentation**. The only way a Greek Christian can come back to God is by **repentance**, complete **renunciation** of their GLO, and separation or **release** from all members (i.e. **they are no longer your friends, brothers, or sisters, but a harvest field. Go get them!!!!!**). GLO's possess a lot of the characteristics of a CHURCH, **but lack the anointing and consecration of The Church**. GLO'S are religious and act as a church by definition and practice because they have **prayer**, require a **belief in a supreme being**, **worship** by performing rituals based on **their** symbols and **beliefs**, **praise** through song and dance, have a written doctrine, and offer a **plan of salvation**. Can anyone say, "Let's have church?"

They often employ the use of the word, "sacred". Sacred and holy are synonymous (i.e. It is not only a religious term, but a Christian term. **Evil things are not TRULY sacred**). GLO's call their brotherhood sacred **though sinners abound**, their temples to be sacred though **idols** are set up in them, the very name of their GLO to be sacred, though only the names by which God has revealed Himself to us are TRULY sacred. Anything that God calls sacred is holy. Sorry GLO's!!!

Religious feelings and practices that have been deeply set in a person may cause them to lose countless blessings. It may even cause them to lose the greatest blessing of all, which is **eternal life.**

HEBREWS 12:17(amp) For you understand that later on, when **he wanted** [to regain title to] his inheritance of the blessing, he was rejected (disqualified and set aside), for he could find **no opportunity to repair by repentance**, [what he had done, no chance to recall the choice he had made] although **he sought for it carefully with [bitter] tears.**

Don't let this be you!! Tears don't move God, sincerity does. He reached the point of no return. His mistakes were irreversible.

SECRECY OF OATHS

Do not be mistaken or deceived, God's wrath is upon GLO's. Plainly stating, the fraternity or sorority you are a member of **IS YOUR GOD**. You take a **secret oath to the GLO** instead of God.

MATTHEW 5:33(amp) Again, you have heard that it was said to the men of old, you shall not **swear falsely**, but you shall perform your oaths **to the Lord** [as a religious duty].

You Worship it, Praise it, Glorify it, Love it, and some even Pray to/for their GLO'S. **GREEK CHRISTIANS!!** You are serving two masters, committing idolatry, breaking the first commandment, and operating in pride. **What are you, who are interested in, agree with, or already belong to a GLO going to do?** Not later! But right NOW!! Many of the doctrines GLO's promote come from evil roots combining them with the Word of God to **try** and make them look good. DO NOT BE FOOLED BROTHERS AND SISTERS IN CHRIST; THE BEST-DRESSED SINNERS GO TO HELL. All they are trying not to do is offend anyone. So by trial and error, some teachings were made up, dropped, and modified, as they went along to suit the needs of each individual. In order to do this, some of their secret information will have to be obtained from many sources; the Koran, Vedas, Book of Mormon, Plato, Socrates, etc., as long as it **sounds** good, and relates to the GLO. Most of their principles come from Greek teachings, as you would expect from a GLO. They take all this (man-made doctrines/myths) and try to blend in the Word of God. This is why Jesus can be so different to so many people. To some He's a god, a mere man, a great prophet like Moses, one of many gods, Lucifer's brother, etc. The problem is Jesus cannot be blended in to fit other religions. Since Jesus is THE TRUTH, He cannot be the truth to one, and a different truth to another.

MATTHEW 24:23 Then if any man shall say unto you, Lo, Here is the Christ, or there; believe it not.

This is why GLO's must keep this information **secret and disguised**, especially from Christians. If they did it openly, their cover would be blown. Read what Paul wrote to Timothy about myths and vain conversation.

II TIMOTHY 4:3-4(amp) For the time is coming when [people] will not tolerate (endure) sound and wholesome instruction, but, having ears itching [for something pleasing and gratifying], they will gather to themselves one teacher after another to a considerable number, chosen to **satisfy their own liking and to foster the errors** they hold, and will **turn aside from hearing the truth** and **wander off** into **myths** and **man-made fictions.**

Christians!! Don't let this be you or happen to you, but if you belong to a GLO this is you. GLO'S and their members will use the Bible (out of context), The Koran, **Greek Mythology**, Satan, or even their own mind and make-up whatever they desire. Greek Christians feel like they can and do create their own knowledge, even though GLO's have people in positions to make these decisions. Individual members seldom feel any accountability to their president. Why should they? They don't fear God, so why should they fear what man can do to them. Most don't share a personal relationship with their leader, and believe the GLO is theirs to do

COMING APART AT THE SEAMS

with as they please (i.e. they really don't respect their founders or history). If so, they would leave certain information alone. On the other hand, Christians obey their leader because of their personal relationship with HIM (JESUS CHRIST). Christians also obey their earthly spiritual leaders, because the Bible says so (**Hebrews 13:17**). Hey GLO's!! You don't have that scripture do you? Neither do you have the power to enforce such a rule. **Rules without Relationship** breeds **rebellion** and **Relationship without Rules** breed **anarchy (i.e. every man for himself)**. Rules without enforcement breeds disobedience, lawlessness, wickedness, and many other sins. Jesus sits in heaven with the power to enforce His laws. GLO's don't have this power. GLO's were asking for trouble from the very beginning. A GLO cannot enforce its rules, because the leadership has no true relationship with its members, and no support from God. This is why hazing still occurs ten years after its apparent abolishment. When rules cannot and are not enforced, then there are truly no rules. It then becomes a proverbial free-for-all. You initiate people who don't fear the TRUE GOD. What you expect of them, cannot possibly be fulfilled.

JUDGES 21:25(amp) In those days there was **no king** in Israel: every man did what was right **in his own eyes**.

PROVERBS 14:12(amp) There is a way which **seems right to a man** and appears straight before him, but at **the end** of it **is** the way of **death**.

Now why would a true Christian, who has the richness of God's Word, wisdom, knowledge, and truth, want to yoke to mythology (complete lies about false gods) and man-made fictions (fairy tales)? **Answer**: Curiosity of what the symbols mean and what the **secrets** are all about, and for this reason a person will put Jesus on the back-burner to partake in these ungodly organizations. They will not preach Christ for fear of criticism and persecution, which is what a **true Christian** will receive for keeping the truth.

GALATIANS 4:16 (amp) Have I then become your enemy by telling the truth to you and dealing sincerely with you?

The problem with human wisdom is that it only goes so far before falling flat on its face. **Secrecy** breeds evil imaginations and thoughts. Examples of those who follow or followed their own way are Hitler, Lenin, Darwin (who supposedly repented of or **denounced** his belief in evolution accepting Jesus and biblical creation), Mohammed, Farrakhan, Mary Madeline O'Hare, Margaret Sanger, Jane Roe (Who is now saved!!!) and the list goes on. The movements these people started were **created and originated in secrecy**. Human intellect is one of the main barriers to salvation, because it requires proof by one or more of the five senses (i.e. the seeing is believing attitude). All of these men and women hated, or refused to believe in the true God, because they sought their own desires. Some later were sorry and repentant for what they had done.

I JOHN 2:16 (amp) For all that is in the world- the lust of the flesh, [craving for sensual gratification] and the lust of the eyes [greedy longings of the mind] and **the pride of life [assurance in one's own resources or in the stability of earthly things]**-these do not come from the Father but are from the world [itself].

This pride coupled with man's wisdom; refuses to give credit to or accept **Jesus' work on the cross**. It's I, I, I, me, me, me and we, we, we, instead of Jesus. Examples of this

COMING APART AT THE SEAMS

trust in man or earthly things are seen in the following passage.

"**Faith** shall have to be **manifested** in an unshakable **belief in Kappa Alpha Psi**, **its** ideals, **its** purposes, **its** membership, **its** programs, and **its** forward movement". (William L. Crump, THE STORY OF KAPPA ALPHA PSI, A History Of The Beginning And Development Of A College Greek Letter Organization, 1911-1983, Third Edition, 1983, p.267.)

They put their assurance in earthly things instead of spiritual things. These are the types of things that Christians can observe. Christians should take heed and obey the Lord. How? By denouncing or rebuking their interest in joining a GLO. Although this passage above appears in a history book, the damage is done **in secret** through the pledge process. As soon as the person becomes a member, whether they were once saved or unsaved, have a biased view towards their GLO.

COLOSSIANS 2:8,18-23(amp) See to it that no one carries you off as spoil or makes you yourselves captive by his so-called philosophy and intellectualism and vain deceit (idle fancies and plain nonsense), following human tradition (men's ideas of the material rather than the spiritual world), just crude notions following the rudimentary and elemental teachings of the universe and disregarding [the teachings of] Christ (the Messiah). Let no one defraud you by acting as an umpire and declaring you unworthy and disqualifying you for the prize, **insisting on self-abasement** and worship of angels, taking his stand on visions [he claims] he has seen, vainly puffed up by his sensuous notions and inflated by his unspiritual thoughts and fleshly conceit, And not holding fast to the Head, from Whom the entire body, supplied and knit together by means of its joints and ligaments, grows with a growth that is from God. If then you have died with Christ to material ways of looking at things and have escaped from the world's crude and elemental notions and teachings of externalism, why do you live as if you still belong to the world? [Why do you submit to rules and regulations? -such as] Do not handle [this], Do not taste [that], Do not even touch [them], Referring to things all of which perish with being used. To do this is to **follow human precepts and doctrines**. Such [practices] **have** indeed the **outward appearance [that popularly passes] for wisdom**, in promoting self-rigor of devotion and **delight in self-humiliation** and **severity of discipline of the body**, but they are of **no value** in checking the indulgence of the flesh (the lower nature). [Instead, **they do not honor God** but **serve only to indulge the flesh**.]

All bold type represents so many of the **secret** practices and characteristics of GLO's. They do insist on self-abasement and self-humiliation by pledging you (**explained in chapter 3**), and after you become a member to follow human precepts and doctrines. The last sentence of the scripture sums it up for Greek Christians. If being in a GLO is the only thing that separates you from God, then you need to stop making excuses right now. If you don't denounce now, you may never denounce. The consequences will not last only a lifetime, **but an eternity!!!!**

By using **secrecy**, GLO's succeed at leading people into captivity. The problem with the Greek Christians (IGNORANT AND/OR REBELLIOUS) in these groups is that many of their **works** do not back up the Christian **faith** according to the Word of God. These **works are hazing, secrecy, rituals, parties, drinking, profanity, unequal yoking**, etc. (see chapter 4 part 2).

JAMES 2:14-20(amp) What is the use (profit), my brethren for anyone to **profess to have faith** if he has **no [good] works** [to show for it]? Can

[such] faith save [his soul]? If a brother or sister is poorly clad and lacks food for each day, and one of you says to him, Good-bye! Keep [yourself] warm and well fed, without giving him the necessities for the body, what good does that do? So also faith, if it does not have works (deeds and actions of obedience to back it up), by itself is destitute of power (inoperative, dead). But someone will say [to you then], You [say you] have faith, and I have [good] works. Now you show me your [alleged] faith apart from any [good] works [if you can], and I by **[good] works [of obedience]** will show you my faith. You believe that God is one; you do well. So do the demons believe and shudder [in terror and horror such as make man's hair stand on end and contract the surface of his skin]! Are you willing to be shown [proof], you foolish (unproductive, spiritually deficient) fellow, that faith apart from [good] works is inactive and ineffective and worthless?

GLO's beliefs (their faith) are dead and hypocritical, because their works, especially their **secret works,** are dead and hypocritical. Greek Christians do not perform works of obedience. Neither do they perform the commandments of God, but instead the commandments of men (dead works).

A SPIRITUAL NEED CANNOT BE FILLED WITH A PHYSICAL SUBSTANCE AND VICE-VERSA!

MATTHEW 16:18 And Jesus answered and said unto him, Blessed art thou Simon Bar-jona: for **flesh and blood** hath not **revealed** it unto you, but my Father which is in heaven.

Salvation is by faith (spiritual), not a good work (physical).

GOD SAYS IN **II TIMOTHY 3:7** CERTAIN PEOPLE ARE **EVER LEARNING,** AND **NEVER ABLE TO COME** UNTO THE KNOWLEDGE OF THE TRUTH. GREEK CHRISTIANS

RENDER THEMSELVES **INCAPABLE** OF SPIRITUAL FULFILLMENT BY SEARCHING FOR AN EARTHLY, TEMPORAL, AND PERISHING KNOWLEDGE.

When the REVEALED Word of God does not satisfy a person, neither will their SECRET KEEPING GLO. If the Word of God does not satisfy, nothing else will ever be able to fill the void.

EPHESIANS 5:12-14(amp) For it is **a shame** to even speak of or mention the things that [such people] **practice in secret**. But when anything is **exposed and reproved** by the light, it is made visible and clear; and where everything is visible and clear there is light. Therefore he says, awake o sleeper, and arise from the dead, and Christ shall shine (make day dawn) upon you and give you light.

The scripture clearly shows again the futility, foolishness and unholiness that **secrecy** produces. If Greek Christians do not AWAKE out of their wickedness, they will not receive LIGHT.

Read those scriptures on secrecy again and be honest with yourself.

    1.) Does God practice secrecy the way GLO's do? **NO!**
    2.) Do GLO's practice secrecy for evil purposes? **YES!**
    3.) Does God move in mysterious ways? **NO!**
It's People who do not understand God that say such things.
    4.) Do GLO's move in mysterious ways? **YES!** And they do it primarily in secret.

The Bible says, "Not by might, nor by power, but **by my Spirit** saith the Lord." (**ZECHARIAH 4:6**)

COMING APART AT THE SEAMS

God tells you here how He does things.

MATTHEW 6:1-6 was grossly misinterpreted ignorantly and purposely to try and justify that God's view of the secrecy (occult/cult) practiced by GLO's is acceptable, BUT the truth in His Word is **absolutely** opposite. When the truth comes forth and exposes secrecy, we see the events in **ACTS 5:1-11, ACTS 7:54-60,** and **ACTS 19:11-20** come to pass. Unfortunately, some do not want to even hear the truth. **One truth being that GLO's are not for Christians.**

IF YOU BELIEVE THIS CHAPTER DOESN'T DIRECTLY DESCRIBE GREEK FRATERNITIES AND SORORITIES, I SAY READ ON. I ALSO SAY! CHRISTIAN OR GREEK CHRISTIAN AND SINNERS! YOU ARE DECEIVED, OR YOU KNOW THE TRUTH AND EXCHANGE IT FOR A LIE (i.e. you refuse and rebel to believe). BECAUSE YOU LOVE NOT THE TRUTH, GOD HAS OR WILL SEND STRONG DELUSION THAT YOU WILL BELIEVE THE LIE. DON'T WAIT TOO LONG! DENOUNCE AND RECEIVE JESUS BACK OR ACCEPT HIM FOR THE FIRST TIME. **UNBELIEF IS SIN.**

JOHN 16:8-9(amp) And when He comes, He will convict and convince the world and bring demonstration to it about sin and about righteousness (uprightness of the heart and right with God) and about judgment: **About sin, because they do not believe** in me [trust in, rely on, and adhere to me];

ONCE ONE HAS BEEN PRESENTED WITH THE TRUTH THEY EITHER ACCEPT IT OR REJECT IT.

MATTHEW 22:29 Jesus answered and said unto them, Ye do **err, not knowing the scriptures**, nor the power of God.

Notes

FREDERIC L. HATCHETT

CHAPTER 3
PART 1

ORIGIN OF GREEK-LETTERED ORGANIZATIONS

Lets hear the origin of GLO's (Greek-Lettered Organizations) from a GLO.

"Our founders were well aware of the need to transfuse the ideals of Greek moral virtues with the **later** concepts of brotherhood and love. That is why they clearly wrote: 'We are a sisterhood founded on

COMING APART AT THE SEAMS

Christian principles...'"
(DELTA SIGMA THETA SORORITY, INC., GRAND CHAPTER, CANDIDATE SYLLABUS, 1990, p.30.)

The problem with this quote is that Christianity is not and can never be transfused with Greek moral virtues because they don't uphold God's standards. The church at Corinth is the best example of the problem when one does with Christianity what they want, and not how the Bible says so.

I TIMOTHY 4:7(amp) But refuse and avoid irreverent legends (profane and impure and **godless fictions**, mere grandmother's tales) and **silly myths** and express your disapproval of them. Train yourself toward godliness (piety), [keeping yourself spiritually fit].

II CORINTHIANS 6:14-18 Be ye not unequally yoked together with unbelievers: for what fellowship has righteousness with unrighteousness? and what communion hath light with darkness? And what concord hath Christ with Belial? Or what part hath he that believeth with an infidel? **And what agreement hath the temple of God with idols**? for ye are the temple of the living God; as god hath said, I will dwell in them; and I will be their God, and they shall be my people. Wherefore come out from among them and be ye separate, saith the Lord, and touch not the unclean thing; and I will receive you, I will be a Father unto you, and ye shall be my sons and daughters, saith the Lord Almighty.

Both scriptures prove that the Delta's beliefs are wrong and sinful. They **yoke themselves to Minerva both a myth and idol.**

Another quotation from the same GLO also shows their closest descendant concerning from whom GLO's got their practices.

"The most direct line of descent from Greek societies to America is the Freemasons (called Masons). Historians of American fraternities and sororities trace most of our rituals, ceremonies and rites to the Masons. An examination of Masonic rituals open to scholars suggest that our Founders were also

COMING APART AT THE SEAMS

influenced by Masonic ritual, symbolism and initiation experiences."
(DELTA SIGMA THETA SORORITY, INC., GRAND CHAPTER, CANDIDATE SYLLABUS, 1990, p.30.)

The significance of this quote is where did the GLO's get their symbolism, ritual, and initiation ceremonies from (i.e. what is the **origin**)? In reading this chapter, you will find out that it is not Judaism, Christianity, Jesus, or the Word of God. **The origin is Satan**. This quote is self-incriminating for GLO's who claim Christian founded principles. For it is well documented that Masonic Orders are cults, practice occultism and extreme idolatry.

THE IMPORTANCE OF ESTABLISHING ORIGIN IS THE KEY TO THIS WHOLE BOOK. IF IT WERE TO BE FOUND THAT THESE ORGANIZATIONS HAD AN INITIAL FOUNDATION IN GOD, MY BOOK WOULD BE USELESS, BECAUSE THEY WOULD HAVE A WAY TO RE-ESTABLISH THEMSELVES THROUGH REPENTANCE. YET, IF THE **ORIGIN** IS EVIL, SO ARE GLO'S THROUGHOUT THEIR ENTIRE EXISTENCE. MANKIND WAS NOT INITIALLY EVIL, BECAUSE WE WERE CREATED BY GOD. MAN BECAME A SINNER (i.e. his work of disobedience broke God's command.) ALL PEOPLE INHERIT SIN AS A RESULT OF ADAM'S SIN IN THE GARDEN-**ROMANS 5:12**. WE HAVE NO POWER TO CHANGE OUR SIN NATURE, BUT SINCE OUR ROOT AND SEED (CHRIST) IS NOT EVIL, WE

CAN BE SAVED. IT IS BECAUSE OF AND THROUGH JESUS; WE ARE MADE RIGHTEOUS THROUGH FAITH IN HIM. THERE IS **NO** REMEDY (**NO MAN** OR **WOMAN)** THAT CAN MAKE THESE SECRET SOCIETIES RIGHT WITH GOD, BECAUSE THEIR ORIGIN IS DEMONIC FROM THE VERY START (i.e. they were accursed from the very beginning). GLO's ORIGINATED FROM DOCTRINES OF DEMONS.

I TIMOTHY 4:1-2(amp) But the [Holy] spirit distinctly and expressly declares that in latter times some will turn away from the faith, giving attention to deluding and seducing spirits and doctrines that demons teach, Through the hypocrisy and pretentions of liars whose conscience and seared (cauterized).

THEY CAN HAVE ALL THE COMMITTEES, BOARDS, RESEARCH GROUPS, FORUMS, TO MAKE CHANGES TO IMPROVE. **PLEASE DON'T BELIEVE FOR ONE MOMENT THAT THEY WILL DISCUSS JESUS AND HOLINESS AS THE <u>SOLE</u> SOLUTION. FOR GLO's TO DO THIS, WOULD MEAN TO CEASE EXISTENCE AS AN ORGANIZATION. POSITIVE CHANGES DO NOT IMPROVE AND CANNOT IMPROVE THE SIN PROBLEM, NOR CAN MAN CHANGE OUR SIN NATURE WITH ANY OF HIS INNOVATIONS.** CHRIST DIDN'T FORM A COMMITTEE TO ABOLISH SIN AND DIE SO THAT WE COULD STAY IN SIN (i.e. MEMBERSHIP IN GLO'S). HE DIED FOR US, THE SINS OF THE WORLD, AND THE CHURCH, NOT FALSE IMITATIONS (GLO's). MAN'S ORIGIN, ANGEL'S ORIGIN, THE CHURCHES' ORIGIN, ANIMAL'S ORIGIN, ANGELS' ORIGIN, ETC. IS NOT EVIL. GOD CREATED THEM AND GAVE THEM

THEIR PURPOSE AND NATURE. OUR ORIGIN IS IN HIM. MEN AND ANGELS **CHOSE AND CHOOSE** TO BE AND DO GOOD OR EVIL. SATAN, BECAUSE OF HIS IRREVERSIBLE SIN, IS CONSIDERED THE ORIGIN OF EVIL. ALTHOUGH CREATED PERFECT, HIS EVIL CONDITION IS IRREVERSIBLE, AS WELL AS THE ANGELS THAT FOLLOWED HIM.

REVELATION 12:7 And there was war in heaven: Michael and his angels fought against the dragon; and the dragon fought and his angels, And prevailed not; **neither was their place any more found in heaven.**

A BELIEVER, NATION, CHURCH, OR CHRISTIAN ORGANIZATION GONE BAD CAN BE MADE RIGHT AGAIN BECAUSE JESUS IS THE ROOT. A SINNER CAN BE MADE RIGHT BECAUSE GOD IS THEIR ORIGIN **AND REDEEMER**, BUT AN ORGANIZATION NOT FOUNDED IN CHRIST ALONE HAS NO CHANCE FOR A COVENANT BLESSING. **GOD BEING LORD OVER HIS CREATION, HAS AND RESERVES THE RIGHT TO REDEEM AND NOT REDEEM WHO HE DESIRES. HE CHOSE NOT TO AND DID** NOT **REDEEM SATAN AND** THE FALLEN ANGELS OR GIVE ANIMALS A SPIRIT. THE FALLEN ANGELS' FINAL DESTINATION WILL BE HELL BY WAY OF THE EARTH.

HEBREWS 2:15-16(amp) And also that he might deliver and completely set free all those who through the [haunting] fear of death were held in bondage throughout the whole course of their lives. For, as we all know, he [Christ]

did not take hold of angels [the fallen angels, to give them helping and delivering], but he **did** take hold of [THE FALLEN] descendants of Abraham [to reach out to them a helping and delivering hand].

SATAN AND ONE-THIRD OF THE ANGELS BLEW IT. WE ARE THE ONLY CREATIONS THAT HAVE SINNED AND CAN COME BACK TO GOD, BUT ONLY THROUGH CHRIST JESUS CAN IT BE DONE. IT WAS NEVER IN GOD'S PLAN TO OFFER SALVATION TO ANGELS. THOUGH MANY CHURCHES AND CHRISTIANS ARE FAILING TO UPHOLD GODLY STANDARDS, ALL THEY WOULD HAVE TO DO IS REPENT TO BE RESTORED TO GOD, AND **REVELATIONS 1:11-3:22 AND II CHRONICLES 7:14** IS PROOF.

ORIGIN OF THE GREEKS AND THE CULT SYSTEM

NIMROD

BEFORE ENCOUNTERING THE HISTORICAL AND SPIRITUAL ORIGIN OF THE GREEKS, LET'S FIRST EXAMINE THEIR EARTHLY SPIRITUAL FATHER, NIMROD.

NIMROD IS VERY WELL KNOWN AS THE FATHER OF THE ANCIENT MYSTERY CULT SYSTEM. THE FIRST BEING, "THE BABYLONIAN MYSTERY RELIGIONS." HE WAS CALLED "THE APOSTATE", BECAUSE HE LED MEN AWAY FROM THE CONSCIENCE OF GOD AS A JUDGE. IT WAS BASED ON NONE OTHER THAN HIS "GOOD WORKS". WHAT EXACTLY DID HE DO? HE BUILT WALLED CITIES AND HUNTED DANGEROUS ANIMALS. HE OFFERED PROTECTION AND

COMING APART AT THE SEAMS

COMFORT. REALIZING HIS POWER OVER THE PEOPLE, **HE** ESTABLISHED HIS **OWN KING**DOM. **HIS AND MODERN DAY GLO'S SHARE MUCH IN COMMON. LET'S SEE THE SIMILARITIES FROM THE LATE REV. ALEXANDER HISLOP IN THE NEXT SEVEN PARTS.**

1.) **SECRECY** WAS A TOOL USED THEN AND NOW TO EASE INITIATES INTO **IDOLATRY.**

"Their (The Babylonian mystery systems) primary object was to introduce privately, by little and little, **under the seal of secrecy** and sanction of an oath, what it would not have been safe all at once and openly to propound." THE TWO BABYLONS OR PAPAL WORSHIP: Proved to be THE WORSHIP OF NIMROD AND HIS WIFE, LOIZEUAX BROTHERS, INC., AMERICA, SECOND AMERICAN EDITION, 1959, adapted, p. 5.)

The pledge period, intake included, is how they introduce their ungodly information privately, by little and little, by means of one or more oaths. With Greek organizations two oaths are usually performed. One oath is to be in the pledge club, and the other at initiation into the membership of the organization.

"It was a matter, therefore, of necessity, if idolatry were to be brought in, and especially such foul idolatry as the Babylonian system contained in its bosom, that it should be done **stealthily and in secret**." (THE TWO BABYLONS OR PAPAL WORSHIP: Proved to be THE WORSHIP OF NIMROD AND HIS WIFE, LOIZEUAX BROTHERS,

INC., AMERICA, SECOND AMERICAN EDITION, 1959, p. 7.)

Idolatry is idolatry. GLO's bring it in the same way cults did about 4,000 years ago as mentioned in bold. One who is honest cannot ignore the similarity unless they want to ignore it. But I do not see how a Christian can ignore such plain facts.

"Therefore it (idolatry) was brought in secretly, and by little and little, one corruption being introduced after another, as apostasy proceeded, and **the backsliding Church** became prepared to tolerate it, till it has reached the gigantic height we now see, when in almost every particular the system of the Papacy is the very antipodes of the system of the primitive Church." (THE TWO BABYLONS OR PAPAL WORSHIP: Proved to be THE WORSHIP OF NIMROD AND HIS WIFE, LOIZEUAX BROTHERS, INC., AMERICA, SECOND AMERICAN EDITION, 1959, adapted, p. 8.)

The same backsliding, tolerant Church exists in 1999. Pastor's, if you can call them that, wear their Greek paraphernalia in the pulpit as they preach. Greek Christians are Church leaders and Sunday school teachers. While at the same time, they are idolaters. If you believe your pastor is ignorant to the TRUTH about GLO's, bless him or her by buying this book for them.

2.) OATHS ARE A NECESSITY PRIOR TO GREEK-LETTERED ORGANIZATION MEMBERSHIP

COMING APART AT THE SEAMS

AND REVEALING OF THEIR SECRET KNOWLEDGE AND WISDOM. **NO COMPLETE INITIATION COULD EVER TAKE PLACE IN THE BABYLONIAN SYTEM WITHOUT THE OATH.**

"In that system, **secret confession** to the priest, according to a **prescribed form**, was required of all who were admitted to the "Mysteries;" and till such confession had been made, no complete initiation could take place." (THE TWO BABYLONS OR PAPAL WORSHIP: Proved to be THE WORSHIP OF NIMROD AND HIS WIFE, LOIZEUAX BROTHERS, INC., AMERICA, SECOND AMERICAN EDITION, 1959, p. 9.)

GLO's operate the same way. Everyone takes the same oath, and is not admitted until they do so.

3.) THE SYSTEM IN THE BABYLON SYSTEM WAS TO HAVE A HIERARCHY OVER THE INITIATE. THIS IS EQUAL TO THE BIG BROTHER/BIG SISTER SYSTEM OF GLO's TODAY OVER THEIR INITIATES.

"That object was to bind all mankind in a blind and absolute submission to a **hierarchy** entirely dependent on the sovereigns of Babylon." (THE TWO BABYLONS OR PAPAL WORSHIP: Proved to be THE WORSHIP OF NIMROD AND HIS WIFE, LOIZEUAX BROTHERS, INC., AMERICA, SECOND AMERICAN EDITION, 1959, p. 7.)

The pledge process of Greek-lettered organizations has been almost flawless at establishing this blind allegiance. Anyone who would allow themselves to be kicked, slapped and beaten with paddles must be in blind, absolute submission. The initiates of GLO's desire so much to know the secrets and other mysteries that they literally lose their minds or just simply give their minds to Big Brother Mike or Big Sister Mary. How many people will step off the edge of anything the first time without looking first?

4.) ASSUMED STATE OF DARKNESS OR IGNORANCE OF ANYONE WHO IS NOT A MEMBER. THE ONLY WAY OUT OF DARKNESS WAS TO JOIN NIMROD'S CULT.

"The priests were the only depositories of religious knowledge; they only had the true tradition, by which writs and symbols of the public religion could be interpreted; and without blind and implicit submission to them, what was necessary for salvation could not be known." (THE TWO BABYLONS OR PAPAL WORSHIP: Proved to be THE WORSHIP OF NIMROD AND HIS WIFE, LOIZEUAX BROTHERS, INC., AMERICA, SECOND AMERICAN EDITION, 1959, p. 7.)

GLO's CLAIM THAT ONE COMES OUT OF DARKNESS INTO THEIR LIGHT DURING AND/OR AFTER THE INITIATION CEREMONIES. THERE HAVE BEEN SEVERAL EXAMPLES OF THIS CLAIM ALREADY, AND MORE ARE FOLLOWING. THE BIG BROTHERS AND SISTERS ARE THE PRIESTS TO THE INITIATES. THEY HAVE THIS KNOWLEDGE THAT CAN ONLY BE OBTAINED BY BLIND AND IMPLICIT SUBMISSION TO THEM. THE SECTION ON HAZING SHOWS THE EXTENT OF THIS BLINDNESS. I HAVE ONE QUESTION TO ALL

COMING APART AT THE SEAMS

GLO's, "WHERE DOES YOUR WISDOM COME FROM, AND WHO DID YOU RECEIVE YOUR LIGHT FROM?" WHAT ARE THE UNINITIATED IGNORANT OF? BY READING YOUR RITUALS AND OBSERVING THE FRUIT YOU PRODUCE, IT CAN COME FROM NO ONE OTHER THAN LUCIFER. NIMROD WORSHIPED LUCIFER, BUT HE HIMSELF RECEIEVED WORSHIP AND CAUSED OTHERS TO WORSHIP SATAN. BY PRACTICING OCCULTISM, HE WAS INFLUENCED AND INDOCTRINATED BY THE DEVIL (**I TIMOTHY 4:1**).

5.) THIS IS THE MOST STRIKING EVIDENCE OF A COMPLETE TRANSPLANTATION OF THIS RELIGIOUS SYSTEM ALL THE WAY TO THE PRESENT.

"After referring to the fact that Egyptian priests claimed the honour of having transmitted to the Greeks the first elements of **polytheism**; he thus concludes: 'These positive facts would sufficiently prove, even without conformity of ideas, that the mysteries transplanted to Greece, and their united with certain number of local notions, never lost the character of their **origin** derived from the cradle of the moral and religious ideas of the universe.'"
(Ouvaroff's Eleusinian Mysteries, sect. ii., p. 20, THE LATE REV. ALEXANDER HISLOP, THE TWO BABYLONS OR PAPAL WORSHIP: Proved to be THE WORSHIP OF NIMROD AND HIS WIFE, LOIZEUAX BROTHERS, INC., AMERICA, SECOND AMERICAN EDITION, 1959, p.13.)

THE EGYPTIAN AND GREEK ORIGIN'S BEING FOUND IN BABYLON ARE ALSO **THE SOURCE OF MODERN SECRET SOCIETIES**

INCLUDING GLO'S (i.e. THE MYSTERIES MENTIONED ABOVE HAVE BEEN TRANSPLANTED TO THE GLO'S OF TODAY). THE SYMBOLISM AND DOCTRINES OF GLO's SUPPORT THIS.

6.) IN NIMROD'S CULT AND THE ONE'S THAT FOLLOWED,

"Men were led to believe that a real spiritual change of heart was unnecessary, and that so far as change was needed, they could be generated by **external means."** (THE LATE REV. ALEXANDER HISLOP, THE TWO BABYLONS OR PAPAL WORSHIP: Proved to be THE WORSHIP OF NIMROD AND HIS WIFE, LOIZEUAX BROTHERS, INC., AMERICA, SECOND AMERICAN EDITION, 1959, p. 55.)

BIBLICALLY THIS IS A LIE, AND GROUNDS FOR GLO's BEING A NON-CHRISTIAN ORGANIZATION. SO GREEK CHRISTIAN, WHAT ARE YOU STILL DOING IN ONE? GREEK CHRISTIANS AND THE GLO's THEY BELONG TO BELIEVE IN WORKS (EXTERNAL MEANS), NOT SALVATION BY FAITH REQUIRED BY GOD.

7.) HERE IS THE FINAL SIMILARITY BETWEEN ANCIENT CULTS AND GLO's TODAY. THIS QUOTE IS EXACT WHEN DESCRIBING GLO's AND THE MEMBERS AS WELL (CONFESSING CHRISTIANS INCLUDED).

"**All traditions** from the earliest times bears testimony to the apostasy of Nimrod, and to his success in leading men away from their patriarchal faith, and delivering their minds from the awe of God and fear of the judgments of

COMING APART AT THE SEAMS

heaven that must have rested on them while yet the memory of the flood was recent. And according to all the principles of depraved human nature, this too, no doubt was one grand element in his fame; For men will **readily** rally behind any one who can give the least appearance for plausibility to **any doctrine which will teach** that **man can be assured of happiness and heaven** at last, though their **hearts and nature** are **unchanged,** and though they live without God in the world." (THE LATE REV. ALEXANDER HISLOP, THE TWO BABYLONS OR PAPAL WORSHIP: Proved to be THE WORSHIP OF NIMROD AND HIS WIFE, LOIZEUAX BROTHERS, INC., AMERICA, SECOND AMERICAN EDITION, 1959, p. 52.)

WHEN I READ THIS QUOTE, I KNEW I HAD TO BUY THE BOOK. WHEN I BOUGHT THE BOOK, MY HEART PUMPED, KNOWING THAT GOD HAD PLACED ANOTHER VESSEL BEFORE ME TO HELP ME IN THE QUEST FOR SOULS IN GLO's. I HAVE NO DOUBT THAT GREEK-LETTERED ORGANIZATIONS DERIVED THEIR ORIGINS FROM THE SEVEN CATEGORIES LISTED ABOVE. GLO's CANNOT DENY THE SIMILARITIES, BECAUSE THE FACTS ABOUT THEM CRY LOUDLY. GREEK CHRISTIAN; IF YOU HAVE NOT READ YOUR RITUAL, YOU NEED TO. IF YOU HAVE, READ IT AGAIN. IF YOU DON'T FEEL THE NEED TO, HELL IS JUST A DEATH AWAY. THE SOURCE, THE ROOT, THE ORIGIN, AND THE **NATURE OF GLO's IS MADE CLEAR.** JUST AS GOD's NATURE IS UNCHANGEABLE, SO IS THE **EVIL NATURE OF ALL SECRET SOCIETIES**. GOD SENT HIS SON TO DESTROY THE WORKS OF THE DEVIL NOT THE DEVIL'S NATURE.

I JOHN 3:8 He that committeth (practices) sin is of the devil; for the devil sinneth from the beginning. For this purpose the Son of God was manifested, that he might destroy the works of the devil.

THE ORIGIN OF THESE SECRET SOCIETIES MUST BE KNOWN TO HAVE A SOLID ARGUMENT AGAINST THEM. ARE THEY EVIL ROOTS OR GOOD ROOTS???? THIS IS WHAT **FIRST** MUST BE DETERMINED, BECAUSE IF ONE COULD ESTABLISH A GOOD ROOT, THIS WHOLE BOOK WOULD BE WORTHLESS. THE ORIGINS OF THESE GROUPS WILL HELP ONE TO UNDERSTAND WHY PEOPLE IN GLO's THINK, TALK, AND ACT THE WAY THEY DO. EVEN A CHRISTIAN BECOMES **ENSLAVED BY SECRECY.** ALTHOUGH SOME KNOW SECRECY IS WRONG, THEY ARE STILL WILLING TO PARTAKE IN THE WICKEDNESS OF GLO's. THE GREEK-LETTERED ORGANIZATIONS KNEW ABOUT THE ANTI-MASONIC/SECRET ORGANIZATION MOVEMENT. PHI BETA KAPPA FELT ITS STING AND APPARENTLY SUCCUMBED TO THE PRESSURE, AND BANISHED ITS SECRECY (SO THEY SAY). ORIGIN AS WE WILL SEE IS **THE DETERMINING FACTOR OF WHETHER SOMETHING IS OF GOD OR NOT.** FOR GREEK-LETTER ORGANIZATIONS, **THEIR ORIGINS DO NOT BEGIN WITH THEIR FOUNDING FATHERS.** THE INSPIRATION GOES FAR BEYOND FELLOWSHIP AND PHILANTHROPY.

"In 1400 B.C. the Minoan civilization collapsed, probably due to a natural phenomena such as an earthquake, whereupon the Greeks took over Crete and **adopted** Cretan **mythology.**" (Kathleen N. Daly, Greek and Roman Mythology form A to Z: A Young Reader's

COMING APART AT THE SEAMS

Companion, New York: Facts on File, 1992, introduction-p. iv.)

"Little is certain about the first Greek settlers except that they brought with them Zeus, their sky god, father of gods and men, lord of the weather, and protector of the household-characteristics that he kept throughout the classical period." (Mark Morford, Greece: Religion and Mythology, Encyclopedia Americana, Grolier, Inc. 1999, p.429.)

Zeus is a mythological god.
LOOK MYTHOLOGY UP!!- IT'S ABSOLUTELY NON-CHRISTIAN, ABSURD AND FORBIDDEN BY GOD.

II TIMOTHY 4:7(amp) But **refuse** and **avoid** irreverent legends (profane and impure and godless fictions, mere grandmother's tales) and **silly myths** and **express your disapproval of them.** Train yourself toward godliness (piety), [keeping yourself spiritually fit].

MYTHOLOGY IS ALSO **IDOLATRY BECAUSE IT GIVES TO OTHERS WHAT BELONGS TO GOD.**

EXODUS 20:3 Thou shalt have no other **gods** before me.

THIS IS THE FIRST COMMANDMENT, AND MANY FRATERNITIES AND SORORITIES (**MEMBERS INCLUDED**) HAVE BROKEN IT BY **DIRECTLY** ASSOCIATING THEMSELVES WITH OTHER gods THROUGH SYMBOL OR IN WRITING. SOME OF THEM ARE: **AURORA** (SIGMA GAMMA RHO), **MINERVA** (DELTA SIGMA THETA), **THE SPHINX** (ALPHA

FREDERIC L. HATCHETT

PHI ALPHA), **APOLLO** (TAU KAPPA EPSILON), **THE CENTAUR** (IOTA PHI THETA), AND **ATLAS** (ALPHA KAPPA ALPHA).

There is another piece of Greek history that needs attention when dealing with **modern day** GLO's.

"Greek religion generally, apart from the mystery religions, did not have a body of doctrine. It required of its worshipers the correct observance of ritual, performed in the correct frame of mind. There were regular civic religious festivals, at which sacrifices, athletic contests, processions, and dramatic performances might take place. Participation in these festivals was both a religious and political act. But the great civic occasions, such as the Panatheanic Festival at Athens did not satisfy the religious needs of the ordinary individual. There was a host of private and domestic religious acts." (Mark Morford, Greece: Religion and Mythology, Encyclopedia Americana, Grolier, Inc. 1999, p.431.)

ANYONE WHO HAS SOME KNOWLEDGE ABOUT GLO's, KNOWS THAT THEY REQUIRE ITS MEMBERS (THE WORSHIPERS) TO GO THROUGH RITUALS. EACH PLEDGE PERIOD HAS A CERTAIN TIME WHERE THE RITUAL IS THE CENTER OF ATTENTION. YOU ARE ACCEPTED AS A PLEDGE, INITIATED, AND ARE BURIED ACCORDING TO THE GLO's RITUAL.

"Greek-letter organizations have regular festivals like the ones recorded in Greek history: step-shows, which are ritual dance routines, are performed at local and national gatherings." (Elder James P. Tharrington Jr., Should Christians Pledge Fraternities and Sororities, For His Glory Printing And Publishing, 1990, p.6.)

RITUAL PRACTICES ARE **DESIGNED TO** IMPRINT THE TEACHINGS AND PRINCIPLES OF THE GLO ON THE MINDS OF THE INITIATES; THEY DO THIS THROUGH REPETITION OF ACTS, SONGS, AND RECITATION OF HISTORY AND POEMS ON DEMAND. THE **PURPOSE OF RITUALS** IS TO:

1.) GIVE IMPORTANCE AND MEANING TO WHO OR WHAT IS BEING WORSHIPED. (THE GLO) EXPLAIN THE EVENTS BASED ON NATURAL REASONING, **NOT GOD'S WORD**.

ALL RITUALS THAT ARE NOT PERFORMED ACCORDING TO THE WORD OF GOD, ARE DEMONIC. IT IS THE WORSHIP OF A FALSE god.

THE SAME **demonic** INFLUENCES BEHIND THE GREEKS, EGYPTIANS, BABYLONIANS, etc., IN ANCIENT TIMES ARE THE SAME THAT EXIST IN THESE GROUPS TODAY. **THE DEMONIC INFLUENCES ARE UNDENIABLE BECAUSE THEIR (GLO's) ACTIONS ARE INDISPUTABLE. FOR A LIST OF THOSE ACTIONS, SEE THE CHAPTER 3 PART 2 ON HAZING.**
THE EGYPTIAN, GREEK, AND BABYLONIAN RELIGIONS ARE RITUAL BASED **(predominantly occult)** WITH A HIGHLY FLEXIBLE SET OF BELIEFS**(diversity)**. THIS

DIVERSITY IS DUE TO MAN'S VIVID IMAGINATION WHICH LEADS TO COMPROMISE, PRIDE, THEIR REFUSAL TO ACCEPT THE **DEITY OF JESUS, AND TO REFUSE A DEITY THAT REQUIRES HOLINESS AS WELL**, ALL OF WHICH ARE **SIN**. ANCIENT CULTS AND GLO'S **DID NOT** AND **DO NOT** WANT A HOLY GOD AT THE CENTER OF THEIR PRINCIPLES. THE CHRISTIAN'S GOD WAS ONE THE GREEKS WERE NOT WILLING TO **WORSHIP**, THE SAME BEING FOR **GLO'S TODAY**. BECAUSE OF THEIR EXTREME DIVERSITY IN THEIR BELIEFS SUCH AS RELIGIOUS TOLERANCE, SO WAS THE RITUALISTIC **WORSHIP** OF THE GREEK RELIGIOUS SYSTEM. A **RITUAL** IS A FORM OF **CONDUCTING WORSHIP. IN ALL WORSHIP, THERE IS THE PRESCENCE OF A DEITY.** WORSHIP DOES NOT MEAN YOU HAVE TO GET DOWN ON YOUR KNEES TO DO IT. WORSHIP OR IDOLATRY CAN BE VERY SUBTLE AND IS NOT TOTALLY DETERMINED BY THE POSITION OF THE BODY, OR JUST BY HAVING A BUDDHA DOLL ON YOUR TABLETOP. IDOLATRY OR WORSHIP CAN EXIST IN THE MIND (THOUGHTS) WITHOUT AN INITIAL EXTERNAL MANIFESTATION. AN EXAMPLE IS GREED AND COVETOUSNESS BOTH OF WHICH ARE IDOLATRY.

COLOSSIANS 3:5(amp) So kill (deaden, deprive of power) the evil desire lurking in your members [those animal impulses and all that is earthy in you that is employed in sin]: sexual vice, impurity, sexual appetites, unholy **desires**, and **all greed and covetousness**, for that **is idolatry (the deifying of self and other created things instead of God)**.

COMING APART AT THE SEAMS

THESE CAN EXIST IN THE HEART AND MIND LONG BEFORE THEY ARE MADE MANIFEST TO THE NAKED EYE. MANY WHO CLAIM A RELATIONSHIP WITH CHRIST HAVE MORE GLO STICKERS ON THEIR CARS AND OBJECTS IN THEIR HOMES THAT RELATE TO THEIR ORGANIZATIONS RATHER THAN TO GOD. THE RITUALISTIC ACTIVITIES CONDUCTED BY THESE GROUPS **ARE IDOLATROUS BECAUSE THEIR RITUALS ARE NOT BASED ON, FOUND IN, AND DO NOT WORSHIP THE ONE, TRUE AND LIVING GOD.** RITUALS ARE HOW ONE WORSHIPS **God,** a god, or gods. IT DEPENDS ON THE NATURE OF THE RITUAL AS TO WHICH god THEY ARE WORSHIPPING. RITUALS THAT DO WORSHIP THE TRUE GOD ARE IN THE BIBLE AND SOME ARE BAPTISM, COMMUNION, CONSECRATION (OF PERSONS OR THINGS), ORDAINING, etc. **WHICH ARE NOT TO BE** CONFUSED WITH UNGODLY FRATERNAL INITIATIONS, BURIAL RITES, STEP SHOWS, BRANDING, OR PLEDGE/INTAKE PERIODS. WHAT'S THE DIFFERENCE BETWEEN THEIRS AND OURS? OURS ARE BIBLICALLY BASED AND WE DO OURS **PUBLICLY, WHILE** THEIRS ARE CULT BASED AND PRIMARILY DONE IN **SECRET-BEHIND CLOSED DOORS** (OCCULT FASHION). **SECRECY ALLOTS ONE THE ABILITY TO WARD OFF GODLY JUDGMENT BY OTHERS, BECAUSE OF THEIR LACK OF KNOWLEDGE OF WHAT GOES ON. WHETHER DONE IN THE OPEN OR NOT, IT IS OBVIOUS BY THE ACTIONS OF MEMBERS AND THE RESULT OF LEAKING INFORMATION THAT THEY ARE NOT GODLY.** THEY CHOOSE THE RITUALS THEY DO OPENLY THAT HAVE A FORM OF GODLINESS SUCH AS FUNERAL SERVICES OR ONES THAT APPEAL TO THE WORLD AND THE THINGS IN THE WORLD. **THE LUST OF THE**

EYES (IT LOOKS GOOD), **THE LUST OF THE FLESH** (APPEALS THROUGH EMOTIONS-**FEELS GOOD**) AND **THE PRIDE OF LIFE** (THE GLORY IS NOT GIVEN TO GOD).

I JOHN 2:16 For all that is in the world, the lust of the flesh, and the lust of the eyes, and the pride of life, **is not of the Father**, but is of the world.

THE DEVIL HAS GAINED SUCH A STRONG FOOTHOLD AND WIDESPREAD ACCEPTANCE **THROUGH PRIDE** THAT THEY ARE NOW DOING SOME OF THEIR SECRET RITUALS IN PUBLIC. RITUALS THEY HAD ALREADY BEEN DOING PUBLICLY ARE STEP SHOWS, PARTIES, etc. DANCING RITUALS WERE PERFORMED IN ANCIENT GREECE AS A PART OF THEIR WORSHIP. STEPPING AND WORLDLY PARTIES ARE OBVIOUSLY SINFUL, BECAUSE THEY GIVE GLORY TO THE GLO. STEP SHOWS HAVE BEEN GIVEN A STATUS OF **"PRE-PROTECTION TO SIN" BY GREEK CHRISTIANS** FOR THE PURPOSE TO RAISE FUNDS FOR GOOD CAUSES. THE BIBLE SAYS,

II PETER 2:16(amp) [Live] as free people, [yet] without employing your freedom **as a pretext for wickedness;** but **[live at all times]** as servants of God.

ROMANS 14:16 Let not then your good be evil spoken of.

GOD REVEALS AND **SATAN CONCEALS**. GOD WILL **REVEAL AND DESTROY GLO's** FROM

COMING APART AT THE SEAMS

THEIR ORIGIN TO NOW ALL THAT SATAN TRIES TO HIDE.

MATTHEW 10:26 So have no fear of them; for nothing is concealed that will not be revealed, or kept secret that will not become known.

I JOHN 3:8 He that commiteth (practices) sin is of the devil; for the devil sinneth from the beginning. For this purpose the Son of God was manifested, that he might destroy the works of the devil.

THE SECRECY PRACTICED BY GLO'S IS A WORK OF THE DEVIL, AND WILL CAUSE YOU TO LOSE YOUR ETERNAL LIFE. GREEK CHRISTIANS! IT'S TIME TO DENOUNCE!!!

JOHN 18:20(amp) Jesus answered him, I have always taught in a synagogue and in the temple [area], where the Jews [habitually] congregate (assemble); and I have spoken nothing **secretly**.

FRATERNITIES, SORORITIES, MASONS, EASTERN STARS, ETC. YOUR 50-200 YEARS OF SECRECY/CONCEALMENT IS OVER!!! BETTER TO BE EXPOSED NOW THAN AT THE GREAT WHITE THRONE OF JUDGMENT!!! PERHAPS YOU WILL DENOUNCE AND REPENT. I MADE A VOW **TO GOD** THAT IF MORE MEMBERS ARE ACQUIRED BY GLO's, IT WILL NOT BE BECAUSE OF IGNORANCE AND DECEPTION. ALL PEOPLE WHO READ THIS BOOK WILL KNOW EXACTLY WHAT THEY ARE GETTING THEMSELVES INTO, AND HAVE NO EXCUSE OF IGNORANCE OR DECEPTION, BUT

WILL BE IN UNBELIEF. THERE IS TOO MUCH SCRIPTURAL PROOF TO THIS POINT TO SAY THAT I AM RENDERING AN **OPINION**. IF THESE ORGANIZATIONS HAD ANY INTEGRITY, FAITH, RIGHTEOUSNESS, GOOD WILL TOWARD MEN, AND ANY DECENCY **THEY WOULDN'T HAVE TO HIDE ANYTHING**. THEY WOULD TELL THE INTERESTED PERSON EVERYTHING SO THEY COULD MAKE A WISE DECISION BASED ON ALL THE FACTS. INSTEAD THEY ARE MADE TO GO THROUGH A PROCESS OF SPIRITUAL DECEPTION, BIASED OPINIONS, PHYSICAL PUNISHMENT, AND MENTAL HUMILIATION FROM SINNERS AND THOSE WHO CLAIM TO BE SAVED. SHOULD IT NOT STRIKE YOU FUNNY THAT A "CONFESSING CHRISTIAN" IS PADDLING YOU OR SLAPPING YOU AROUND? IF WHAT THEY POSSESS IS SO AWESOME, WHY NOT REVEAL IT? OUT OF THE MOUTHS OF ABOUT 30 PROFESSING CHRISTIANS IN GLO'S I HAVE ASKED THIS QUESTION: THEY HAVE NOT AND WILL NOT, BECAUSE THEY CANNOT. THEY KNOW WHAT THEY HAVE IS NOT POPULAR WITH GOD AND SO DOES THE DEVIL WHO INSPIRED IT. THERE IS NO SUCH THING AS GOOD SECRECY WHEN IT COMES TO GLO's. BUT WHAT THE TRUE BELIEVER POSSESSES IS A NAME THAT IS ABOVE EVERY NAME AND HAS NO PROBLEM **REVEALING** THAT NAME AND HIS PURPOSE FOR ALL MEN AND WOMEN.

ACTS 4:10-12 Be it known unto you all, and to all the people of Israel, that by the name of **Jesus Christ** of Nazareth, whom ye crucified, whom God raised from the dead, even by him doth this man stand here before you whole. This is the stone which was set at naught of ye builders, which is become the head of the corner. Neither is there salvation in any other: for there is **none other name** under heaven given among men, whereby we must be saved.

THE NAME OF A GLO CAN'T DO WHAT THE NAME OF JESUS CAN. THERE IS NO SALVATION IN ANY GLO, YET MANY CLAIM IT. THEY BELIEVE THAT SERVICE (**WORKS**) DONE FOR A GLO IS ENOUGH TO GO TO HEAVEN AND JUSTIFY THEIR EXISTENCE. THIS IS WHAT SOME SAY IN THEIR WRITINGS. REMEMBER THOSE SEVEN SIMILARITIES; HERE'S PROOF.

"Their immortality is assured throughout all eternity as each generation of Deltas continues the organization's **good works**. The lighted candles in our beloved Sigma represent the nine Cardinal Virtues by which our departed Sorors sought to pattern their lives. As these lights are extinguished, symbolizing **the passage of these Sorors into Omega Omega."** (DELTA SIGMA THETA SORORITY, INC., GRAND CHAPTER, RITUAL, 1990, p.70)

Omega Omega is where the deceased sorors go after death. This excerpt speaks of **"assured" immortality**, a rite of passage into some eternally favorable place for doing good works. **Works salvation is a false gospel preached by the GLO's**, and many Christians are led astray by this deceitful flattery. Jesus is nowhere to be found in this excerpt, as if his judgment means nothing. You consider your rebellious ways by remaining in your GLO. **None** of The nine

Cardinal Virtues is faith, salvation, repentance, evangelism, etc. All of their Virtues point toward the sorority and its members, not toward the God of the Bible, **but instead toward the goddess Minerva.**

Omega Psi Phi makes the same type of statement during their memorial service for deceased brothers:

"<u>Chaplain</u>: 'The souls of the righteous are in the hands of God, and there shall no torment touch them.'"

"<u>Response</u>: 'In the sight of the unwise they seem to die; and their departure is taken for misery.'"

"<u>Chaplain</u>: 'And their going from us to be utter destruction; but they are in peace.'"

"<u>Response</u>: **God proved them and found them worthy for Himself.'"**
(OMEGA PSI PHI FRATERNITY (Incorporated 1914), THE RITUAL, 1970, pp. 35-36.)

There is no mention of this member's salvation, and relationship with Jesus. By what did **they say** God proved them and how did they attain righteousness? It was by their lives **in Omega.** They say these words in vain, because your worth is not in a GLO. They are clearly making an assumption and a false one at best. They cannot help that persons eternal destiny, only hinder it, neither should they lie by saying they can. Their "brother" is in hell. The only way to have **peace** with God is by accepting Jesus' sacrifice on the cross, and living the life according to that belief. If they are in peace, Omega is implying that all of their deceased brothers go to heaven. This is NEVER the case. I plead with any Greek Christian to stop being deceived. Look at the evidence so far, do what is right and denounce. Chapter 10 Part 3, "Denouncing My Organization", tells you how to denounce and repent.

WE (TRUE CHRISTIANS) DO NOT NEED ANOTHER BOOK TO PERFORM OUR RITUALS OR TEACH OUR DOCTRINES, BECAUSE OUR RITUALS AND DOCTRINES ARE **ORIGINA**TED BY **GOD THE FATHER** AND **GOD THE SON** WHICH ARE WRITTEN (OPENLY) IN HIS WORD THROUGH THE INSPIRATION OF **GOD THE HOLY GHOST.** THE GREATEST 1-2-3 PUNCH COMBINATION EVER. NOT ONLY THAT, WE PERFORM OUR RITUALS OPENLY. THESE GROUPS HAVE RITUALS AND DOCTRINES THAT **NEVER WERE** AND **NEVER WILL BE** ROOTED IN GOD OR AS THEY SAY FOUNDED UPON CHRISTIAN PRINCIPLES. THE SECRET SOCIETIES OF THE GREEKS AND BABYLONIANS OF OLD, AND THE **SECRET ORGANIZATIONS OF THE NOW** SHARE A COMMON TRAIT: THEY NEVER COULD GET ENOUGH FROM **THEIR OWN** DOCTRINES, FESTIVALS, SACRIFICING, BELIEFS, OR THEIR gods (all of their gods were not enough!!!). THEY (THE GREEKS ESPECIALLY, LIKE ALL SECRET GROUPS) JUST KEEP MAKING UP STUFF AS

THEY GO ALONG. UNSATISFIED, REBELLIOUS CHRISTIANS ARE THE ONES OFTEN FOUND IN FRATERNITIES, SORORITIES, AND OTHER WORLDLY ORGANIZATIONS, BUT TRUE CHRISTIANS ARE SATISFIED WITH THE WORD OF GOD AND THEIR LOCAL CHURCH AND DO NOT NEED A HYPOCRITICAL CHANGE OF PACE FOR THEIR BELIEFS. **THE TRUE CHRISTIAN'S GOD, WHO IS THE WORD THAT WAS MADE FLESH:** IS ALONE SUFFICIENT FOR US. WHEN WE WANT TO KNOW SOMETHING, WE SEEK **HIS** FACE AND WE FIND HIM. WE ASK **HIS** BLESSINGS AND RECEIVE THEM WITH JOY. WE KNOCK ON **HIS** DOOR AND HE OPENS IT. WE THANK **HIM** FOR **HIS** STRIPES THAT HAVE HEALED US AND WE ARE HEALED. WE SEARCH **HIS** WORD (**A HISTORICALLY RELIABLE DOCUMENT**) AND FIND MANY TREASURES, AND WE SEEK FELLOWSHIP WITH OTHER CHRISTIANS, **NOT OUR OWN MIND, OR UNSAVED FRATERNITY OR SORORITY MEMBERS.**

PSALMS 1:1-6 Blessed is man that walketh not in the counsel of **the ungodly**, nor standeth in the way of **sinners**, nor sitteth in the seat of the **scornful**. But his delight is in the law of the Lord; and in His law doth he meditate day and night. And he shall be like a tree planted by the rivers of water, that bringeth forth his fruit in season; his leaf shall not wither; and whatsoever he doeth shall prosper. **The ungodly are not so**: but are like the chaff which the wind driveth away. Therefore, the ungodly shall not stand in judgment, nor sinners in the congregation of the righteous. For the

Lord knoweth the way of the righteous: but the way of the ungodly shall perish.

BESIDE THIS, DO YOU KNOW THE WRITERS OF YOUR RITUALS AND THEIR STATUS WITH CHRIST? I doubt it. **I'M NOT TALKING ABOUT THEIR TITLES** (i.e. BISHOP, PASTOR, PROPHET, ETC.), BUT THEIR LIFESTYLES. ACCORDING TO THEIR HISTORY, MEMBERS PARTICIPATED IN UNGODLY SOCIAL ACTIVITIES, AND THE FACT THAT GREEK PHILOSOPHY, MYTHOLOGY, SYMBOLISM ARE ALL INCLUDED IN THE RITUALS PROVES MOST PROBLEMATICAL FOR THE GREEK CHRISTIAN TO USE THIS AS A PLAUSIBLE ARGUMENT FOR AN ORGANIZATION OF GODLY ORIGIN. FOR ANY MINISTER OF GOSPEL TO TOLERATE MYTHS AND UNGODLY PHILOSOPHIES AS APART OF ANY GROUP, **MUST** COMPROMISE THE GOSPEL. WE **KNOW** THE AUTHOR AND **ORIGIN OF GOD'S WORD, THE EARTH AND OURSELVES**. HE BACKS IT UP IN THE BIBLE, HIS WORD.

II TIMOTHY 3:16- All scripture is given by inspiration of **God**, and is profitable for doctrine, for **reproof**, for correction, and instruction in righteousness:

JOHN 1:3- For **all things were made by him**; and without him was not any thing made that was made.

A CHRISTIAN ALREADY KNOWS WHERE HE COMES FROM (PAST), WHO HE IS (PRESENT), AND WHERE HE IS GOING WHEN

HE DIES (FUTURE). A CHRISTIAN ALSO KNOWS THAT THE BIBLE IS A PERFECT DOCUMENT, AND THAT IT IS HISTORICALLY RELIABLE.

THE HISTORY YOU LEARN AS A PLEDGE IS ACHIEVEMENTS AND STRUGGLES OF PAST MEMBERS AND THE GROUP AS A WHOLE. WHY NOT REVEAL ALL OF THEIR HISTORY? IN THE HISTORIES OF SOME THAT I HAVE READ, IT NEVER ONCE MENTIONS THE SAVING OF SOULS THROUGH SALVATION BY FAITH IN JESUS CHRIST, EVANGELISTIC CRUSADES, OR DOOR-TO-DOOR WITNESSING. A THANKSGIVING DINNER WAS MORE IMPORTANT TO GIVE THAN TO WITNESS ABOUT JESUS CHRIST. ONE COULD NOT READ THEIR HISTORY BOOKS AND HAVE A CONVICTION TO BE SAVED OR THAT JESUS WAS THE MAIN FOCUS. THE ONLY CONVICTION ONE COULD HAVE IS TO JOIN OR DENOUNCE. FROM COVER TO COVER, IT'S ALL ABOUT THEIR FRATERNITY OR SORORITY. **THIS IS PRIDE.** JESUS HIMSELF SAYS IN,

JOHN 12:32 And I, if I be lifted up from the earth, will draw all men unto me.

GLO'S CONSTANTLY LIFT THEMSELVES UP, NOT JESUS. SO WHO DO THEY EXPECT TO DRAW TO THEM? MEN AND WOMEN WHO ARE NOT ROOTED AND GROUNDED IN GOD'S WORD AND SINNERS WILL BE DRAWN TO GLO'S. EVEN THOUGH THESE GROUPS ARE NOT A CHURCH, INDIVIDUAL CHRISTIANS ARE CHARGED BY GOD TO BE SOUL WINNERS.

THIS COMMAND FROM GOD IS CORPORATE AND INDIVIDUAL. GLO's DO NOT HAVE SOUL WINNING AS PART OF THEIR PRINCIPLES, BECAUSE THEY ARE RELIGIOUSLY TOLERANT. **RELIGIOUS TOLERANCE** CANNOT BE A CHARACTERISTIC OF ORGANIZATIONS THAT CLAIM TO BE FOUNDED UPON CHRISTIAN PRINCIPLES. **FOUNDERS THAT WERE CLERGY** MISSED GOD ON THIS ONE.

PROVERBS 11:30 (amp) The fruit of the [**uncompromisingly**] righteous is a tree of life, and he who is wise captures human lives [for God, as a fisher of men he gathers and receives them for eternity].

THE CAPTURING OF HUMAN LIVES (SOUL WINNING) IS A USELESS ENDEAVOR FOR THE GREEK CHRISTIAN. **HOW CAN A SINNER (A GREEK CHRISTIAN) "WIN" SOULS TO CHRIST? IT'S A CONTRADICTION OF TERMS. IT'S A CASE OF THE BLIND LEADING THE BLIND.**

II CORINTHIANS 5:18&20 (amp) And all things are of God, who has reconciled us to himself by Jesus Christ, and hath given unto **us** the ministry of reconciliation; **Now** then **we are ambassadors for Christ**, as though God did beseech you by us: we pray you in Christ's stead, be ye reconciled to God.

THE SAVED ARE THE AMBASSADORS, NOT THOSE IN GLO's. A TRUE AMBASSADOR DOES NOT COHABITATE WITH THE ENEMY.

YOU KNOW WHY SOUL WINNING IS NOT WRITTEN IN THEIR HISTORY OR RITUALS? BECAUSE THESE GROUPS DO NOT PROMOTE THE GOSPEL **IN ITS ENTIRETY IN MANY MORE WAYS THAN JUST SOUL WINNING**; BUT LOOK AT WHAT THE BIBLE SAYS.

I JOHN 2:5(amp) But he who keeps (treasures) His Word [who bears in mind His precepts, who observes His message **in its entirety**], truly in him has the love of and for God been perfected (completed, reached maturity). By this we may perceive (know, recognize, and be sure) that we are in Him:

IF YOUR CHURCH IS NOT A SOUL WINNING BODY, IT IS NOT A CHURCH OF GOD. GLO's HAVE NO NEED FOR CHRISTIANITY IN THEIR RITUALS, BECAUSE THEY DO NOT PRACTICE CHRISTIANITY OR **THEIR OWN PRINCIPLES**; THEY ARE NOTHING BUT A BUNCH OF HYPOCRITES AND A PACK OF LIARS. IT DOES NOT TAKE A CHRISTIAN TO DO A GOOD DEED (**LUKE 11:11-13**), BUT A SINNER THAT DOES THE GOOD DEED IS NOT REWARDED BY GOD. ONLY THE RECEIVER OF THE DEED BENEFITS, THE SINFUL GIVER HAS NO REWARD FROM GOD. YET, GLO's TRY TO RESTORE AND MAKE THE WORLD BETTER BY THEIR OWN EFFORTS, BUT ONLY A TRUE CHRISTIAN WANTS TO AND KNOWS THAT THIS CAN ONLY BE ACHIEVED BY THE TRUTH OF THE GOSPEL ALONE. IT'S A SHAME TO DO GOOD, AND HAVE GOD NOT ONLY IGNORE IT, BUT SEND YOU TO HELL. (**MATTHEW 7:21-23**).

LUKE 11:11-13(amp) What father among you, if his son ask for a loaf of bread, will give him a stone; or if he ask for a fish, will instead of a fish give him a serpent? Or if he ask for an egg, will give him a scorpion? If you then, evil as you are, know how to give good gifts [**gifts that are to their advantage**] to your children, how much more will your heavenly father give the holy spirit to those who ask and continue to ask!)

JOHN 8:32 And ye shall know the truth, and the truth shall make you free.

IT'S NOT AA OR THE NICOTINE PATCH THAT FREES ONE FROM THEIR ADDICTION. IT'S JESUS, THE TRUTH.

II TIMOTHY 2:20-22(amp) But in a great house there are not only vessels of gold and silver, but also [utensils] of wood and earthenware, and some for honorable and noble [use] and some for menial and ignoble [use]. So whoever cleanses himself [from what is ignoble and unclean, who separate himself from contact with contaminating and corrupting influences] will [then himself] be a vessel set apart and useful for honorable and noble purposes, consecrated and profitable to the Master, **fit and ready for any good work.** Shun youthful lusts and flee from them, and aim and pursue at righteousness (all that is virtuous and good, right living, conformity to the will of God in thought, word, and deed); [and aim at

FREDERIC L. HATCHETT

and pursue] faith, love, [and] peace (harmony and accord with others) in fellowship with all [Christians], who **call upon the Lord out of a pure heart.**

When one belongs to a GLO, they are ignoble and unclean, and **not fit or ready for any good work. When they denounce, they are fit and ready for any good work.**

TITUS 1:15-16(amp) To the pure [in heart and conscience] all things are pure, but to the defiled and corrupt and unbelieving **nothing is pure**, their very minds and consciences are defiled and polluted. They profess to know God [to recognize, perceive, and be acquainted with him] but deny and disown and denounce him by what they do; they are detestable and loathsome, unbelieving and disobedient and disloyal and rebellious, and [they are] **unfit and worthless for good work (deed or enterprise) of any kind.**

CHRISTIANITY IN THE RITUALS IS THE DEVIL'S PLOT TO DECEIVE. THEY DO NOT OBEY THE GREAT COMMISSION (**MATTHEW 28:19-20**), MINISTRY OF RECONCILIATION (**II CORINTHIANS 5:17-21**, JUSIFICATION BY FAITH (**HEBREWS 6:1**), etc., etc. SINCE GLO's DO NOT OBEY THESE TRUTHS, CHRISTIANS SHOULD NOT BE A PART OF THEM. THERE IS NO SUCH THING AS A 25%, 75%, OR 90% CHRISTIAN.

MATTHEW 6:22-23(amp) The eye is the lamp of the body. So if your eye is sound, your entire body will be full of light. But if your eye is unsound, your whole body will be full of darkness. If then the light in you [**your conscience**] is darkened, how dense is that darkness!

WHEREVER SPIRITUAL DARKNESS (the unsound eye) IS CONDONED, THERE CAN BE **NO SPIRITUAL LIGHT**; JUST AS THEIR CAN BE NO LIGHT WITHOUT ELECTRICITY. WHEN ONE HAS LOST THE ABILITY TO **RECEIVE** SPIRITUAL LIGHT BECAUSE OF COMPROMISE, DOUBT, REBELLION AND UNBELIEF (the characteristics of an **UNSOUND EYE**), THE **CONSCIENCE IS DARKENED** LEADING TO A WILL FOR THE DEVIL.

JAMES 1:5(amp) If any of you is deficient in wisdom, let him ask of the giving God [who gives] to everyone liberally and ungrudgingly, without reproaching or faultfinding, and it will be given him.

ONCE YOUR CONSCIENCE IS ABANDONED, SO WILL YOUR LIFESTYLE. BEING IN A GLO DOES THIS BECAUSE THE WORD SAYS IN,

I CORINTHIANS 15:33(amp) Do not be so deceived and misled! Evil companionships (communion, associations) corrupt and deprave good manners and morals and character.

SINCE GLO'S ARE INNATELY AND INHERENTLY EVIL, SO WILL YOU EVENTUALLY BECOME EVIL. A CHRISTIAN WHO JOINS A GLO SURROUNDS THEMSELF WITH SINNERS. THESE **EVIL**

COMPANIONSHIPS WILL BRING YOU DOWN. YOU CAN'T SEE GOD WITH AN EVIL EYE, NEITHER CAN YOU HEAR GOD WITH AN EVIL EAR. THE," I DON'T CARE," ATTITUDE TAKES ROOT, AND REBELLION SETS ITSELF UP IN YOU. MANY HEAR AND KNOW THE TRUTH ABOUT GLO's AND STILL JOIN ANYWAY. AN INDIVIDUALS' REBELLION OF **THE TRUE GOD** IS WHAT MAKES A GLO THEIR god. GOING TO CHURCH, WITNESSING THE LOST TO CHRIST, AND HELPING THE POOR, ALONG WITH PARTIES, UNEQUAL YOKING, RITUAL CEREMONIES, AND TAKING OATHS CAUSES THAT LIGHT WITHIN THEE TO BE DARKNESS.

I CORINTHIANS 10:21-23(amp) You **cannot** drink the Lord's cup and the demons' cup. You **cannot** partake of the Lord's table and the demons' table. Shall we thus provoke the Lord to jealousy and anger and indignation? Are we stronger than he [that we should defy him]? All things are legitimate (permissible), [and we are free to do anything we please], but not all things are helpful (expedient, profitable, and wholesome). All things are legitimate, but not all things are constructive [to character] and edifying [to spiritual life].

MEMBERSHIP IN A GLO IS NOT CONSTRUCTIVE OR EDIFYING. ANY CHRISTIAN IN A GLO IS LEADING A DOUBLE, YET SINGLE LIFE. THEY TRY TO LIVE FOR THE DEVIL AND GOD (DOUBLE LIFE), BUT THIS EQUATES ITSELF TO LIVING FOR THE DEVIL (SINGLE LIFE).

GOD SAYS TO SERVE HIM WITH SINGLENESS OF HEART. FEEDING THE POOR AND COMMUNITY CLEAN-UPS ARE GREAT IN THE NATURAL, BUT THESE ARE ONLY WORKS AND DO NOT EXCLUDE THE GLO MEMBER FROM THE MANY OTHER SPIRITUAL COMMANDMENTS OF THE BIBLE.

MATTHEW 5:20 For I say unto you, that except your righteousness shall exceed the righteousness of the scribes and Pharisees, ye shall in no case enter into the kingdom of heaven.

MATTHEW 15:1-9 Then came to Jesus scribes and Pharisees, which were of Jerusalem, saying Why do thy disciples transgress the tradition of the elders? for they wash not their hands when they eat bread. But he answered and said unto them, Why do ye also transgress the commandment of God by your tradition? For God commanded, saying, Honour thy father and mother: and, He that curseth father or mother, let him die the death. But ye say, Whosoever shall say to his father or his mother, It is a gift, by whatsoever thou mightest be profited by me; And honour not his father or his mother, he shall be free. Thus have ye made the commandment of God of none effect by your tradition. Ye hypocrites, well did Esa'ias prophesy of you, saying, This people draweth nigh unto me with their mouth, and honoureth me with their lips; but their heart is far from me. But in vain they do worship me, teaching for doctrines the commandments of men.

MATTHEW 23:23 Woe unto you, scribes and Pharisees, **hypocrites**! for ye pay tithe of mint and anise and cummin, and have omitted the weightier matters of the law, judgment, mercy, and faith: these ought ye to have done, and not to leave the other undone.

WORKS ARE NOT A COVERING FOR YOUR SINS. THIS IS ONE REASON THERE ARE SO MANY DIFFERENT SECRET SOCIETIES AS WELL AS CHURCH DENOMINATIONS. SECRET SOCIETIES AND DENOMINATIONS OR (WATERED DOWN CHRISTIANITY) ARE **INVENTIONS OF MEN (NOT GOD)** WHICH CAN BE ATTRIBUTED TO THE **RELATIVISM AND DIVERSITY** OF AN INDIVIDUAL'S BELIEFS. CHRISTIANS ARE TO BE FOCUSED ON ONE PERSON, ONE WAY, ONE TRUTH, AND ONE LIFE: JESUS CHRIST. **BOTTOM LINE:** FRATERNITIES, SORORITIES, MASONS, EASTERN STARS, SHRINERS, ETC. ARE NOT ABOUT CHRIST, BUT **ARE MAN'S WORK**, NOT GOD'S. IF THEY WERE CHRIST-CENTERED, THEY WOULD PROMOTE GODLY THINGS **EXCLUSIVELY: NO OATHS, RITUALS, PARTIES, UNGODLY SYMBOLISM, GREEK MYTHOLOGY, DEATH RITES CEREMONIES, INITIATION RITES CEREMONIES,** etc., etc. ONLY TRUE CHRISTIANS (i.e. THOSE WHO LIVE FOR JESUS AND DO THE WILL OF THE FATHER EXCLUSIVELY) WILL RECEIVE REWARD FOR THEIR LABORS (REVELATION 14:13), AND ONLY THOSE WHO SEEK GOD DILIGENTLY BY FAITH (HEBREWS 11:6) NOT

COMING APART AT THE SEAMS

GOD AND THEIR GLO. REAL CHRISTIANS ARE RULED BY, "WHAT DOTH SAITH THE LORD", NOT WHAT THEY DESIRE. THIS IS WHY THE SCRIPTURE TELLS US NOT TO BE ASHAMED OF THE GOSPEL OF JESUS CHRIST, BECAUSE WE KNOW IT IS THE ONLY WAY FOR ALL OF MANKIND'S REDEMPTION.

ROMANS 1:16 For I am not ashamed of the gospel of Jesus Christ: for it is the power of God unto Salvation to everyone that believeth; to the Jew first, and also to the Greek.

I HAVE NO NEED TO APOLOGIZE OR BE ASHAMED FOR WHAT I SAY IN THIS BOOK, BECAUSE IT'S BASED ON THE TRUE GOSPEL. THE GOSPEL OF THE GLO's DOES NOT LEAD TO ETERNAL SALVATION. INSTEAD IT LEADS TO ETERNAL DAMNATION. IF ONE SAYS THAT I AM BEING JUDGMENTAL, I HAVE GOD'S AUTHORITY TO DO SO, **BECAUSE I AM SAVED.** ON THE OTHER HAND, GLO's ARE SPIRITUALLY EVIL, AND A PERSON IN ONE HAS NO AUTHORITY TO JUDGE ME, OR ANYTHING FOR THAT MATTER, BECAUSE **THEY ARE NOT SAVED.**

I CORINTHIANS 2:14-16(amp) But the **natural, unspiritual** man does not accept or welcome or admit into his heart the gifts and teachings and revelations of the Spirit of God, for they are folly (meaningless nonsense) to him; and **he is incapable of knowing them** [of progressively recognizing, understanding, and becoming better acquainted with them] **because they are spiritually**

discerned and estimated and appreciated. But **the spiritual man tries all things** [he examines, investigates, inquires into, questions, and discerns all things], yet is himself to be put on trial and judged by no one [he can read the meaning of everything, **but no one can properly discern or appraise or get insight into him**]. For who has known or understood the mind (the counsels and purposes) of the Lord so as to guide to instruct him and give him knowledge? **But we have the mind of Christ** (the Messiah) and do hold the thoughts (feelings and purposes) of His heart.

THE UNSAVED DO NOT HAVE THE MIND OF CHRIST. THE UNSAVED CANNOT UNDERSTAND SPIRITUAL THINGS. THEREFORE, HOW CAN THEY JUDGE ANYTHING?

JOHN 3:19-20(amp) The [basis of the] judgment (indictment, the test by which men are judged, the ground for sentence) lies in this: the Light has come into the world, and people loved the darkness rather and more than the Light, for their works (deeds) were evil. For every wrongdoer hates (loathes, detests) the Light, and will not come out into the Light but shrinks from it, lest his works (his deeds, his activities, his conduct) be exposed and reproved.

GLO's WORKS AND SECRECY ARE EVIL AND MUST BE REPROVED (EXPOSED) AND REBUKED. THEY MUST MAKE EXCUSES FOR THEIR PARTYING ON SATURDAY IN CHURCH

ON SUNDAY MENTALITY, DRINKING, SEXUAL IMMORALITY, HAZING, AND BLATANT HYPOCRISY. THEY GET MAD BECAUSE OF GUILT, CONDEMNATION, REVELATION, AND CONVICTION. WHEN **THE LIGHT** CONFRONTS THEIR **DARKNESS**, THEY DON'T WANT TO COME TO THE LIGHT(TRUTH), BECAUSE THEIR DEEDS ARE EVIL. WHEN EVIL IN A GLO IS **REVEALED**, A GREEK CHRISTIAN WILL DO ONE OF **THREE** THINGS IN THE FACE OF TRUTH. THEY WILL LIE SOME MORE AND **REFUSE** THE TRUTH, GET ANGRY AND ARGUE TO **AVOID** THE TRUTH, OR DO WHAT THE BIBLE SAYS LIARS SHOULD DO: REPENT, **BELIEVE** THE TRUTH, AND BE BAPTIZED.

ACTS 2:38 Then Peter said unto them Repent, and be baptized every on of you in the name of Jesus Christ for the remission of sins, and ye shall receive the gift of the Holy Ghost.

REVELATIONS 21:8 But the fearful, and **unbelieving**, and the abominable, and murderers, and whoremongers, and sorcerers, and **idolaters**, and **all liars**, shall have their part in the lake which burneth with fire and brimstone: which is the second death.

HOPEFULLY REVELATION WILL LEAD TO CONVICTION TO CAUSE REPENTANCE. THE BIBLE ALSO DESCRIBES THE GOSPEL AS FOOLISHNESS TO THE GREEKS, BECAUSE THE GREEKS SEEK AFTER WISDOM THAT COMES NATURALLY, BUT NOT THE WISDOM OF CHRIST WHICH IS SUPERNATURALLY BY

FAITH (i.e. without the five senses). GREEKS WERE MATERIALISTS (i.e. THEY DID NOT ACKNOWLEDGE SPIRITUAL THINGS). THE NEXT FIVE SCRIPTURES SHOW THAT HUMAN KNOWLEDGE AND GODLY KNOWLEDGE IN THE WRONG PERSPECTIVE IS DANGEROUS. GREEK CHRISTIANS HAVE A STRONG DESIRE FOR KNOWLEDGE, BUT NOT FOR RIGHTEOUSNESS.

LOVE IS GREATER THAN KNOWLEDGE; KNOWLEDGE WITHOUT LOVE AND SELF-CONTROL LEADS TO PRIDE, AND KNOWLEDGE WITHOUT CHRIST IS WORTHLESS.

I CORINTHIANS 8:1 Now as touching things offered unto idols, we know that we all have knowledge. **Knowledge puffeth up**, but charity edifieth.

EPHESIANS 3:19- And to know **the love of Christ, which passeth knowledge**, that ye might be filled with all the fullness of God.

II PETER 1:5-6 And beside this, giving all diligence, add to your faith virtue; and to virtue knowledge; **And to knowledge temperance**; and to temperance patience; and to patience godliness;

KNOWLEDGE WITHOUT TEMPERANCE (self-control) LEADS TO PRIDE.

COLOSSIANS 2:18 Let no man beguile you of your reward in a voluntary humility and worshipping of angels, intruding into those things which he hath not seen, **vainly puffed up by his fleshly mind.**

I CORINTHIANS 1:22-23 For the Jews require a sign, and the **Greeks seek after wisdom**: But we preach Christ crucified, unto the Jews a stumblingblock, and **unto the Greeks foolishness;**

THIS SAME PROBLEM EXISTS WITH THE GLO's NOW. **WHY?** BECAUSE THEY BELIEVE IN ACQUIRING KNOWLEDGE OR WISDOM THE SAME WAY THE GREEKS DO: **WITHOUT THE TRIUNE GOD. A MAN** WHO **SAID** HE WAS SAVED TOLD ME THAT THE BIBLICAL POINT OF VIEW RELATING TO HIS FRATERNITY, **Omega Psi Phi**, WAS NOT IMPORTANT TO HIM AND THAT IT IS NOT PROPER TO JUDGE AN ORGANIZATION OR THE PEOPLE IN IT BY THE WORD OF GOD. GREEK CHRISTIANS OFTEN QUOTE SCRIPTURES IN DEFENSE OF GLO's HAVING NO REVELATION FROM GOD ON WHAT THEY MEAN. INSTEAD THEY INTERPRET IT ACCORDING THEIR OWN INTELLECT AND EXPERIENCE. THIS IS BECAUSE THEY ARE NOT SPIRITUAL, NOT SAVED, AND CANNOT UNDERSTAND SPIRITUAL THINGS. GREEK CHRISTIANS DON'T STUDY TO SHOW THEMSELVES APPROVED UNTO GOD. WHENEVER YOU WITNESS TO A GREEK CHRISTIAN, REMEMBER THAT YOU ARE THE ANOINTED ONE.

I CORINTHIANS 2:15-16(amp) But the spiritual man **tries all things** [he examines, investigates, inquires into, questions, and discerns all things], yet is himself to be put on trial and judged by no one [he can read the meaning of everything, but no one can properly discern or appraise or get insight into him]. For who has known or understood the mind (the counsels and purposes) of the Lord so as to guide to instruct him and give him knowledge? But we have the mind of Christ (the Messiah) and do hold the thoughts (feelings and purposes) of His heart.

THIS MAN IS A HERETIC AND A PREDICTABLE ONE. HE KNOWS THE TRUTH, BUT WILLFULLY REJECTS THE TRUTH. HE KNOWS, BUT APPARENTLY REFUSES TO BELIEVE THAT he EXISTS AND IS KNOWN BY THE **SPOKEN WORD:**

GENESIS 2:7 And the Lord God formed man of the dust of the ground, and breathed into his nostrils the breath of life; and man became a living soul.

HEBREWS 1:3 Who being the brightness of his glory, and the express image of his person, and upholding all things by the word of his power, when he had by himself purged our sins, sat down on the right hand of the Majesty on high;

HEBREWS 4:12 For the word of God is quick, and powerful, and sharper than any two-edged sword, piercing even to the diving asunder of soul and spirit, and of the joints and marrow, and is **a**

discerner of the thoughts and intents of the heart.

HIS REJECTION OF GOD'S WORD MEANS HE HAS TO REJECT THE HOLY GHOST AND JESUS AS WELL FOR HE **IS THE WORD**. REMEMBER, THAT WHICH WAS WRITTEN BY MEN CAME FIRST FROM GOD TO MAN BY INSPIRATION OF THE HOLY GHOST.

II PETER 1:19-21 We have also a more sure word of prophecy; whereunto ye do well that ye take heed, as unto a light that shineth in a dark place, until the day dawn, and the day star arise in your hearts: Knowing the first, that no prophecy of the scripture is of any private interpretation. For the prophecy came not in the old time by the will of man: but holy men of God spake as they were moved by the Holy Ghost.

THE GREEK'S PHILOSOPHY ABOUT WHO GOD IS AND HOW TO DEFINE HIM HAS BEEN TAKEN ON BY GLO's. YOU WOULD THINK AN ORGANIZATION FOUNDED UPON CHRISTIAN PRINCIPLES WOULD BE ABLE TO GIVE A BIBLICAL DESCRIPTION OF GOD. BUT THEY LIKE THEIR ANCIENT MENTORS HAVE FAILED. **II PETER 1:19-21** IS IN DIRECT CONFLICT WITH THE **GREEK'S PHILOSOPHY**, WHICH TRIES TO **EXPLAIN** THINGS BASED ON NATURE, EXPERIENCES, AND THEIR SURROUNDINGS; **BUT NOT BY FAITH.** BY ONLY USING THEIR **OWN NATURAL MINDS** AND **NATURAL** SENSES, THEY DO NOT USE FAITH AND DO NOT HAVE FAITH AS DEFINED BY THE WORD OF GOD IN (**HEBREWS 11:1**). THE

ACQUIRING OF KNOWLEDGE WITH THE FIVE SENSES IS CALLED EMPIRICISM WHICH IS AN EXTERNAL, **FAITHLESS** MENTALITY. GOD CAN NEVER BE TRULY **KNOWN** WITHOUT FAITH. MENTAL ASCENT IS NOT ENOUGH TO TRULY KNOW THE GOD OF THE BIBLE.

I CORINTHIANS 2:14(amp) But the **natural, non-spiritual** man does not accept or welcome or admit into his heart the gifts and teachings and revelations of the Spirit of God, for they are folly (meaningless nonsense) to him; and **he is incapable** of knowing them [of progressively recognizing, understanding, and becoming better acquainted with them] because they are spiritually discerned and estimated and appreciated.

YET, GOD **REQUIRES FAITH IN HIM, FOR HIM TO MOVE ON YOUR BEHALF** (**HEBREWS 11:6**), BUT THIS IS DEFINITELY NOT THE FAITH THESE GLO's EXHIBIT. THEY BELIEVE THAT NOT ONLY IS THEIR GLO A REWARDER OF THEIR DILIGENCE TO THEM, BUT SO IS GOD. THE GREEKS OF OLD BELIEVED THEIR gods WERE SUPERHUMANS IN CONTROL OF NATURAL FORCES OR DIVINE BEINGS IN HUMAN FORM WHICH IS DISPLAYED BY THE ABUNDANCE OF THEIR IDOLS. IDOLS WERE HOW GREEKS FELT THEY COULD HAVE THEIR gods NEAREST TO THEM. THE BIBLE SHOWS THE IGNORANCE AND FOOLISHNESS OF IDOLATRY AND **THE GREEK'S PHILOSOPHY** ABOUT DIVINE THINGS. YOU THINK CHRISTIANS WOULD SEE THE IGNORANCE AND FOOLISHNESS TO AND

COMING APART AT THE SEAMS

STOP JOINING GLO's. UNFORTUNATELY, THEY DO NOT, CANNOT, OR MOST OFTEN REFUSE TO SEE THE TRUTH.

ACTS 17:22-25 Then Paul stood in the midst of Mar's hill, and said, Ye men of Athens, I perceive that in all things ye are too superstitious. For as I passed by, and beheld your devotions, I found an altar with this inscription, **TO THE UNKNOWN GOD.** Whom therefore ye ignorantly worship, him declare I unto you. God that made the world and all things therein, seeing that he is Lord of heaven and earth, dwelleth not in temples made with hands; Neither is worshipped with men's hands, as though he needed any thing, seeing he giveth to all life, and breath, and all things;

Devotions- The objects or gods of their worship.

THE GREEKS BELIEVED THEY KNEW WHAT THE gods WERE THINKING BASED ON THEIR OWN FEELINGS (EMOTIONS) AND god-likeness. THEY CENTERED THEIR LIVES AROUND MYTHOLOGY, WHICH IS NOTHING BUT A BUNCH OF LIES. IT IS ALSO SINFUL TO GIVE HEED TO MYTHS, AND CHRISTIANS ARE COMMANDED TO REFUSE MYTHS. IT IS TO THOSE CHRISTIANS THAT DO NOT ENDURE SOUND DOCTRINE AND STRAY FROM THE TRUTH THAT SHALL BE TURNED TO **FABLES AND MYTHOLOGY.** THIS MEANS THERE ARE A LOT OF CHRISTIANS WHO DO NOT ENDURE SOUND DOCTRINE. THEY ALLOW THE DESIRES OF THEIR HEART TO LEAD AND GUIDE THEM,

INSTEAD OF THE HOLY GHOST. **THE SPIRIT DOES NOT LEAD ANY CHRISTIAN INTO GLO's, AND I WISH THEY WOULD STOP LYING ON GOD. ANYONE CAN PRAY TO GOD ALL THEY WANT ABOUT JOINING A GLO, HE'LL ALWAYS ANSWER THEM, NO!!!!!**

I TIMOTHY 1:4(amp) Nor to give importance or occupy themselves with legends (fables, myths) and endless genealogies, which foster and promote useless speculations and questionings rather than acceptance in faith of God's administrations and the divine training that is in faith (in that leaning of the entire personality on God in absolute trust and confidence)

II TIMOTHY 4:7(amp) But refuse and avoid irreverent legends (profane and impure and godless fictions, mere grandmother's tales) and silly myths and express your disapproval of them. Train yourself toward godliness (piety), [keeping yourself spiritually fit].

AS A MATTER OF FACT, CHRISTIANITY IN NO WAY ESTEEMS MYTHOLOGY OR USES ANY OF ITS DOCTRINES OR TEACHINGS <u>AS TRUTH</u>. CHRISTIANS SHOULD AND ARE ADVISED TO DO THE SAME. THEREFORE, ALL GLO's ARE GUILTY OF DISOBEDIENCE TO SCRIPTURE, AND IF THEY ARE GUILTY THEN SO ARE CHRISTIANS WHO JOIN THEM. ALL REFERENCES TO MYTHOLOGY IN THE BIBLE ARE NEGATIVE AS WOULD BE EXPECTED, SEEING THAT IT IS IDOLATRY.

COMING APART AT THE SEAMS

THOSE WHO PROFESS TO BE CHRISTIANS IN GLO's (i.e. **GREEK CHRISTIANS**) HAVE LITTLE TO CONSIDER. REMAIN A MEMBER AND RECEIVE ETERNAL DAMNATION, OR DENOUNCE AND REPENT TO RECEIVE ETERNAL LIFE. IT'S REALLY NOT A HARD CHOICE.

ANOTHER PHILOSOPHY OF THE ANCIENT GREEKS WAS TO PLEASE THE gods **BY HUMAN DEEDS**. THIS PHILOSOPHY HAS CARRIED OVER TO THE MODERN DAY GLO's. IT'S CALLED,"**SALVATION BY WORKS**," WHICH IS BLASHPEMY, AND IS A HEINOUS CRIME AGAINST THE WORK BY JESUS ON CALVARY (HIS DEATH ON THE CROSS).

I HAVE REALIZED HOW DEEP ROOTED AND INTERWOVEN GLO'S ARE IN EFFECTING THE SAINTS. PASTORS, MINISTERS, ELDERS, AND THOSE WHO HAVE BEEN IN THE MINISTRY ATLEAST 20 YEARS STILL HOLD ON TO THEIR **ABOMINABLE** GLO's. SATAN HAS REALLY PLANTED SOME DEEP ROOTS IN GLO's AND THOSE WHO BELONG TO THEM, BUT THE HOLY GHOST IS ABLE TO REACH DOWN AND PULL UP EVERY ROOT. **WHERE DOES THE BONDAGE (DEEP ROOTS) START?** IT STARTS AFTER AN INTERESTED PERSON TELLS A MEMBER. THE MEMBER TELLS THEM NOT TO TELL ANYONE WHAT THEY WANT TO PLEDGE, AND THAT THEY WANT TO PLEDGE. THANK GOD, MANY TELL SOMEBODY.

NOW JESUS, **WHO IS GOD**, CAME **IN** THE LIKENESS OF MAN (NOT A STATUE) AND CAN ONLY BE SOUGHT **BY FAITH EVEN THOUGH HE WAS VISIBLE.**

MATTHEW 16:15-17(amp) He said to them, But who do you [yourselves] say that I am? Simon Peter replied, You are the

Christ, the Son of the living God. Then Jesus answered him, Blessed (happy, fortunate, and to be envied) are you, Simon Bar-Jonah. For **flesh and blood [men]** have **not revealed this** to you, but My Father Who is in heaven.

NOT ONLY THIS, HE PROVED TO THE PEOPLE IN WORD AND DEED OF THAT TIME AND TODAY THROUGH THE SCRIPTURES THAT HE WAS THE TRUE GOD, TRUE WISDOM, AND THE ONLY REDEEMER OF THEIR SOULS. MANY JUST REFUSE AND REBEL TO BELIEVE WHO HE WAS AND IS;

1.) GOD IN THE FLESH (**JOHN 1:1,14**)
2.) THE PERFECT MAN (**I PETER 2:24**)
3.) THE PERFECT SACRIFICE (**I PETER 2:24**)
4.) SOMEONE THAT NONE OF US COULD EVER BE IN THE FLESH (i.e. SINLESS-**I PETER 2:24**)
5.) WORTHY OF WORSHIP, PRAISE, GLORY, AND HONOR THAT ONLY GOD CAN RECEIVE (**JOHN 20:28/REVELATION 4:11**).

THE DIFFERENCE BETWEEN JESUS AND THE GREEK gods IS **LIVING vs. DEAD, REAL vs. MYTH, TRUE vs. FALSE**, AND **GOD vs. SATAN**. YOU SEE, ANYONE CAN LOOK AT NATURE AND FIGURE OUT THERE IS A REAL GOD WHO **CREATED** IT (**ROMANS 1**), BUT WHO GOD IS, THAT'S MUCH DIFFERENT. THE GREEKS COULD NOT UNDERSTAND THROUGH EXPERIENCE, OR NATURE, WHO GOD IS BECAUSE THEY DID NOT REALIZE (RECEIVE THE REVELATION) THAT ONLY BY FAITH CAN ONE KNOW HIM AND HAVE

COMING APART AT THE SEAMS

A **RELATIONSHIP** WITH HIM. JESUS DOES KNOW US AND WHAT WE ARE GOING THROUGH. FOR HE IS TRULY GOD AND IS TRULY MAN.

HEBREWS 4:14-15(amp) Inasmuch then as we have a great High Priest Who has [already] ascended and passed through the heavens, Jesus the Son of God, let us hold fast our confession [of faith in Him]. For we do not have a High Priest Who is unable to understand and sympathize and have a shared feeling with our weaknesses and infirmities and liability to the assaults of temptation, but One Who has been tempted in every respect as we are, yet without sinning.

HE **HIMSELF** DIED FOR THE MISTAKES OF HIS OWN CREATION (NOT HIS MISTAKE) AND REMAINED SINLESS. HIS SINLESS LIFE PROVED THAT HE DID NOT MAKE ANY MISTAKES IN CREATING MAN, BUT HE PROVED THAT IT WAS POSSIBLE FOR A MAN (EVEN ADAM) TO LIVE WITHOUT COMMITTING ONE SIN IF THEY **WANTED** TO BY TOTAL SUBMISSION TO THE HOLY SPIRIT. THE OLD TESTAMENT HOLDS GREAT WITNESS THAT MAN, ALTHOUGH BORN WITH A SIN NATURE, WAS WORTHY OF HEAVENLY GLORY. ENOCH AND ELIJAH WERE TAKEN DIRECTLY TO HEAVEN. GOD WITHHELD DESTRUCTION OF THE WHOLE HUMAN RACE FOR THE SAKE OF ONE MAN, NOAH.

GENESIS 6:8-9(amp) But Noah found grace in the eyes of the Lord. These are the generations of Noah: Noah was a just man and perfect (blameless) in his generations, and Noah walked with God.

EVIL IS NOT GOD'S FAULT. **GOD PROVED THROUGH JESUS CHRIST THAT THE SIN NATURE, AND HENCEFORTH EVIL, DID NOT HAVE TO COME INTO EXISTENCE. NO MAN** CAN CLAIM ANY GLORY. **JESUS** TOOK UPON **HIMSELF** OUR SINS AND GAVE US HIS RIGHTEOUSNESS.

I PETER 2:24- Who his own self **bare our sins** in his own body on the tree, that we, being dead to sins, should live unto righteousness: by whose stripes ye were healed.

ROMANS 3:26- To declare, I say, at this time **his righteousness**: that he might be just, and the justifier of him which **believeth in Jesus.**

BUT WE CAN ONLY RECEIVE HIS RIGHTEOUSNESS BY FAITH WITHOUT WORKS. WE PROVE THAT WE HAVE RECEIVED HIS RIGHTEOUSNESS IN US BY THE WORKS WE DO.

EPHESIANS 2:8-9 For by grace are ye saved through faith; and that not of yourselves: it is the gift of God: Not of works; lest any man should boast.

TITUS 3:5- Not by works of righteousness which we have done, but according to his mercy he saved us, by the washing of regeneration, and renewing of the Holy Ghost.

HOW DARE ANYONE, ESPECIALLY A "CHRISTIAN", TRAMPLE THE GREATEST WORK OF UNCONDITIONAL LOVE AND OBEDIENCE **IN HISTORY** (THE CRUCIFIXION), YET THIS IS WHAT GLO's, FROM THEIR **ORIGINATION,** AND THEIR MEMBERS (INCLUDING PROFESSING CHRISTIANS) DO BY LIFTING UP AND SERVING THEIR godless ORGANIZATIONS!!! IF ONE THINKS THAT A CANNED FOOD DRIVE OR GIVING A SCHOLARSHIP CAN EVER BE CLOSE, I DARE YOU TO TAKE UP **THE REAL CROSS**, AND GO INTO YOUR NEXT MEETING DEMANDING THAT YOUR GLO RAISE THE STANDARD OF HOLINESS AND BECOME A CHRIST-CENTERED SERVICE ORGANIZATION. TELL THEM: ALL OF US MUST REPENT, AND ALL THAT DO NOT MUST GO, NO MORE PARTIES, RAFFLES, FORNICATION, ETC. UNFORTUNATELY, THIS WILL NEVER WORK WITH GLO's BECAUSE THE SINNERS WILL REBEL. YOU'LL JUST BE WASTING YOUR TIME. THIS SOLUTION WILL NOT WORK WITH MAN TRYING TO SOLVE HIS OWN PROBLEMS WITHOUT GOD (i.e. THEY DON'T WANT GOD INVOLVED). THE SITUATION IS CHAOTIC. FROM HAZING, TO DRIVE-BYS, TO WORLD WARS, TO MIND CONTROL AND WE ARE SUPPOSED TO BE THE MOST INTELLIGENT CREATURES ON EARTH. SO WHY DO GLO's HAZE? WHY DO MEN FIGHT WARS? THEY DO IT TO KEEP ORDER AND CONTROL OR TAKE CONTROL. POWER IS NOT JUST GIVEN AWAY!! YOU WERE, ARE NOW, WILL BE, **OR DECIDE NOT TO BE** MENTALLY OR PHYSICALLY **COERCED** TO CONFORM TO A

SET OF MAN'S RULES WITH **NO BIBLICAL FOUNDATION. REFUSAL TO BE HAZED OR GO THROUGH SOME TYPE OF UNGODLY INITIATION (i.e. SUBMIT TO THE POWERS THAT BE)** WILL **RESULT** IN YOU BEING AN **OUTCAST** BY YOUR OWN SO-CALLED BROTHERS OR SISTERS, OR NEVER BEING IN THAT FRATERNITY OR SORORITY. IF YOU QUIT PLEDGING OR DENOUNCE YOUR MEMBERSHIP, YOU ARE SEEN BY GLO MEMBERS AS WEAK AND TREATED WITH CONTEMPT. BUT GOD SEES THE CHRISTIAN AS AN OVERCOMER WILLING TO PUT OFF THE CHAINS OF BONDAGE.

HEBREWS 12:1-3 Wherefore seeing we also are compassed about with so great a cloud of witnesses, let us lay aside every weight, and the sin which so easily beset us, and let us run with patience the race that is set before us. Looking unto Jesus the author and finisher of our faith; who for the joy that was set before him endured the cross, despising the shame, and is set down at the right hand of the throne of God. For consider him that endureth such contradiction of sinners against himself, lest ye be wearied and faint in your minds.

VOLUNTEERING TO BE PUT THROUGH **ANY TYPE** OF PLEDGING PROCESS HAS MANY CONSEQUENCES. IF THE MEMBERS ARE SUCCESSFUL AT MOLDING THE INITIATES, THEY WILL BE WELL-TRAINED **IDIOTS** DOING EXACTLY AS THEY HAVE BEEN PROGRAMMED TO DO (**BARK, MEOW, EE-YIP, OO-OOP, YO-**

YO, 06, SKEE-WEE, BLUE-PHI). CONFORMING TO MAN WILL KEEP ORDER AND CONTROL, BUT ONLY FOR A LITTLE WHILE. WHEN THE GREEKS SAW A STORM OR THEY GOT SICK, IT MEANT THEIR gods WERE MAD. TO KEEP ORDER (i.e. GAIN BACK FAVOR FROM THE gods) THE PEOPLE WOULD DO **ANYTHING SUCH AS MURDER (BY SACRIFICING), WHIP, HAVE ORGIES, BURN THEIR SKIN, OR DO ANY <u>WORK</u> TO OBTAIN THIS FAVOR.** JUST AS A BIG BROTHER WITH A PADDLE CAUSES THE PLEDGES TO BELIEVE THAT THEIR god (THE BIG BROTHER, THE FRAT, OR HIS PADDLE) IS MAD; THESE PLEDGES WILL DO JUST ABOUT ANY **WORK** TO APPEASE THEIR MASTERS. THEY WILL PERFORM SKITS, BEG, OR SOMETIMES JUST TAKE THE PADDLING. BUT WHAT HAPPENS WHEN A PLEDGE OR A MEMBER DECIDES HE HAS HAD ENOUGH AND BECOMES DEFIANT, REBELLIOUS, MAD, OR SAVED LIKE MANY OTHERS AND MYSELF? THEY CAN CAUSE SERIOUS PROBLEMS. THESE MEN WANT **THEIR** POWER BACK. THEY WANT THEIR **FREEDOM BACK.** INSTEAD OF REMAINING AN "omega man", I GOT SAVED TO BECOME A REAL MAN. NOW, I AM CAUSING PROBLEMS ON PURPOSE. WHY? BECAUSE GOD IS USING ME TO CAUSE THESE ORGANIZATIONS TO REAP WHAT THEY HAVE SOWN. YEARS OF **VIOLENCE, LIES,** AND **DECEPTION** ARE RISING UP AGAINST THEM IN THE FORM OF LAWSUITS, DENUNCIATIONS, REVEALING OF SECRETS, and the rise of many anti-Greek ministries.

GALATIANS 6:7- Be not deceived; God is not mocked: for whatsoever a man soweth, that shall he also reap.

HOSEA 8:7 IF YOU SOW TO THE WIND, YOU WILL REAP A WHIRLWIND.

MANY OTHERS AND I ARE THOSE WHIRLWINDS EXPOSING THE TRUTH ABOUT GREEK LETTERED ORGANIZATIONS, AS DID JOHN THE BAPTIST EXPOSE THE TRUTH ABOUT HEROD.

MARK 6:17-18 For Herod himself had sent forth and laid hold upon John, and bound him in prison for Herodias' sake, his brother Phillip's wife: for he had married her. For John had said unto Herod, It is not lawful for thee to have thy brother's wife.

HE WAS A MAN WHO REFUSED TO COMPROMISE GOD'S WORD AND SO ARE WE TO HAVE THIS SAME ATTITUDE KNOWING THAT WE BEING PERSECUTED WILL BE GREATLY REWARDED. FOR THE BIBLE SAYS, "THAT IN DUE SEASON WE SHALL REAP IF WE FAINT NOT."(**GALATIANS 6:9**). WORLDLY MEN HAVE A, "KILL THE MESSENGER ATTITUDE", THINKING THAT BY DOING SO THEY WILL KILL THE MESSAGE. THE GOSPEL IS 2000 YEARS OLD, AND STILL VERY MUCH ALIVE. JESUS IS STILL ALIVE. THE MESSAGE THAT GLO's ARE UNGODLY IS ALIVE AND WELL AND ABOUT TO EXPLODE. **THERE ARE SOME TRUE PASTORS, MINISTERS, ELDERS, AND OTHER LEADERS IN THE CHURCH WHO ARE TOTALLY AGAINST GLO's. THEY ARE NOT**

AFRAID OF LOSING CHURCH MEMBERS OR THEIR MONEY FOR THE TRUTH. YET, **ALL COMPROMISERS** OF THE FAITH WILL JOIN OR STAY WITH GLO's TO ESCAPE AND FLEE IN FEAR FROM THE GOOD FIGHT OF FAITH AND **THE PERSECUTION** THAT COMES ALONG WITH BEING A **TRUE BELIEVER.**

ACTS 7:9-10 And the patriarchs, moved with envy, sold Joseph into Egypt; but **God was with him, And delivered him out of all his afflictions, and gave him favour and wisdom** in the sight of Pharaoh king of Egypt; and he made him governor over Egypt and all his house.

ACT 16:22 And the multitude rose up together against them: and the magistrates rent off their clothes, and commanded to beat them.

READ THIS SCRIPTURE THROUGH VERSE 34. IF THIS DOES NOT ENCOURAGE AND FIRE YOU UP TO DENOUNCE, KEEP READING. A MAN GOT SAVED BECAUSE OF THE EXAMPLE OF TRUE BELIEVERS.

II TIMOTHY 2:12 If we suffer, we shall also reign with him: if we deny him, he also will deny us:

II TIMOTHY 3:12 Yea, and all that will **live godly in Christ Jesus** shall suffer persecution.

I PETER 4:12-19 Beloved, think it not strange concerning the fiery trial which is to try you, as though some strange thing happened unto you: But rejoice, inasmuch as ye are partakers of Christ's sufferings; that, when his glory shall be revealed, ye may be glad also with exceeding joy. If ye be reproached for the name of Christ, happy are ye; for the spirit of glory and of God resteth upon you: on their part he is evil spoken of, but on your part he is glorified. But let none of you suffer as a murderer, or as a thief, or as an evildoer, or as a busybody in other men's matters. **Yet, if any man suffer as a Christian, let him not be ashamed**; but let him glorify God on this behalf. For the time is come that judgment must begin at the house of God: and if it first begin at us, what shall the end be of them that obey not the gospel of God? and if the righteous scarcely be saved, where shall the ungodly and sinner appear? Wherefore let them that suffer according to the will of God commit the keeping of their souls to him in well doing, as unto a faithful Creator.

MANY GREEK CHRISTIANS CLAIM TO SUFFER THE SAME PERSECUTION AS TRUE CHRISTIANS WHEN THEIR MEMBERSHIP IN A GLO IS QUESTIONED OR REPROACHED. THEY FAIL TO SEE THAT IT'S NOT BEING A CHRISTIAN THAT THEY ARE PERSECUTED; IT'S FOR BEING IN A GLO. NOTICE HOW THE SCRIPTURE CONTRASTS SUFFERING AS A CHRISTIAN AS OPPOSED TO AN EVILDOER. SUFFERING AS A CHRISTIAN IS TO BE EXPECTED AND RECEIVED WITH JOY. SUFFERING AS AN EVILDOER IS TO BE

COMING APART AT THE SEAMS

AVOIDED BECAUSE IT'S NOT THE WILL OF GOD FOR CHRISTIANS TO SUFFER FOR DOING WRONG. GREEK CHRISTIAN!!! YOU DESERVE TO BE PERSECUTED FOR YOUR AFFILIATION WITH A GLO, **BUT IT'S NOT BECAUSE YOU ARE A CHRISTIAN.** THE GREEK CHRISTIAN'S **RESPONSE** TO BEING QUESTIONED ABOUT THEIR GLO AFFILIATION IS NEVER THE WAY IT'S DESCRIBED ABOVE. INSTEAD OF GLORIFYING GOD AND BEING HAPPY, THEY BECOME **UNRIGHTEOUSLY** DEFENSIVE AND ANGRY, AND THIS GLORIFIES THE DEVIL. THEIR ANGER IS NOT WHAT THE BIBLE CONSIDERS RIGHTEOUS INDIGNATION.

JUDE 3-5 Beloved, when I gave all diligence to write unto you of the common salvation, it was needful for me to write unto you, and exhort you that ye should **earnestly contend for the faith** which was once delivered unto the saints. For there are certain men crept in unawares, who were before of old ordained to this condemnation, ungodly men, turning the grace of our God into lasciviousness, and denying the only Lord God, and our Lord Jesus Christ. I will therefore put you in remembrance, though ye once knew this, how that the Lord, having saved the people out of the land of Egypt, afterward destroyed them that believed not.

GREEK CHRISTIANS WOULD RATHER CONTEND FOR THE GREEK SYSTEM THAN FOR THE FAITH IN JESUS.
TRUE CHRISTIANS WILL ATTACK (CONTEND) THE SOURCE OF SIN, THE

DEVIL. THEY WILL NOT SIT IDLY BY WATCHING PEOPLE GO TO HELL. PEOPLE WHO DO NOT COMPROMISE ARE SUBJECT TO THREATS, LOSS OF FRIENDS AND RELATIVES, AND THOUGHT OF AS TROUBLEMAKERS. TRUE PASTORS, **NOT HIRELINGS**, WILL PREACH AGAINST GLO's REGARDLESS OF WHAT THE CONGREGATION SAYS OR EVEN THREATENS TO DO. STILL, TRUE CHRISTIANS DO IT WITH NO REGRET AND WITHOUT FEAR. CHRISTIANITY IS CLOSE TO 2000 YEARS OLD, CHRIST AND HIS FOLLOWERS SUFFERED THEN AND STILL SUFFER MUCH PERSECUTION NOW, AND AS ALWAYS WE ARE IN TOTAL CONTROL AND STILL HERE. THERE WILL ALWAYS BE TRUE SOLDIERS OF CHRIST WILLING TO GO THROUGH THE FIRE FOR HIM. PERSECUTION IS THE "BAD WEATHER" OR THOSE MATERIAL THINGS THE GREEKS SAW AS JUDGMENT FOR WRONGDOINGS, BUT WE COUNT OUR PERSECUTIONS ALL JOY. **NOW**, THE "GOOD WEATHER" ARE THOSE MATERIAL INDICATORS THAT GAVE THE GREEKS THE BELIEF THAT THE gods WERE PLEASED WITH THEM. THINGS SUCH AS FINANCIAL PROSPERITY, NATIONAL WELFARE (ALL NATURAL OR TEMPORAL OCCURENCES) MEANT THE gods WERE PLEASED WITH THEIR WORSHIP, ADORATION, AND THEIR LIFESTYLES. JUST BECAUSE SOMEONE IS HEALTHY AND BLESSED FINANCIALLY DOES NOT MEAN THEY ARE **LIVING IN OBEDIENCE** TO AND PLEASING GOD (SPIRITUAL OCCURRENCES). THIS IS THE DOMINANT CLAIM OF THE GLO'S; "WE DO GOOD." BUT GOD WANTS AND REQUIRES OBEDIENCE TO HIS WORD, AND THEN GOOD WORKS. DRUG DEALERS, THE MAFIA, AND

EXTORTIONERS ARE BLESSED FINANCIALLY AND PERFORM SOME GOOD DEEDS, BUT CANNOT BE BLESSED SPIRITUALLY, BECAUSE THEY DO NOT OBEY GOD'S WORD. THIS MINDSET IS WHAT CAUSES **SPIRITUAL REGRESSION** AND **MORAL DEGRADATION** IN THE LIVES OF THOSE CONFESSING CHRISTIANS IN GLO'S. THE BELIEF THAT BEING GOOD AND DOING GOOD WORKS PREVAILS OVER OBEDIENCE AND FAITH IS THE REASON WHY PROFESSING CHRISTIANS IN GLO'S FALL RIGHT INTO THE CATEGORY OF SPIRITUAL REGRESSION AND MORAL DEGRADATION.

GREEK CHRISTIANS WILL STOP READING THE BIBLE, PRAYING, FASTING, AND WILL START TO DOUBT, CONTRADICT AND DISBELIEVE GOD'S WORD. THEY WILL START CONFORMING TO THIS WORLD AND ACTING LIKE SINNERS.

THERE ZEAL FOR GOD IS DAMPENED BY THE LOSS OF RELATIONSHIP WITH HIM BY 1.) BY YOKING TOGETHER WITH UNBELIEVERS, 2.) BY RITUAL WORSHIP, 3.) IDOLATRY, 4.) FOLLOWING AFTER MAN, NOT GOD (**JEREMIAH 17:5**), AND 5.) SEXUAL IMMORALITY TO NAME SOME. THIS MEANS THAT NO MEMBER OF A GREEK-LETTERED ORGANIZATION **CAN WORSHIP** THE ONLY TRUE GOD. SPIRITUAL DISOBEDIENCE WILL ALWAYS PAY THE WAGE OF ETERNAL DEATH, AND WILL SOMETIMES CAUSE IMMEDIATE PHYSICAL DEATH WHICH TO THE SINNER IS ETERNAL DAMNATION. THE BABYLONIAN CAPTIVITY OF THE JEWS IN JEREMIAH IS THE PERFECT EXAMPLE OF RELYING ON NATURAL BLESSINGS AS A

BENCHMARK FOR YOUR RELATIONSHIP WITH GOD. MANY MAY GO A LONG TIME WITHOUT LOSING THEIR ZEAL FOR GOD, BUT THAT DOES NOT MEAN YOU ARE ABIDING IN THE TRUE VINE.

JOHN 15:1-6 I am the true vine, and my father is the husbandman. Every branch in me that beareth not fruit he taketh away: and every branch that beareth fruit, he purgeth it, that it may bring forth more fruit. Now ye are clean through the word which I have spoken unto you. Abide in me, and I in you. As the branch can not bear fruit of itself, except it abide in the vine; no more can ye, except ye abide in me. I am the vine, ye are the branches: He that abideth in me, and I in him, the same bringeth forth much fruit: for without me ye can nothing. If a man abide not in me, he is cast forth as a branch, and is withered; and men gather them, and cast them into the fire, and they are burned.

MANY, ONCE TRULY SAVED PERSONS ARE WITHERED AND DO NOT KNOW IT. GOD ALLOW'S HIS BLESSING'S TO FALL ON THE JUST (COVENANT) AND THE UNJUST (NO COVENANT), BUT NOT FOR THE SAME REASONS (**MATTHEW 5:45**). GLO's MAY BE DOING WELL FINANCIALLY, AND ARE WELL LIKED BY THE COMMUNITY, AND THEY DO HAVE MANY PROMINENT PEOPLE IN THEM. BUT THIS DOES NOT MEAN THE INDIVIDUALS OR THE GLO ARE OBEDIENT TO AND SHARE A RELATIONSHIP WITH JESUS CHRIST. GOD ENTHRONES ALL KINGS/RULERS. MANY KINGS

WERE RICH AND PROSPEROUS, AND AT THE SAME TIME CRUEL AND WICKED. GOD BLESSED THOSE KINGS AND BLESSES SINNERS TODAY, BECAUSE THE GOODNESS OF GOD LEADS TO REPENTANCE (**ROMANS 2:4**). IT'S NOT BECAUSE THEY ARE DOING GOD'S WILL. IT'S BECAUSE GOD IS GOOD REGARDLESS OF WHAT PEOPLE DO. ONE MUST REMEMBER THAT THESE GROUPS WERE FOUNDED ON THE **WILL** OF MEN AND WOMEN ACCORDING TO **THE FLESH** NOT GOD'S WILL. THE PROBLEM IS NOT ONLY HUMAN ORIGIN, BUT IT IS ALSO A FACT THAT GLO's DON'T REQUIRE OF THEIR MEMBERS THE SAME AS A HOLY GOD REQUIRES OF HIS PEOPLE. THIS MEANS "GREEK CHRISTIANS" ARE NOT LIVING **CHRIST-CENTERED LIVES, AND GLO's CANNOT BE CHRIST-CENTERED ORGANIZATIONS.** TO MAKE IT PLAINER, IF THE ORGANIZATION IS NOT CHRIST-CENTERED, NEITHER **WILL** OR CAN THE PEOPLE THAT BELONG TO THEM. THE BIBLICAL PRINCIPLE OF GUILTY BY ASSOCIATION OR UNEQUAL YOKING REIGNS TRUE IN COUNTLESS SCRIPTURES. HERE ARE SOME OF THEM.

I CORINTHIANS 15:33(amp) Do not be so deceived and misled! Evil companionships (communion, associations) corrupt and deprave good manners and morals and character.

II CORINTHIANS 6:14-18 Be ye not unequally yoked together with unbelievers: for what fellowship has righteousness with unrighteousness? and what communion hath light with darkness?

And what concord hath Christ with Belial? Or what part hath he that believeth with an infidel? And what agreement hath the temple of God with idols? for ye are the temple of the living God; as god hath said, I will dwell in them; and I will be their God, and they shall be my people. Wherefore come out from among them and be ye separate, saith the Lord, and touch not the unclean thing; and I will receive you, I will be a Father unto you, and ye shall be my sons and daughters, saith the Lord Almighty.

Hebrews 7:26 For such an high priest became us, who is holy, harmless, undefiled, **separate from sinners** and made higher than the heavens;

IT IS IMPORTANT TO UNDERSTAND THESE SCRIPTURES FOR **WITNESSING PURPOSES**. WHEN YOU TELL A GREEK CHRISTIAN THAT THEY ARE UNEQUALLY YOKED, THEY DO NOT UNDERSTAND THAT IT HAS NOTHING TO DO WITH BEING SURROUNDED BY SINNERS. THEY FAIL TO REALIZE THAT **IT'S THE FELLOWSHIP OR SPIRITUAL ASSOCIATION** WITH THEM THAT RESULTS IN THE UNEQUAL YOKE. THE GREEK CHRISTIAN IS VERY QUICK TO POINT OUT THAT SOME PEOPLE ON THE JOB ARE NOT CHRISTIANS. AGREE WITH THEM; BUT LET THEM KNOW THAT YOU DO NOT HAVE TO **FELLOWSHIP** WITH THEM IN ANY MANNER WHATSOEVER. JESUS, HIMSELF, REMAINED SEPARATE FROM SINNERS. YET SHOWED THEM HIS LOVE AND TRUTH. A CO-WORKER THAT CONFESSES JESUS AS THEIR LORD, BUT PRACTICES SIN IS NOT TO BE ASSOCIATED WITH BY ANOTHER CHRISTIAN. THE FELLOWSHIP INITIATES THE UNEQUAL **YOKE**. A CHRISTIAN WORKING IN THE MIDST OF SINNERS DOES NOT MEAN FELLOWSHIP OR SPIRITUAL ASSOCIATION. **BEING IN A GLO DOES. BY OATH, A SPIRITUAL YOKE IS BEGUN. WE ARE LIVING**

IN A WORLD FULL OF SINNERS, BUT THAT DOES NOT MEAN WE HAVE TO FELLOWSHIP OR CONFORM OURSELVES TO THEIR WAYS. WE ARE IN THE WORLD, NOT OF THE WORLD (i.e. ASSOCIATED WITH THE WORLD). THE FOLLOWING SCRIPTURE EXPLAINS THIS.

I CORINTHIANS 5:9-13 I wrote unto you in an epistle **not to company with fornicators**: Yet not altogether with the fornicators **of this world**, or with the covetous, or extortioners, or with idolaters; **for then must ye needs go out of the world**. But now I have written unto you not to keep company, if **any man that is called a brother** be a fornicator, or covetous, or an idolater, or a railer, or a drunkard, or an extortioner, with such an one not to eat. For what have I to do judge them also that are without? do not ye judge them that are within? But them that are without God judgeth. Therefore put away from among yourselves that wicked person.

PSALMS 1:1-6 Blessed is man that walketh not in the counsel of **the ungodly**, nor standeth in the way of **sinners**, nor sitteth in the seat of the **scornful**. But his delight is in the law of the Lord; and in His law doth he meditate day and night. And he shall be like a tree planted by the rivers of water, that bringeth forth his fruit in season; his leaf shall not wither; and whatsoever he doeth shall prosper. **The ungodly are not so**: but are like the chaff which the wind driveth away. Therefore, the ungodly shall not stand in judgment, nor sinners in the congregation of the righteous. For the Lord knoweth the way of the righteous: but the way of the ungodly shall perish.

GREEK CHRISTIANS WILL NEVER BE TRUE CHRISTIANS UNTIL THEY DENOUNCE; GRANTED THEY ARE PRACTICING NO OTHER SIN. HOW DOES A SAFE SEX SEMINAR GLORIFY JESUS?

FLESH IS MAN'S NATURE **WITHOUT THE HOLY SPIRIT.** THEREFORE, GREEK CHRISTIANS ARE AND MUST BE JUDGED BY THEIR **ACTIONS AND NOT INTENTIONS ALONE, BECAUSE OF NO SPIRITUAL DISCERNMENT.** THE INDIVIDUAL'S HEART IS SOMETHING MAN IS UNABLE TO JUDGE WITHOUT OUTWARD MANIFESTATIONS. BUT GOD KNOWS YOUR HEART AND **ITS NATURE.** THE HOLY SPIRIT DOES ENABLE TRUE CHRISTIANS, **AT HIS WILL**, TO KNOW A MAN'S HEART WITHOUT ANY ACTIONS. WHY IS THIS IMPORTANT? GLO's CAN ONLY DEAL WITH ITS MEMBERS ONCE THE OFFENSE HAS OCCURRED. YET, CHRISTIANS ARE GIVEN THE ABILITY TO DISCERN SPIRITS. TRUE CHRISTIANS ARE ABLE TO KNOW CERTAIN THINGS PRIOR TO THERE OCCURRENCE.

JEREMIAH 17:9 The heart is deceitful above all things, and desperately wicked: who can know it?

HE IS ALSO THE ONLY ONE WHO HAS THE POWER TO CHANGE IT. GLO's CLAIM THEY CAN CHANGE THE HEART, BUT THEY CANNOT! IT IS IMPOSSIBLE FOR CHRISTIANS TO

KNOWINGLY AND DELIBERATELY <u>PRACTICE</u> SIN. GREEK CHRISTIANS DO KNOWINGLY AND DELIBERATELY PRACTICE SIN BY REMAINING IN A GLO. IF YOU'RE IN A GLO AND YOU DIDN'T KNOW THEN, YOU SURELY KNOW NOW.

I JOHN 3:9(amp) No one born (begotten) of God [**deliberately, knowingly,** and **habitually**] practices sin, for God's nature abides in him [His principle of life, the divine sperm, remains permanently within him]; and he cannot practice sinning because he is born (begotten) of God.

SINCE BEING IN A GLO IS AT THIS POINT **KNOWN** TO BE SIN, TO REMAIN MAKES IT **DELIBERATE** ALSO. ANY CHRISTIAN THAT HAS THE TRUTH REVEALED TO THEM ABOUT GLO'S AND REFUSES TO DENOUNCE IS A BACKSLIDER AND A SINNER. ONLY A REDEEMED HEART IS CAPABLE OF WORSHIP AND TOTAL OBEDIENCE. REPENT AND DENOUNCE BEFORE YOUR EVIL DAY COMES, FOR GOD ASSUREDLY KNOWS YOUR THOUGHTS FOR WHICH YOU WILL BE JUDGED ALSO.

ROMANS 2:16(amp) On that day when, as my Gospel proclaims, God by Jesus Christ will judge men in regard to the things which they conceal (their hidden thoughts).

Members of these groups do not have to feel any accountability to God for their actions because they believe their doctrines are sufficient to live by and change the heart. Therefore, they do not have or feel the need to **trust or really believe** God nor fear His judgment (see opening of chapter 3). But True Christians know God is a judge and fears His judgments. True Christians know their total being exists in God.

Acts 17:28 For in him we live, and move, and have our being; as certain also of your own poets have said, For we are also his offspring.

IT IS IMPOSSIBLE TO DO ANY EVIL **IN THE NAME** OF JESUS, BECAUSE EVIL IS NOT A PART OF HIS NATURE. BY NOT TRULY BEING FOUNDED UPON CHRISTIAN PRINCIPLES, FRATERNITIES AND SORORITIES PRACTICE EVIL BECAUSE THEY HAVE AN ANTAGONSTIC RELATIONSHIP WITH JESUS CHRIST (i.e. THEY JUST CANNOT AND WILL NOT EVER GET ALONG). BECAUSE OF THEIR DIFFERENT NATURES, THE TRUE BELIEVER BY VIRTUE OF THEIR CHRISTLIKE NATURE SHOULD NOT REMAIN IN A GLO, KNOWING THAT THEIR BELIEFS ARE ALREADY COMPROMISED AND ARE CONTRADICTORY TO THE PRINCIPLES OF GLO's. IF THEY DECIDE TO LEAVE, THEY WILL EVENTUALLY BE OSTRACIZED BECAUSE GLO's DO NOT HAVE GOD'S UNCHANGEABLE NATURE.

HEBREWS 13:8 Jesus Christ is the same; yesterday, today, and forever more.

HOPEFULLY BY CONVICTION THEY WILL REPENT AND DENOUNCE AS MANY HAVE CHOSEN, REALIZING THEY HAVE MADE A

MISTAKE. YET, THOSE WHO ONCE CALLED YOU BROTHER OR SISTER, MAY OR MAY NOT EVER SPEAK TO YOU AGAIN. TO THIS I SAY, SO WHAT!!! THAT PERSON IS BACK IN RELATIONSHIP WITH CHRIST. LASTLY, A GLO HAS **LIMITED AUTHORITY TO JUDGE** A MEMBER'S INTENTIONS AND HIS ACTIONS, BECAUSE NO MAN IS OMNISCIENT, AND NO GLO CAN GIVE JAIL TIME. THIS IS A VERY DANGEROUS LACK OF CONTROL, BECAUSE THERE IS NO FEAR INVOLVED. THE THREAT TO THOSE WHO YOU SUSPECT WILL HAZE CAN ONLY BE FOLLOWED BY; "YOU BETTER NOT GET CAUGHT". BUT AN ACT OF HAZING MUST BE COMMITTED BEFORE ANY JUDGMENT CAN TAKE PLACE. MAN'S JUDGMENT IS NEVER FINAL AND MAN ALONE HAS NO POWER TO DESTROY SPIRITUAL YOKES. SO ONE CAN NEVER REALLY LOSE HIS MEMBERSHIP STATUS WITH THEIR GLO, EXCEPT AT DEATH OR DENUNCIATION. WHILE DIVINE JUDGMENT IS FINAL AT DEATH, YOU CAN LOSE YOUR MEMBERSHIP IN CHRIST'S BODY IN THIS LIFE, BUT GET IT BACK ONLY IN THIS LIFE. IF LOST AT DEATH, IT'S ETERNAL. MOST OATHS (WHICH CONTAIN A STATEMENT OF JUDGMENT, IF YOU BREAK IT) REQUIRE SECRECY IN ALMOST ANY SITUATION SUCH AS ADULTERY, HAZING, LIES, EVEN MURDER WHEN POSSIBLE. WITH CHRISTIANITY, THE JUDGMENT BY GOD ON SIN BEGINS WHEN IT IS CONCEIVED IN THE HEART.

MATTHEW 15:18-19(amp) But whatever comes out of the mouth comes from the heart, and this is what makes a man unclean and defiles him. For out of the heart come evil thoughts such as murder, adultery, sexual vice, theft, false witnessing (lying), slander, and irreverent speech.

GLO's REALLY HAVE NO ACCOUNTABILITY FOR THEIR MEMBERS BECAUSE THEIR AUTHORITY CANNOT DEAL WITH THE SPIRIT AND SOUL OF A MAN, NOR ARE THEY THE FINAL JUDGES. SINCE CHRIST IS THE HEAD OF THE CHURCH AND THE HEAD OF MAN, MEMBERS OF HIS CHURCH AS WELL AS ALL THE REST OF HIS CREATION HAVE TOTAL ACCOUNTABILTIY TO HIM (EVEN THE SECRET THINGS PEOPLE DO). **THE MEMBERSHIP (TEMPORARY)** OF A PERSON EXCOMMUNICATED BY A FRATERNITY OR SORORITY IS THE ONLY THING AT STAKE WHEN PUNISHED, BECAUSE HE OR SHE IS GOING TO HELL ANYWAY FOR BEING A SINNER, EVEN IF HE IS REINSTATED TO THE MEMBERSHIP. THE ONLY WAY FOR ONE TO SEPARATE FROM A GLO IS TO REPENT AND DENOUNCE.

MATTHEW 10:28 And fear not them which kill the body, but are not able to kill the soul: but rather fear him which is able to destroy both soul and body in hell.

THE LIFE (ETERNAL) OF AN EXCOMMUNICATED CHURCH MEMBER IS PURPOSELY HANDED OVER TO SATAN THAT HE MAY NOT LEARN TO BLASPHEME SO THAT THE **SOUL (ETERNAL)** MAY BE SAVED.

I TIMOTHY 1:19-20 Holding faith, and a good conscience; which some having put away concerning faith have made shipwreck: Of whom is Hymenaeus and

Alexander; whom I have delivered unto Satan, that they may learn not to blaspheme.

I CORINTHIANS 5:5 To deliver such a one unto Satan for the destruction of the flesh, that the spirit may be saved in the day of the Lord Jesus.

THE POWER STRUCTURE, RULES, PRINCIPLES, DOCTRINES, AND NATURE OF THE CHURCH, AS ONE CAN SEE, ARE MUCH DIFFERENT FROM GLO's.

PLEASE OBSERVE HERE AND THROUGHOUT THIS BOOK, HOW THE WORD OF GOD SAYS ONE THING AND GLO's SAY ANOTHER.

TO STATE IT PLAINLY: GREEK-LETTERED ORGANIZATIONS HAVE NOTHING ETERNALLY FAVORABLE TO OFFER.

Notes

FREDERIC L. HATCHETT

CHAPTER 3
PART 2

THE ORIGIN OF HAZING

HAZING RITUALS HAVE THEIR **ORIGIN** BETWEEN THE 8TH AND 5TH CENTURY B.C. IN ANCIENT GREECE.
(Mark Morford, Greece: Religion and Mythology, Encyclopedia Americana Grolier, Inc., 1999, p.397.)

"THE FIRST RECORDED DEATH FROM HAZING IS 1838, IN THE STATE OF KENTUCKY," (Esther Wright, Torn Togas: the dark side of Greek life/ Minneapolis: Fairview Press, 1996, p.22.)

THIS IS ABOUT 60 YEARS AFTER THE FIRST GLO (**Greek-Lettered Organization**) WAS ESTABLISHED IN THE U.S. **THESE HAZING (PHYSICAL) RITUALS HAVE DEMONIC (SPIRITUAL) FORCES AT THEIR ROOT.** THESE SAME DEMONIC SPIRITS ARE THE ONES INFLUENCING HAZING IN GLO's TODAY. HAZING STARTED WITH THE GREEKS AND IT CONTINUES WITH THE GREEKS (i.e. PRESENT DAY GLO's). GREEK CHRISTIANS CANNOT BE LIVING UP TO THE COMMANDMENT TO LOVE GOD AND OTHERS WHEN THEY HAVE KNOWLEDGE OF OR PARTICIPATE IN HAZING. BY VIRTUE OF THE FACT THAT HAZING WHETHER IT BE PHYSICAL OR MENTAL EXISTS, SHOULD ALARM ANYONE WHO IS A TRUE CHRISTIAN. FOR THE NATIONAL BODIES OF THESE ORGANIZATIONS TO CASUALLY PASS HAZING OFF ON SOME RENEGADE INDIVIDUALS IS GROSSLY IRRESPONSIBLE. THEY ARE YOUR BROTHERS REGARDLESS OF WHAT YOU SAY. **NO GLO** HAS THE **ABILITY OR POWER** TO STOP HAZING. WHATEVER A FEW IGNORANT BOYS OR GIRLS DO, THE OTHERS WILL ALWAYS BE IDENTIFIED WITH THEM. CHRISTIANS! YOU BELONG TO GOD. YOU HAVE NO BUSINESS ALLOWING

YOURSELVES TO BE HAZED OR PLEDGED. CHRISTIANS! YOU ARE THE TEMPLE OF GOD.

I CORINTHIANS 3:16 Know ye not that ye are the temple of God, and that the Spirit of God dwelleth in you?

I CORINTHIANS 6:16 What? know ye not that he which is joined to a harlot is one body? for Two, saith he, Shall Be One Flesh.

CHRISTIANS SHOULD NOT BE A PART OF ANYTHING THAT IS UNHOLY. GLO's ARE UNHOLY ORGANIZATIONS, AND CHRISTIANS CANNOT ASSOCIATE WITH THEM AND STILL BE CHRISTIANS.

LUKE 10:27-28 And he answering said, thou shalt love the Lord thy God with all thy heart, and with all thy soul, and with all thy strength, and with all thy mind; **and thy neighbor as thyself.** And he said unto him, thou hast answered right: this do, and thou shalt live.

YOU CAN'T LOVE YOUR NEIGHBOR WHEN YOU'RE USING SOMETHING (YOUR GLO) TO ASSUME AUTHORITY THAT'S NOT GIVEN BY GOD, OVER HIM.

MATTHEW 5:44-48 But I say unto you, Love your enemies, bless them that curse you, do good to them that hate you, and pray for them which despitefully use you, and persecute you; That ye may be the children of your Father which is in heaven: for he maketh his sun rise on the evil and on the good, and sendeth

FREDERIC L. HATCHETT

rain on the just and on the unjust. For if ye love them which love you, what reward have ye? do not even the publicans the same? And if ye salute your brethren only, what do ye more than others? do not even the publicans so? Be ye therefore perfect even as your Father which is in heaven is perfect.

HAZING (INCLUDING THE NEW INTAKE PROCESS) VIA MANIPULATION AND INIMIDATION, FOR THE PURPOSE OF DOMINATION OR CONTROL IS DEFINED AS WITCHCRAFT OR THE SPIRIT THEREOF. SO IF ANY OF YOUR BROTHERS OR SISTERS DO IT, YOU ARE A PARTAKER THROUGH YOUR SPIRITUAL FELLOWSHIP WITH THEM (CHAPTER 7). HAZING CLEARLY FITS THE DEFINITION OF WITCHCRAFT. EVEN THE NEW INTAKE PROGRAMS ARE FILLED WITH MANIPULATION AND INTIMIDATION. THE CONTROLLING FACTOR IS SUBTLE, YET OBVIOUS TO ONE WHO HAS EXPERIENCED THE PROCESS. THEY HAVE WHAT YOU WANT, AND THEY TELL YOU TO DO IT THEIR WAY OR IT'S NO WAY.

Judge for yourself as to whether this initiation ritual is godly or ungodly. **Who does the ritual worship?**

"**Initiation**- The alumnae Anti-Basileus shall assist in the initiation ceremony. The following activities **may be** adhered to by the presiding officer.

Part I- Stunts. There shall be **no hazing** or paddling.

    a.) **Blindfold** the initiates for stunts.
    b.) Eat Sigma "worms".
        (Cooked unseasoned spaghetti.)
    c.) Drink "Sigma Tea" (Salt, oil, pepper, **etc.**)
    d.) Brand the Sigma Letters on thighs. (With ice, or candle wax, mercurochrome)
    e.) Remove blindfold."

COMING APART AT THE SEAMS

(The Handbook of Sigma Gamma Rho Sorority, Inc., 1980, pp. 33-34.)

Jesus does not command this of you to come into His kingdom, nor should a church require you to do any of the acts mentioned above. **This is** mental, physical, and spiritual **hazing**. The purpose of blindfolding is to invoke fear in the initiates (mental). The blindfolding, the initiate's state of darkness represents ignorance (spiritual). Eating, drinking, and branding are (physical). Performing this type of ritual is the worship of a false god (spiritual idolatry). In the excerpt, the phrase, **"may be"**, opens up a lot of room for creativity. This may seem harmless, but spiritually it is fatal, **lest you repent and denounce.** Just look at all the creativity mentioned below in the 25+ ways to haze. The fear that these ceremonies invoke is unscriptural. The Bible says that, "perfect love casts out fear"(**I JOHN 4:18**). Hazing in any form is not an expression of God's love. Since this is true, there can be no possible benefit to hazing whether giving or receiving. So all that stupid talk about hazing, breaking down and building up a person or group of persons, is just another one of the many lies a GLO will tell an unsuspecting victim. What's more unfortunate is the amount of GLO alumni who still feel that physical hazing is a good thing.

Part D of the Sigma Gamma Rho initiation is similar to an act that **used to be** performed by Omega Psi Phi. The exception is that they used Iodine to write the Greek letters on the initiate's chest. **Yet, many undergraduate chapters will do things the old way.**

FREDERIC L. HATCHETT

LISTED HERE ARE SOME OF THE ACTUAL METHODS OF HAZING. REMEMBER THAT THESE ARE COLLEGE STUDENTS WITH GPA'S OF 2.5 AND ABOVE, MARRIED MEN WITH FAMILIES, MEN AND WOMEN WHO HAVE NATIONAL RECOGNITION, AND SOMETIMES OFFICERS OF THEIR OWN ORGANIZATION.

1.) **SLAPPING** THE NECK, BACK, FACE, (COMMONLY RESULTS IN A RUPTURED EAR DRUM) AND CHEST WITH ONE OR BOTH HANDS.
2.) PADDLING WITH **WOODEN PADDLES**, 3.) BEATEN WITH **RUBBER TIRES**, 4.) BEATEN WITH **TREE VINES**, 5.) PADDLED WITH **TABLE LEGS**, 6.) WHIPPED WITH COAT HANGERS, AND ANYTHING ELSE IMAGINABLE.
7.) **HANGING**, "WITHOUT THE INTENTION TO CAUSE DEATH", 8.) **BURNING** (NOT THE VOLUNTARY BRANDING), 9.) **RUSSIAN ROULETTE**, 10.) STEALING, 11.) DRINKING (SOMETIMES TO DEATH), 12.) BLINDFOLDING 13.) **KICKING**, 14.) HITTING OVER THE HEAD WITH A **FRYING PAN,** 15.) STUNNED WITH STUN GUNS, 16.) PUNCHING ALL OVER, INCLUDING THE FACE. 17.) **FORCED** TO CUT THE HAIR A CERTAIN WAY FOR RITUALISTIC PUPROSES SUCH AS PLEDGING, STEPPING, OR ANY OTHER REASON. 18.) HAVING TO TAKE AN OATH THAT GOES AGAINST YOUR RELIGIOUS PRINCIPLES, 19.) CONSTANT REPETITION OF WORDS AND PHRASES (i.e. **MANTRA**, 20.) EATING FOODS (onions, butter, and Tabasco sauce at once) THAT WOULD MAKE A PIG THROW UP. 21.) JUMPING OUT 5 STORY WINDOWS, 22.) BEING BEATEN WITH A **HAMMER.** 23.) GETTING SPAT ON 24.) ABANDONMENT (TAKEN TO THE MIDDLE OF NOWHERE TO FIND YOUR WAY BACK), 25.) INVOLUNTARY BRANDING, AND 26.) RELIGIOUS RIDICULE. I SEE IT LIKE THIS: IF MAN KILLED GOD, HE'S CAPABLE OF ANYTHING. MANY HAVE DIED AND GONE TO HELL **PLEDGING, NOT EVEN BECOMING A MEMBER. THEY CROSSED THE BURNING SANDS ALL RIGHT!** WHILE THEIR **MURDERERS** ARE STILL ALIVE AND POSSIBLY STILL HAZING, BUT PRAYERFULLY THEY ARE SAVED. THE MAIN REASON PEOPLE KEEP PLEDGING IS BECAUSE THEY WOULD FEEL STUPID

AFTER GETTING BEAT DOWN TO QUIT. SO THEY CONVINCE THEMSELVES ALONG WITH THE HELP OF THEIR BIG BROTHERS AND LINE BROTHERS THAT THEY ARE DOING THE RIGHT THING. THESE BOYS AND GIRLS DO NOT CARE OR HAVE ANY LOVE FOR YOU, ESPECIALLY VISITING BROTHERS OR SISTERS FROM OTHER SCHOOLS. THE LORD JESUS HIMSELF AND THROUGH THE CHURCH REQUIRES OBEDIENCE BUT NOT THROUGH BRUTALITY, **OBLIGATORY OATHS**, AND BLINDFOLDED CEREMONIES WHICH ARE ALL BONDAGE AND DEMONIC IN NATURE. INSTEAD IT IS SPIRITUAL OBEDIENCE BASED ON THE WORD OF GOD WHICH LIBERATES AND GIVES ETERNAL LIFE (**JOHN 8:32,10:10**). THIS INWARD OBEDIENCE SHOWS ITSELF OUTWARDLY TO THE NATURAL EYE BY THE FRUIT OF THE SPIRIT, AND THAT SAME SPIRIT IS THE ONE THAT CHANGES SOULS FROM ETERNAL DEATH TO ETERNAL LIFE.

GALATIANS 5:22-23 But the fruit of the spirit is love, joy, peace, long-suffering, gentleness, goodness, faith, Meekness, temperance: against such there is no law.

WHERE DOES HAZING FIT IN THIS SCRIPTURE?

THE CHURCH IS THE LORD'S INSTRUMENT TO BRING SAVED PEOPLE TO PERFECTION THROUGH HIM ALONE. THIS IS WHERE TRUE CHRISTIANS BELONG. THEY HAVE NO BUSINESS BEING IN A CULT (A GLO).

EPHESIANS 4:11-12 And he gave some, apostles; and some, prophets; and some evangelists; and some, pastors and teachers; For the perfecting of the saints, for the work of the ministry, for the edifying of the body of Christ:

THE CHURCH IS ALSO FOR THE UNSAVED. THEY NEED TO GO AND HEAR THE GOSPEL PREACHED, SO PERHAPS THEY WOULD REPENT.

ROMANS 10:17- Faith cometh by hearing, and hearing by the Word of God.

FAITH WILL NEVER COME THROUGH SOME GREEK-LETTERED ORGANIZATION, PREACHING A FALSE GOSPEL, TO THE POINT THAT PEOPLE WILL REPENT. THE CHURCH IS THE ONLY PLACE IN THE WORLD MADE SPECIFICALLY BY GOD TO HELP MESSED UP PEOPLE, AND BUILD UP GODLY PEOPLE. ALL OTHER GODLY ORGANIZATIONS ARE THE BRANCHES OF THE CHURCH. **GLO's ARE NOT ONE OF THESE BRANCHES.** THESE GROUPS ARE REALLY NO DIFFERENT THAN THE SECULAR HUMANISTS WHO BELIEVE THAT MAN CAN PERFECT THEMSELVES, SOCIETY AND EVENTUALLY THE WHOLE WORLD THROUGH WORKS. **GLO's AND ANYTHING ELSE (INCLUDING A CHURCH) THAT OPERATES WITHOUT THE HOLY SPIRIT IS STERILE OR DEAD (i.e. UNABLE TO PRODUCE FRUIT).**

ZECHARIAH 4:6 Not by might, nor by power, but by My Spirit, saith the Lord.

WHATEVER A MAN BUILDS WITH HIS OWN HANDS, UPON ANY FOUNDATION OTHER THAN JESUS, HE LABORS IN VAIN, AND BY LOOKING AT WHAT HE HAS DONE HE PUFFS UP WITH PRIDE (**READ DANIEL 4:33-37**). HAZING IS **MAN'S WILL**. HAZING IN ANY FORM IS A MEANS TO CONTROL BY POWER (WITCHCRAFT SPIRIT). TO DO ANYTHING BY THE WILL OF MAN ALONE IS NOT PRODUCTIVE, BECAUSE JESUS IS NOT THE FOUNDATION.

PROVERBS 14:12 There is a way that seemeth right unto a man, but the end thereof are the ways of death.

MATTHEW 7:24-27 Therefore whosoever heareth these sayings of mine, and doeth them, I will liken him unto a wise man, which built his house upon a rock: And the rain descended, and the winds blew, and beat upon that house; and it fell not: for it was founded upon a rock. And everyone that heareth these sayings of mine, and doeth them not, shall be likened unto a foolish man, which built his house upon the sand: And the rain descended, and the winds blew, and beat upon that house; and it fell: and great was the fall of it.

ALL GLO'S HAVE **MAN-MADE** RULES AND REGULATIONS THAT MUST BE FOLLOWED, BUT WILL THAT WHICH GLO'S HAVE BUILT BE ABLE TO STAND IN THE PRESENCE OF GOD, TESTED BY THE WORD OF GOD, TRIED IN THE FIRE AND BE PERFECTED? **NO!! A DEMONIC ROOT CAN NEVER PRODUCE GOOD FRUIT.** ALL SECRET SOCIETIES ARE ALREADY GUILTY, AND HAVING FAILED THE TEST, LEAVE BEHIND ASHES AND SMOKE AS THEIR TESTIMONY, INSTEAD OF PURIFIED GOLD AND SILVER. THOSE DESIRING TO BE, WHO ARE MEMBERS NOW, AND WHO NEVER DENOUNCED BEFORE OR DENOUNCE **RIGHT NOW WILL BE JUDGED ACCORDINGLY.** CHRISTIANS WHO HAVE A DESIRE TO JOIN A GLO CANNOT SERVE GOD WITH A DIVIDED HEART. YET, GOD IS FAITHFUL TO CALL US TO REPENTANCE. GREEK CHRISTIANS NEED TO REPENT AND DENOUNCE (TURN AWAY FROM YOUR IDOLS).

EZEKIEL 14:1-6(amp) THEN CAME certain of the elders of Israel and sat before me. And the word of the Lord came to me: Son of man, these men have set up their idols in their hearts and put a stumbling block of their iniquity and guilt before their faces; should I permit Myself to be inquired of at all by them? Therefore speak to and say to them, Thus says the Lord God: Every man of the house of Israel who takes his idols [of self-will and unsubmissiveness] into his heart and puts a stumbling block of iniquity [idols of silver and gold] before his face, and yet comes to the prophet [to inquire of him], I the Lord will answer him, answer him according to the multitude of his idols, that I may lay hold of the house of Israel in the thoughts of their own mind and heart, because they are all estranged from Me through their idols. Therefore say to the house of Israel, Thus says the Lord God: Repent and turn away from your idols, and turn your faces from all your abominations.

    CHRIST NOT ONLY SAID TO SERVE HIM ALONE: HE ALSO SET UP A MEANS TO DO THIS SERVICE THROUGH, AND IT'S CALLED **THE CHURCH**. WHEN YOU'RE ON THE JOB, AT HOME, IN ANOTHER COUNTRY, OR IN PRISON, YOU ARE TO SERVE AND GLORIFY GOD ALONE. THIS CAN'T BE DONE BY GLO's, BECAUSE THEY ALWAYS DESIRE TO GET SOME OF THE GLORY FOR THEMSELVES. HE IS SAYING, SERVE ME THROUGH THAT WHICH I DIED FOR, YOU, THE LIVING CHURCH.

ROMANS 12:1-2 I beseech you therefore, brethren, by the mercies of God, that ye present your bodies a living sacrifice, holy acceptable unto God, which is your reasonable service. And be not conformed to this world: but be ye transformed by the renewing of your mind, that ye may prove what is good, and acceptable, and perfect, will of God.

    ONE ALSO SERVES THE LOCAL CHURCH THEY BELONG TO, BUT NOT THE WAY YOU WANT; LIKE THROUGH A GLO. GOD SAYS TO DESIRE HIM ALONE. HAZING IS JUST A WAY TO COERCE AND NEGATIVELY REINFORCE **SERVICE FOR THE GLO, NOT FOR THE LORD**. SERVICE MUST BE TO GOD ALONE, OUT OF A WILLING HEART. HAZING IS ABOUT CONFORMITY TO MAN'S WILL. CONFORMITY TO CHRIST IS GOD'S WILL.

    HERE ARE SOME ACTUAL ACCOUNTS OF HAZING.

THIS FIRST INCIDENT WAS AT THE UNIVERSITY OF MARYLAND. THIS REPORT WAS ACTUALLY A CONFIRMATION TO WHAT I HAD ALREADY KNOWN (i.e. BEFORE IT WAS MADE PUBLIC).

"SIX BOYS PLEDGING OMEGA PSI PHI FRATERNITY WERE BRUTALIZED IN HAZING SESSIONS THAT LASTED ABOUT TWO MONTHS." MAY I COMMENT THROUGH EXPERIENCE THAT THESE "SESSIONS" CAN LAST FROM 2-6 HOURS AT A TIME. "THESE BOYS WERE KICKED, PUNCHED, BEATEN, AND WHIPPED. ALL SIX WERE HOSPITALIZED WITH INJURIES SUCH AS A RUPTURED SPLEEN, COLLAPSED LUNG, PUNCTURED EARDRUM, CRACKED RIBS, A BROKEN ANKLE, LIVER DAMAGE, AND A CONCUSSION." (Ronald E. Childs, BLACK GREEK FRATERNITIES IN THE '90S: ARE THEY STILL CULTURALLY RELEVANT? Ebony Man, Volume 8, Number 10, Johnson Publishing Company, August 1993, pp. 44&51.)

I FOUND OUT LATER THAT ONE OF THE MEN WON A $375,000 LAWSUIT. THE FRATERNITY WAS SUSPENDED FOR ONLY FIVE YEARS. BY THE TIME THIS BOOK IS DONE, THEY WILL BE BACK ON CAMPUS. NOW ONE SHOULD SEE WHY THE HAZING DOES NOT STOP. CRIMINAL LIABILTY? WHAT CRIMINAL LIABILTY?

"SOUTHERN UNIVERSITY IN BATON ROUGE LOUISIANA: A MEMBER OF PHI BETA SIGMA HITS A PLEDGEE, DERONE WALKER OVER THE HEAD WITH A FRYING PAN, BLINDING HIM. DOCTORS DO NOT KNOW WHETHER HE WILL EVER SEE AGAIN." (Ronald E. Childs, BLACK GREEK FRATERNITIES IN THE '90S: ARE THEY STILL CULTURALLY

FREDERIC L. HATCHETT

RELEVANT? Ebony Man, Volume 8, Number 10, Johnson Publishing Company, August 1993, pp. 44&51.)

"AT ILLINOIS STATE UNIVERSITY, ARMED GANG-LIKE CONFRONTATIONS BETWEEN MEMBERS OF ALPHA PHI ALPHA, KAPPA ALPHA PSI, AND OMEGA PSI PHI FRATERNITIES HAVE LOCAL LAW ENFORCEMENT PERPLEXED." (Ronald E. Childs, BLACK GREEK FRATERNITIES IN THE '90S: ARE THEY STILL CULTURALLY RELEVANT? Ebony Man, Volume 8, Number 10, Johnson Publishing Company, August 1993, pp. 44&51.)

AT THE UNIVERSITY OF SOUTH FLORIDA, ZETA PHI BETA **SORORITY** WAS SUSPENDED FOR HAZING.

"There were beatings using wooden paddles, serious enough to cause bruises and physical discomfort." (Linda Chion Kenny, USF sorority suspended for hazing, Saint Petersburg Times, Saint Petersburg Times Publishing Company, April 9, 1999.)

I WAS SENT A LETTER FROM MY OWN FRATERNITY TO HELP BY PAYING MY DUES AGAIN (Reclamation). IN IT I READ SOMETHING VERY DISTURBING. A YOUNG WAS SUING OMEGA PSI PHI FRATERNITY, BECAUSE **HIS RECTUM COLLAPSED** FROM EXCESSIVE PADDLING. (Blackston v. Omega Psi Phi Fraternity Case Summary)

IF YOU WANT TO KNOW MORE ABOUT HAZING INCIDENCES, YOU CAN FIND PLENTY ON THE INTERNET. YOU WILL SEE THAT I WAS NOT JOKING ABOUT SOME OF THE METHODS. I HIT ABOUT 15 SITES ON HAZING IN ONE DAY.

DOES HAZING SOUND UPLIFTING, BOND BUILDING, HONORABLE, RIGHTEOUS, AND CHRISTLIKE? **CERTAINLY NOT!**

THE GENERAL PUBLIC REALLY HAS NO IDEA HOW HARD THESE PADDLES GET SWUNG ON THE BUTTOCKS, LEGS, AND SOMETIMES THE BACK; HOW MANY EARDRUMS GET BUSTED; HOW MANY KIDNEYS GET DAMAGED AND HOW MANY PEOPLE GET MAIMED FOR LIFE. AT RANDOM, I AM JUST GOING TO WRITE ALL THAT I KNOW TO HAVE HAPPENED DURING HAZING "SESSIONS." TWO BLACK EYES, KNOCKED OUT TOOTH, BROKEN LEG, RUPTURED SPLEEN, BEARD SET ON FIRE, HIT OVER THE HEAD WITH A PADDLE, BROKEN JAW, BRUISED DIAPHRAGM, BUSTED EARDRUMS, BURNED HANDS, ICE-PICKED IN THE FACE AND HIT OVER THE HEAD WITH A BASEBALL BAT AND LEFT-FOR-DEAD. THE LAST THREE LISTED APPLY TO THE ONE PERSON. THE SORORITIES HAZE ALSO. I HAVE SEEN IT AND HEARD ABOUT IT FROM THEIR MOUTHS. THEY HIT WITH PADDLES, SLAP, AND HUMILIATE PLEDGES MENTALLY.

MANY HAZING INCIDENCES NEVER MAKE IT PUBLIC. THE MEMBERS, INITIATES, AND GRADUATE CHAPTERS COVER THEM UP, BECAUSE PUBLICITY WOULD HURT **THEIR IMAGE. ALL DUE TO THE ME, MYSELF, AND I ATTITUDE,** MANY LIVES HAVE BEEN DESTROYED WITHOUT PROPER RETRIBUTION. AS I HAVE BEEN WRITING THIS BOOK, I WAS MADE AWARE OF A HAZING INCIDENT. THIS GLO HAS TWO GREEK CHRISTIANS IN IT. ONE CLAIMS TO BE A CHRISTIAN MINISTER, AND IS INVOLVED DIRECTLY WITH THE HAZING. AT THE SAME TIME, THIS CAMPUS HAS THREE OTHER GLO's PLEDGING ITS INITIATES. I INFORMED THE NATIONAL OFFICE OF ONE OF THE GLO's. THE MAN SAID THE PERSON THAT HANDLES THOSE INCIDENCES IS OUT OF TOWN, AND FOR ME TO CALL BACK LATER. DOESN'T SOUND LIKE CONCERN TO ME.

NOW ISN'T THIS HYPOCRITICAL FAITH? THIS MAN IS A MINISTER OF THE GOSPEL BY DAY, AND A HAZER BY NIGHT. ONE

CANNOT BELIEVE **LUKE 10:27-28**, AND CONDONE OR TAKE PART IN HAZING. BY REMAINING A MEMBER, YOU ARE CONDONING HAZING (i.e. YOU ARE GUILTY BY ASSOCIATION). LIKE ME AT ONE TIME BEING A FOOL, I THOUGHT I HAD THE RIGHT TO HAZE SOMEONE. BY WHAT AUTHORITY COULD I DO IT? BY ANOTHER PERSON GIVING THE AUTHORITY? IT STILL DOES NOT MAKE IT RIGHT FOR THEM TO SUBMIT, AND ME TO INDULGE. WHY? BECAUSE WE ARE ALL CREATED BY GOD. ANYONE WHO HAZES IS A FOOL, AND ANYONE WHO ACCEPTS IT IS EVEN A BIGGER FOOL, AND I HAVE BEEN BOTH. THERE IS ALSO HAZING THAT GOES ON AMONG MEMBERS OF GLO's. ONE FORM IS "PROPHYTE". THIS IS WHEN YOU HAVE REACHED A LEVEL ABOVE A NEOPHYTE (BRAND NEW MEMBER). YOU ARE REQUIRED TO GO THROUGH SOME FORM OF HAZING TO BE GIVEN THE TITLE OF PROPHYTE. HERE IS PROOF OF HAZING BY MEMBERS OF THE SAME FRATERNITY.

TWO **MEMBERS, "BROTHERS"**, OF PHI BETA SIGMA BEAT EACH OTHER TO SEE WHO COULD TAKE THE MOST. ONE OF THEM HAD TO BE HOSPITALIZED FOR KIDNEY DIALYSIS. (Copyright 1999- Minerva Computer Services. http://deltasigmatheta.com/haze14.htm)

THERE IS ANOTHER FORM OF HAZING CALLED **WRECKING**. THIS IS WHEN BOYS OR GIRLS IN THE SAME GLO HAZE THEIR OWN BROTHERS AND SISTERS BECAUSE THEY DON'T KNOW ENOUGH INFORMATION ABOUT THE GLO. THEIR BROTHERS AND SISTERS WILL OFTEN RIP THEIR SHIRTS OR TAKE

PARAPHERNALIA BY PHYSICAL FORCE. NO TRUE CHRISTIAN WOULD EVER WANT TO BE ASSOCIATED WITH THIS KIND OF BEHAVIOR.

IF YOU ESCAPE THE HAZING AND BECOME A MEMBER, OR QUIT PLEDGING, EXPECT TO BE AN OUTCAST. BELIEVE ME, FORGIVENESS IS VERY RARE AMONGST YOUR SO-CALLED BROTHERS AND SISTERS. BUT THE BIBLE SAYS TO FORGIVE AS GOD FORGAVE, IF YOU WANT GOD TO FORGIVE YOU.

MATTHEW 6:14-15 For ye forgive men their trespasses, your heavenly Father will also forgive you: But if ye forgive men not their trespasses, neither will your Father forgive your trespasses.

OTHER SO-CALLED BROTHERS OR SISTERS FEEL CHEATED AND STUPID BECAUSE YOU DIDN'T GET HAZED, HUMILIATED, AND BECOME A SLAVE LIKE THEM. THIS ATTITUDE OVERFLOWS TO RESENTMENT, TO BITTERNESS, AND FINALLY HATRED. THE ONES WHO DON'T MAKE IT ARE PUNKS, SISSIES, OR BOYS (i.e. THEY ARE NOT REAL MEN OR WOMEN). PEOPLE EVEN BRAG ABOUT HOW MUCH WORSE (HARDER IS WHAT THEY SAY) THEY WERE HAZED THEN YOU. IF THAT'S NOT BRAINWASHING, THEN WHAT IS? PLEDGING **IN ANY FORM** IS ALSO PROOF THAT ACCEPTANCE IS BY WORKS, NOT FAITH WHICH IS WHY THESE PEOPLE BOAST (CHRISTIANS INCLUDED). EVEN WITHOUT PLEDGING, THERE ARE WORKS REQUIRED TO BE ELIGIBLE FOR MEMBERSHIP. ELIGIBILITY FOR MEMBERSHIP IN THE

KINGDOM REQUIRES NO WORKS AND CAN NEVER BE EARNED. GLO's CANNOT EXIST WITHOUT **POWER AND CONTROL (HAZING)** WHETHER IT BE SPIRITUAL, PHYSICAL, OR MENTAL (i.e. BRAINWASHING, BRUTALITY). YET, GLO's DO NOT HAVE THE POWER TO STOP HAZING EITHER. SO WHEN YOU DECIDE TO PLEDGE REMEMBER ONE THING, **YOU ARE PUTTING YOUR OWN LIFE ON THE LINE**. SINCE GLO's DO NOT HONESTLY PROMOTE A SAVING RELATIONSHIP WITH CHRIST, THEY CLAIM TO BE FOUNDED ON CHRISTIAN PRINCIPLES AS A **RELIGIOUS FRONT**. THE REASON IS GLO's KNEW A CHRISTIAN IMAGE WAS NECESSARY. THE CHURCH WAS PERSECUTING SECRET ORGANIZATIONS DURING THE 1700'S. WHITE GLO's OF THE LATE 1700'S AND BLACK GLO's OF THE EARLY 1900'S KNEW OF THE ANTI-SECRET ORGANIZATION MOVEMENT. CHRISTIAN PRINCIPLES WERE USHERED IN TO REDUCE PERSECUTION AND ATTRACT "PEOPLE OF FAITH". **GLO's NEVER INTENDED TO STOP BEING SECRET, OR EXCLUDE SINNERS FROM MEMBERSHIP, AND THEY DON'T NOW**. THIS IS THE REASON FOR THE MORAL DEGRADATION, DRUNKENESS, BRUTALITY, IDOLATRY, HAZING, FORNICATION, AND OTHER SINS. THE **SECRECY** MIXED WITH THE CHRISTIAN **RHETORIC** BLINDED THE BELIEVER FROM THE TRUE EVIL. GREEK CHRISTIANS ARE JUST TOOLS OF THE DEVIL TO RAPE MORE PEOPLE OUT OF THE KINGDOM OF GOD.

All of these activities are not confined to just the college campuses. The **graduate chapters** also engage in these ungodly actions. There are many **pastors, ministers, and other church leaders** who feel it's okay to be members and are members of these groups. Some are still actively involved with their respective groups. I know some personally, but I no longer **associate** myself with them anymore. Their excuse is that it is based on Christian principles. As you have seen, this is a Biblically incorrect statement. All clergy are not going to make it in to heaven. The Word of God is what you must follow, not what a man says.

MATTHEW 7:21-23 Not every one that saith unto me, Lord, Lord, shall enter into the kingdom of heaven; but he that doeth the will of my Father which is in heaven. Many will say to me in that day, Lord, Lord, have we not prophesied in thy name? and in thy name have cast out devils? and in thy name done many wonderful works? And then I will profess unto him, I never knew you: depart from me, ye that work iniquity.

FOR BETTER OR FOR WORSE: HAZING'S SPIRITUALLY-VIOLENT PARTNER

"THE NEW INTAKE PROCESS"

"IF YOU CAN'T BEATEM, BRAINWASHEM"

THE INTAKE PROCESS WAS ENACTED IN 1990 BY MOST OF THE BLACK GLO's BECAUSE OF SO MANY HAZING CRIMES. IT WAS DESIGNED TO

ELIMINATE PHYSICAL HAZING BY CONCENTRATING MORE ON THE NON-VIOLENT RITUALS. SINCE THEN, I BELIEVE IT HAS GOTTEN WORSE.

THE NEW INTAKE PROCESS IS MORE DANGEROUS AND DAMAGING THAN PHYSICAL HAZING BECAUSE IT ATTACKS THE MIND AND THE SPIRIT TO A GREATER DEGREE.

THE NEW INTAKE PROCESS IS SO DANGEROUS BECAUSE IT DEALS MORE ON A SPIRITUAL AND MENTAL LEVEL. WORDS MIXED WITH DESIRES ARE A POWERFUL COMBINATION. INSTEAD OF BEING THREATENED WITH A PADDLE, YOU ARE THREATENED WITH THE PENALTY OF NOT BECOMING A MEMBER. THEIR THREATENING WORDS AND THE PLEDGES DESIRE TO JOIN COLLIDE. WHO WILL COMPROMISE? THEY TURN YOUR DESIRE INTO BONDAGE AND COVETOUSNESS. ONE WANTS TO BE A MEMBER SO BAD EVEN A CHRISTIAN WILL DO WHATEVER THEY ARE TOLD, WHETHER IT'S BIBLICALLY CORRECT OR NOT. MANY WHO HAVE BEEN TURNED DOWN BECOME DEPRESSED, CRY, AND GET MAD. SOME GET MAD ENOUGH TO CALL THE NATIONAL OFFICE AND CRY FOUL PLAY. YET, THE SCENARIO IS ALWAYS THE SAME, IF YOU DO NOT DO WHAT WE SAY, YOU'LL NEVER BE A MEMBER. IF YOU BECOME A MEMBER BY, "DROPPING DIME" OR CALLING NATIONALS, WE WILL NEVER TRULY ACCEPT YOU.

THE NO HAZING POLICY HAS MADE IT MORE ACCEPTABLE AND PALATABLE TO THOSE WHOM DESIRE MEMBERSHIP KNOWING THEY DO NOT HAVE TO BE BEATEN. NOW MANY WHO WOULD NOT HAVE JOINED AT THE UNDERGRADUATE LEVEL, BECAUSE THEY FEARED PHYSICAL PAIN WOULD JOIN. THE NO HAZING POLICY IS THE

MAIN REASONS WHY MANY CHRISTIANS FEEL THEY CAN SAFELY JUSTIFY BEING IN A GLO. THEY FAIL TO REALIZE THAT THE SPIRITUAL ASPECTS OF GLO's CAN NEVER CHANGE. GLO's CONCENTRATE EVEN MORE ON THE MIND OF THE INITIATE. THEY DO IT USING A CLEVERLY DISGUISED ANTI-CHRIST INDOCTRINATION. THEY EVEN TEACH THEM TO BEWARE OF THE CHRISTIAN WITNESSING METHODS. THEY WARN THE INITIATES THAT THEY MAY RUN INTO CHRISTIANS WHO OPPOSE GLO's. THEY TELL THEM HOW TO ANSWER QUESTIONS, NOT TO REALLY LISTEN, AND HOW TO GET THEIR "2 CENTS IN". THE ONE THING GLO's AND THE "GREEK CHRISTIANS" CAN NEVER SEEM TO COME UP WITH TO DEFEND THEMSELVES IS SCRIPTURE. YOU KNOW WHY? BECAUSE THERE AREN'T ANY SCRIPTURES THAT DEFEND GLO's. I AM NOT SAYING GREEKS DO NOT USE SCRIPTURE, IT'S JUST THAT WHEN THEY DO IT'S GROSSLY MISAPPLIED AND NO GOOD FOR A DEFENSE. I'LL PUT IT TO THE "GREEK CHRISTIAN" AND ALL GLO's THIS WAY; IT'S GREAT THAT CHRISTIANS **HAVE APPROXIMATELY 400-500 SCRIPTURES** IN THEIR DEFENSE OF THE FAITH TOWARD GLO's, BECAUSE THAT'S WHAT I HAVE IN THIS BOOK, AND THERE ARE PLENTY MORE.

THE INTAKE PROGRAM IS NOTHING MORE THAN AN IN WRITING, FORMAL COVER-UP FOR HAZING. IT IS ALSO DONE IN SECRECY (IN SIN) TO HIDE SOMETHING. **THOSE WHO OPPOSE THE INTAKE WILL CONTINUE TO HAZE.** MANY FOR THE INTAKE ARE THE ONES WHO ALREADY HAD THEIR HAZING DAYS, OR FEAR THE BANKRUPTCY OF THEIR GLO FROM LAWSUITS. A HOUSE DIVIDED CANNOT STAND. THE

COMING APART AT THE SEAMS

BICKERING OVER HOW TO PLEDGE WILL NEVER END. IT WILL BE THE NEVER ENDING THORN IN THE SIDE OF GLO's. HAZING HAS NOT CEASED. SINCE THE NEW-INTAKE PROCESS **9** YEARS AGO, I KNOW OF **FIVE DEATHS**, BROKEN LEGS, PUNCTURED LUNGS, AND **EXTENDED HOSPITALIZATIONS**, BUT NOT ONE **PERMANENT REMOVAL** OF THOSE GLO's FROM A PARTICULAR CAMPUS. EVEN WHEN MANY CHAPTERS ARE REVOKED, THE PRESENT BROTHERS OR SISTERS STILL PLEDGE AND ILLEGITIMATELY INITIATE PEOPLE ANYWAY. LATER, THEY BECOME "LEGITIMATE" (i.e. PAY INITIATION FEES) MEMBERS IN A GRADUATE CHAPTER. RIGHT NOW MANY GRADUATE CHAPTERS ARE FULL OF THESE **RENEGADE** MEMBERS. THE ULTIMATE QUESTION IS WHY? WHY WOULD ANYONE (ESPECIALLY A CHRISTIAN) AFTER THE FIRST BEATING, ENDURE MORE ACTS OF BRUTALITY? **THE ANSWER IS IDOLATRY.** A PERSON'S DESIRE TO BE IN THE GLO OVERSHADOWS ALL OTHER PRIORITIES IN LIFE INCLUDING JESUS. JESUS IS SOMETIMES ASKED OR TOLD TO BE SECOND PLACE UNTIL THE HAZING IS OVER. UNFORTUNATELY, HIS RANKING DROPS AFTER INITIATION. **IDOLATRY IS THE ROOT TO THE ENDURANCE OF BRUTALITY.** EVERY BREATH THEY TAKE IS ABOUT THEIR GLO. THEY ACT LIKE PARAKEETS, REPEATING EXACTLY WHAT THEY ARE TOLD TO REPEAT. **MONKEY SEE, MONKEY DO SUMS UP THE MENTALITY OF THE PLEDGE.** WHY ELSE WOULD ONE TAKE THE STUFF YOU READ ABOUT ABOVE EXCEPT IT BE TO BECOME A GREEK? THE ANSWER-**IDOLATRY!!!** INSTEAD OF THE CHRISTIAN HAVING THEIR EYES FIXED ON JESUS, IT IS FIXED ON SOME HELLISH GLO. AFTER READING ABOUT ALL THE METHODS, DEATHS AND

INJURIES, DON'T EVEN THINK TWICE. YOU PUT YOUR **PHYSICAL AND ETERNAL LIFE** AT STAKE BY JUST BEING INTERESTED IN A GLO. IF YOUR PASTOR PREACHES AGAINST GLO's, AND YOU JOIN ONE ANYWAY, THAT PERSON IS NOT YOUR PASTOR. YOU CANNOT RECEIVE OR BENEFIT FROM THE WORD HE PREACHES, BECAUSE OF YOUR REBELLION AGAINST HIM. TO REBEL AGAINST HIM IS THE SAME AS REBELLING AGAINST GOD. THE STEPS TO AND BECOMING A MEMBER OF A GLO **DESTROYS THE SPIRITUAL LIFE OF A TRUE CHRISTIAN.**

IN CONCLUSION, HAZING IS SUPPOSED TO BUILD BONDS, PROMOTE BETTER RELATIONSHIPS THROUGH SIMILAR EXPERIENCES, AND TO LEARN HOW TO ENDURE HARDSHIPS. **SINCE HAZING IS TRULY UNRIGHTEOUS DISCIPLINE**, IT DOES THE FOLLOWING:

- a.) Provokes one to **ANGER**
- b.) Produces **BONDAGE**
- c.) Leads to **BITTERNESS**
- d.) **Desensitizes the conscience** of both the **PLEDGEE** and **MEMBER** (i.e. Right or wrong makes no difference. It's a part of the process. It's **TRADITION**)
- e.) **Serves no TRUE purpose.**
- f.) Breeds **REVENGE**

RIGHTEOUS DISCIPLINE DOES THE FOLLOWING:

- a.) Shows **LOVE- HEBREWS 12:5-11**
- b.) Can save the **SPIRIT- I CORINTHIANS 5:5**

c.) Leads to **RIGHTEOUSNESS- HEBREWS 12:5-11**

Cleanses away EVIL- PROVERBS 20:30

Notes

CHAPTER 3
PART 3

IDOLATRY

ALL IDOLATRY IS DEMON-INSPIRED AND DEMON-LED. WHERE THERE IS AN IDOL, THERE'S A DEMON. MANY EMBLEMS OF GLO's (Greek-Lettered Organizations) HAVE gods ON THEM. MOST OF THEIR DOCTRINES AND PRINCIPLES ARE CENTERED AROUND THEIR SYMBOLS (i.e. THEY IDOLIZE THEMSELVES).

Key Scripture

ISAIAH 42:8 I am the Lord: and my glory will I not give to another, neither my praise to graven images.

"The Greeks unlike the Egyptians, made their gods in their own image." (Edith Hamilton, Mythology, Boston: Little, Brown, and Company, 1969, p. 15.)
THE GREEKS EMBRACED SUCH FOOLISH PRIDE. THIS PRIDE IS IDOLATRY OF MAN HIMSELF.

COMING APART AT THE SEAMS

The next step for man's PRIDE IS TO TAKE HIM TO THE NEXT LEVEL which is making themselves gods, as they did with Paul and Barnabas in **ACTS 14:11-20**; BUT THEY DID NOT CLAIM THIS **ELITE** POSITION WHICH COULD HAVE GIVEN THEM GREAT WEALTH AND ABUNDANCE OF PLEASURES. IDOLATRY OR AN IDOL IS ANYTHING WE KEEP IN OUR HEARTS IN THE PLACE WHICH GOD OUGHT TO BE, WHETHER IT BE AN IMAGE OF WOOD, STONE, SILVER, GOLD, OR MONEY, **DESIRE** FOR FAME, THE LOVE OF PLEASURE, FRATERNITY, SORORITY, OR SOME SECRET SIN YOU WILL NOT GIVE UP. GOD MUST OCCUPY THE HIGHEST PLACE IN OUR HEARTS. IF SOMETHING ELSE DOES, IT IS AN IDOL (**ACTS 17** GIVES A CLEAR EXPLANATION OF WHAT THESE **DESIRES** CAN DO TO THE MIND). IDOLATRY MANIFESTS ITSELF IN GLO'S BY THOUGHT, WORD, DEED, SYMBOLISM, AND RITUALS. REMEMBER CHRISTIANS! YOU ARE NOT IMMUNE TO THE ATTACK OF IDOLATRY. HERE IS THE PROBLEM WITH **ANY IDOLATRY** ACCORDING TO:

JOSHUA 24:14-16 Now therefore fear the Lord, and serve Him in sincerity and truth: and put away the **gods** which your fathers served on the other side of the flood, and Egypt; and serve ye the Lord. And if it seem evil unto you to serve the Lord, choose this day whom you will serve; whether the gods which your fathers served that were on the other side of the, or the gods of the Amorites, in whose land ye dwell: but as for me and my house, we will serve the Lord. And the people answered and said, God forbid that we should forsake the Lord, to serve other gods.

SECRET CEREMONIES ARE NOT, NOR ARE THEY BASED ON THE TRUTH. ALL GLO's ARE IDOLATROUS BASED ON THEIR TEACHINGS, RITUALS, SONGS, POEMS, SERVICE etc. GLO's ARE THE gods, AND THE MEMBERS ARE THE WORSHIPERS. GOD DOES TOLERATE THIS.

DEUTERONOMY 6:14 Ye shall not go **after other gods,** of **the gods of other people** which are round about you.

THE MEMBERS EVEN COVET THEIR OWN SECRETS. I BELIEVE SOME WOULD DIE (IN VAIN) BEFORE GIVING UP THE SECRETS. I HAVE SEEN PEOPLE BEATEN UP FOR KNOWING A GLO's SECRETS, BUT NOT BEING A MEMBER. IDOLATRY WILL CAUSE PEOPLE TO DO VERY CRAZY THINGS. I WARN ANY PERSON NEVER TO PERPETRATE BEING IN A GLO. YOU WILL END UP WITH MORE THAN YOUR FEELINGS HURT. MY WARNING IS THE SAME FOR GREEK CHRISTIANS. STOP PERPETRATING YOUR RELATIONSHIP WITH CHRIST.

IT'S ONE SIDE OR THE OTHER. **YOUR GLO OR JESUS.**

NOT LATER

PROVERBS 27:1 BOAST NOT thyself of tomorrow; for **thou knowest not what a day may bring forth.**

JAMES 4:13-15 Go to now, ye that say, Today or tomorrow we will go into such a city, and continue there a year, and buy and sell, and get gain: Whereas **ye know not what shall be on the morrow.** For what is your life? It is even a vapour, that appeareth for a little time, and then vanisheth away. **For ye ought to say, If the lord will,** we shall live, and do this, or that.

RIGHT NOW

II CORINTHIANS 6:2 (For he saith, I have heard thee in a time accepted, and in the day of salvation have I succoured thee: behold, **now is the time**; behold, **now is the day of salvation.**)

REPENT AND DENOUNCE BEFORE IT'S TOO LATE.

LUKE 16:19-31 REALLY POINTS OUT THE IDEA ABOUT BEING ON ONE SIDE OR THE OTHER. THERE IS A GREAT GULF DURING THIS LIFE THAT IS NOT FIXED, AND A GREAT GULF **FIXED** AFTER YOU DIE. THE DIFFERENCE BETWEEN THE ONE ON EARTH AND AFTER DEATH IS **ONE IS TEMPORARY** AND **THE OTHER PERMANENT**. WHILE LIVING, YOU CAN CROSS THE GREAT GULF BY CROSSING OVER ON THE BLOOD OF JESUS (HOW DO YOU GLO'S CROSS-OVER? I KNOW IT'S NOT ON JESUS' BLOOD!!! PERHAPS SOME OF YOUR OWN YOU THINK?). AFTER DEATH, THE GREAT GULF IS **FIXED** FOR ETERNITY. GOD **CANNOT** HELP YOU!!!!!!!!!!

JOSHUA 24:22-23 And Joshua said unto the people, ye are **witnesses against yourselves** that ye have chosen the Lord, to **serve him**. And they said, we are witnesses. Now therefore **put away**, said he, **the strange gods** which are among you, and **incline your heart unto the Lord** God of Israel.

I CORINTHIANS 5:9-13 I wrote unto you in an epistle not to company with fornicators: Yet not altogether with the fornicators of this world, or with the covetous, or extortioners, or with idolaters; for then must ye needs go out of the world. But now I have written unto you **not to keep company**, if any man that is called a brother be a fornicator, or covetous, or **an idolater**, or a railer, or a drunkard, or an extortioner, with such an one not to eat. For what have I to do judge them also that are without? do not ye judge them that are within? But them that are without God judgeth. Therefore **put away from among yourselves that wicked person.**

I CORINTHIANS 6:9-10 Know ye not that the unrighteous **shall not inherit the Kingdom of God**? Be not deceived: neither fornicators, **nor idolaters**, nor adulterers, nor effeminate, nor abusers of themselves with mankind, Nor thieves, nor covetous, nor drunkards, nor revelers, nor extortioners, shall inherit the kingdom of God.

THE SYMBOLS OF GLO'S-THE AURORA (SIGMA GAMMA RHO), MINERVA (DELTA SIGMA THETA), THE SPHINX (ALPHA PHI ALPHA), APOLLO (TAU KAPPA EPSILON), THE CENTAUR (IOTA PHI THETA), THE DOGS (OMEGA PSI PHI), ATLAS (ALPHA KAPPA ALPHA), PROMETHIUS (PHI BETA SIGMA), CATS (ZETA PHI BETA) ETC, PROVE SECRET SOCIETIES ARE IDOLATROUS. GOD HAS A PROBLEM WITH ALL OF THIS.

ISAIAH 42:8 I am the Lord: and my glory will I not give to another, neither my praise to graven images.

THEY MAY NOT NAME A SPECIFIC god OR DISPLAY A SYMBOL OF ONE, BUT THE IDOLATRY EXISTS AND CAN ALSO BE SEEN IN THOUGHT, WORD AND DEED. ALL GLO'S ALSO COMMIT IDOLATRY

COMING APART AT THE SEAMS

THROUGH THE PERFORMING OF RITUALS, BECAUSE **RITUALS ARE AN ACT OF WORSHIP**. GLO'S RITUALS ARE AN **ALTERNATE** FORM OF WORSHIP WHICH IS IDOLATRY BECAUSE THEY ARE NOT WORSHIPPING THE GOD OF ABRAHAM, ISAAC, AND JACOB IN SPIRIT AND IN TRUTH, BUT ATTEMPTING TO DO IT THROUGH **OBJECTS** (CANDLES), OTHER TYPES OF **RITUALS** (DEATH RITES), AND **SYMBOLS** (THE GREEK LETTERS, STARS, SWORDS, etc.). WORSHIP BELONGS TO GOD **ONLY.**

MATTHEW 4:10 Then saith Jesus unto him, Get thee hence, Satan: for it is written, Thou shalt **worship the Lord thy God, and him only shalt thou serve.**

THERE ARE RITUALS OR ACTS OF WORSHIP IN THE CHURCH WHICH CLEARLY WORSHIP THE TRUE GOD, AND ARE BIBLICALLY SUPPORTED. WATER BAPTISM, COMMUNION, AND ORDAINMENT ARE A FEW. INSTALLATIONS, REDEDICATIONS, AND INITIATIONS ARE RITUALS PERFORMED BY GLO's. THE RITUALS ARE CENTERED AROUND THE GLO ITSELF; NOT GOD AND JESUS. THEY MAY APPEAR BY FORM AND FASHION TO BE BIBLICAL, AND THEIR WORDS SEEM GODLY, EVEN USING SCRIPTURE, BUT THE ORIGIN AND HISTORICALLY RELIABLE EVIDENCE PROVE THAT THESE RITUALS, **CLEARLY IDOLATROUS**, ARE NOTHING MORE THAN ANCIENT GREEK CULT CEREMONIES (SUCH AS THE AKA GREEK GODDESS RITUAL THEY PERFORM FOR THEIR INITIATION). IN ESSENCE, IT'S GOING FROM BEING YOU, TO BEING YOU THE GREEK CHRISTIAN **WITHOUT TRULY CHANGING**. TO THE RELIGIOUS PERSON EVERYTHING IS FINE. BUT TO THE ONE WHO TRULY BELIEVES IN CHRIST, AND SEEKS HIM DAILY, WILL BE CONVICTED AND DENOUNCE. THE RITUALS, SHIELDS, OR BADGES OF THESE GROUPS ARE BLATANT IDOLATRY AND SATANIC SYMBOLISM. THE AKA's HAVE **ATLAS (a mythological god)** ON THEIR SHIELD, SIGMA GAMMA RHO HAS **"RHOMANIA."** A RITUAL OF THE SORORITY WHEREIN A DAY IS SET ASIDE TO DO

GOOD WORKS, BUT IT IS ACTUALLY A CELEBRATION OF THE goddess OF THE NEW DAWN, **AURORA**.) THEY ALSO HAVE THE SKULL AND CROSS BONES ON THEIR BADGE THAT IS A SYMBOL OF DEATH AND DECEPTION. ALPHA PHI ALPHA HAS THE **SPHINX** (**IDOL GOD** OF THE EGYPTIANS) ON ITS BADGE. MOST BADGES OR SHIELDS ALSO CONTAIN WREATHES WHICH ARE SYMBOLIC OF DEATH, BUT TO THE GREEKS IT'S A SYMBOL OF VICTORY. THEIR WAS ONLY ONE TO HAVE VICTORY OVER DEATH, AND HIS NAME IS JESUS. THE ONLY WAY AN INDIVIDUAL IS GIVEN THIS SAME VICTORY IS BY **BELIEVING IN JESUS AND LEAVING THOSE OTHER IDOLS AND GLO's BEHIND.**

I JOHN 5:21 Little children, **keep yourselves from idols.** Amen.

ACTS 15:20 But we write unto them, that they **abstain from** pollutions of **idols**, and from fornication, and from things strangled, and from blood.

CHECK OUT THE DICTIONARY AND ENCYCLOPEDIA. **IF SYMBOLISM MEANS NOTHING, THEN WHY ADVERTISE? SYMBOLISM IS AT THE HEART OF THE BELIEFS OF THESE ORGANIZATIONS** AND IS ALSO A DIRECT RESULT OF THE WITCHCRAFT SPIRIT. THIS IS A CONTROLLING SPIRIT OR ONE THAT CAUSES THINGS TO BE IRRESISTIBLE. THE SYMBOLS, COLORS, AND BAGDE DESIGNS APPEAL TO THE NATURAL SENSES, NOT THE SPIRITUAL SENSES. ASK MANY WHY THEY JOINED, AND OFTEN THEIR FIRST REPLY IS "I DON'T KNOW, THERE WAS JUST SOMETHING ABOUT IT". THE SECOND REPLY USUALLY HAS SOMETHING TO DO WITH AN APPEAL FOR SYMBOLS OR COLORS. **IT IS SO MUCH THAT THE HANDBOOKS/RITUALS OF THESE GROUPS, FOR THE PURPOSE OF POLITICAL CORRECTNESS AND "CHRISTIAN APPEAL",** TWIST THE MEANINGS OF THE SYMBOLS AND WARN MEMBERS AND PLEDGES TO KNOW THEM OR FACE PUNISHMENT. A **CHARACTERISTIC OF CULTS IS MAKING**

PROFANE THINGS APPEAR SACRED AND HOLY. INSTEAD OF THE **MYTHOLOGICAL** goddess **MINERVA** BEING AN IDOL, SHE IS MADE TO **SYMBOLIZE** GOOD WISDOM. DELTA SIGMA THETA CRAFTILY BRINGS MINERVA TO LIFE, YET DENOUNCE OTHER SYMBOLS OF THEIR SORORITY (i.e. ELEPHANTS AND DUCKS). **DELTA SIGMA THETA IS IN CLEAR TRANSGRESSION OF THE FIRST COMMANDMENT, BUT FOR THEM TO GET RID OF MINERVA WOULD BE TO DESTROY THE FACT OF WHO DELTA SIGMA THETA TRULY IS.** THIS IS CLEAR, BLATANT IDOLATRY. HOW THE DELTAS PORTRAY MINERVA IS A LIE, AND YOU "GREEK CHRISTIANS" SAY IT'S OK TO BE IN IT. **IF ANYONE, INCLUDING A CHRISTIAN, CAN JUSTIFY THIS SIN IN THEIR LIFE, THEY CAN JUSTIFY ALL SIN.**

II CORINTHIANS 4:18 IS PROOF OF THE **FOOLISHNESS** OF SYMBOLISM.

II CORINTHIANS 4:18 While we look not at the things which are seen, but at the things which are not seen: for **the things which are seen are temporal**; but the things which are not seen are eternal.

GLO's adore, **covet**, protect, and **wrongfully define their symbols** to suit their need and conscience. They take what is evil, and try to make it appear good, deceiving others and deceiving themselves.

This symbolic wisdom of MINERVA is not from above, but rather human and **demonic wisdom from below.**

FREDERIC L. HATCHETT

JAMES 3:14-16(amp) But if you have bitter jealousy (envy) and contention (rivalry, selfish ambition) in your hearts, do not pride yourself on it and thus be in defiance of and false to the truth. This [superficial] wisdom is not such as comes down from above, but is earthly, unspiritual (animal), even devilish (demonical). For where there is jealousy (envy) and contention (rivalry, selfish ambition) there will also be confusion (unrest, disharmony, rebellion) and all sorts of evil and vile practices.

While God's wisdom is described as coming from above.

JAMES 3:17-18(amp) But **the wisdom from above is first all pure (undefiled)**; then it is **peace-loving, courteous** (considerate, gentle). [It is willing to] yield to reason, **full of compassion** and **good fruit**, it is **wholehearted and straightforward**, impartial and unfeigned **(free from doubts, wavering, and insincerity)**. And the harvest of righteousness (of conformity to God's will in thought and deed) is [the fruit of the seed] sown in peace by those who work for and make peace [in themselves and in others, that peace which means concord, agreement, and harmony between individuals, with undisturbedness in a peaceful mind free from fears and agitating passions and moral conflicts].

INSTEAD OF GOD BEING THE ONE TO PRAY TO, a former Zeta says that **ZETA PHI BETA HAS TAKEN HIS PLACE.**

"WE PRAY FOR ZETA, FERVENTLY."
(Minister J. Davis. Interviewed by author. Original quote by B. Stover, 1998.)

If the sorority wants to refute this quote, read Chapter 10 Part 6.

COMING APART AT THE SEAMS

PHI BETA SIGMA CALL THEMSELVES, "THE SONS OF FIRE AND BRIMSTONE"; NEED I SAY MORE. YES! I KNOW THE SIGMA'S EXPLANATION FOR THIS TITLE. IT IS VERY RELIGIOUS AND SOUNDS GOOD, BUT TO THE MATURE CHRISTIAN IT'S "HOGWASH" AND I WON'T EVEN WASTE TIME WITH THIS OBVIOUS DEMONIC REPRESENTATION. WHY IS THE SYMBOL OF THE OMEGAS A DOG? 1.) THEY SAY THE DOG REPRESENTS "TENACITY" AND 2.) THE MIRROR IMAGE OF GOD (i.e. DOG SPELLED BACKWARDS). HERE THEY TRY TO MAKE THE DOG A GREAT MASCOT. THE TRUTH BE KNOWN: IT'S A SYMBOL OF STUPIDITY AND LUST. IMAGINE WALKING ACROSS A COLLEGE CAMPUS, AND HEARING TWO BOYS BARKING AT EACH OTHER. WHAT THEY SAY THE DOG REPRESENTS, AND THE BEHAVIOR THEY EXHIBIT ARE TWO WORLDS APART. BIBLICALLY, THERE ARE ABSOLUTELY NO POSITIVE REPRESENTATIONS OF DOGS. THE BIBLE SAYS DOGS ARE MALE TEMPLE PROSTITUTES OR HOMOSEXUALS FOR HIRE.

DEUTERONOMY 23:18 Thou shalt not bring the hire of a whore, or the price of a **dog**, into the house of the Lord thy God for any vow: for even both these are abomination unto the Lord thy God.

DOGS ARE PEOPLE WHO WILL FOREVER BE EXCLUDED FROM THE NEW JERUSALEM. LOOK AT THE COMPANY THEY KEEP.

REVELATION 22:15 For without are **dogs**, and **sorcerers**, and **whoremongers**, and **murderers**, and **idolaters**, and whosoever loveth and maketh a **lie**.

DOGS ARE THOSE TYPE OF PEOPLE WHO ARE **MORALLY IMPURE**. DOMESTICATED DOGS MAY BE MAN'S BEST FRIEND, BUT TO GOD THEY ARE SEEN IN THE **MORAL** SENSE AS SOMETHING TO BE DISGUSTED. DOGS IN THE BIBLE ARE SEEN **AS** CARNIVOROUS, BLOOD-EATING, DANGEROUS, **UNCLEAN**, **SATANIC**, FALSE TEACHERS,

HYPOCRITES, ETC., ETC. OMEGA PSI PHI, HAS OFFICIALLY (ON PAPER) ABOLISHED THE DOG AS A SYMBOL, BUT IT IS STILL VERY MUCH ALIVE IN THE HEARTS OF MANY OMEGAS, **REGARDLESS OF THE NATIONAL SANCTION. THE PEN THOUGH IS NOT MIGHTIER THAN SPIRITS.** THEY MAY HAVE ABOLISHED IT ON PAPER, BUT **THE SPIRIT** OF THE DOG IS NOT GONE. OLD AND YOUNG OMEGAS STILL BARK ANYWAY. MAN CALLED DOGS MAN's BEST FRIEND. GOD'S WORD DOESN'T SAY IT. **THIS IS TYPICAL OF THE GLO MENTALITY IN TRYING TO PRESENT A CASE TO A DISAPPROVING SOCIETY THAT THEIR SEEMINGLY UNMANLY BEHAVIOR IS ACTUALLY TASTEFUL, GODLY, AND MANLY.** THE BIBLE WARNS US TO GUARD OUR EARS AND EYES FOR THEY ARE THE GATEWAYS TO OUR FLESH, SOUL, AND SPIRIT.
II PETER 2:8-(amp) (For that righteous man dwelling among them, in **seeing and hearing**, vexed his **righteous soul** from day to day with their unlawful deeds;)

SYMBOLISM AND IMAGES, WORDS, SONGS, POEMS, etc., MUST BE EXAMINED WITH ALERT EYES AND EARS THAT HAVE BEEN TRAINED BY THE WORD OF GOD AND A HUMAN SPIRIT THAT IS SENSITIVE TO AND CONTROLLED BY THE HOLY SPIRIT.

SEE CHAPTER 4 PART 2 FOR WORDS TO SONGS AND POEMS

MOST GLO RITUALS ARE HARMLESS PHYSICALLY WITH THE EXCEPTION BEING HAZING. YET, THEY ARE ABSOLUTELY DEMONIC SPIRITUALLY. **JEREMIAH 10:1-9** SHOWS THE FACT THAT THE PHYSICAL IDOL ITSELF IS INCAPABLE OF DOING HARM OR GOOD. GOD SAYS THAT IT IS STUPID TO WORSHIP SOMETHING THAT CANNOT SPEAK WHEN IT CHOOSES OR HAS TO BE CARRIED (i.e. SOMETHING THAT IS DEAD), ESPECIALLY WHEN THERE IS A LIVING GOD. ALL IDOLS ARE **NOT TRULY** gods, BUT HAVE DEMONS THAT INSPIRE A PERSON TO WORSHIP WHATEVER THE IDOL MAY BE AS A god. DEMONIC SEDUCTION IS WHY ONE WILL SEE THE THOUGHT

LIFE OF A "GREEK CHRISTIAN" SINK INTO THE DEPTHS OF IDOLATRY AND REBELLION. THEY WILL IDOLIZE THEIR GLO, A MEMBER OF THEIR OWN GLO, AND OFTEN SOME SHIRT, JACKET, OR TRINKET THEY BOUGHT. YOU WILL NOTICE A COMPROMISING ATTITUDE TOWARD GOD'S WORD BASED ON EMOTIONS INSTEAD OF TRUTH. ALL OF A SUDDEN THEIR CHURCH ATTENDANCE WILL DROP OFF. **ONE SURE THING TO LOOK FOR IS THE LACK OF CONVERSATION ABOUT JESUS. THE USE OF THE BIBLE AS THE FINAL AUTHORITY WILL BECOME FOREIGN TO THE "GREEK CHRISTIAN". THEY WILL SEEK OTHER SOURCES FOR ANSWERS OTHER THAN GOD'S WORD.** INSTEAD OF MAKING STATEMENTS OF **TRUTH WHICH NEED NO VERIFICATION**, OR **FACTUAL STATEMENTS THAT HAVE PROOF** TO **VERIFY THEM. THE MAJORITY OF WHAT ONE WILL HEAR FROM GREEK CHRISTIANS IS OPINIONATED STATEMENTS. OPINIONATED STATEMENTS** ARE GENERALLY CHARACTERIZED BY EMOTIONAL OUTBURSTS THAT HAVE **NO PROOF** TO VERIFY **THEM. GREEK CHRISTIANS CANNOT AND FEEL NO NEED TO SUPPORT THEIR OPINIONS BIBLICALLY, BECAUSE THEY HAVE CUT THEMSELVES OFF FROM JESUS. OBSERVE THEIR REACTIONS, AND I GUARANTEE THEY WILL BE OPINIONS JUST AS DESCRIBED ABOVE.** MEMBERS OF GLO's GO FROM **THE MIND OF CHRIST TO THE MIND OF FOOLISHNESS, FROM GOD'S WISDOM, TO THEIR GLO's WISDOM.** THIS BECOMES AN ALL TOO OFTEN AND UNFORTUNATE MEANS OF REASONING FOR THE "GREEK CHRISTIAN" WHEN ASKED TO GIVE BIBLICAL SUPPORT FOR WHY AND WHERE GOD SAYS IT'S OK FOR HIS CHILDREN TO BE MEMBERS OF A GLO. THE WHOLE THOUGHT PROCESS OF A GREEK CHRISTIAN IS REVAMPED. IT IS **RESHAPED AND MOLDED** BY SATAN THROUGH RITUALS, SYMBOLS, GOOD WORKS, SONGS, POEMS, CHANTS, AND HAZING. REMIND THEM **HOW JESUS ANSWERED THE DEVIL.** IT WAS **WITH THE WORD OF GOD, NOT HIS OWN** THOUGHTS, DEEDS, OR WORKS. HE MADE IT CLEAR THAT HE DID THE WILL OF HIS FATHER, AND NO ONE ELSES **INCLUDING HIS OWN. JESUS**

NEVER MADE ONE OPINIONATED STATEMENT IN HIS LIFE. TRUE CHRISTIAN?? YOUR FORMER BROTHER OR SISTER IN CHRIST, WHO ONCE USED THE WORD TO CUT THE DEVIL'S KINGDOM DOWN, IS NOW IN ALLEGIANCE WITH SATAN. THE TRANSFORMATION FROM HOLY ROLLER TO HELL RAISER MAY TAKE A WHILE, BUT GOD'S WORD GUARANTEES IT WILL TAKE PLACE.

I CORINTHIANS 15:33(amp) Do not be so deceived and misled! Evil companionships (communion, associations) corrupt and deprave good manners and morals and character.

BY ANSWERING WITH OPINIONATED, HUMANISTIC, NON-BIBLICAL STATEMENTS, IDOLATRY HAS TRULY MADE ITS HOME IN THE GREEK CHRISTIAN'S HEART. **AN UNWILLINGNESS TO SEEK THE WORD OF GOD FOR ANSWERS MEANS TO THAT PERSON THAT GOD MUST NOT HAVE THE ANSWERS. I HAVE NEVER WITNESSED WHERE A "CONFESSING CHRISTIAN" IN A GLO HAS REMAINED HOLY OR USED THE WORD OF GOD PROPERLY OR TRUTHFULLY TO PROVE A POINT CONCERNING GLO's BEING RIGHT WITH GOD. THEY TRY TO CONVERT THE GLO's COMMUNITY SERVICE AS DOING SERVICE FOR GOD. THE BIBLE SAYS, IF JESUS BE LIFTED UP, HE WILL DRAW ALL MEN UNTO HIM. THE BANNER OF THE GLO MAKES IT CLEAR WHO'S BEING LIFTED UP.** FOR YOU AS AN INDIVIDUAL, TO CLAIM IT FOR GOD **IS HYPOCRITICAL TO THE GLO YOU BELONG TO.** WHOSE SIDE ARE YOU ON, THEIRS OR GOD'S? WHO ARE YOU SERVING? GOD OR A GLO/THE DEVIL.

JAMES 1:8(amp) [For being as he is] a man of **two minds** (hesitating, dubious, irresolute), **[he is] unstable** and **unreliable** and **uncertain about everything** [he thinks, feels, decides].

YOU'RE WEARING A GLO SHIRT, SINGING GLO SONGS, BUT ARE YOU DOING IT FOR GOD?? THE BIBLE SAYS TO BE OF ONE MIND AND ON ONE ACCORD.

THE CHURCH AND CHRISTIANS ARE NOT IMMUNE TO WRONG DOING EITHER. REVELATION 2&3 (THE CHURCH), ACTS 4 (ANANIAS & SAPPHIRA), AND GALATIANS 2:15-16 (PETER) ARE CLEAR EVIDENCE THAT THE WORD OF GOD RULES, AND NOT WHAT YOU SEE OTHER CHURCHES OR INDIVIDUALS DOING. THIS WILL BE NO EXCUSE FOR YOU AT THE GREAT WHITE THRONE OF JUDGMENT. YOU ARE ACCOUNTABLE FOR YOURSELF. WHEN YOU ARE **PRACTICING** SIN, IT'S BEST YOU POINT NO FINGERS AT ANYONE ELSES SINS. THIS IS A COMMON PRACTICE OF THE "GREEK CHRISTIAN". YOU WHO WITNESS BE AWARE OF THIS TACTIC ACCUSING YOU OF CASTING STONES. CAST A BIG ROCK AT THEM: **JESUS.** THE BOTTOM LINE, FOR YOU AS A WITNESS, IS TO **MAKE THEM PROVE** ALL THINGS BY THE WORD OF GOD. IF THEY CANNOT, YOUR WITNESS IS TO GIVE THEM THE WORD. IF THEY DON'T REPENT, DON'T WORRY. IF THEY REPENT, REJOICE!!!!! THE TRUE CHRISTIAN WITNESS IS NOT CASTING ANY STONES; THE WORD OF GOD IS WHAT'S BOTHERING THEM, NOT YOU.

IT IS VERY CLEAR THAT THE INSPIRATION OF MODERN DAY GLO's ARE CONCENTRATED ON THE RELIGIOUS PRACTICES OF ANCIENT GREEK CIVILIZATIONS. ANCIENT GREEKS DID NOT WORSHIP THE JEWS' GOD (JEHOVAH, YAHWEH, ELOHIM, EL SHADDAI, THE RIGHTEOUS BRANCH, etc.). THEY WORSHIPPED MANY gods, AND GLO's FOLLOW RIGHT IN THEIR FOOTSEPS.

Notes

CHAPTER 4
PART 1

ARE YOU RELIGIOUS OR A CHRISTIAN?

TRUE CHRISTIANS ALLOW GOD TO BE WHO HE IS, GOD. CHRISTIANS KNOW THAT WHO GOD IS, IS BASED ON WHAT HIS WORD SAYS. **CHRISTIANS COMFORT THEIR CONSCIENCE BY** ACCEPTING THE **TRUTH**, WHETHER IT IS SWEET AS HONEY OR BITTER AS WORMWOOD, BECAUSE CHRISTIANS KNOW THAT THE TRUTH MAKES YOU FREE. WHY? GOD'S WORD SAYS IT IN **JOHN 8:32**. CHRISTIANS KNOW THAT WHEN A PERSON SEEKS JESUS THERE ARE NO BIBLICAL EXCUSES FOR REJECTING HIM JUST AS THERE ARE NO BIBLICAL JUSTIFICATIONS FOR BEING IN A GLO (Greek-Lettered Organization). **RELIGIOUS PEOPLE PUT GOD IN A BOX**, THEY DO THIS BY DELETING HIM AS A JUDGING GOD, AND MAKING HIM INTO ONLY A LOVING GOD **TO SOOTH THEIR CONSCIENCE**. WHEN A RELIGIOUS PERSON HEARS THE TRUTH AND KNOWS IT'S THE TRUTH, THEY TRY TO LIMIT WHO GOD IS BY NOT GIVING

THE FULL SCOPE OF HIS ATTRIBUTES. TO ACCOMPLISH THIS, **ONE MUST IGNORE SCRIPTURE.** RELIGIOUS PEOPLE SAY THINGS SUCH AS GOD IS A LOVING GOD, GOD UNDERSTANDS MY HEART, I DO GOOD THINGS, JESUS SAT WITH THE SINNERS, etc. THEY LEAVE OUT THAT THE LORD IS OUR JUDGE (**ISAIAH 33:22**), HE KNOWS MAN'S HEART IS DESPERATELY WICKED (**JEREMIAH 17:9**), THAT ALL OF OUR WORKS ARE AS FILTHY RAGS (**ISAIAH 64:6**), AND THAT JESUS' INTENTION WAS NOT TO BECOME A PART OF THEIR GROUP (**MATTHEW 9:11-13**). RELIGIOUS PEOPLE DESPISE THE WORD OF GOD. THEY CHOOSE THE BITS AND PIECES THEY WANT AND SPIT OUT THE REST WHICH IS CONTRARY TO THE WAY THEY DESIRE. **ALL SCRIPTURE** IS GIVEN BY THE INSPIRATION OF GOD (**II TIMOTHY 3:16**).

A RELIGIOUS PERSON is easy to define. It is a person who relies on self, does not believe the whole Word of God, boasts about <u>their works and the works of others</u>, and lives by faith in the world, not by faith in God.

EPHESIANS 2:8-9 says, It is by grace ye are saved through faith, and that not of yourselves: It is the gift of God: Not of works, lest any man should BOAST.

Grace is God's unmerited gift to man (i.e. you cannot earn it). Grace also means that, saved or unsaved, works do not earn or keep one saved: It is grace you are saved and stay saved. It is impossible for a sinner to perform a work of righteousness, because God does not see them in Christ. A person who is religious can be morally good, **try** to keep the Ten Commandments, be baptized, or give money to the church. But this does not mean they are Christians according to scripture. A TRUE CHRISTIAN IS NOT TO BE CONCERNED WITH HIS WORKS, BUT WITH THE WORK (THE CROSS) THAT JESUS PERFORMED IN THE EARTH AS A MAN. WITHOUT HIS WORK, OUR WORKS WOULD BE USELESS. WE FOLLOW CHRIST AND HIS WORKS, NOT OUR WORKS, JUST LIKE THE BIBLE COMMANDS. **BESIDES, CHRISTIAN SERVICE CAN ONLY BE PERFOMED BY A TRUE BORN-AGAIN BELIEVER.**

I CORINTHIANS 3:10-15 According to the grace of God which is given unto me, as a wise master builder, I have laid the foundation, and another buildeth thereon. But **let every man take heed how he buildeth thereupon.** For **other foundation can no man lay than that is laid**, which is **Jesus Christ.** Now if any man build upon his foundation gold, silver, precious stone, wood, hay, stubble; Every man's work shall be manifest: for the day shall declare it, because it shall be revealed by a fire; and the fire shall try every man's work of what sort it is. **If any man's work abide** which he hath built thereupon, **he shall receive a reward.** If any man's work shall be burned, he shall suffer loss: but he himself shall be saved; yet so as by fire.

ISAIAH 64:6(amp) For we have al become like one who is unclean [ceremonially, like a leper], and all our righteousness (**our best deeds of rightness and justice**) is like filthy rags or a polluted garment; we all fade like a leaf, and our iniquities, like the wind, take us away [far from God's favor, hurrying us toward destruction].

NO ACCOUNT IS MADE FOR YOUR WORKS ALONE. IT IS NOT UNTIL YOU GET SAVED AND **CONSECRATE** YOURSELF TO SERVE GOD ALONE THAT YOU WILL RECEIVE REWARD FOR YOUR WORKS.

ISAIAH 57:12- I will declare thy righteousness, and thy works; for they shall not profit thee.

Isaiah 59:2 But your iniquities have been separated between you and your God, and your sins has hid his face from you, that he will not hear.

TITUS 3:5 Not by works of righteousness which we have done, but according to his mercy he saved us, by the washing of regeneration, and renewing of the Holy Ghost.

I CORINTHIANS 3:11-15 for other foundation can no man lay than that is laid, which is Jesus Christ. Now if any man build upon his foundation gold, silver, precious stone, wood, hay, stubble; Every man's work shall be manifest: for the day shall declare it, because it shall be revealed by a fire; and the fire shall try every man's work of what sort it is. If any man's work abide which he hath built thereupon, he shall receive a reward. If any man's work shall be burned, he shall suffer loss: but he himself shall be saved; yet so as by fire.

Salvation is present and future, not what you did in the past.

I CORINTHIANS 15:57-58 But thanks be to God, which gives us the victory through our Lord Jesus Christ. Therefore, my beloved brethren, be ye steadfast, unmovable, always abounding **in the work of the Lord**, forasmuch as ye know your work is not in vain **in the Lord.**

GLO's (Greek-Lettered Organizations) believe that by works one can be right with God. The Word of God (Old and New Testament clearly contradicts that belief). Salvation is by faith, not by works. Once in Christ, the works must be done for Christ (in thought, word, and deed.)

The deeds you did prior to salvation are not rewarded. Only one who believes **by faith** that Jesus Christ is Lord and **continues** in that faith and abides in Christ is a Christian.

JOHN 8:31(amp) So Jesus said to those Jews who had **believed in Him**, if you abide in **My** word [hold fast to **My** teachings and **live in accordance with them**], you are **truly My** disciples.

As a Christian, God commands us to live according to His word and attribute all we do to Him. Fraternities and sororities out of pride do service, live, and attribute that which they do to themselves or their GLO, but not Christ. Most "Greek Christians" will say they are doing it for Christ. This means that they are not in agreement with the unsaved members or their GLO's who are doing it to the GLO's glory and honor. How can you be unified without agreement? You can't! Therefore, a "Greek Christian" must compromise his or her beliefs in Christ to be in **true agreement** with their organization (i.e. they must go to meetings, parties, commit ungodly information to memory, etc.), and thereby are in disagreement with God. This violates **John 8:31**, and they are no longer Christ's disciples. One way or the other, they are hypocrites. If they don't compromise their faith in Jesus, they are making a statement of disapproval with certain

COMING APART AT THE SEAMS

practices that their brothers and sisters do. I would not want to **remain yoked** to a fraternity brother or sorority sister who refuses to stop fornicating. I would not call him or her something he is not, my brother or sister in Christ. Fortunately, a true Christian can break fellowship with a rebellious Christian without having to denounce their faith in Christ. **With the Greek Christian, this is not so.** A Greek Christian must break fellowship with **all members and the GLO they belong to.** When one SEES the truth of the above statement, **denouncing will be an easy decision.**

I CORINTHIANS 5:17-20(amp) But all things are from God, who though Jesus Christ reconciled us to himself [received us into favour, brought us into harmony to himself] and gave to us the ministry of reconciliation [that **by words and deed** we might aim to bring others in harmony with him]. It was God [personally present] in Christ, reconciling and restoring the world to favour with himself, not counting up and holding against [men] their trespasses [but canceling them], and committing to us the message of reconciliation (of the restoration of favour).

A person in a GLO cannot fulfill this scripture, because an ambassador is one who represents the country in which he has citizenship. A true Christian's citizenship is in heaven, but a Greek Christian's citizenship is in the earth. Therefore, he or she is not fit to represent the Kingdom of God in the earth. Besides, the words and deeds they **practice** will prove that they don't possess heavenly citizenship. It's not the committing of the sinful act that proves you're not a Christian; it's the practicing of sin (transgression) that proves this fact. GLO's and their members are guilty of practicing sin.

By remaining a member of a GLO, you are **practicing** idolatry, unequal yoking, occultism, lying, deception, and defiling the temple of the Holy Ghost which temple you are supposed to be.

PROVERBS 11:30 (amp) The fruit of the [uncompromisingly] righteous is a tree of life, and he who is wise captures human lives [for God, as a fisher of men he gathers and receives them for eternity].

If members in GLO's can't fulfill I Corinthians 5:17-20, they can't **truly** fulfill this one either. This means that anyone in a GLO is not wise. Because a Greek Christian is not righteous, they can't have the tree of life either. If your conscience is bothering you, now is the best time to repent and denounce. Don't let the devil steal your right to the tree of life, and surely don't let him keep making a fool out of you.

Soul winning, the most important and first ministry of all saved people, IS NOT ON THEIR LIST OF PRINCIPLES, SERVICE, GOALS, etc.

MATTHEW 6:33 But seek ye first the kingdom of God, and righteousness; and all these shall added unto you.

You will not see the appearance of this scripture in any GLO constitution and by-laws that I know of, and **I challenge any GLO to prove it.** All these lame Greeks tell us is that they **include** God in their organization. **If God is not the head or center, then the devil is in full control.** Because GLO's are not Christ-centered, demonic forces have a playground of millions with their souls as toys. Any organization and the persons in it must be founded upon the Rock, who is Christ. His church is founded upon Him, and once people realize this, GLO's will cease to exist. People may approve of what you do, but does God approve? NO! The Bible says not to do things to please man, but to please the Father which is in heaven. The Omega Psi Phi Fraternity claims that without faith it is impossible to please God **and man.**

(OMEGA PSI PHI FRATERNITY (Incorporated 1914), THE RITUAL, 1970, p. 17.)

This is not SCRIPTURAL TRUTH. THEREFORE, IT IS A LIE. Omega is clearly serving to masters, and the devil (the father of the **LIE**) is one of them. The Bible clearly states not to do things for men to glorify you or to see.

MATTHEW 6:1-8 Take heed that ye do not your alms before men, to be seen of them: otherwise ye have no reward of your father which is in heaven. Therefore when thou doest thou alms, do not sound a trumpet before thee, as the hypocrites do in the synagogues and in the streets, that they may have glory of men, Verily I say unto you, They have their reward. But when thou doest alms, let not thy left hand know what thy right hand doeth: That thine alms might be in secret: and thy father which seeth in secret himself shall reward thee openly. And when thou prayest, thou shalt not be as the hypocrites are: for they love to stand praying in the synagogues and in the corners of the streets, that they may be seen of men. Verily I say unto you, They have their reward. But thou, when thou prayest, enter into the closet, and when thou hast shut thou door, pray to thy father which is in secret; and thy father which seeth in secret shall reward thee openly. But when ye pray, use not vain repetition, as the heathen do: for they think that they shall be heard for their much speaking. Be not ye therefore like unto them, for your father knoweth what things you have need of, before ye ask him.

The Bible also says pride goeth before destruction. Pride is a clearly seen characteristic of the religious person.

PROVERBS 16:18 Pride goeth before destruction, and a haughty spirit before a fall.

Pride is how the Devil got kicked out of heaven, why Pharaoh wouldn't let God's people go, why Marvin Gaye and Elvis are in hell right now, IF THEY WERE NOT ABLE TO REPENT. This was why some of the greatest kings like Nebuchadnezzar end up eating with the beasts of the field in total humiliation (**DANIEL 4:30-37 It was his response to his punishment that's important**). GLO's knew about the churches' stand against secret societies, but still formed them anyway out of pride. The founders refused to listen to the voice of the church. What has occurred as a result? People have been maimed, killed, and many lives destroyed in ways seen and unseen. Reader, when you had set your eyes upon the hazing section of this book, **how could you ever look at a GLO (Greek-lettered organization) the same?** There are many other examples of pride, destruction, and salvation by works that will **always** manifest itself as PRIDE. The RELIGIOUS group or RELIGIOUS person's creed is "I" did this and that, or "we" did this and that. Salvation by FAITH gives no place for pride and neither does GOD. Any boasting must be done in the Lord (i.e. "It had to be God, if it weren't for God, or thank you Jesus.") The scripture that best illustrates how a Christian should look at WORKS **is,**

JAMES 2:14-20(amp) What doth it profit my brethren, though a man say he hath faith, and have not works? Can faith (this type) save him?

If a brother or a sister be naked, and destitute of daily food, and one of you say unto them, Depart in peace, be ye warmed and filled; notwithstanding (nevertheless) ye give them not those things which are needful to the body; what doth it profit? Even so faith, if it has works, is dead, being alone. Yea, a man may say, Thou hast faith, and I have works: shew me thy faith without thy works, and I will shew thee my faith by my works. Thou believest that there is one God; thou doest well: the devils also believe, and tremble. But will thou know, O vain man that faith without works is dead.

This scripture is letting all people know that works share an inseparable relationship to faith, but that **salvation is not and cannot be received by works**. Religious people are guilty of salvation by works. They use God instead of allowing God to use them. They say things about God and His Word that the Bible does not say. Religious people put God in a box, not realizing they are under the microscope of the Omniscient God. They try to reveal God instead of allowing God to reveal Himself to them. Religious people try to justify everything they do that the Word says not to do. Religious people, not being Word-Centered, will always attempt to try and use a logic, humanistic approach to

God's Word. The true Christian knows that the Holy Ghost is the only teacher. It is not by might, nor by power, but by My Spirit, saith the Lord (**ZECHARIAH 4:6**). The religious persons' desires mean more to them than God. It is by justification of faith in Christ that one is made RIGHTEOUS. God will test/prove your faith. It is by your works of obedience to God that your faith is made whole. For even the devils believe in God, but their works do not prove their belief to be real (i.e. they are not justified by works, because their deeds are unrighteous). Therefore, their faith and their works are in vain. Evolution without transitional fossils is dead. Therefore, evolution is a belief on faith alone with out any evidence (works) to support it; rendering it DEAD. A person's works will manifest what he or she truly believes. Fraternities and sororities are guilty of hypocritical faith (i.e. IN CHURCH ON SUNDAY AFTER PARTYING ON SATURDAY. THOSE GREEK-LETTER CHRISTIANS WHO DID NOT PARTY ARE GUILTY OF ANOTHER SIN, UNEQUAL YOKING. THE SAME WOULD APPLY TO THE

TRUE CHRISTIANS WHO KNEW THEIR FELLOW BROTHERS AND SISTERS WERE DOING THE SAME WITH NO DESIRE TO REPENT, AND WOULD NOT BREAK FELLOWSHIP).

What Greek Christians claim to be about is a far cry from what they really represent.

II TIMOTHY 3:5(amp) For [although] they hold a form of piety (true religion), they deny and reject and are strangers to the power of it [their conduct belies the genuineness of their profession]. Avoid [all] such people [turn away from them].

The Greek-Letter Christian claims a relationship with Jesus, yet their conduct identifies themselves with other gods and other forms of worship through rituals. How many of you "Christian" members have **truly studied** the **origins** of these ritual practices? "Christian" AKA's, If you really knew about the Ivy Leaf and the origin of the rituals based on it (**The Two Babylons, pp.49-50.**), and the goddess ceremony you all perform, you may think twice about this false worship, and remaining a member of your GLO.

Performing rituals, observing certain religious days makes one feel religious and justified. This is why religious people do not use the Word of God in their defense of membership. They use works and famous members to justify their organizations, while ignoring the lifestyle of those individuals and the antichrist nature of the works GLO's do.

JOHN 4:23 But the hour cometh, and now is, when the true worshippers shall worship the Father in spirit and in truth: for the Father **seeketh** such to worship him.

The Father is waiting for you to denounce, so that you can worship Him. Unfortunately, most of the rituals GLO's do, are an addition to ones done in ancient times. Still, **none originate from God's Word.** Even most sinners know that the reason they are breathing is because of Him, so how dare they boast about what they do, and then attribute it to themselves or their organization. It is obviously the **pride (self-exaltation)** that began with LUCIFER. Look at him now. He can't even help himself. Jesus' work on the cross and His resurrection was based on faith being spoken prophetically by David 1,000 years before it occurred.

PSALM 16:10 For thou wilt not leave my soul in hell; neither wilt thou suffer thine Holy One to see corruption.

This is why we (true believers) must believe this scripture also. If a Greek Christian was a true Christian, the unsaved members should hate them, because they serve opposing masters. However, this is not the case, because the once true Christian becomes a Greek Christian by making a compromising adjustment, and is expected to do so to keep the peace in the group. This is religious tolerance. **Religious tolerance** is a coveted principle of GLO's and the world. It's so ironic that we (true Christians) are always expected to change our convictions while others can keep theirs. It's most unfortunate that many true Christians have already done it. **They were converted from true Christians to Greek Christians.**

FREDERIC L. HATCHETT

They compromise the Word of God and give up their eternal life for a religious, demonic, and worldly organization called a Greek fraternity or sorority.

The true Christian knows that the Word of God is the only confirmation of any fact or opinion. Ask a religious person to prove it by the Word of God, and prepare for the 10 excuses, because they can't give you any scripture. Religious people have no spiritual authority, and have no power to fight the devil. Therefore, they walk in fear. This is why many will not denounce. They see, **know**, and hear the truth about GLO's, but they remain faithful to their GLO (i.e. their god), because of fear. They fear to take an uncompromising position on a godly issue. This is why religious people have to set their own standards. They don't want to serve God on His terms, so they suppress their conscience to truth and attempt to satisfy God in their own way. A true Christian chooses to be a Greek Christian. A Greek Christian compromises their beliefs and becomes religious to satisfy their desires, or else be ostracized by their brothers and sisters. They choose the lies over the Truth (Jesus).

Notes

CHAPTER 4 PART 2

THE SCRIPTURAL ASSAULT OF GREEK LETTERED ORGANIZATIONS

THERE ARE MANY THAT PROUDLY SAY THAT THERE IS A LACK OF SCRIPTUREAL EVIDENCE TO CLAIM THAT GLO's ARE UNGODLY. I STRONGLY OPPOSE THIS CLAIM DUE TO THE FACT THAT THERE ARE **200-300 DIFFERENT** SCRIPTURAL REFERENCES IN THIS BOOK TO PROVE IT. HERE'S WHY GREEK CHRISTIANS MAKE THIS CLAIM!

IT IS THEIR POOR REASONING, STUBBORNESS, AND **LACK OF READING AND STUDYING THE WORD OF GOD** AND UNBELIEF.

I am now adding more scriptures to the ones you have seen already to support my claim that will total about 400-500 scriptures. There is no way based on the Word of God that a Christian can, should, or want to be in a GLO.

First, I want to list **some** of the activities (i.e. works of the flesh ACCORDING TO **GALATIANS 5:19-21**) that are common in these organizations being a result of the demonic forces that control them. Just as the activity of the unseen Holy Spirit will result physical manifestations of His power, so will unseen demonic activity result in physical manifestations of their nature (**ACTS 10:38**). **Immorality, sexual perversion, impurity, pride, prejudice, division, idolatry, drunkenness, carousing, sects with peculiar opinions, witchcraft, heresies, indecency, revelry/banquetings (i.e. partying spirit), deception,** and **lying.**

I PETER 4:1-6(amp) So, SINCE Christ suffered in the flesh for us, for you, arm yourselves with the same thought and purpose [patiently to suffer wrath than fail to please God]. For whoever have suffered in the flesh [having the mind of Christ] is done with [intentional] sin [has stopped pleasing himself and the world, and pleases God], so that he can no longer spend the rest of his natural life living by [his] human appetites and desires, but [he lives] for what God wills. For the time that is past already suffices for doing what the Gentiles like to do living [as you have done] in shameless, insolent wantonness, in **lustful desires**, drunkenness, reveling, drinking bouts and abominable, **lawless idolatries**. They are astonished and <u>**think it very queer**</u> that <u>**ye do not now run hand in hand with them**</u> in the <u>**same**</u> excesses of dissipation, <u>**and they abuse [you]**</u>. But they will have to give an account to Him Who is ready to judge and pass sentence on the living and the dead. For this is why the good news (the Gospel) was preached [in their lifetime] even to the dead, that though judged in fleshly bodies as men are, they might live in the spirit as God does.

When I denounced my GLO, people thought something was wrong with me. Some did, and many still abuse me now for doing it. God will judge them for it.

GALATIANS 5:19-21(amp) Now the doings (practices) of the flesh are clear (obvious): they are immorality, impurity, indecency, **Idolatry**, sorcery, enmity, strife, jealousy, anger (ill-temper), selfishness, divisions (dissensions), party spirit (factions, sects with peculiar opinions, heresies), Envy, **drunkenness**, **carousing**, and the like. I warn you beforehand, just as I did previously, that those who do such things shall not inherit the kingdom of God.

All of these practices were known among ancient Greeks, Babylonians, Egyptians, Sumerians and many current civilizations **including our own U.S.A.** If these are the roots, you can imagine the fruits that grow from them!!!! The spiritual influences are already in place. If hazing was not an initial purpose of Greek-Lettered Organizations, this begs the question, where did it come from, and what influenced them to do it? ABSOLUTELY NOT GOD!! Some person did not just say come let's haze. Either they had read or heard about from somewhere, or **an evil spirit** told them to do it for a SEEMINGLY good reason, because the Bible does not condone it. Regardless, hazing originated from the devil. People for some reason believe that their thoughts are their own. Well, they are not. The source of your thoughts is either from God or the devil. It is what you DO with your thoughts that make the difference.

PROVERBS 3:5-6 Trust in the Lord with all thine heart; and lean not unto thy own understanding. In all thy ways acknowledge him, and he shall direct thy paths.

The Devil tells you a thought, and you think it is your own, but it is not. He is trying to manipulate your emotions. Nevertheless, it was introduced into the heart.

MATTHEW 15:19 For out of the **heart** proceed evil thoughts, murders, adulteries, fornications, thefts, false witness, blasphemies:

PROVERBS 6:12(amp) A worthless person, a wicked man, is he who goes out with a perverse (contrary, wayward) mouth.

PROVERBS 6:14(amp) Willful and contrary in his **heart**, he devises trouble, vexation, and evil continually; he lets loose discord and sows it.

For a Christian to even consider hazing, whether giving, receiving, or not standing against it to the point of denouncing the organization is either ignorant or foolish. **Only a wicked person** could haze someone.

JAMES 4:17 Therefore to him that knoweth to do good, and doeth it not, to him it is sin.

I AM GOING TO INTRODUCE **TITUS 1:15-16** TO PROVE THE POINT THAT **NO MATTER WHAT YOUR MOTIVES ARE, PURITY OR HOLINESS MUST ENCOMPASS**

COMING APART AT THE SEAMS

EVERY ASPECT OF WHO YOU ARE, WHAT YOU DO, AND WHAT YOU ARE A PART OF:

I WILL ALSO INTRODUCE II CORINTHIANS 10:3-5 TO ENCOURAGE ALL CHRISTIANS TO BRING **EVERY THOUGHT** IN THEIR MIND AND COMPARE IT TO GOD'S WORD.

WHEN **WITNESSING** TO A PERSON IN A GLO, REMEMBER THAT **THEY ARE UNDER GREAT PEER PRESSURE**. THEY ARE PROGRAMMED TO RESPOND WITH CERTAIN ANSWERS, EVEN IF IT MEANS LYING. IF YOU DON'T KNOW ANY OF THEIR SECRETS, DON'T WORRY; **SECRECY IS SINFUL**. GREEK CHRISTIANS TAKE THE OATH OF SECRECY MORE SERIOUSLY THAN THE EIGTH COMMANDMENT.

MATTHEW 10:26-27 So have no fear of them; for nothing is concealed that will not be revealed, or kept secret that will not become known. What I say to you in the dark, tell in the light; and what you hear whispered in the ear, proclaim upon the housetops.

PROOF OF NOT BEING ABLE TO MAKE A DECISION ON THEIR OWN TO REVEAL SECRETS FOR THEIR OWN AND OTHER'S **WELL BEING** SHOWS HOW SERIOUS THEIR DEDICATION IS. THEIR DEDICATION CAN BE EQUATED TO IDOLATRY. THEY CHOOSE NOT TO DO GOOD.

JAMES 4:17 Therefore to him that **knoweth to do good**, and **doeth it not, to him** it is sin.

TITUS 1:15-16 (amp) To the pure [in heart and conscience] all things are pure, but to the defiled and corrupt and unbelieving nothing is pure, their very minds and consciences are defiled and polluted. They **profess to know God** [to recognize, perceive, and be acquainted with him] but **deny** and **disown** and **denounce him by what they do**; they are detestable and loathsome, unbelieving and disobedient and disloyal and rebellious, and [they are] **unfit and worthless for good work** (deed or enterprise) **of any kind.**

SIMPLY PUT, THE WORKS THAT MEMBERS OF FRATERNITIES AND SORORITIES DO WILL BE REJECTED BY GOD'S JUDGEMENT. THEY ARE CORRUPT AND DEFILED. THIS IS WHY A "GREEK-LETTERED CHRISTIAN" BELIEVES THEY CAN BE IN A **GLO AND DO GOOD WORKS THAT PLEASE GOD.** THEY ARE DOUBLE-MINDED. ON ONE HAND THEY ATTEMPT TO **SERVE GOD,** WHILE ON THE OTHER HAND THEY **SERVE THEIR GLO.**

JAMES 1:8(amp) [For being as he is] a man of **two minds** (hesitating, dubious, irresolute), [he is] **unstable** and **unreliable** and **uncertain** about **everything** [he **thinks, feels, decides**].

THE BIBLE SAYS A CHRISTIAN IS COMMANDED TO RENEW HIS MIND.

ROMANS 12:1-2 I beseech you therefore, brethren, by the mercies of God, that ye present your bodies a living sacrifice, holy acceptable unto God, which is your reasonable service. And **be not conformed to this world:** but **be** ye **transformed** by the **renewing of your mind**, that ye may prove what is good, and acceptable, and perfect, will of God.

THE MAIN PROBLEM WITH THE GREEK CHRISTIAN IS FAILING TO RECOGNIZE THAT **THEY ARE SINNERS.** THEY FAIL TO REALIZE THEIR PURPOSE IN CHRIST, AND WILL NEVER BE ABLE TO REACH FULL SPIRITUAL MATURITY. **REPENTANCE AND DENUNCIATION** IS THE ONLY POSITIVE DECISION FOR A GREEK CHRISTIAN. NOTHING ELSE THEY DO IN LIFE WILL MATTER UNTIL THEY DO.

COMING APART AT THE SEAMS

JAMES 4:8(amp) Come close to God and He will come close to you. [**Recognize that you are**] **sinners, get** your soiled hands **clean;** [**realize** that you have **been disloyal**] **wavering** individuals with **divided interests,** and purify your hearts [of your **spiritual adultery**].

EPHESIANS 2:10 For we are **his workmanship**, created in Christ Jesus unto good works, which God hath before ordained that we should walk in them.

COLOSSIANS 3:10(amp) And you are in Him, full and having come to fullness of life [in Christ you are filled with the God head-Father, Son, and Holy Spirit-and **reach full spiritual stature**]. And He is the head of all rule and authority [of every angelic principality and power].

THE QUESTION IS CAN A GREEK CHRISTIAN BE A TRUE CHRISTIAN WHILE BEING A MEMBER OF A GLO?

THE ANSWER IS **NO**.

LET'S SEE WHY!!!!!

II CORINTHIANS 10:3-5 For though we walk in the flesh, we do not war after the flesh: (For the weapons of our warfare are not carnal, but mighty through God to the pulling down of strongholds;) Casting down imaginations, and every high thing that exalteth itself against the knowledge of God, and bringing into captivity every thought to the obedience of Christ;

NOT **DOING** THIS SCRIPTURE IS WHY ABORTION WAS LEGALIZED, WHY WE HAVE THE FALSE TEACHING OF

SEPARATION OF CHURCH AND STATE, AND WHY WE HAVE DOCTOR ASSISTED SUICIDE. ALL OF THESE ARE UNSCRIPTURAL IMAGINATIONS AND HIGH THINGS. BECAUSE CHRIST IS PERFECT, PURE, TRUE, AND RIGHTEOUS, **EVERY THOUGHT THAT DOES NOT MATCH UP TO HIM AND HIS WORD SHOULD BE CAST DOWN.** ALL GOOD AND PERFECT GIFTS COME FROM ABOVE. WHETHER IT IS SINGING, BASKETBALL, FOOTBALL OR BOOK WRITING, THE **TALENT** TO DO IT COMES FROM GOD. THE DEVIL IS A STEALER, A KILLER, AND A DESTROYER. ALL THE DEVIL DOES, WITH GOD'S PERMISSION AND YOUR WILLINGNESS, IS TAKE THE GIFT GOD HAS GIVEN YOU, AND USE IT FOR ONE PURPOSE; TO RAPE YOU, AND AS MANY AS WILL FOLLOW, OF THEIR ETERNAL LIFE. HE WILL PERVERT YOUR GOD-GIVEN GIFT TO BE USED FOR HIS GLORY. **THE DEVIL HAS USED GLO's** TO RECEIVE THE GLORY FROM THE MULTI-TALENTED GREEK CHRISTIANS AND ACCOMPLISH HIS PURPOSE. INSTEAD OF GOD GETTING THE GLORY FOR THEIR TALENTS AND ACCOMPLISHMENTS, THE DEVIL BY WAY OF A GLO RECEIVES IT (e.g. **Thurgood Marshall-Supreme Court Justice** and member of **Alpha Phi Alpha** Fraternity **helps to pass a law** that has resulted in the **murder of 35 million babies.** This is the most notable example. Yet, in the Alpha's history book, he is praised for his great success for getting as far as he did being A Black Man during segregation and I thank him too. Of course, they failed to mention his support for abortion/murder. I hope he repented for that approval vote of Roe vs. Wade, and gave his life to Christ as well. Unfortunately, more babies are being slaughtered.

HOW COME A GREEK CHRISTIAN CAN'T BE A TRUE CHRISTIAN?

THIS CHAPTER WILL **REVEAL ONLY A FEW** THE **DEEP SECRETS** OF ALL GLO'S BY USING INFORMATION FROM ONLY SEVERAL OF THEM. HEREIN LIES THE REASON WHY

COMING APART AT THE SEAMS

ANY ONCE TRUE CHRISTIAN IS LEFT WITHOUT EXCUSE FOR BEING IN A GLO. BLAMING THE CHURCH, THE DEVIL, YOUR FRIENDS, YOUR PASTOR, YOUR CONSCIENCE, AND EVEN GOD IS NO GOOD. IF YOU BLAME THE WORD OF GOD, YOUR TESTIMONY AS A CHRISTIAN IS SHOT TO HELL!!!!!! (LITERALLY). READ **II CORINTHIANS 13:5** AND VERY CAREFULLY CONSIDER IF GLO's ARE ORGANIZATIONS THAT CHRISTIANS SHOULD JOIN. THE SECRECY HAS BEEN UNCOVERED. NOW, I CAN SAY THIS WITH AUTHORITY, DECEIVING AND LYING GLO's; YOUR COVER IS BLOWN, AND TO GOD BE THE GLORY. MANY OTHERS AND MYSELF ARE DISGUSTED WITH THE **LIES AND DECEIT** THAT THEY HIDE BEHIND THEIR VEILS OF SECRECY. WE WANT **OUR** BROTHERS AND SISTERS BACK.

THAT'S RIGHT!! **OUR** BROTHERS AND SISTERS BACK. WE WANT THEM BACK IN THE LOVING ARMS OF JESUS AND OUT OF THE STEALING, KILLING, DESTROYING GRASP OF THE DEVIL BY WAY OF GLO's. IF YOU WANT TO FIGHT, THAT'S FINE! MY CHOICE OF WEAPONRY IS **THE BLOOD OF JESUS, THE NAME OF JESUS, AND THE WORD OF GOD vs.** THE PUNY RITUALS OF YOUR GLO's.

ALL NUMBERED SCRIPTURES ARE THE MAIN SCRIPTURES. WHILE ALL OTHERS UNDER THEM ARE SUPPLEMENTAL.

1.) HEBREWS 10:1-39 For the law having a shadow of good things to come, and not the very image of the things, **can never** with those sacrifices which they offered year by year continually make the comers thereunto perfect.

PLEASE READ THIS SCRIPTURE IN ITS ENTIRETY.

This scripture shows that Christ by **His deity**, His **nature**, His **humanity**, and His **works** prove to be **superior** to our nature, humanity, and WORKS. Man being a **deity** should never enter one's mind. Faith in Him is superior to our efforts (WORKS) to get His acceptance. This proves the inferiority of GLO's. They try to portray their goodness on what they do, but actually they usher in a false sense of security to sinners and Christians alike. They do this by putting on a false face of righteousness not knowing that righteousness comes through Christ ONLY. These GLO's have no business trying to mimic **their** need to society by **their** works. This is **PRIDE.** Greek Christians are saying I do not need God to help people, to get to heaven or be good, and the language in their rituals, handbooks, and history books prove it.

"Their **immortality is assured** throughout all eternity as each generation of Deltas continues the organization's good works. The lighted candles in our beloved Sigma represent the nine Cardinal Virtues by which our departed Sorors sought to pattern their lives. As the lights (candles) are extinguished, symbolizing **the passage** of these Sorors into Omega Omega (or Haven of **Rest**)." (DELTA SIGMA THETA SORORITY, INC., GRAND CHAPTER, RITUAL, 1990, p. 70)

REST IS A WORD THE BIBLE USES FOR THOSE WHO HAVE DIED IN THE LORD. **HEBREWS 4:1-11** speaks of the TRUE REST. Some will enter it and some will not.

GREEK CHRISTIANS WILL NOT ENTER BECAUSE OF DISOBEDIENCE (**HEBREWS 4:6**). THEIR REST IS UNREST, TORMENT AND PAIN.

NONE OF THE NINE THE CARDINAL VIRTUES IS FAITH, AND WITHOUT FAITH IT IS **IMPOSSIBLE TO PLEASE GOD. THE DELTAS' HAVEN OF REST IS NOT HEAVENLY GLORY.**

This next excerpt from Kappa Alpha Psi shows the arrogance and pride that a works religion produces:

"In 1953, we are no longer called upon to defend our organizational existence against the destructive onslaught **of any adversary**; we are on the offensive. We are **heterogeneous in** racial and **religious composition**. We see and are **demonstrating our worth in terms of service:**" (William L. Crump, THE STORY OF KAPPA ALPHA PSI, A History Of The Beginning And Development Of A College Greek Letter Organization, 1911-1983, Third Edition, 1983, p. 249.)

Works (**service**) do not determine righteousness or demonstrate worth. If you're worthless spiritually, you're good to no one, not even yourself. The belief that works make you good reveals pride. Little do they know, but **Jesus is one of their adversaries**.

My comment is short and clear; I know who your master is Greek Christian, and it definitely is not Jesus.

The Christian is not needed in GLO's; THEY AND THEIR SERVICE BELONGS IN THE CHURCH, but the Greek Christian believes that the

COMING APART AT THE SEAMS

church is not enough. They are not listening to the Holy Spirit, the God that brought them with a price. This is the exact same frame of mind the ancient Greeks attended to. A holy God, in their eyes, was too restrictive for the human mind and will. GLO's, by far, are not even a shadow of good things to come. As long as these groups are able to exist, there will be more **deaths**, blindings, punctured lungs, beatings, and ungodly secret rituals, because the level of man's creativity is vast. Do you want this to be you? Has it already happened to you? Are you one of those who have done this to someone or know someone it has happened to? COWARDS HAZE! FOOLS ALLOW THEMSELVES TO BE HAZED! I WAS A COWARD AND A FOOL, BUT I AM SO THANKFUL I NEVER HURT ANYONE SERIOUSLY. Mankind, for some reason, seems to have to put others to the test, either collectively or on a personal level. A true Christian will stand up and say, "Hazing is wrong," and leave the GLO. Since God's ANOINTING will not come upon these organizations, they need to stop asking Him for it, because these types of behavior do not meet God's approval. These ungodly activities will **always occur, and their proposed solutions will always be fruitless**. Threaten your members all you want. Set up all the laws you please. GLO's don't understand that obedience **TO GOD** is better than sacrifice (i.e. MAN'S PLEASING GOD BY HIS OWN EFFORTS, INSTEAD OF OBEYING HIS WORD IN SPIRIT, SOUL AND BODY.) **If GLO's, as an organization do not obey God's Word, why would they expect their members to?**

I THESSALONIANS 5:23 And the very God of peace sanctify you **wholly**; and I pray God your whole **spirit** and **soul** and **body** be preserved blameless unto the coming of our Lord Jesus Christ.

GLO's do not obey this command. This is why these organizations will never meet God's standards. It is hypocritical to demand of others what you do not follow yourself. I'm not talking about hazing alone. I'm talking about right living according to the Word of God.

The Obedience that God commands has conditions, and is not decreed by force. Man is both willing and obedient or rebellious and stiff-necked. The results match the condition.

ISAIAH 1:19-20 If ye be willing and obedient, ye shall eat the good of the land: But **if** ye refuse and rebel, ye shall be devoured with the sword: for the mouth of the Lord hath spoken it.

Man's efforts can neither perfect him in the Father's eyes any more than a man's actions can remit sin.

HEBREWS 10:11-12(amp) Furthermore **every [human]** stands [at his altar service] ministering daily, offering the same sacrifices over and over again, which **never are able to strip** [from every side of us] **the sins** [that envelope us] and take them **away**. Whereas this One [Christ], after He had offered a single sacrifice for our sins [that shall avail] for all time, sat down at the right hand of God;

HEBREWS 10:18(amp) Now where there is absolute remission (forgiveness and cancellation of the penalty) of these [sins and lawbreaking), there is no longer any offering made to atone for sin.

No priest enters through the veil for us anymore. Jesus did it once and for all for us. Only by the **BLOOD OF JESUS** are our sins forgiven and we made holy. A GLO is unable to make one holy or enforce true holiness, because they are not the author and source of holiness, and they know it. God told us to be holy, because He is holy. Besides, some GLO's have already **chosen your god for you**, but not a real, holy, or living God (e.g. **Delta Sigma Theta/Sigma Alpha Epsilon-MINERVA, Sigma Gamma Rho- AURORA, Delta Delta Delta- POSEIDON, and Tau Kappa Epsilon-APOLLO**). Their works and their gods cannot save. They are inferior to Jesus. They are not even real gods.

2.) **I CORINTHIANS 10:31** Whether therefore ye eat, or drink, or **whatsoever ye do**, do all to the glory of God.

COLOSSIANS 3:17 And whatsoever ye do in **word and deed**, do **all in the name of the Lord Jesus**, giving thanks to God and the Father by him.

AND

ISAIAH 42:8 I am the Lord: and **my glory will I not give to another**, neither my praise to graven images (idols).

GREEK CHRISTIANS CAN NEVER FULFILL THESE SCRIPTURES FOR 3 REASONS:

- A.) THEIR **ASSOCIATION** WITH A GLO.

- B.) THEIR ASSOCIATION TO MEMBERS WHO HAVE NEVER BEEN SAVED. (THIS BEING **BASED ON THE FALSE ASSUMPTION** THAT YOU CAN BE A GREEK AND A TRUE CHRISTIAN AT THE SAME TIME.)

- C.) GLO's IN WORD AND **DEED** GLORIFY THEMSELVES THROUGH SONG, HYMNS, POETRY, SYMBOLS, AND RITUALS.

Pledging, hymns, community service, and rituals done by GLO's are not to the glory of God, but to the praise, honor, and glory of men and the GLO. This is **IDOLATRY, PRIDE, AND <u>DISOBEDIENCE TO GOD'S WORD</u>.**

II CORINTHIANS 10:5-6 Casting down imaginations, and every high thing that exalteth itself against the knowledge of God, and bringing into captivity every thought to the obedience of Christ; And having a readiness to revenge all disobedience, when **your obedience** is fulfilled.

A MEMBER OF A GREEK-LETTERED ORGANIZATION CAN NEVER FULFILL VERSE 6 BECAUSE OF **II CORINTHIANS 6:14-18**(unequal yoking) and **I CORINTHIANS 10:31**(pride and idolatry).

HERE'S A PERFECT EXAMPLE WHEN ONE DOES NOT CAST DOWN IMAGINATIONS, AND BRING THEIR THOUGHTS INTO CAPTIVITY EVERY THOUGHT **TO THE OBEDIENCE OF CHRIST OR GOD'S WORD.**

This next poem shows a mind that did not bring thoughts to the obedience of Christ's Word.

A DISCONTENTED MAN

It's no sin to be discontented
With the world and the role men play,
For it's only then **men will take their tools**
And build a better day.

Socrates was discontented
With the teachings of his time,
So he went about the city states
With a message **more divine.**

Jesus Christ was discontented
With the lives of men on earth,
So he came from heaven to teach the world
"Man is saved by the second birth."

It was Gandhi, the man of India,
Who was discontented too,
And he brought peace to his native land,
Which no army could ever do.

So it seems our world is waiting
For a discontented man,
To lead this world in paths of peace,
Pray tell me-**who else can**?
        Alpha Alpha Alpha Chapter
        Phi Beta Sigma Fraternity

        George Eggleston
        Virginia State College
        Petersburg, Virginia

(Phi Beta Sigma Fraternity, Inc., THE CRESCENT: Official Organ of the Phi Beta Sigma Fraternity, Inc., Spring 1951, p. 43.)

It is a sin to be discontented, because we are commanded to be content in whatever our present condition. How could God ever be discontent being omniscient (all-knowing). This is saying that Jesus has always been and planned His own discontentment. He came because He loved us (**Romans 5:8**), not because He was discontent.

PHILIPPIANS 4:11-12 Not that I speak in respect of want: for I have learned, in **whatsoever state** I am, therewith **to be content**. I know both how to be abased, and I know how to abound: every where in **all** things **I am instructed** both to be full and to be hungry, both to abound and suffer need.

I TIMOTHY 6:6 But godliness with contentment is great gain. For we brought nothing into this world, and it is certain that we can carry nothing out. And having food and raiment let us therewith be content.

EPHESIANS 2:6(amp) And He raised us up together with Him and made us to sit down together [giving us **joint seating with Him**] in the heavenly sphere [by virtue of our being] in Christ Jesus (The Messiah, The Anointed One).

Since this is true, how can one claim to be discontent, and in

COMING APART AT THE SEAMS

heavenly places at the same time. Discontent people will have a faulty prayer life, loss of hope, depression, etc. None of which are the characteristics of Jesus or a true Christian. If there was any discontent with Jesus, then he had to be the origin of all discontentments, because He is **unchanging**. Did He create us to later become discontent with us? Certainly Not!! He created none of us to be discontent, and to be discontent is to blame God for your circumstances. JOHN 10:10 tells you who is the **source** of your discontentment and contentment. Your relationship with God is out of line when you are discontent, and this man was out of line to say that Jesus was discontent. A true Christian is not going to be discontent, because this means there is inner spiritual unrest. How can we claim the peace and joy of Christ while being discontent at the same time? How can one whom never sinned be discontent? Where is there discontent with perfection? Why does this man and other Greek Christians say such foolish things? They try to employ human wisdom and philosophy to spiritual circumstances just like the ancient Greeks. The **apparent** foolishness and weakness of God is greater than the wisdom/philosophy/stupidity and strength of man (**Read I CORINTHIANS 1:18-31 KJV/Amplified**). No true Christian would ever dare to compare or contrast Jesus with sinful men. Jesus became man without taking upon man's sinful nature, but retained His nature as a perfect God.

Jesus Christ was never discontent, and how dare anyone compare The Son of God with these, or any other man. THIS IS PRIDE AND BLASPHEMY, THE BY-PRODUCTS OF NOT GIVING GLORY TO GOD. The last stanza also says that Jesus failed in bringing peace. Any man who would even imply the Savior of the world as a failure is a FOOL.

IF YOU ARE A TRUE CHRISTIAN THAT DIDN'T HAVE A PROBLEM WITH GLO's, IT'S TIME TO SOUND THE ALARM. GLO's ARE IDOLATROUS. TRUE CHRISTIANS, ESPECIALLY THOSE IN THE PULPITS, MUST **NOT STOP** TELLING PEOPLE IT IS AGAINST GOD. IT ALSO MEANS THAT AS A TRUE CHRISTIAN ONE MUST ALWAYS PUT EVERYTHING SIDE-BY-SIDE WITH

THE WORD OF GOD TO SEE IF IT'S RIGHT. **IT'S TIME TO REVENGE DISOBEDIENCE. DENOUNCE!!!!!!!!! AND FULFILL YOUR OBEDIENCE FIRST.**

HERE ARE SOME EXAMPLES OF HOW GLO's DISOBEY GOD'S WORD BY NOT DOING ALL THINGS TO THE GLORY OF GOD. **THE ALPHA KAPPA ALPHA NATIONAL SONG BY J. Marjorie Jackson** DOES NOT GIVE GLORY, PRAISE, OR HONOR TO GOD. THE AKA's HAVE THE AUDACITY TO SING A SONG THAT SAYS THEY SHOULD DO THINGS TO BRING THEIR SORORITY HONOR AND GLORY. A PART OF THE FIRST STANZA SETS THE STAGE OF WHO IS TO BE HONORED AND GLORIFIED. SO WHENEVER YOU SEE THE WORD, ***"THY"***, IT'S A SUBSTITUTE FOR ALPHA KAPPA ALPHA, NOT GOD:

"O, Alpha Kappa Alpha
Dear Alpha Kappa Alpha"

THE SECOND STANZA READS AS FOLLOWS:

So together anew
We will pledge our faith
And United we'll forge away
Greater laurels to win
Greater tasks to begin

For thy honor and thy glory today."

Delta Sigma Theta Sorority displays this lack of glorifying God, and the gross idolatry that results from not giving Him glory. Notice how they use the word mentor instead of **god**. Minerva is a Delta's head and not the tail. So how can a Delta who says she's saved, that Jesus is the head and not the tail? That is correct, they cannot, but they do. How? By ignoring the quote below, and saying it does not apply to them. If not, then they are not a Delta. Can you say, "HYPOCRITE"? It is what I call, **"the crazy double standard"**. They accept from Delta Sigma Theta, who **gave them** the title of "soror", whatever they choose and reject whatever they desire. It's like denying your parents are your parents. You claim they are your parents when the will is read, but deny their existence while they are living.

"Question: What is the **ultimate goal**, then?
Answer: **Wisdom**! The college educated woman seeks to become wise

rather than smart. That is why **MINERVA, the Goddess of Wisdom, is our Sorority mentor."** (DELTA SIGMA THETA SORORITY, INC., GRAND CHAPTER, MEMBERSHIP INTAKE PROGRAM, 1990, p. 106.)

The partial excerpts from the Kappa Alpha Psi Hymn are full of self-praise and glory.

Words by   Music by
Elder Watson Diggs   Kenneth Billups

"O noble Kappa Alpha Psi, The **Pride** of all our hearts. **The source** of our delights and joys, and happiness thou art. Still **we will honor, love, and sing Thy praises** o'er and o'er. we'll live for thee, we'll strive for thee, we'll all thy ways adore." (William L. Crump, THE STORY OF KAPPA ALPHA PSI, A History Of The Beginning And Development Of A College Greek Letter Organization, 1911-1983, Third Edition, 1983, p. iii.)

The pride and glory (vainglory) of Kappa speaks for itself. This wording of this song and doctrines of so many other GLO'S are what make them incredibly powerful strongholds. That is why our greatest weapon against these strongholds is **prayer and solid presentation of the truth.**

FREDERIC L. HATCHETT

These excerpts from the hymn of **Alpha Phi Alpha** are as all others; Full of **Pride**.

"Alpha Phi Alpha, the **pride** of our hearts and **loved by us dearly** art **thou**,

We cherish **thy** precepts, **thy** banner shall be raised.
To **thy** glory, **thy** honor, and renown.
We hold ever aloft, noble ideals and aims,
Carrying out earth's and heaven's grand command.
Our true hearts ever strive, success' goal to gain, That **our fraternity's praises** may be sung."

Words by Brother Abram L. Simpson
Music by Brother John J. Erby
Xi Chapter

(Charles H. Wesley, The History of Alpha Phi Alpha-Development in College Life,
14th printing, 12th ed. (Chicago, Illinois, 1981.)

Alpha Phi Alpha is clearly at the center of its members' lives, NOT CHRIST. As a matter of fact, I

COMING APART AT THE SEAMS

don't see Jesus anywhere in their song.

Alpha Phi Alpha also demonstrates pride and the giving of glory to itself in this excerpt from their history book.

"Brother Dickinson, the General President, was quite active in pushing forward the interests of the fraternity along all lines. Said he '**Think** Alpha Phi Alpha, **talk** Alpha Phi Alpha, **promote** Alpha Phi Alpha, **and labor for** the broad principles of idealism for which **Alpha Phi Alpha** was created, so that **all humanity** shall look on us as **a body worthwhile'**". (Charles H. Wesley, The History of Alpha Phi Alpha- Development in College Life, 14th printing, 12th ed. (Chicago, Illinois, 1981, p.94)

WHERE IS JESUS???

This is the President of the fraternity making such statements of pride and idolatry. To an Alpha, there is no other god but Alpha Phi Alpha. They preferred to have man see their deeds rather than God. They want the glory, honor, and praise of men. When you do things to receive rewards of men, you miss out on the rewards that come from above (**MATTHEW 6:2,5**).

IF YOU WANT SUCCESS, DON'T LOOK TO MAN FOR IT.

JOSHUA 1:8(amp) This Book of the Law shall not depart out of your mouth, but you shall meditate on it day and night, and that you may observe and **do according to all that is written in it**. For then you shall make your way prosperous, and then you shall deal wisely and have good success.

It does not say that success comes from a body worthwhile, but from the Word of God.

Alpha Delta Pi exhibits the same attitude of not glorifying God in this excerpt from The Creed of Alpha Delta Pi found on the Internet Website (http://www.geocities.com/CollegePark/Union/1348/History.html). It states that,

"I believe that the principles established by our founders in 1851 are enduring attributes, exemplifying the highest ideals of Christian womanhood. I believe that

COMING APART AT THE SEAMS

I must strive to become a well-balanced person by following the dictates of the four points symbolized by our diamond-shaped badge: first, strengthening my own character and personality; second, watching my attitudes toward my fellow beings; third, recognizing the value of high educational standards: and fourth, developing faith and loyalty. I believe that these four guide-posts, **guarded by the stars and friendly hands clasped in the Adelphean bonds of fellowship**, will lead me to achieve a rich and useful life."

All statements are centered on Alpha Delta Pi and its symbols. This creed itself does not exemplify Christianity, nor does it try to uplift the name of Jesus in any shape of form or fashion. I want to know how they plan to achieve the second and fourth guide-posts. There is no safety in the **stars** or hands clasped in Adelphean bonds.

PSALM 46:1 God is our refuge and strength, and very present help in trouble.

Any "confessing Christian" in this sorority is not walking in agreement with God.

3.) LUKE 10:27-28 And he answering said, Thou shalt **Love the Lord thy God** with **all** thy **heart**, and with all thy **soul**, and with all thy **strength**, and with all thy **mind**; and **thy neighbour as thyself.**

And he said unto him, Thou hast answered right: this **do**, and thou shalt live.

If Christians do not practice this scripture, they will get into pride and idolatry.

GLO's require of its members the same things that Jesus requires of you. One must choose to give Jesus all to have eternal life.

Let's listen to some GLO'S on this scripture. The **Sigma Gamma Rho** Pledges National Aurora Hymn States:

"One life I pledge **to thee**,
O Sisterhood, of service brave and true;
My love, my loyalty, my dreams I give **to Thee**,
With humble heart and faith anew.
Firmly stand I with head held high hoping to find the key that opens the door for all who seek noble cause **for Thee**.
Teach me Dear God by **Thy precepts** the path to walk
Place in my hands the light.
Grant that I may be worthy in Thy sight for this new Sigma life."

COMING APART AT THE SEAMS

(The Handbook of Sigma Gamma Rho Sorority, Inc., 1980, p.32. Quoted from Elder James P. Tharrington, Jr., Should Christians Pledge Fraternities and Sororities, For His Glory Printing And Publishing, 1990, p. 48)

Who is God in this excerpt? The words

"thee" and "thy" obviously refer to the sorority, not God.

"Our founders were well aware of the need to **transfuse** the ideals of Greek moral virtues with later concepts of brotherhood and love. That is why they clearly wrote: 'We are a sisterhood founded upon Christian principles...'

Any new ritual and intake program would then **combine** the best of Greek virtues with the highest Judeo-Christian ideals." (DELTA SIGMA THETA SORORITY, INC., GRAND CHAPTER, CANDIDATE SYLLABUS, 1990, p. 30)

How can you live and believe **LUKE 10:27-28** and Greek virtues, when God commands us to leave myths and false stories alone?

I TIMOTHY 4:7(amp) But refuse and avoid irreverent legends (profane and impure and godless fictions, mere grandmother's tales) and silly myths and express your disapproval of them. Train yourself toward godliness (piety), [keeping yourself spiritually fit].

Christianity will not accept this so-called transfusion of Greek moral values, which were at best detestable.

Kappa Alpha Psi's history book gives perfect clarity on who they should love first, and it's not Jesus.

"It must stress first things first, and maintain a continuing realization **that the only first in Kappa Alpha Psi is Kappa Alpha Psi itself.**" (William L. Crump, THE STORY OF KAPPA ALPHA PSI, A History Of The Beginning And Development Of A College Greek Letter Organization, 1911-1983, Third Edition, 1983, p. 268.)

Alpha Kappa Alpha tells its members in their oath whom they are to serve:

"**To thee O Alpha Kappa Alpha** I pledge my **heart**, my **mind**, and my **soul** to foster **thy teachings** and to **obey thy laws** and to make **thee supreme** in service to all mankind." (Fred Hatchett, quoted by Minister J. Davis, 1998.)

Any individual in a GLO, especially an AKA, can never obey **LUKE 10:27-28**.

Hazing is another factor to consider when reading **LUKE 10:27-28, I CORINTHIANS 10:31**, as well as **I CORINTHIANS 3:16 & 6:16**.

If you have already read the chapter on hazing, anyone should see that its spiritual, mental, and physical humiliations are closely related to gangs. The inhumanity of hazing has reached deep enough for it to cause the deaths of **one** too many individuals. The purpose of hazing may not be to kill, but it has certainly succeeded. However, many still believe it is positive to build strong bonds. If so, husbands need to be hazing their wives!!! **No Christian** can be a part of an organization that hazes, pledges, or intakes **in any manner**. Since there is and always will be hazing, a Greek Christian has only one recourse, **TOTAL DENUNCIATION** OF HIS OR HER GREEK-LETTERED ORGANIZATION!!!! Hazing represents a destructive behavior.

COMING APART AT THE SEAMS

JOHN 10:10 The thief cometh not, but to steal, and to kill, and to destroy, but I have come that they may have life, and have it more abundantly.

Hazing fits in perfectly with the thief's (Satan) part of this scripture.

WHAT'S LEFT FOR THE GLO? TOTAL ABOLISHMENT!!!!!

I GUARANTEE THAT MORE PEOPLE WILL DIE FROM HAZING.

ISAIAH 14:12 How have you fallen from heaven, O "light bringer and daystar, son of the morning! How you have been cut down to the ground, you who weakened and laid low the nations [O **blasphemous**, satanic king of Babylon!]

Lucifer loved himself, not the Lord thy God.

The fraternities, sororities, and other "secret societies" all sing hymns of praise to themselves. One even **prays for/to itself, ZETA PHI BETA SORORITY.** They memorize poems that say **loving** their GLO is above anything else. The love for their GLO is in direct contradiction to God's agape love. The deep-rooted love or idolatry for their organization originates in

Luciferian Pride. Greek Christians are sure to be cut down like Lucifer for their deep-seated pride.

4.) I JOHN 5:21(amp) Little children, **keep yourselves from idols (false gods)-[from anything and everything** that would occupy the place in your heart due to God, from **any sort of substitute for Him that would take first place in your life].** Amen (so let it be).

GLO's are idols based on the fact that they only **include** God in their organization. Jesus is **not first** in GLO's, and I have never heard a Greek Christian admit it, nor is it in the doctrines or principles of any GLO that I know about. Even if GLO's put God first in writing, it would be pure hypocrisy, based on what GLO's practice.

Most GLO'S claim to take initiates out of darkness and give them light or the GLO itself claims **to be or give light.**

Alpha Phi Alpha claims to be "The Light of the World".

COMING APART AT THE SEAMS

A verse of the National Hymn of **Delta Sigma Theta** reads; "The bright gleam of thy vision has lighted the world;" (DELTA SIGMA THETA SORORITY, INC., GRAND CHAPTER, RITUAL, 1990, p. 7.)

Thy in this excerpt is Delta Sigma Theta.

The Bible clearly states that JESUS **alone** is the **Light** of the world. **PRIDE AND IDOLATRY again!!!** To any TRUE Christian, this statement is an insult. It says your Savior is a lie, by not being The Light, and that Christians are still in darkness, when they have received the only True Light (**JOHN 1:9**). That true Christians are in darkness, when they have the only true Light is contradictory. Even John the Baptist confessed not to be that Light which is Christ.

JOHN 1:20 And he confessed, and denied not; but confessed, I am not the Christ.

Confessing Christians in Alpha Phi Alpha, Omega Psi Phi, Delta Sigma Theta, Alpha Delta Pi, Pi Kappa Alpha, etc. it's time to go.

Anything you put before or replace God with in thought, word, or deed is idolatry. Your organizations stink in the nostrils of God. God is light, life, and love. He doesn't need to haze you, or force you to memorize songs and poems to prove it. How can a "Greek Christian" quote **LUKE 10:27-28** meaningfully and live it??

Read **II CORINTHIANS 10:3-5** again concerning membership in a GLO. If you decide to remain, write me and justify everything about your GLO by scripture and a copy of all secret material. Do not compare your GLO to the church, Christians and society; but compare to the Word of God ONLY.

5.) AMOS 3:3 Can two walk together, except they be agreed?

AND

I KINGS 18:21 And Elijah came unto all the people, and said, How long halt ye between two opinions? If the Lord be God, follow him: but if Baal, then follow him. And the people answered him not a word.

How do all these different organizations walk together having different principles that they follow? How do they walk in agreement with God when they **allow sinners into their organizations**, and at the same time claim a foundation upon Christian principles? The Bible clearly states that only saved people can be true members of His church, the body of Christ. Their excuse is that they can't make people be Christians. TRUE, **but you can exclude them if they are not and do not want to be**. Any Christian based organization must set standards based on the Word of God. You Greek Christians need to consider your ways and stop straddling the fence. God's Word has given you a choice to follow whoever you believe is God. True Christians know that the Lord is God and follow Him only. Greek Christians in turn try to follow the Lord God and a false god at the same time. Too bad! It can't be done.

Here is the fence straddling mentality found in Delta Sigma Theta Sorority, and in all other GLO's.

National President: "WE believe in a spiritual life, **but** WE leave to the individual the **selection** of the MEDIUM for its outward manifestation." (DELTA SIGMA THETA SORORITY, INC., GRAND CHAPTER, Ritual, 1990, p. 30.)

This means a Delta can be a witch, psychic, palm reader, Buddhist, Hindu, Muslim, etc... A true Christian cannot be in agreement with any of the above religions or professions. How can you (Delta Christian) believe that you could belong to this sorority **and be saved**? IT HAS TO BE UNBELIEF IN GOD'S WORD. Deltas are saying that, **JOHN 14:6** and **ACTS 4:12** mean nothing.

JOHN 14:6 Jesus saith unto him, **I am** the way, the truth, and the life: no man cometh unto the father, **but by me.**

ACTS 4:12 Neither is there salvation in **any other**: for there is **none other name** under heaven given among men, whereby we must be saved.

All GLO's deny scripture in many ways. God said that His Word shall never pass away. Guess what? GLO's will pass away.

A statement from, "The Story of Kappa Alpha Psi" concerning a need of the fraternity is:

1.) "To **integrate** along social, **religious** and nationality lines" (William L. Crump, THE STORY OF KAPPA ALPHA PSI, A History Of The Beginning And Development Of A College Greek Letter Organization, 1911-1983, Third Edition, 1983, p. 258.)

A Christian cannot integrate with anyone that does not believe or follow the doctrine of Christ.

II JOHN 9-10 Whosoever **trangresseth the doctrine of Christ, hath not God.** He that abideth in the doctrine of Christ, he **hath both the Father and the Son. If** there come **any** unto you, and **bring not this doctrine, receive him not** into your house, **neither bid him God speed.**

The lyrics to this next song show that there is no way a Christian can be an Alpha **unless he leaves Christ first**. Either that or be an idolater. It reads:

"**Mighty Sphinx** in Egypt standing Facing eastward toward the sun,

Glorified and e'er **commanding
Your children** bravely on.
Be to us a bond of union
held fast by Peace and Right."
CHORUS:
**"Alpha Phi Alpha our fraternity,
Be to us a guiding light,**
Instill within us love and purity
Through fraternal hope held bright."
  (Charles H. Wesley, The History of Alpha Phi Alpha-Development in College Life, 14th printing, 12th ed. (Chicago, Illinois, 1981, p. 100.)

   The symbol and idol god of Alpha Phi Alpha is the Sphinx. In the chorus, Alpha Phi Alpha claims to give what it does not possess; **LIGHT.** Either Alpha Phi Alpha is God and Jesus was an Alpha. Since neither is true, **ALL Alpha's are IDOLATERS.** Idolaters shall not inherit the kingdom of God. Therefore, how can they claim to be in agreement with God, or say that they are founded upon Christian principles? How can some Alphas profess one way to salvation, and be in this fraternity? **The answer is, "They cannot," and neither can any other GLO. I don't care what meaning they give to the Sphinx, God has already condemned it. To man it may have great meaning and** significance, but to God it is a worthless idol. I beg all true Christians to carefully read this song. Almost every line contradicts the Word of God.

EXCERPTS FROM **THE OATH OF THE OMEGA PSI FRATERNITY** DO NOT AGREE WITH THE WORD OF GOD AND THE LIFE OF A TRUE CHRISTIAN. IT CLAIMS THAT WHATEVER A BROTHER TELLS YOU THAT YOU ARE TO KEEP TO YOURSELF AS IF YOU NEVER HEARD IT. LISTEN TO THIS PART OF THE OATH:

"and hold his secrets when communicated to me as such, as sacred and inviolable in my breast as they were in his before communicated". (OMEGA PSI PHI FRATERNITY (Incorporated 1914), THE RITUAL, 1970, p. 22.)

The most important decision one will ever make in their life is to choose Christ. The second most important decision is whom an individual decides to marry. Husbands and wives, this warning is to you more so than friends of Greeks, or brothers and sisters in GLO's. Consider the betrayal with those you profess to love. If the secrets of their GLO are more important than you, there is a serious problem of priority. A husband or wife wants to and has the right to know any and everything you do. He or she has the right to read your ritual, constitution and by-laws, diary, etc. **Who's more important to you, your spouse or your GLO**? Wives and husbands, some of you would be appalled, probably furious if you knew what went on behind some of those closed-door meetings. The strippers, profanity, and drinking. Wives and husbands? If you're not worried, you ought to be! Often, the worst enemies, are your fellow members. Why would a true Christian want to be a part of this? How can he or she be in agreement with such vile behavior?

THERE ARE THREE AREAS TO LIFE WE SEE, BUT TO GOD THERE ARE ONLY TWO: WE SEE RIGHT, WRONG, AND BOTH, BUT GOD SEES RIGHT AND WRONG ONLY. TRUE CHRISTIANS CAN STAND ON ONE SIDE ONLY TO OBTAIN ETERNAL LIFE: THE RIGHT SIDE. The Bible, history, GLO quotes, and CURRENT OBSERVATION render these organizations guilty before God. Even outsiders not knowing the secrets can see by observation, what a poor example these organizations represent as a **whole (i.e. they see the EVIL fruits of GLO's more than the apparent good.)** How can organizations with different secrets possibly trust each other or be in agreement? They can't and this causes **DIVISION**. Since Christ cannot truly be divided, GLO's are either completely for God or against Him.

I CORINTHIANS 1:13 Is Christ divided? Was Paul crucified for you? Or were you baptized in the name of Paul?

Their works prove they are against Him from their founding, too now, and forever. Proof that Christ cannot be divided is based on this truth: He is the same yesterday, today, and forever (**HEBREWS 13:8**). He is coming back for A CHURCH without spot or wrinkle, not a divided CHURCH (see chapter 5). He will separate the tares (the bad) from the wheat (the righteous). Therefore, Christians cannot agree, walk together, be partakers in, commune, or have interdependent relationships with good (Jesus) and evil (Satan/GLO's) at the same time. Christians are commanded to hate the evil (Satan) and love the good (Jesus). Division often occurs **within** the same group of so-called brothers and sisters causing arguments, envy, and strife within a GLO. You Greeks know exactly what I am talking about, don't you? Some want hazing and some do not. While others want parties, girls, and drinking, others do not. The lack of trust these groups have for one another is manifest by their gang mentality toward each other.

1.) "Phi Beta Sigma and Kappa Alpha Psi fought with fists, canes, and **exchanged gunfire** over who were the **best steppers** and **who donned the finest clothing.**" (Ronald E. Childs, BLACK GREEK FRATERNITIES IN THE '90S: ARE THEY STILL CULTURALLY RELEVANT? Ebony Man, Volume 8, Number 10, Johnson Publishing Company, August 1992, p. 51.)

2.) **"Armed, gang-like** confrontations occurred between Alpha Phi Alpha, Omega Psi Phi at Illinois State University." (Ronald E. Childs, BLACK GREEK FRATERNITIES IN THE '90S: ARE THEY STILL CULTURALLY RELEVANT? Ebony Man, Volume 8, Number 10, Johnson Publishing Company, August 1992, p. 51.)

3.) A feud between two **GLO'S** where I went to college caused the **best of friends to become overnight enemies**. Guys were kicking in each other's doors and carrying knives. I saw one guy in a neck brace that said he had been jumped at another school. The feud on this campus spilled over onto at least 2 other campuses. Stupid, stupid, stupid!!! If you went on a campus with purple and gold on, you'd better know if theirs a feud going on. WHY? Because **pride**, secret knowledge, and loyalty are beaten, brainwashed, and branded (voluntary) into you. Recently, the branding has been **involuntary**.

GLO's CLAIM TO HAVE A COMMON PURPOSE ON PAPER, BUT IN PRACTICE THEY ARE DIVIDED. IT'S A FACT THAT PEOPLE IN THESE ORGANIZATIONS DON'T EVEN FOLLOW THE SAME GOD. HOW DO YOU EXPECT THEM TO GET ALONG WHEN THERE IS NO TRUE SUBMISSION TO **ANY AUTHORITY**? GLO's CONFIRM THE TRUTH OF, **AMOS 3:3. I KINGS 18:21** CALLS **GREEK CHRISTIANS** TO THE TABLE OF **CHOICE**. THE **ONLY** RIGHT CHOICE IS **THE LORD GOD**.

6.) I CORINTHIANS 6:15-16, 20

Know ye not that your bodies are the members of Christ? Shall I then take the members of Christ, and make them the members of an harlot? God forbid. What? Know ye not that he which is joined to an harlot is one body? For two, saith he, shall become one flesh. For ye are bought with a price: therefore glorify God in your body, and in your spirit, which are God's.

IT'S LIKE A MOUTH BEING WHERE THE EAR IS LOCATED, OR THE BODY OF CHRIST HAVING THE MORMON CHURCH ON ONE ARM AND JEHOVAH'S WITNESSES ON THE OTHER ARM. IT DOES NOT BELONG ON CHRIST'S BODY. THEREFORE, THE BODY WOULD NOT BE ABLE TO FUNCTION PROPERLY. UPON READING THESE EXAMPLES ABOUT THE MEMBERS OF CHRIST'S BODY, HOW CAN A CHRISTIAN BE IN ANY AGREEMENT WITH GLO's?

A MEMBER OF THE BODY OF CHRIST HAS NO PLACE **AGREEING WITH** OR BEING A MEMBER OF ANY SECRET SOCIETY, BECAUSE OF THEIR SINFULNESS. GREEK CHRISTIANS DO NOT AND CANNOT GLORIFY GOD IN THEIR SPIRIT, FOR THEY HAVE NOT THE SPIRIT OF CHRIST. EVEN IF THEY REMAIN DISTANT FROM

THE PARTIES, DRINKING AND SEX, THEY ARE STILL JOINED SPIRITUALLY TO THE MEMBERS. THEY ARE NOT ABLE TO SEPARATE THEMSELVES FROM SPECIFIC MEMBERS WHO ARE NOT SAVED **WITHOUT SEPARATING FROM THE WHOLE GROUP (i.e. The entire GLO.)**

HOW DOES ONE CLAIM MEMBERSHIP IN A GLO, WHILE AT THE SAME TIME CLAIM SEPARATION FROM CERTAIN MEMBERS? **THROUGH HYPOCRISY!** THE WORD OF GOD SAYS IT'S IMPOSSIBLE.

I CORINTHIANS 12:16 And if the ear shall say, Because I am not the eye, I am not of the body; is it therefore not of the body?
Answer for yourself.

I pose one final question to all GLO'S; Could Jesus join your GLO, before going to the cross? Keep in mind that he had to be without sin to be the PERFECT sacrifice.

7.) LUKE 11:11-13 What father among you, if his son asks for a loaf of bread, will give him a stone; or if he asks for a fish, will instead of a fish give him a serpent? Or if his asks for an egg, will give him a scorpion? If you then, evil as you are, no how to give good gifts [gifts that are to their advantage] to your children, how much more will your heavenly Father give the Holy Spirit to those who ask and continue to ask Him!

This scripture clearly shows that one being evil (sinful) can do ACTS OF KINDNESS (works), but that the receiver benefits, not the giver. The giver is still evil. FOR PEOPLE IN GLO's, **IT SOOTHES THEIR CONSCIENCE** and gives them an excuse FOR ANY AND ALL THE EVIL THEY DO. Even a Christian, who does a good work, must have a proper intention motivating him to do it. If the intention is bad, it is not done out a pure heart (**TITUS 1:15-16**). Doing good is a common reason given by many as an excuse for their evil ways. Doing good works does not keep one from being evil, wicked, perverse, etc. This is **DECEPTION**. No reception of revelation is what deception really means, and Satan is the cause of one being deceived.

II CORINTHIANS 4:4(amp) For the god of this world has blinded **the unbelievers' minds** [that they should not discern the truth], **preventing them from seeing** the illuminating light of the Gospel of the glory of Christ (the Messiah), Who is the image and Likeness of God.

Many had the opportunity to look at The Truth (JESUS) face-to-face, and still did not see It/Him, because they are spiritually discerned. Without godly authority or the respect for it, every man will do what he thinks is right in his own eyes, instead of following the truth.

JUDGES 21:25 In those days there was no king in Israel: every man did that which was right in his own eyes.

The Bible says, "the way of the **transgressors** is hard" (**PROVERBS 13:15**).

My point is simple. Salvation is never obtained by good works or kept simply by doing good works. The principle of salvation by works, taught by GLO's is transgression or simply put **"stepping over the line that God has drawn."** Only the righteous receive a profitable reward for doing a work of righteousness, but the unrighteous person is rewarded only for their works of unrighteousness, because God does not see Christ in the person. Right+Wrong=WRONG.

REVELATIONS 20:11-15 And I saw a great white throne, and him that sat on it, from whose face the earth and the heaven fled away; and **there was found no place for them**. And I saw the dead, small and great, stand before God; and the book was opened: and another book was opened, which is the book of life:

and the dead were judged out of those things which were written in the books, **according to their works**. And the sea gave up the dead which were in it; and death and hell delivered up the dead which were in them: and **they were judged every man according to their works**. And death and hell were cast into the lake of fire. And whosoever was not found in the book of life was cast into the lake of fire.

The GOOD WORKS done by a GLO and its members are good, but the intent is to glorify the GLO itself. This misguided intention, even by a Greek Christian is not received by God, nor will He reward them for it. The receivers benefit from the good work, but the doer receives a reward of condemnation.

Think long and hard Greek Christian on those bold excerpts of scripture. It is you to whom the Word of God speaks. If you do not believe that being in a GLO is wrong, I hope you at least believe this scripture. Perhaps, it will stir you up to **research your rituals, handbooks and songs bringing you to repentance**.

7.) MATTHEW 5:33-37 (v.37*)

Again, ye have heard that it hath been said by them of old time, thou shalt not **forswear** thyself, but shalt perform unto the Lord thine oaths: But I say unto you, **swear not at all**; neither by heaven; for it is God's throne: Nor by the earth; for it is his footstool: neither

COMING APART AT THE SEAMS

by Jerusalem; for it is the city of the great King. Neither shall thou swear by thy head, because thou canst not make one hair white or black. But let your communication be, Yea, yea; Nay, nay: for **whatsoever is more** than these **cometh from the evil one.**

JAMES 5:12 But above all things, my brethren, swear not, neither by heaven, neither by earth, **neither by any other oath**: but let your yea be yea; and your nay, nay; **lest ye fall into condemnation.**

MATTHEW 10:32-33 Whosoever therefore shall confess me before men, he will I confess also before my Father which is in heaven. But whosoever shall deny me before men, him will I also deny before my Father which is in heaven.

MATTHEW 12:36-37 But I say unto you, That **every idle word** that **men shall speak**, they shall **give account** thereof **in the day of judgment.** For **by thy words** thou shalt be **justified**, and **by thy words** thou shalt be **condemned.**

MY OATH WAS OF THE EVIL ONE, AS WELL AS ALL OTHERS WHO WILL JOIN OR HAVE JOINED A GLO. YOU WILL HAVE TO GIVE AN ACCOUNT FOR THOSE WORDS.

Your word should be your word. LET ME SAY THAT BIBLICALLY **OATHS AND SWEARING** ARE NOT THE

SAME AS **VOWS AND PROMISES**. **OATHS AND SWEARING** HAVE TO DO WITH **ADJURATIONS.**

An **adjuration (horkizo-Greek)** is, **"to cause** to swear, to lay under **the obligation** of an oath."[2]

In the case of adjurations, one has or desires you to swear to do something in God's name. Using God's name in this manner is using His name profanely and in vain. The third commandment tells us not to use His Name in vain. These are the types of oaths GLO's have you repeat prior to membership.

BELIEVE ME, IT'S NOT SWEARING ON OR OFF THE BIBLE THAT MAKES A DIFFERENCE TO GOD, IT IS SWEARING THAT DOES. A LIE IS A LIE PERIOD. THE OATH YOU TAKE IS THE REASONING BEHIND SOMEONE BEING **A GREEK FOR LIFE.** "ONCE A SIGMA ALWAYS A SIGMA!" THIS IS ONE WAY THEY FOOL YOU INTO BONDAGE. SIMPLY PUT; SWEARING AN OATH IS MEANT TO PLACE ONE IN BONDAGE WHICH IS A CURSE, but;

Christ has redeemed from the curse of the Law, being made a curse for us. (**Galatians 3:13**)

If You allow yourself to believe such statements as, **"Once a Sigma always a Sigma,"** as being the truth, Why don't you believe Jesus and His words? It's because the deception of Satan is so strong. This bondage and deception begins with pledging. The oath, poems, songs, symbols and other teachings are meant to brainwash you to believe that the GLO is the most important thing in life. Being redeemed from bondage through Christ is why you can DENOUNCE your GLO without any feeling of condemnation (**Romans 8:1**). Do IT NOW!!!! or fall deeper into bondage. Wash your brains clean with the Word of God. DO IT NOW!!!! And then you can say, "I was a Sigma, Delta, Alpha, etc." When I tell people I used to be a "Que or a Mason," the first thing most say is, "you were a Que. I thought you are one for life." I let them know that I was but never will be again, because I have been redeemed by Christ. I realized my oath was not eternally binding, and could be broken by denouncing it in **JESUS' NAME.** GLO's are nothing but bondage machines, but lack the power to keep you locked in chains. Still, some people are unreachable from the Christian witness (i.e. their minds are reprobate). Even after denouncing, people will notice a residual effect of the GLO in their life. That's just the Devil trying to regain that stronghold. **Soon there will be no more love for what you used to love so dearly. God washes your mind from all that opposes Him as long as you seek after Him, read His Word, pray and fast, and FELLOWSHIP with TRUE CHRISTIANS.** When you join a GLO, their words are your words, their sin is your sin, their master is your master. Although you may have never read that Delta Sigma Theta worships MINERVA, hearing that name in association to them is enough to make you responsible. It's just the same with a Christian. When we hear the Word, we must do the Word. (James 1:22)

One should never take the type of oaths **warned against in scripture** at any time. Although you may only say yes or no at the end of the oath, or don't say it at all does not mean it's okay. It is whatever you orally and/or non-verbally **agree to or with** that makes a difference. You have become a member (yoked) to that which your mouth has spoken, or by simply identifying yourself as a member of a GLO. If you don't repeat the oath, remain active, become inactive, or whether you pay your dues or not, your yoke to them is in your heart **if you do not deny membership**. Besides, what's the need of joining a GLO if you don't want complete identification with it, or its members? This is hypocrisy. What? Are you ashamed of some things your GLO does? If so, why join? Why should a Christian join? Your identity with a GLO establishes your yoke to **the GLO and all of its members**. I remember going to a friend's house with my Omega Psi Phi shirt on. The lady just went off on me, because of what some of my X-brothers had done. Just as a TRUE Christian is inseparable from Christ (the HEAD), so are you inseparable from all of its constituents (the BODY-all **TRUE Christians**). Your membership in a GLO connects you to that whole organization, its principles, doctrines, **members**, symbols, etc. Therefore, as an individual you are inseparable from the body (**The GLO**) and all of its individual constituents (other brothers or sisters whether they confess Christ or are sinners. Sinners are able to be good members. Therefore, they are acceptable to the GLO and considered good brothers and sisters). Greek-Christian? What do you say to that? You are in covenant with sinners of good reputation with the standards of your GLO (i.e. you have no reason to ostracize them for being hazers or not meeting their financial obligations.) GLO's have no standards against fornicators, idolaters, parties, etc. So how can a Greek Christian have a problem with them? HYPOCRISY!!

Next, you will read excerpts of oaths taken by one fraternity (**Omega Psi Phi**) and one sorority (**Alpha Kappa Alpha**). In them, a true Christian **should see** why it's ungodly, **but** the question is, **will they**? Truly, there's only one logical choice.

The prelude to the oath of Omega Psi Phi will show you the stress GLO's place on this part of the initiation. The oath of Omega also proves my point that I made about serving two masters. This oath asks you to serve Omega; not God through Omega, as many Greek Christians will try to proclaim. **I KINGS 18:21 (scripture #5)** strongly states that the service to God is a one-way street, and that's His way. I can say authoritatively, that GLO'S ways are not God's ways.

"The District Representative shall proceed to talk on the value, sacredness, and significance of **the oath**. 'My friends, we are now about to go through the **most sacred** part of the entire initiation; you are about to take upon yourself an oath which will **bind you <u>most</u> intimately to <u>every</u> brother** of the Omega Psi Phi Fraternity, and enlist you in a cause with which you will at all times be expected to sympathize, **whose principles** you will uphold and defend, **whose name** you will **honor**, and to which you will give full support. The taking of this oath is not a matter of mere formality, but a far more serious transaction.'" (OMEGA PSI PHI FRATERNITY (Incorporated 1914), THE RITUAL, 1970, pp. 21-22.)

The oath states: "I (full name), uninfluenced by mercenary motives and imbued with a desire to serve

COMING APART AT THE SEAMS

mankind, in the name and presence of Almighty God, and all I hold sacred, and under the sacred seal of the Omega Psi Phi Fraternity, do solemnly and sincerely promise and swear that I will always help a worthy distressed brother; protect his family, warn him of any approaching danger, and hold his secrets when communicated to me as such, as sacred and inviolable in my breast as they were in his before communicated. I further promise and swear that I will **support** the Constitution of **Omega Psi Phi Fraternity**, maintain **its** standards, and never prove traitor to **any trust** imposed in me **by** the **Omega Psi Phi** Fraternity; binding me under no less a penalty if I forsake thee O Omega, than to have my right hand lose her cunning and my tongue cleave to the roof of my mouth." (OMEGA PSI PHI FRATERNITY (Incorporated 1914), THE RITUAL, 1970, pp. 22-23.)

This oath also portrays another theme mentioned everywhere throughout this book. The fact that once you join, you are joining yourself to all members. Unequal yoking will take place and you are without recourse to choose which brothers and sisters you associate with, because it has been chosen for you. Every Christian, before they became a Greek Christian, is now unequally yoked with unbelievers and an unbelieving organization (i.e. everyone in a GLO was a believer and now an unbeliever, or has always been an unbeliever). Who is the Almighty God at the beginning of the oath? If Omega Psi Phi is an organization founded upon Christian principles as they claim, why not put, in the name and presence of **Jesus**? I know why, and they know it too. Everyone that joins is not a Christian, and may be offended by using Jesus' name. So what does Omega and other GLO's do? They play the coward to another person's god, by not putting Jesus' name in controversial parts of their rituals. Jesus' name is purposely omitted from their documents where it would cause controversy. In doing this they compromise, which is sin. **If it's not done in Jesus' Name, it's all in vain.** GLO's treat Jesus and Christianity just like any other religion. They deny the truth about His deity, and to deny Christ means he will deny you before the Father (**MATTHEW 10:32-33**). All GLO's deny Jesus; Who He is, Who He says He is, and Who the scriptures say He is, and that is fullness of the Godhead bodily (i.e., God in the flesh- **COLOSSIANS 2:9**). To confess Him on one part and deny Him on the other is hypocrisy that results in Him never knowing you.

MATTHEW 7:21-23 Not every one that saith unto me, Lord, Lord, shall enter into the kingdom of heaven; but he that doeth the will of my Father which is in heaven. Many will say to me in that day, Lord, Lord, have we not prophesied in thy name? and in thy name have cast out devils? and in thy name done many wonderful works? And then I will profess unto him, I never knew you: depart from me, ye that work iniquity.

These false prophets were guilty of the same sin of hypocrisy that "you!" Greek Christians are guilty of today.

The oath of **Alpha Kappa Alpha** as given to me by a former member states:

"To thee O Alpha Kappa Alpha I pledge my **heart**, my **mind**, and my **soul** to foster **thy teachings** and to **obey thy laws** and to make **thee supreme** in service to all mankind." (Fred Hatchett, quoted by Minister J. Davis, 1998.)

How can an AKA or any other Greek Christian quote LUKE 10:27-28? They have no right or need to quote it, because the scripture won't do them any good anyway. As a matter of fact, it looks like the one who wrote it quoted LUKE 10:27 and added AKA and other words as needed. Another thing I noticed about most of the oaths I've read is the constant use of the words, Thee and Thy. These oaths are not made to God; they are made to man and the DEVIL.

You are not even promised tomorrow so remember what you say, think, or do because it will effect your eternity. To set the record straight, whether you agree or disagree with something the Bible says, it will not change the ungodliness of these GLO's or the righteousness of Christ. Truth is absolute, immutable, incorruptible, never changing, etc. Therefore, your opinion is nothing, unless the Word of God supports it.

On that note, let's define this next set of words and their use **in scripture.**

THE WORD **OATH** IN THE SCRIPTURES ABOVE COMES FROM THE GREEK (**horkos**) WHICH MEANS,

"A fence, enclosure, or that which restrains a person. The Lord's command in Matt. 5:33 was a condemnation of the minute and arbitrary restrictions imposed by the scribes in the matter of **adjurations** by which **God's Name was profaned.**"[3]

An **adjuration (horkizo)** is, "**to cause** to swear, to lay under **the obligation** of an oath."[4]

This is the same type of oaths GLO's have their initiates perform. Look at the words restrain, obligation, restrictions, and enclosure. All of these words are synonymous with bondage. Bondage is of the Devil.

The word FORSWEAR in the Greek is (**epiorkeo**) which means,

"to swear falsely."[5]

The word SWEAR in the Greek is (**omnumi**) which means, "accompanied by that by which one swears."[6]

In other words, they get you to swear to certain terms with certain conditions. In **MATTHEW 5:34**, notice the person must swear by something. The word forswear in verse 33 is used, based on the fact of man swearing by something he **cannot keep**.

There are always **terms** in the oaths that you must swear to abide by in GLO's. Believe me, most initiates are not even thinking about what they are swearing about, neither do they care. All they want is those Greek letters.

The next two words are often used by society as equals. The Bible defines them basically the same. Neither word requires coercion, restriction, restraint, etc. It's a free choice. You promise and vow or you don't. It's as simple as that. One does not promise or vow **by things**, one does these acts by faith alone. Promises and vows are free will. There's no coercion, compulsion, or necessitation to bind yourself by something.

THE WORD **PROMISE** COMES FROM THE GREEK WORD (**epangelia-homologeo-exomologeo**) WHICH MEANS,

"An announcement or proclamation. Not a pledge <u>secured by negotiation</u>, but <u>given freely</u>."[7]

THE WORD **VOW** COMES FROM THE GREEK WORD (**euche**) WHICH MEANS,

"A wish, expressed as a petition to God." (James Strong, ST.P, L.L.D., Strong's Exhaustive Concordance of the Bible, MACDONALD PUBLISHING COMPANY, MCLEAN, VIRGINIA 22102, p. 34.)

SWEARING OATHS FOR GLO'S ARE **UNCONDITIONAL** AND STRESSED AS A **NECESSITY FOR MEMBERSHIP (i.e. THEY LET YOU KNOW YOU MUST SWEAR).** THE OATH IS **THE SEAL OF YOUR YOKE TO ALL BROTHERS AND SISTERS. IT IS HOW YOU BECOME PHYSICALLY IDENTIFIED AND SPIRITUALLY YOKED TO ALL MEMBERS.**

An oath establishes a covenant, but so do promises. As God and a Christian have a covenant with each other, so is there one with husband and wife. Both are based on promises. Would you want your husband or wife to establish a covenant with another man or woman?

God forbid. God does not want a Christian to establish a covenant with a GLO either.

MANY WILL SAY THAT WE ALL MUST SWEAR AN OATH IN A COURT OF LAW OR TO SERVE IN THE ARMED FORCES, OR EVEN TO BE PRESIDENT. THIS IS NOT TRUE, AND THERE ARE MANY CHRISTIANS WHO **DO NOT SWEAR** AND **WILL CONTINUE NOT TO SWEAR.** WHAT TRUE CHRISTIANS WILL DO IS CONTINUE REFUSING TO BOW DOWN TO MAN, HIS gods AND SATAN. SINCE THAT WOULD CAUSE THEM TO DISOBEY THEIR GOD, THE COURTS WILL EITHER COMPROMISE, OR TRUE CHRISTIANS WILL GO TO JAIL. ONE SHOULD NEVER ALLOW MAN TO FORCE THEM TO SWEAR AN OATH AS GLO's DO. THERE IS A GODLY ALTERNATIVE. LET YOUR YEA BE YEA, AND YOUR NAY, NAY! THIS ALTERNATIVE WOULDN'T LET YOU OFF THE HOOK OF BEING UNEQUALLY YOKED. JESUS DOES NOT MAKE US SWEAR BY ANYTHING TO BE SAVED. ALL CONVERSATIONS WHERE I MENTIONED MY MEMBERSHIP IN THE PAST TENSE, WERE MET WITH THE, "ONCE ONE ALWAYS ONE" COMMENT. THIS IS BONDAGE. IF YOU WILLFULLY CONFESSED YOUR MEMBERSHIP, WHY CAN YOU NOT WILLFULLY RECANT AND REALIZE YOU WERE IN ERROR ABOUT GLO's. MY GOD!

COMING APART AT THE SEAMS

EVEN CHRISTIANS CAN DENY GOD, AND TELL HIM THEY DON'T WANT HIM ANYMORE. NOT EVEN GOD FORCES HIS HAND IN YOUR CONFESSION OF HIM, NOR WILL HE STRONG ARM ANYONE **TO LEAVE** HIM. IF SO, EVERYONE WHO CONFESSED JESUS AS LORD COULD BE FORCED TO DENY HIM (i.e. WE WOULD NO LONGER BE ABLE TO EXERCISE OUR FREE WILL.) JUST BECAUSE YOU CONFESS JESUS AS LORD AND SAVIOR ONCE, DOES NOT MEAN YOU STAY A CHRISTIAN FOR LIFE. **IT'S A CHOICE** TO BE A CHRISTIAN, **IT'S A CHOICE** TO KEEP BEING A CHRISTIAN, AND **IT'S A CHOICE TO STOP** BEING A CHRISTIAN. **IT'S A CHOICE** TO JOIN A GLO, **IT'S A CHOICE** TO REMAIN IN A GLO, AND **IT'S A CHOICE TO STOP** BEING IN A GLO. AFTER READING THIS BOOK, YOU DECIDE TO PLEDGE, AND MANAGE TO GET IN WITHOUT SAYING THE OATH. SO WHAT!! YOU ARE STILL UNIVERSALLY ATTACHED TO ALL MEMBERS AND ALL THE PRINCIPLES. ONCE INITIATED, YOU **INVOLUNTARILY** ADOPTED EVERYTHING ABOUT THAT ORGANIZATION. UNEQUALLY YOKING COMES BY ASSOCIATION.

THE OATH OF ALPHA KAPPA ALPHA DIRECTS ITS FOCUS AND DIRECTION TOWARDS THE IMPORTANCE OF THEIR ORGANIZATION, NOT JESUS. PLEASE

READ IT AGAIN CAREFULLY AND ASK THE QUESTION, IS THERE ANYTHING IN IT THAT'S GODLY?

8.) II CORINTHIANS 6:14-18
Be ye not unequally yoked together with unbelievers: for what fellowship has righteousness with unrighteousness? and what communion hath light with darkness? And what concord hath Christ with Belial? Or what part hath he that believeth with an infidel? And what agreement hath the temple of God with idols? for ye are the temple of the living God; as god hath said, I will dwell in them; and I will be their God, and they shall be my people. Wherefore come out from among them and be ye separate, saith the Lord, and touch not the unclean thing; and I will receive you, I will be a Father unto you, and ye shall be my sons and daughters, saith the Lord Almighty.

Sons and daughters:

Sounds like God draws the lines as to who can be brothers and sisters.

If you are related by blood, you are brother and sister by **natural, involuntary** means: not by some **voluntary or involuntary** oath you take. Whether or not one is related by blood, one cannot be your **true** brother or sister **unless you are saved.** If you are saved, only those who are saved are your true brothers and sisters through faith in Jesus: whether you are related

COMING APART AT THE SEAMS

or not. This is **supernatural**, **voluntary** brotherhood and sisterhood.

LUKE 8:21 And he answered and said unto them, My mother and my brethren are these which **hear** the word of God and **do** it.

In these scriptures, the point is clear that brotherhood/sisterhood in Christ is the new and true standard of relationships established by Jesus and that blood relation or GLO bonds are purely backseat to the Gospel. Christian's are the only representation of **true** brotherhood and sisterhood **combined**, while GLO's represent a **fake** system of brotherhood and sisterhood. AT CHURCH OR RELIGIOUS EVENTS, MANY MEMBERS IN GLO's WHEN GIVEN THE CHANCE, TAKE PRIDE IN MENTIONING THE FACT THAT BESIDE BEING A BROTHER OR SISTER IN CHRIST, THAT THIS IS ALSO MY alpha brother or my delta sister. THIS TYPE OF PROCLAMATION COULD ONLY BE MADE IN A "GREEK FRIENDLY" CHURCH. THIS PROVES THAT GREEK CHRISTIANS ARE AWARE THAT TRUE CHRISTIANS DO NOT APPROVE OF THEM. IT'S WHAT I SAID BEFORE; IT'S A RELIGIOUS COVER-UP, AND AN ATTEMPT TO HAVE PEOPLE ACCEPT GLO's AS GODLY ORGANIZATIONS. **NOT ONLY IS IT PRIDE, IT IS DECEITFUL.**

This scripture tells the saved not to have **fellowship** (i.e. an ongoing relationship, partake, associate) with sinners (**II CORINTHIANS 6:14-18**) and the scripture below says for true Christians not to fellowship with **unrepentant** Christians. Therefore, true Christians can't fellowship with Greek Christians and Greek Christians should not be fellowshipping with sinners. Greek Christians do have fellowship with sinners and freely admit it. Jesus **did not fellowship** with sinners.

Hebrews 7:26 For such an high priest became us, who is holy, harmless, undefiled, **separate from sinners** and made higher than the heavens;

I CORINTHIANS 5:11-13 But now I have written unto you **not to keep company, if any man that is called a brother be** a fornicator, or covetous, or an **idolater**, or a railer, or a drunkard, or an extortioner, with such an one no not to eat. For what have I to do to judge them also that are without? do not ye judge them that are **within**? But them that are without God judgeth. Therefore **put away** from among yourselves **that wicked person.**

Now, if God commands us to break covenant and/or fellowship with someone who is called a Christian, because they continue in sin, why should one think they should keep covenant with a Greek Christian who confesses Christ, but continues in sin, **much less the sinners in GLO's**. The ways they try to explain associating with sinners away is fascinating, but to no avail. GLO's end up using what they so vigorously deny, "excuses". There is a saying pledges are told to learn. It says,

COMING APART AT THE SEAMS

"Excuses are tools of incompetence, they build monuments of nothingness; those who often specialize in them are good for nothing but, excuses, excuses, excuses." (Lampados Club of Omega Psi Phi Fraternity, 1990.)

To prove a point about one's inability to separate from only the bad apples in their GLO, read these excerpts personally from a GLO.

"The bonding of new members is a sacred **obligation** which we **share with Deltas throughout the world**. As we induct new members into the sisterhood, we assure Delta's **everlasting** future and strengthen the **Minerva Circle** of Delta sorors who are pledged to work together in sisterly love to build a better world." (DELTA SIGMA THETA SORORITY, INC., GRAND CHAPTER, RITUAL, 1990, p. 53.)

Delta even issues a stern warning or threat to those who decide to denounce:

"**The induction of new members into Delta Sigma Theta is the Sorority's Most Sacred Trust.**
The breaking of this trust becomes an organizational taboo. As is true of any organization **of this**

239

kind, there must be **strong sanctions against** those who break a Sacred Trust. One does not tamper with organizational taboos." (DELTA SIGMA THETA SORORITY, INC., GRAND CHAPTER, CANDIDATE SYLLABUS, 1990, P. 24.)

SOMEONE BROKE THIS TRUST, AND I MUST ASK: WHAT WOULD YOU DO TO THIS PERSON? KILL THEM, REPRIMAND THEM, BEAT THEM UP OR PUT A HIT OUT ON THEM? SOMEONE TAMPERED WITH THIS TABOO BECAUSE THEY HAVE THE SAME CONVICTION ABOUT GLO's AND DELTA SIGMA THETA AS I DO. THEY'RE UNGODLY, EVIL, AND DECEPTIVE.

Once you took that oath, you were universally **yoked** to the organization, its beliefs, its symbols, and to every member of that organization whether you wanted to be or not, and whether you knew it or not. Go back and read the definition of an oath. Based on what the oaths of GLO's say, it's easy to see why you can't be in one and be a Christian. The only way to break the bond is to completely break the yoke by denouncing the GLO in question. Just to say, "I do not associate with the bad people and things, or "I am not active" does not settle it with God. You're either for HIM or against HIM. The Greek Christian excuses his or herself by staying away from the obvious sinners, going to church, or holding a Bible study. This does nothing. All members in a GLO are sinners anyway. **There is not one excuse for the Greek Christian.** Get out of the kingdom of darkness and into the kingdom of God, because to remain in both means to remain in darkness.

MATTHEW 6:23 But If thine eye be evil, thy whole body shall be full of darkness. If therefore the light that is in the be darkness, how great is that darkness!

A Christian who **voluntarily** joins himself to evil will assume the nature and become a part of that evil.

I CORINTHIANS 15:33(amp) Do not be so deceived and misled! **Evil companionships** (communion, **associations) corrupt and deprave** good manners and **morals** and **character**.

As a person observes these groups, they hear and see mostly one side. They know about the parties and drinking, easy sex, and a general acceptance of their bad behavior as a trade-off for their small contribution to the community and needy people. The minuscule amount they do along with a desire to know what the secrecy is all about is enough to lead any person astray. Man has the nature and curiosity to seek the supernatural, and anything he can't get by natural methods. Even the church has welcomed them, their money, and their false doctrines. This causes deception and confusion among Christians and the unsaved. This excerpt shouldn't confuse any Christian or any Pastor.

"A woman who becomes a Candidate is under the shadow of **Minerva**, and in no way could we offend one who is under **her grace!**" (DELTA SIGMA THETA SORORITY, INC., GRAND CHAPTER, CANDIDATE SYLLABUS, 1990, p. 38.)

Idolatry, Idolatry, Idolatry!!! Greek Christian, you are **UNEQUALLY YOKED** with unbelievers whom you call "brother and sister," as well as **an unbelieving organization**. What's your excuse now???? Get out while you are still under the TRUE God's grace. Quickly I say, Quickly!! Delta Sigma Theta, Kappa Alpha Psi, Sigma Nu, and all of you other GLO's do not state publicly that Jesus is Lord of All, and that He's the only way to heaven. You do not acknowledge in **word and deed** that the Bible is the rule by which you run your organizations. I plead with all of those who believe they can be Greek and Christian at the same time: Please observe what the Bible says and what they say. There is **no agreement and no yoke between the Word of God and GLO's**.

The Bible warns against and commands us to avoid **myths and fables**. Kappa Alpha Psi and other GLO's **failed** to adhere to this command. Yet, they have absolutely no problem claiming to be founded upon Christian principles.

"The founders of Kappa Alpha Psi were so concerned with the authenticity and uniqueness of their ritual, emblems, and ceremonies that they took classes in **Greek mythology and Greek heraldry."** (William L. Crump, THE STORY OF KAPPA ALPHA PSI, A History Of The Beginning And Development Of A College Greek Letter Organization, 1911-1983, Third Edition, 1983, p. 4.)

Either they totally ignored God's command about avoiding myths and fables, or were totally ignorant of it. Nevertheless, the excuses are now useless for any GLO. They all in some way touch on Greek mythology or philosophy. True Christians must totally separate themselves from these types of philosophies and persons of the GLO. Failure to separate, means to disobey **II CORINTHIANS 6:14-18**. How can you separate from one who is still your brother or sister? Your choice of who to hang with does not change the reality that you are still yoked **spiritually** to each and every individual in your GLO.

EXTREME SEXUAL PERVERSION, DRUNKENNESS, REVELRY or **PARTYING, and DECEPTION** have already placed GLO's in the **worldly picture**. They have even come into the church causing discord among the brethren; striving about the Word of God, and having Christians ask foolish questions. These are things, which God commands us to avoid, and to deal with the judgment of those erring brothers.

TITUS 3:9-11(amp) But **avoid stupid and foolish controversies** and genealogies and dissensions and wrangling about the Law, for they are

COMING APART AT THE SEAMS

unprofitable and futile. [As for] a man who is factious [a heretical sectarian and cause of divisions], after admonishing him a first and second time, **reject [him from your fellowship and have nothing else to do with him]**, Well aware that the such a person has utterly changed (is perverted and corrupted); he goes on sinning [though he] is convicted of guilt and self-condemned.

For a Pastor to knowingly allow members of any secret society, to become members of their church is disobedient to the Lord Jesus Christ and His Father Who sent Him, as well as the Holy Spirit Who inspired the Word of God. I do believe in a person being given some time to examine the truth and repent, but their decision determines whether they will or will not become a member of the church. During that time, they should not discuss their view with other members to try and sway them to believe it's all right to be Greek and a Christian too. If one who is already a member of the church is found to be in a GLO, it must be exposed to the Pastor. I do believe that space and some time to repent should be given after hearing the truth. How long should

the pastor allow this person's fellowship continue? This is a personal decision by the pastor. If you know the person, how long should you maintain fellowship? **After the first and second admonition!** Once your friend realizes your conviction, the relationship will change. I believe as long as there is a genuine effort in examining what they have seen and been told, one should show love, patience and mercy. The Word of God is so clear that it may be the day you show them. The length of time will vary from person to person, but proceed with caution, not to be caught in a trap.

GALATIANS 6:1 BRETHREN, IF any man be overtaken in a fault, ye which are spiritual, restore such an one in the spirit of meekness; **considering thyself, lest thou also be tempted.**

From the **worldly picture**, parties are the main forms of fundraising for these groups. Step shows and "T-shirt and panties contests" are some of the crude and vulgar displays by these groups. These activities include profanity, sexual lewdness, and making fun of other GLO's. What happens at these events seems funny, but has so often turned into violence, ranging from fist fights to gun battles. The strongholds and evil influences in GLO's are very powerful and **very much supernatural**. These organizations influence individuals to make very poor and irrational spiritual decisions such as joining the organization. The Black Greeks are usually the only source of entertainment on the college campus for blacks. This is what results in such a widespread acceptance of GLO's, especially by non-Greeks. If you remove the "Greeks," you remove the main social outlet for black students. The strongholds go much deeper than parties. I know a man who was willing to divorce his wife, the most important part of his natural life, if she didn't take a back seat to his Masonic organization. I know people in GLO's who were willing to do the same. This is how strong the **influence (A STRONGHOLD)** of these groups can be. SIN, LIKE A DEMON, NEEDS A BODY TO PERFORM ITS DEEDS.

THEREFORE, A CHRISTIAN MUST SEPARATE FROM ANOTHER WHO CALLS HIMSELF A CHRISTIAN AND PRACTICES (WILLINGLY COMMITS) SIN, AND DOES NOT WANT TO REPENT. ONCE A SAVED PERSON REJECTS CHRIST BY **CONTINUING IN SIN**, OR AN UNSAVED PERSON REJECTS AN INVITATION TO COME TO CHRIST, YOU SHOULD NO LONGER HAVE ANY **HABITUAL FELLOWSHIP** WITH THEM. INVITE THEM TO CHURCH, WITNESS TO THEM OR TAKE THEM OUT TO EAT A COUPLE OF TIMES, BUT THAT'S ABOUT AS FAR AS ONE SHOULD GO. YOU WILL KNOW IF THEY WANT CHRIST OR NOT. IF NOT, SEPARATION SHOWS GOD AND MAN THAT YOU REFUSE TO BE IDENTIFIED WITH HYPOCRITES AND OTHER SINNERS THAT CHOOSE NOT TO REPENT. GREEK CHRISTIANS FALL INTO ONE OR BOTH OF THESE CATEGORIES. THERE ARE THOSE WHO CALL THEMSELVES CHRISTIANS, BUT THE HEAD OF CHRISTIANITY HAS STRIPPED THEM OF THAT IDENTITY FOR REFUSING TO REPENT. THIS IS WHY **II CORINTHIANS 6:14-18 MUST BE OBEYED**. NOTE: **TRUE** CHRISTIANS CAN NEVER BE UNEQUALLY YOKED, IF SO, THEN CHRIST IS NOT UNIFIED. THIS MEANS THAT JESUS IS NOT WHO HE CLAIMS TO BE. ONE COULD SAY THAT CHRIST'S RIGHTEOUSNESS HAS DIFFERENT LEVELS

AND IS NOT EQUALLY DISTRIBUTED TO ALL BELIEVERS.

UNEQUAL YOKING IS CAUSED BY MAN'S WILL TO DO AS HE CHOOSES, OR IN IGNORANCE. I WROTE THE BOOK SO THE IGNORANT COULD BE KNOWLEDGEABLE, AND BRING THE KNOWLEDGEALBE TO REPENTANCE.

EPHESIANS 5:3-7 (amp) But immorality (sexual vice) and all impurity [of lustful, rich, wasteful living] or greediness must not even be named among you, as is fitting and proper among saints (God's consecrated people). Let there be no filthiness (obscenity, indecency) nor foolish and sinful (silly and corrupt) talk, nor coarse jesting, which are not fitting or becoming; but instead voice your thankfulness [to God]. For be sure of this: that no person practicing sexual vice or impurity in thought or in life, or one who is covetous [who has lustful desire for the property of others and is greedy for gain] for he [in effect] is an idolater **has any inheritance in the kingdom of Christ and of God. Let no one delude and deceive you with empty excuses and groundless arguments** [for these sins], for through these things the wrath of God comes upon the sons of rebellion and disobedience. So do not associate or be sharers with them.

THIS SCRIPTURE GIVES US AN EXAMPLE OF HOW NOT TO LIVE, ALONG WITH A COMMANDMENT NOT TO BE **ASSOCIATED** WITH PEOPLE WHO DO SUCH THINGS. ALL "GREEK CHRISTIANS", IF THEY WERE TRULY CHRISTIANS WOULD BE GUILTY OF UNEQUAL YOKING WITH UNBELIEVERS. YOKING DOES NOT BEGIN AT THE **PHYSICAL** LEVEL. **IT'S SPIRITUALLY ROOTED.** WHEN YOU HAVE ORGANIZATIONS IMPLYING AND PROFESSING TO GIVE LIGHT, PROVIDING A WAY TO ETERNAL LIFE, OR PROFESSING THAT **A CHRISTIAN IS IN DARKNESS UNTIL THEY JOIN THEIR GLO, AVOID THEM.** IF THEY SAY THAT WE **INCLUDE** GOD, **AVOID THEM.** THIS IS AN ORGANIZATION THAT NEEDS TO BE AVOIDED AND MARKED BY TRUE CHRISTIANS AS DEMONIC. YOU CANNOT BE FOLLOWING GOD IN A GLO. MANY OF THE WORDS IN THIS SCRIPTURE ARE COMMONPLACE IN "GREEKDOM" (i.e. GREEK LIFE.) AN EXAMPLE OF THIS CAN BE IN AN EXCERPT FROM THE RITUAL OF OMEGA PSI PHI FRATERNITY.

"On bringing you **from the darkness** of selfish and self-centered lives **into the** fullness and **light** of life **in Omega**, you first beheld the escutcheon (shield) of Omega, the crossed

COMING APART AT THE SEAMS

swords, the glove of mail and the helmet, by the aid of the four burning candles". (OMEGA PSI PHI FRATERNITY (Incorporated 1914), THE RITUAL, 1970, p. 26.)

Every symbol and act in the ritual center around (i.e. worship) OMEGA, not Christ. This is so with all GLO's. As a Christian, Omega Psi Phi sees you as living or practicing the sin of a selfish, self-centered life, and are in need of **their** light. **Pride, Pride, Pride!!! Professing themselves to be wise, they are fools, and so it is with GLO's.**

Christian's cannot practice sin.

FOR ONE WHO BECOMES A CHRISTIAN AND LEAVES SIN BEHIND, GOD IS NO LONGER YOUR JUDGE IN THE SENSE OF GUILTINESS, HE IS A JUST JUDGE AND A REWARDER OF THOSE FAITHFUL TO HIM. YOU ARE NOT IN NEED OF ANYONE ELSES LIGHT, NOR SHOULD YOU ALLOW A GLO TO CONDEMN YOU OF ANYTHING.

HEBREWS 11:6 But without faith it is impossible to please him: for he that cometh to God must believe that he is, and that he is a rewarder of them that diligently seek him.

NOT ONLY DID JESUS BEAR YOUR GUILT ON THE CROSS, GOD HAS MADE JESUS YOUR PERSONAL ADVOCATE (i.e. YOUR PERSONAL DEFENSE ATTORNEY).

I JOHN 2:1-2 My little children, these things write I unto you, that ye sin not. And if any man sin, we have an advocate with the Father, Jesus Christ the righteous: And he is the propitiation for our sins: and not for ours only, but also for the sins of the world.

WHAT'S IN YOUR HEART WILL MAKE ITSELF MANIFEST IN YOUR BODY (i.e. YOUR ACTIONS). GREEK CHRISTIANS ARE SURROUNDED BY MEMBERS WHO PRACTICE SOME OF THESE SINS. THE GREEK CHRISTIAN CANNOT RECONCILE WITH UNEQUAL YOKING. HE OR SHE IS GUILTY.

MATTHEW 15:18-19 But those things which proceed out of the mouth come forth from the heart; and they defile the man. For out of the heart proceed evil thoughts, murders, adulteries, fornications, thefts, false witness, blasphemies:

GOD HATES THE SIN NOT THE PERSON, BUT SINCE THE TWO ARE ONE, THE PERSON MUST BE JUDGED ALONG WITH THE SIN. THIS IS WHY

COMING APART AT THE SEAMS

YOU NEED HIM AS A PERSONAL DEFENSE ATTORNEY. THIS IS WHY HE SENT HIS ONLY BEGOTTEN SON INTO THE WORLD AND RAISED HIM BACK TO LIFE. HE DID THIS SO THAT BY BELIEVING IN HIM YOU MAY HAVE AN **ETERNAL** RELATIONSHIP WITH HIM. OUR RELATIONSHIP WITH JESUS, BECAUSE OF HIS BLOOD, IS WHAT ALLOWS GOD'S WRATH AND INDIGNATION TO **PASS OVER** US. IT IS BECAUSE OF **HIS WORK** NOT OUR WORK**S** THAT WE RECEIVE HIS MERCY. THESE ORGANIZATIONS JUST WANT THE GLORY FOR WHAT THEY DO. THEIR SONGS, POEMS, HISTORY BOOKS, RITUALS, AND THEIR ACTIONS ARE ENOUGH FOR MANY TO DENOUNCE, BUT BECAUSE GLO's HAVE ONLY "A FORM OF GODLINESS", THEY ONLY ATTRACT THE "CARNAL BELIEVERS", **THE RELIGIOUS CROWD**, WHO LIVE FOR THE WORLD. UNFORTUNATELY, THESE **STUBBORN** AND **REBELLIOUS BACKSLIDERS** REMAIN MEMBERS, **NOT WILLING** TO BELIEVE THE TRUTH. EVEN WHEN ALL GODLY EFFORTS HAVE BEEN EXHAUSTED, THEY TRY TO JUSTIFY SOME WAY TO MAKE GLO's RIGHTEOUS.

9.) TITUS 1:15-16(amp) To the **pure [in heart** and conscience] all things are pure, but **to the defiled and corrupt and unbelieving nothing is pure**, their very **minds** and **consciences** are **defiled** and **polluted**. They profess to know God [to recognize, perceive, and be acquainted with him] **but deny** and **disown** and **denounce** him **by what they do**; they are detestable and loathsome, unbelieving and disobedient and disloyal and rebellious, and [they are] **unfit and worthless for good work** (deed or enterprise) of any kind.

AND

MATTHEW 5:8 Blessed are the **pure** in heart: for they shall see God.

a.) A GODLY MAN OR WOMAN DOES NOT HAZE, HUMILIATE, EXALT HIMSELF ABOVE HIS FELLOW MAN (i.e. Exhibit **Pride**), OR GIVE GLORY TO AN ORGANIZATION, **NOR DO THEY HABITUALLY ASSOCIATE THEMSELVES IN ANY WAY TO A GLO OR THEIR MEMBERS**. THESE THINGS ARE **NOT PURE**. THEREFORE, THEY CAN'T BE PURE.

b.) THE SAVED PERSON IS AWARE THAT THE BEGINNING, DURATION, AND END OF THEIR LIFE MUST BE PURE. THE MOTIVES MUST BE PURE. THE ENDS MUST JUSTIFY THE MEANS. THIS MEANS THAT IF THE ENDS ARE RIGHTEOUS, THEN THE MEANS (ORIGIN) MUST ALSO BE RIGHTEOUS. A MEMBER OF A GLO DOES NOT POSSESS A PURE HEART,

AND THEREFORE, WILL NOT SEE GOD. FROM BIRTH TO DEATH, JESUS WAS SINLESS. HIS RESURRECTION PROVES THIS. PARTIES, RAFFLES, UNEQUAL YOKING, MOCKING, IDOLATRY, DRUNKENESS, FORNICATION AND SECRECY ARE JUST A FEW IMPURE PRACTICES OF GLO'S. A TRUE CHRISTIAN, ONLY BECAUSE OF CHRIST, IS PURE AND ABLE TO STAY PURE. I SAID THIS TO WARD OFF THE STATEMENT THAT NO ONE COULD EVER BE PURE. BY AN INDIVIDUAL'S ABILITY **ALONE**, HE IS INCAPABLE OF BEING PURE, AND UNFIT TO DO ANY GOOD WORK.

Pride is at the root of evil and destroys anything that is pure and holy. A true Christian cannot be yoked to someone in pride. It destroyed Lucifer, who was made perfect in all his ways, but because of pride he rebelled. Yet, pride is a most vital ingredient in any GLO. I believe **Kappa Alpha Psi** states it best;

"All frat men have **pride in themselves** and we should all be realistic enough to note that no man would ever have **pride** in his race unless he first has **pride** in

FREDERIC L. HATCHETT

himself. Frat men also have a deep seated, **irrevocable pride in their organizations.** The critics would never admit it, nevertheless, in each frat man's daily life he **transfers the pride he feels in himself and in his organization to every person he comes in contact with."** (William L. Crump, THE STORY OF KAPPA ALPHA PSI, A History Of The Beginning And Development Of A College Greek Letter Organization, 1911-1983, Third Edition, 1983, p. 402.)

I, being a strong critic, do admit this to be true. I also admit that this is a serious problem for Christians who believe that there's nothing ungodly about GLO's. Another damaging quote from their history book states:

"Fraternities build pride." (William L. Crump, THE STORY OF KAPPA ALPHA PSI, A History Of The Beginning And Development Of A College Greek Letter Organization, 1911-1983, Third Edition, 1983, p. 402.)

This is what the pledge and/or intake process (hazing) is designed to do. Unfortunately, it does the exact opposite. Pride is purely satanic, and totally impure when it comes to Jesus.

Symbolism also plays a significant role in the impurity of

COMING APART AT THE SEAMS

GLO's. Iota Phi Theta's symbolism lacks Christian purity. The Centaur, a half-man-half-horse, is one of many animals in Greek mythology. Idolatry poisons Christianity and the Christian as well, and because of this Iota Phi Theta and its members are declared **impure** in the eyes of Christ. All GLO's condone and/or do not defend many of the moral standards written in God's word. GLO's instead practice and condone many things that the Bible calls immoral, abominable, sinful, etc. Some of the things they do not take a stand of righteousness on are fornication, partying, smoking, drinking, gambling, profanity, etc. All are sinful and impure.

UNEQUAL YOKING IS A SIN THAT GREEK CHRISTIANS CANNOT ESCAPE. IF YOU ARE A CHRISTIAN WITNESS, **DO NOT** ALLOW GREEK CHRISTIANS TO USE HYPOTHETICALS WITH **II CORINTHIANS 6:14-18**: SUCH AS **IF, WHAT IF? HOW ABOUT THIS?**

10.) ACTS 17:23-24 (AMP) For as I passed along and carefully observed your objects of worship, I came also upon an altar with this inscription, To the **unknown god**. Now what you are already worshiping as unknown,

257

this I set forth to you. The God Who produced and formed the world and all the things in it, being Lord of heaven and earth, does not dwell in handmade shrines.

AND

JOHN 4:22 Ye worship ye know not what: we know what we worship: for salvation is of the Jews.

THE ACKNOWLEDGEMENT OF OTHER gods IS DONE BY PERFORMING UNGODLY RITUALS AND THROUGH UNGODLY SYMBOLS. GLO SYMBOLS ARE BLASPHEMOUS AND BRING A CURSE TO YOUR HOME. THE RITUALS THEY PERFORM DO NOT WORSHIP THE TRUE GOD. THEREFORE, SATAN IS BEING WORSHIPPED. EVERY god OTHER THAN THE GOD OF THE BIBLE IS A FALSE, LIFELESS god. Many GLO's are worshipping gods they do not know, and many worship gods of which they do have knowledge. None of which are The Lord Jesus.

PSALM 96:4-5 For the Lord is great, and greatly to be praised: he is to be feared above all gods. For **all the gods** of the nations **are idols**: but the Lord made the heavens.

THERE IS ONLY ONE TRUE GOD. ACCORDING TO PAUL AND JESUS,

WORSHIPPING ANOTHER god IS STUPID OR IGNORANT.

EXAMPLES ARE **THE AKA (ALPHA KAPPA ALPHA) goddess CEREMONY** WHERE THE INITIATE IS SYMBOLICALLY AN IVY LEAF.

"SHE IS CROWNED WITH IVY LEAVES AND INITIATED, AND THEN SHE BECOMES A **goddess** AND A PART OF THE VINE OF AKA." (Fred Hatchett, quoted by Minister J. Davis, 1998.)

THEY DO NOT BECOME A PART OF THE TRUE VINE IN **JOHN 15**. "CHRISTIAN AKA?" HOW CAN YOU BE A PART OF TWO DIFFERENT VINES, WHEN THERE'S ONLY ONE ROOT? HOW CAN TWO WALK TOGETHER EXCEPT THEY BE AGREED? I DO NOT KNOW WHETHER OR NOT ALPHA KAPPA ALPHA STILL PRACTICES THIS RITUAL.

Tau Kappa Epsilon states on the Internet that,

"The mythological ideal or patron of Tau Kappa Epsilon is **Apollo,** one of the most important of Olympian divinities. The Grecian **god** of music and culture, **of light** and the ideals toward which all Tekes must constantly be striving. Typifying the finest development of manhood, the selection of Apollo is most appropriate." (TKEnet: TKE Symbols and Traditions http://ww.tke.org/tkesymb.shtml#Apollo.)

The Candidate Syllabus of **Delta Sigma Theta** states,

"We **turned for guidance to** one of the most ancient initiation rites, **the Elusinian mysteries.** The object of those rites was to ascend through the natural elements to a **'new life'** (being carried forward through all the elements)." (DELTA SIGMA THETA SORORITY, INC., GRAND CHAPTER, CANDIDATE SYLLABUS, 1990, p. 40.)

The Elusinian mysteries are the **worship** of **Demeter and Persephone**, the **goddesses** of the harvest. Any Delta, and any other Greek Christian must simultaneously deny **EXODUS 20:13, I TIMOTHY 4:3, ISAIAH 44:6, PSALM 96:4-5**, and countless other scriptures in order to associate with any group that teaches such blasphemy and idolatry. I challenge; even dare anyone to substantiate the quote above as being scriptural.

One of the tests you must go through to become a member of Omega Psi Phi Fraternity is the test of faith. The result of the test is supposed to teach you to have faith

COMING APART AT THE SEAMS

in your brothers, **not God**. It mentions in the prelude to taking the test that,

"The scriptures say, 'without faith it is impossible to please God.' Without faith it also impossible to please **man"** (OMEGA PSI PHI FRATERNITY (Incorporated 1914), THE RITUAL, 1970, p. 17.)

It is easy to please man without faith. Flash a $100 bill in a person's face, and I guarantee their faith will mean nothing, because they do not need it. The bill is in their face. The quote above is man's opinion, not God's Word. God, not man, tests one's faith. This entire quote by Omega Psi Phi is not a true statement (**read HEBREWS 11:6**). The test is designed to have faith in your brothers and the fraternity, **NOT GOD**. Remember all GLO rituals of worship, praise, adoration, love, and initiation point to the GLO. The test of faith as described in their ritual is nothing more than **a work** to achieve the goal of membership. This is totally opposite to God's way of achieving SALVATION. It is by faith in HIS work on the cross, not a test for us to be faithful in doing something that we receive salvation. With Omega and other GLO's, it is works for God's acceptance. If it were by faith that GLO's rewarded people, then whom would the members pray to for a reward/blessing? That's right, the god of the GLO, which is the god of this world, who the Bible calls the devil. Other GLO's that acknowledge other gods or mythological creatures through symbols or by associating with a god are 1.) Tau Kappa Epsilon (**Apollo**), 2.) Iota Phi Theta (**Centaur**), 3.) Alpha Kappa Alpha (**Atlas**), 4.) Sigma Gamma Rho (**Aurora**), 5.) Delta Sigma Theta and Sigma Alpha Epsilon (**Minerva**), and 6.) Phi Beta Sigma (**Prometheus**). Don't get happy just because your GLO is not on this list. The list is much greater. This list is just to let you, the reader, see it for yourself. Do not let them fool you into saying this information is false. **I have the proof and so do they**. What a shame for a Christian to deny this information. It's called LYING. It is not wise, and it's a SIN. If you're interested and concerned about what you're

COMING APART AT THE SEAMS

getting yourself into, ask them to **prove** what you ask. Don't allow them to make **any** excuses.

EPHESIANS 5:6(amp) Let no one delude and deceive you with **empty excuses** and **groundless arguments [for these sins]**, for through these things the wrath of God comes upon the sons of rebellion and disobedience.

Don't allow them to play games with you. GLO's are good for this. They teach their members to be evasive and adamant about revealing certain information. To the Christian, my advice to you is **never joining**. Yet, if you insist, ask them to show you all of their secrets first.

11.) I PETER 4:3(amp) For the time that has past already suffices for doing what the Gentiles like to do living [as you have done] in shameless, insolent wantonness, in lustful desires, drunkenness, reveling, drinking bouts and abominable, lawless idolatries.

AND

GALATIANS 5:19-21(amp) Now the doings (practices) of the flesh are clear (obvious): they are immorality, impurity, indecency, 20 Idolatry, sorcery, enmity, strife, jealousy, anger (ill temper), selfishness, divisions (dissensions), party spirit (factions, sects with peculiar opinions, heresies), 21 Envy, drunkenness, carousing, and the like. I warn you beforehand, just as I did previously, that those who do such things shall not inherit the kingdom of God.

ALL OF THE SINS MENTIONED IN THESE SCRIPTURES CLEARLY PORTRAY GLO INDULGENCE. ALL OF THE FOLLOWING EXAMPLES, UNTIL THE NEXT NUMBERED SCRIPTURE, CAN FIND THEIR PLACE IN ONE OR BOTH OF THESE SCRIPTURES. REGARDLESS OF DRINKING AGE, GREEKS WILL GET DRUNK. REGARDLESS OF THEIR GPA, GLO'S WILL HAVE PARTIES. AN EXAMPLE IS THE FAMOUS "PRE-EXAM JAM" THAT GLO'S OFTEN EMBARK ON NEAR SEMESTERS END. GLO'S WILL USUALLY HAVE A WEEK WHERE THEY PERFORM REQUIRED FUNCTIONS SET DOWN BY THE NATIONAL HEADQUARTERS. MONDAY-THURSDAY WILL CONSIST OF SEMINARS, BUT FRIDAY AND/OR SATURDAY IS PARTY TIME!!! **SUNDAY** INVOLVES THE TYPICAL AND HYPOCRITICAL "WE DO GO TO CHURCH" SERVICE. IT GOES FROM "GOOD WORKS", TO A LATE NIGHT PARTY, AND THEN TO CHURCH. ON MOST COLLEGE CAMPUSES, IF A BLACK GLO IS NOT SPONSORING A

COMING APART AT THE SEAMS

PARTY, THERE WILL BE NO ENTERTAINMENT FOR THE BLACKS. THEY DOMINATE ALL SOCIAL FUNCTIONS ON CAMPUS. JESUS IS NOT BEING LIFTED UP AT THESE PARTIES, SO THEY CANNOT BE HOLY, GODLY, OR RIGHTEOUS. THEY CLAIM THESE PARTIES ARE TO RAISE MONEY FOR THEIR PROJECTS. IF THEIR PROJECTS ARE SO HONORABLE, PEOPLE NEED NOT BE ENTERTAINED TO SUPPORT IT. THE PEOPLE DRAWN TO THESE PARTIES ARE NOT TRUE CHRISTIANS; NEITHER ARE THEY COMING TO SEEK JESUS THERE. WELL WHAT DO YOU FIND AT A GLO PARTY?? PEOPLE WHO ARE DRUNK, HIGH, FULL OF PRIDE (MOSTLY THE GREEKS), AND FULL OF LUST. **ALL COME EMPTY, AND ALL WILL LEAVE EMPTY.**

HERE ARE SOME EXCERPTS FROM FLIERS THEY POST ON CAMPUS.

A **ZETA PHI BETA** FLIER HAD **"FINER WOMANHOOD"** AT THE TOP. THE PICTURE WAS GRAPHICALLY HYPOCRITICAL TO THEIR SLOGAN. IT WAS A WOMAN IN A G-STRING WITH ALMOST A WHOLE BREAST SHOWING. SHE HAD HER HEAD LEANING BACK WITH AN EXPRESSION OF EXTREME PLEASURE. IF THE PICTURE WEREN'T PROTECTED UNDER COPYRIGHT, I WOULD HAVE PUT IN MY BOOK. THERE WAS NO

PROFESSION SHE COULD HAVE PERFORMED THAT JESUS WOULD BE PLEASED WITH. I WONDER WHAT A PASTOR OF A ZETA WOULD SAY IF SHE WANTED TO PUT THIS ON THE CHURCH BULLETIN BOARD. IF THIS FLYER CAN'T BE BROUGHT BEFORE THE TRUE CHURCH, IT IS UNHOLY. SIX MONTHS EARLIER, THE SAME SORORITY HAD A FLYER UP WITH MALACHI Z. YORK ON IT. THE HEADLINE WAS,

"**THE MASTER TEACHER** WITH A PLAN THAT IS WORKING FOR **THE REBIRTH OF THE gods**".

I SHOWED THIS FLYER TO A YOUNG LADY THAT **WAS INTERESTED IN JOINING.** AFTER SHE SAW THE WORD, **"gods", SHE CHANGED HER MIND.** HER REASON, **"I CAN'T BE YOKED TO THEM"**, AND **GOD'S WORD** SUPPORTS HER REASON.

12.) JOHN 14:6 Jesus saith unto him, I am the way, the truth, and the life: no man cometh unto the father, but by me.

AND

JOHN 12:32(amp) And I, if and when I am lifted up from the earth [on the cross], will draw and attract all men [Gentiles as well as Jews] to myself.

COMING APART AT THE SEAMS

GLO's ARE NOT CHRIST-CENTERED AND HAVE NO HOLY STANDARDS ACCORDING TO THE WORD OF GOD. ONE STANDARD I KNOW THEY DON'T HAVE IS **JOHN 14:6**. WHEN TALKING TO GREEK CHRISTIANS IN GENERAL CONVERSATION, THE CENTER ATTRACTION WILL NOT BE **THE SAVIOR**. TRUE CHRISTIANS SHOULD EXPECT THIS FROM THEM ANYWAY, BECAUSE **JESUS** IS NOT THE WAY OF ANY GLO.

Here is an excerpt from the Candidate Syllabus of **Delta Sigma Theta,**

"A woman who becomes a Candidate is under the shadow of **Minerva**, and in no way could we offend one who is under **her grace!**" (DELTA SIGMA THETA SORORITY, INC., GRAND CHAPTER, CANDIDATE SYLLABUS, 1990, **p. 38.**)

The Ritual of Omega Psi Phi Fraternity, p.34, says that Jesus is not the way to eternal life. Guess who they say is the way, and how to get there? Not a hard question to answer is it?

"It is to vividly recall to each attending brother's mind, the ten basic tenets of our **Omega Life:**

'**Fraternity** is our **chosen way** of life;'" (OMEGA PSI PHI FRATERNITY (Incorporated 1914), THE RITUAL, 1970, p. 34.)

Jesus is not their chosen way of life.

"'By Discretion, Faith, Obedience, Endurance, and Courage we came into that life;'" (OMEGA PSI PHI FRATERNITY (Incorporated 1914), THE RITUAL, 1970, p. 34.)

But this life did not come through the blood sacrifice of Jesus.

"'Friendship is our constant striving and eternal goal.'" (OMEGA PSI PHI FRATERNITY (Incorporated 1914), THE RITUAL, 1970, p. 34.)

Their goal is not the higher calling of God which is in Christ Jesus.

PHILLIPPIANS 2:14-15 I press toward the mark for the prize of the high calling of God in Christ Jesus. Let us therefore, as many as be perfect, be thus minded: and if any thing ye be otherwise minded, God shall reveal even this unto you.

They would rather have the "Omega Life" than eternal life.

MEMBERS OF PHI BETA SIGMA CLAIM TO BE **"THE SONS OF FIRE AND BRIMSTONE"**. NO MATTER WHAT THE REASON, THEY TELL YOU IN WHOM THEY BELIEVE BESIDE THEMSELVES. WHY THIS SLOGAN? IT JUST SHOWS THE MORAL DEGRADATION OF THE MIND OF SOMEONE IN A GLO.

FROM THE WORDS OF A FORMER ZETA OR MEMBER OF ZETA PHI BETA,

"PRAY FOR ZETA FERVENTLY." (Fred Hatchett, quoted by Minister J. Davis. Original quote from B. Stover, 1998.)

WE SEE ON WHOM THEY LOOK TO FOR STRENGTH.

If you are a Greek Christian, you should be on your knees repenting and denouncing.

HEBREWS 12:17 (amp) For you understand that later on, when he wanted [to regain title to] his inheritance of the blessing, he was rejected (disqualified and set aside), for he could find **no opportunity to repair by repentance**, [what he had done, no chance to recall the choice he had made] **although he sought for it carefully with [bitter] tears.**

**REPENT BEFORE IT'S TOO LATE FOR YOU!!!
BEFORE YOU GO SIX FEET UNDER!!!**

THIS SCRIPTURE WILL PORTRAY HOW GLO's HAVE NO HOPE. THEY DO NOT OBEY THE WORD OF GOD IN **SOUL WINNING, LIVING BY FAITH, REPENTANCE, SANCTIFICATION**, etc. IF MEMBERSHIP **REQUIRES** THAT **YOU BELIEVE IN** JUST **A SUPREME BEING** THEN HINDUS, BUDDHISTS, MORMONS, JEHOVAH'S WITNESSES CAN ALL JOIN AN ORGANIZATION FOUNDED UPON "CHRISTIAN PRINCIPLES." THIS INCLUDES GLO'S, BUT AN ORGANIZATION FOUNDED UPON **"TRUE"** CHRISTIAN PRINCIPLES CANNOT EXCEPT THESE PEOPLE **AS MEMBERS**. TO DO THIS ONE MUST TAKE **ACTS 4:12, EXODUS 20:3**, AND **MATTHEW 4:10** OUT OF THE BIBLE. THE GLO CAN'T REFUSE MEMBERSHIP TO ANYONE OF THE PROPER SEX WITHOUT BEING HYPOCRITES. ESAU'S TEARS, HIS EMOTIONS, AS WELL AS OURS ARE NOT SUFFICIENT TO GOD FOR REPENTANCE AND RESTORATION. WE MUST ADMIT THAT WE ARE SINNERS. GLO's LACK OF HOLINESS RENDERS THEM **INSUFFICIENT** OF BEING FOUNDED UPON CHRISTIAN PRINCIPLES.

DON'T TRADE YOUR RELATIONSHIP WITH JESUS FOR A FLESHLY GRATIFICATION (i.e. YOUR GLO) LIKE ESAU TRADED HIS SPIRITUAL BLESSINGS FOR FOOD. HE DID NOT HAVE HIS HEART

SET ON GOD, AND NEITHER DOES THE GREEK CHRISTIAN. IT'S NOT WORTH IT. REPENT AND DENOUNCE, WHILE YOU STILL HAVE THE MIND TO DO SO. REPENT AND DENOUNCE TO STOP LOSING THE SPIRITUAL BLESSINGS YOU ARE MISSING OUT ON BY BEING A GREEK CHRISTIAN. AS LONG AS YOU ARE A GREEK CHRISTIAN, YOUR WORSHIP IS FALSE, YOUR PRAYERS ARE NOT EFFECTIVE, AND YOUR BLESSINGS ARE THOSE FOR THE UNJUST.

ANY ORGANIZATION THAT CLAIMS TO BE FOUNDED UPON CHRISTIAN PRINCIPLES (CHRIST-CENTERED) MUST HAVE SPECIFIC STANDARDS.

THE FIRST STANDARD MUST BE THAT **ALL** MEMBERS ARE BORN AGAIN. IF THIS STANDARD IS NOT UPHELD, NO OTHER STANDARDS CAN BE UPHELD. SIN WILL EVENTUALLY TAKEOVER.

I CORINTHIANS 5:6-7 Your glorying is not good. Know ye not that a little leaven leaveneth the whole lump? Purge out therefore the old leaven, that ye may be a new lump, as ye are unleavened. For even Christ our passover is sacrificed for us.

NO GLO HAS THE "MUST BE BORN AGAIN PRINCIPLE" INTACT; SO NO GLO IS FOUNDED UPON CHRISTIAN PRINCIPLES. CHRISTIAN!! BY JOINING A GLO, YOU ARE BRINGING SIN INTO YOUR OWN HOUSE (YOUR BODY), WHICH IS THE TEMPLE OF THE HOLY GHOST. THE SCRIPTURE SAYS IF YOU DEFILE THE TEMPLE, HIM WILL GOD DESTROY. THE **SECOND STANDARD** THAT MUST BE UPHELD IS THAT **ALL ACTIVITIES MUST BE BIBLICAL.** SORRY GLO's, BUT YOU FAIL THIS BY A LONG SHOT. GLO's ARE NOT HOLY AND THUS BREAKING GOD'S COMMAND TO BE HOLY.

I PETER 1:15-16 But as he which has called you is holy, so **be ye holy** in all manner of conversation; Because it is written, Be ye holy; **for I am holy**,

I ALSO WANTED TO MAKE MENTION OF THE LACK OF HOLINESS IN DRESS. IT'S NOT THE EVERYDAY ROUTINE, BUT WHAT I OBSERVE AT THE PARTIES. IT IS OBVIOUS THAT THERE IS NO SHAME IN LETTING IT ALL HANG OUT AT A PARTY, AND IT SHOULD COME AT NO SURPRISE. PARTIES OF THE WORLD ARE DONE BY AND ATTRACT THOSE OF THE WORLD. GLO's FALL IN THIS CATEGORY OF

ENTERTAINING THESE TYPES OF FUNCTIONS, BECAUSE THEY ARE OF THE WORLD. THE BIBLE SAYS THAT FRIENDSHIP WITH THE WORLD IS ENMITY WITH GOD (JAMES 4:4). GLO's!!!! IF YOU ARE FOUNDED UPON CHRISTIAN PRINCIPLES, HOW COULD YOU ALLOW SUCH MUSIC TO BE PLAYED, PROVOCATIVE ATTIRE TO BE WORN, AND FOUL LANGUAGE TO OCCUR? I KNOW OF THREE REASONS; **1.)** THE DEVIL RUNS YOUR GLO; **2.)** THE MONEY YOU MAKE; AND **3.)** YOU'RE NO DIFFERENT THAN THE PEOPLE WHO ENTER YOUR PARTIES. **GREEK CHRISTIAN!** HOW WILL YOU EXPLAIN YOURSELF TO GOD ABOUT SUCH THINGS? THE MAIN REASON WHY MOST PEOPLE DO NOT LIVE A HOLY LIFE UNTO GOD IS LACK OF PRAYER, AND NOT READING THE WORD OF GOD. WITHOUT PRAYER AND READING THE BIBLE, YOU WON'T KNOW HOW TO LIVE HOLY. YOU WILL BECOME REBELLIOUS AND STUBBORN. AS A WITNESS AND TRUE CHRISTIAN, YOU WILL FIND THIS TO BE THE CASE 100% OF TIME WITH GREEK CHRISTIANS. AS A WITNESS IN THIS SITUATION, THE BEST OPTION IS TO QUOTE SCRIPTURES TO THE INDIVIDUAL(S). ARGUMENTS LEAD NOWHERE, BUT FAITH COMES BY HEARING THE WORD OF GOD. EVEN IF THEY'RE WALKING AWAY, QUOTE THE WORD AND

TELL THEM YOU LOVE THEM, BUT DO NOT FOLLOW BEHIND THEM AND BE A PEST. IF THEY ASK YOU TO LEAVE THEM ALONE, SHAKE THE DUST OFF YOUR FEET.

   THE PROOF THAT THEY ARE NOT HOLY ARE; **1.)** PRACTICE AND COVET SECRECY; **2.)** PARTAKE IN WORLDLY ACTIVITIES SUCH AS PARTIES, WET T-SHIRT CONTESTS, DATING GAMES, RAFFLES (which are gambling), **3.)** HAVE FELLOWSHIP WITH ANTI-CHRISTIAN RELIGIONS SUCH AS ISLAM, MASONIC ORDERS, MORMONS, AND OTHER CULTS; **4.)** ALL MEMBERS ARE NOT SAVED; **5.)** ALL **PRACTICE** SOME TYPE OF SIN, ESPECIALLY THE WORKS OF THE FLESH, MENTIONED IN GALATIANS 5:19-21. WHILE THE BIBLE SAYS IN **I JOHN 2:23**, THAT **NO SAVED** PERSON CAN **PRACTICE** SIN; **6.)** DO NOT PROFESS THAT **JESUS IS GOD; 7.) DO NOT REQUIRE MEMBERS TO BELIEVE IN JESUS, AND 8.) RELIGIOUS TOLERANCE.**
   GLO's (**Greek-lettered organizations**) ARE JUST ASKING FOR SINNERS TO COME AND JOIN. UNFORTUNATELY, MANY CHRISTIANS **CAN**, BUT **MOST DO NOT WANT TO SEE** THE TRUTH ABOUT GLO's. I PRAY THE LORD REVEAL THE TRUTH TO THOSE WHO DON'T KNOW, AND THE HOLY SPIRIT CONVICTS

THOSE WHO DO KNOW THE TRUTH, BUT HAVE REJECTED IT. THESE PEOPLE CONFESS CHRIST AS LORD, BUT ARE RELIGIOUS NOT CHRISTLIKE. THEY FEEL JUSTIFIED BY WHAT **THEY DO**, NOT **WHO DID IT FOR THEM.**

EZEKIEL 14:1-11 Then came certain of the elders of Israel unto me, and sat before me. And the word of the Lord came unto me, saying, Son of man, these men have **set up their idols in their heart**, and put the stumblingblock of his iniquity before their face: should I be inquired of at all by them? Therefore speak unto them, and say unto them, Thus saith the Lord God; Every man of the house of Israel that setteth up his idols; That I may take the house of Israel in their own heart, because **they are all estranged from me through their idols**. Therefore say unto the house of Israel, Thus saith the Lord God; **Repent, and turn yourselves from your idols**; and turn away your faces from all your abominations. For every one of the house of Israel, or for the stranger that sojourneth in Israel, which separateth himself from me, and setteth up his idols in his heart, and putteth the stumbling blocks of iniquity before his face, and cometh to a prophet to inquire of him concerning me; I the Lord will answer him by myself: And I will set my face against that man, and will make him a sign and proverb, and I will cut him off from the midst of my people; and ye shall know that I am the Lord. And if the prophet be deceived when he hath spoken a thing, I the Lord have deceived the prophet, and I will stretch out my hand upon him, and will destroy him from the midst of my people Israel. And they shall bear the punishment of their iniquity: the punishment of the prophet shall be even as the punishment of him that seeketh unto him; That the house of Israel may go no more astray from me, neither be polluted any more with all their transgressions; but that they may be my people, and I may be their God, saith the Lord God.

MATTHEW 6:25(amp) Therefore I tell you, stop being perpetually uneasy (anxious and worried) about your life, what you shall eat or what you shall drink; or about your body, what you shall put on. Is not life greater [in quality] than food, and the body [far above and more excellent] than clothing?

GLO's REQUIRE YOUR DEDICATION, TIME, SERVICE, **LOVE,** AND OTHER FACETS OF LIFE. YET THEY HAVE NO POWER TO CHANGE YOU SPRITUALLY ACCORDING TO THE WORD OF GOD. THE PURPOSE OF PLEDGING IS TO SEE IF YOU HAVE THE WILLINGNESS **TO SERVE THE GLO, NOT GOD.** GREEK CHRISTIANS ARE GUILTY OF A DIVIDED HEART BY WAY OF THEIR IDOLATRY THROUGH DIVIDED ALLEGIANCE. THEY ARE MORE

CONCERNED AND PLACE GREATER IMPORTANCE ON SOCIETIES' PROBLEMS (EARTHLY THINGS) **THAN THEY DO SOULS (SPIRITUAL THINGS)**. GOD IS A JEALOUS GOD, AND YOUR GLO IS IN HIS WAY TO DO FOR YOU WHAT HE PURPOSED YOU TO DO. WHAT WILL GOD DO NOW? BETTER YET, WHAT WILL YOU DO? LOOK AT WHAT GOD DID TO THE FALSE PROPHETS AND THOSE WHO DID NOT REPENT IN EZEKIEL. "GREEK CHRISTIANS" YOUR END WILL BE NO DIFFERENT THAN THEIRS. WILL YOU KEEP TAKING GOD FOR A JOKE? HE'S NOT SLACK CONCERNING HIS PROMISE.

BY THIS JUNCTURE IN THE BOOK, YOU KNOW THE TRUTH AT THIS POINT. REPENTANCE IS A CONFESSION AWAY. DENOUNCING TAKES ABOUT 3 SECONDS. "I DENOUNCE MY GLO IN JESUS NAME, AMEN". THE KEY IS TO **SAY** IT, **BELIEVE** IT, AND **DO** IT. IT MUST SHOW IN YOUR LIFE. MANY OF THE EXCERPTS FROM GLO'S CLEARLY SHOW THAT A GREEK CHRISTIAN HAS A DIVIDED HEART AND MUST BE SERVING TWO MASTERS.

I WILL QUOTE FROM ZETA PHI BETA AND PHI BETA SIGMA ABOUT WHO THEY ARE TO SERVE. ZETA PHI BETA'S SERVICE AND ACCOMPLISHMENTS ARE ALL DONE FOR THEM TO UPLIFT THEIR

FREDERIC L. HATCHETT

REPUTATION AND IMAGE. HERE IS AN EXCERPT FROM THEIR BIOGRAPHICAL DIRECTORY.

"We can take **great pride** in **our sisterhood** and in the distinguished members whose contributions **guarantee our relevance and longevity.**" (Zeta Phi Beta, Biographical Directory, 1976, Foreword.)

THE BIBLE CLEARLY SAYS, CURSED IS THE MAN THAT TRUSTETH IN MAN WHOSE STRENGTH IS IN THE ARM OF THE FLESH (**JEREMIAH 17:5**). THE USE OF **"OUR"** SHOWS YOU WHO IS TO BE UPLIFTED. ANYONE CAN SEE THAT IT'S NOT GOD. FAMOUS ZETAS GET THE LIMELIGHT, WHILE THE LITTLE ONES RECEIVE NO HONOR. THIS SHOWS **ELITISM AND DIVISION** WITHIN THE ORGANIZATION.

The motto of Phi beta Sigma is, "Culture for service, service for humanity." (Phi Beta Sigma Fraternity, Inc., THE CRESCENT: Official Organ of the Phi Beta Sigma Fraternity, Inc., SPRING 1949, p. 42.)

THEY **SERVE MANKIND** BY FIRST SERVING PHI BETA SIGMA. THE GREEK LETTER **BETA** IN PHI **BETA** SIGMA REPRESENTS THE GREEK WORD BOULÉ WHICH MEANS **SERVICE**. REMEMBER WHAT I SAID ABOUT THE SYMBOLS AND LETTERS OF A GLO AND HOW THEY POINT TO THEIR BELIEFS AND PRINCIPLES. I'M NOT WRITING

A FICTION. **UNLESS I NOTATE IT**, I HAVE SEEN IT WITH MY OWN EYES, OR HEARD WITH MY OWN EARS.

I DON'T NEED TO TELL YOU THE ETERNAL REWARD FOR IDOLATRY. THE BIBLE SPELLS IT OUT CLEARLY IN MANY WAYS.

13.) ACTS 26:26 For the king knoweth of these things, before whom I also speak freely: for I am persuaded that none of these things are hidden from him; for this thing was not done in a corner.

JOHN 18:20(amp) Jesus answered him, I have spoken openly to the world, I have always taught in a synagogue and in the temple [area], where the Jews [habitually] congregate (assemble); and I have spoken nothing secretly.

MATTHEW 10:26-28 So have no fear of them; for nothing is concealed that will not be revealed, or kept secret that will not become known. What I say to you in the dark, tell in the light; and what you hear whispered in the ear, proclaim upon the housetops. And do not be afraid of those who kill the body but cannot kill the soul; but rather be afraid of him who can kill both soul and body in hell.

THE WATCHWORD IN THESE SCRIPTURES IS **SECRECY.**

WHAT SHOULD SEND A WARNING SIGN TO ANY CHRISTIAN OR SINNER IS THE **INTENTIONAL SECRECY** PRACTICED BY GLO'S. ESCPECIALLY SINCE THEY CLAIM TO BE SO GREAT AND DO GREAT THINGS. THE CLAIM THAT THEY LIVE AND ACT OUT THEIR SECRETS IS UNPROVEN TO MANY. BUT THEIR UNGODLINESS SHOULD BE OBVIOUS TO THE NON-MEMBER. BY THIS I MEAN, A GLO AND ITS MEMBER'S ACTIONS WILL ONLY TELL ON THEMELVES AND THEIR MEMBERS. NO MATTER HOW HARD A "GREEK CHRISTIAN" TRIES; PROOF OF THEIR ASSOCIATION WITH A GLO CAN ALWAYS BE DETERMINED BY **THE TESTIMONY OF THEIR LIFESTYLE OR THEIR LIPS.** THESE ARE THINGS THEY CAN'T KEEP SECRET. CHAPTER 2 DEALS WITH SECRECY IN DEPTH.

14.) ACTS 17:11(amp) Now these [Jews] were better disposed and more noble than those in Thessalonica, for they were entirely ready and accepted and welcomed the message [concerning the attainment through Christ of eternal salvation in the kingdom of God] in inclination of mind and eagerness **searching and examining the Scriptures daily to see if these things were so.**

THE BEREANS SEARCHED THE SCRIPTURES, **NOT GREEK MYTHOLOGY OR ANY OTHER HUMAN WISDOM OR PHILOSOPHY**, TO SEEK THE VALIDITY OF THE PREACHER'S WORDS. GLO's DO NOT MIND A PERSON READING THEIR HISTORY, BECAUSE IT'S NOT SECRET. YET, THEIR HISTORY BOOKS, CONVERSATIONS AND ACTIONS REVEAL THAT JESUS CHRIST IS A NOBODY. BY NOT MENTIONING HIM ACCORDING TO THE **TRUTH, THE GREEK CHRISTIAN PROVES HE DOES NOT KNOW CHRIST FOR HIMSELF.** WHY? THEY ARE NOT SAVED AND CANNOT UNDERSTAND SPIRITUAL THINGS. THEY ALWAYS SAY WHAT THEY HEARD SOMEONE ELSE SAY ABOUT JESUS.

I CORINTHIANS 2:9-16 But as it is written, eye hath not seen, nor ear heard, neither have entered into the heart of man, the things that which God hath prepared for them that love him. But God hath revealed them unto us by his spirit: for the spirit searcheth all things, yea, the deep things of God. For what man knoweth the things of a man, save the spirit of man which is in him? even so the things of God knoweth know man, but the spirit of God. Now we have received, not the spirit of the world, but the spirit which of God, that we might know the things that are freely given to us of God. Which things also we speak, not in the words which man's wisdom teacheth, but which the Holy Ghost teacheth; comparing spiritual things with spiritual. But the natural man receiveth not the things of the spirit of God: for they are foolishness unto him: neither can he know them, because they are spiritually discerned. But he that is spirit judgeth all things, yet he himself is judged by no man. For who hath known the mind of the Lord, that he may instruct him? But we have the mind of Christ.

A TRUE CHRISTIAN CAN READ GLO HISTORY AND SEE WHY GREEK CHRISTIANS CANNOT BE SAVED. NO TRUE CHRISTIAN SHOULD EVER ENTER INTO A **COVENANT** WITHOUT **GOD'S** REVELATION KNOWLEDGE OF A PERSON OR GROUP. FOR A CHRISTIAN TO ACCEPT GLO's AS GODLY ORGANIZATIONS, THEY MUST BE **CONFUSED** BY THEIR RHETORIC. **FOR A CHRISTIAN BASED ORGANIZATION NOT TO MENTION JESUS AS THE ONLY WAY TO GOD, ARE DENYING JESUS AS THE AUTHOR OF THEIR FAITH. THEREFORE, MEMBERS ARE IN AGREEMENT WITH THIS BELIEF THROUGH MEMBERSHIP WITH THE GLO.**

I CORINTHIANS 14:33(amp) For he [Who is the source of their prophesying] is not a God of confusion and disorder but of peace and order. As [is the practice] in all the churches of the saints (God's people)

HEBREWS 12:2 Looking unto Jesus the author and finisher of our faith; who for the joy that was set before him endured the cross, despising the shame, and is set down at the right hand of the throne of God.

EZEKIEL 28:14-19 Thou art the anointed cherub that covereth; and I have set thee so: thou wast upon the holy mountain of God; thou hast walked up and down in the midst of the stones of fire. Thou wast perfect in thy ways from the day that thou wast created, **till iniquity was found in thee**. By the multitude of the merchandise they have filled the midst of thee with violence, and thou hast sinned: therefore I will cast thee to profane?? out of the mountain of God: and I will destroy thee, O covering cherub, from the midst of the stones of fire. Thine heart was lifted up because of thy beauty, thou hast corrupted thy reason by reason of thy brightness: I will cast the to the ground, I will lay thee before kings, that they may behold thee. thou hast defiled thy sanctuaries by the multitude of thy iniquities, by the iniquity of thy traffick; therefore I will bring forth a fire from the midst of thee, it shall devour thee, and I will bring thee to ashes upon the earth in the sight of all them that behold thee. All they that know thee among the people shall be astonished at thee: thou shalt be a terror, and **never shalt thou be any more**.

LUCIFER IS THE AUTHOR OF SIN (AND CONFUSION). THE ORIGIN DETERMINES THE PRODUCT. THE ROOT DETERMINES THE FRUIT. THE **BASIC** ORIGIN OF GLO's IS AS FOLLOWS:

1.) THE DEVIL
2.) NIMROD
3.) BABYLONIAN CULTS

4.) EGYPTIAN CULTS
5.) GREEK CULTS (POLYTHEISM)
6.) MASONIC ORDERS
7.) GREEK-LETTERED ORGANIZATIONS

TRUE CHRISTIANS KNOW THEIR ORIGIN IS IN CHRIST (**JOHN 1:3**). HE IS ALSO THE AUTHOR AND FINISHER OF OUR FAITH. YOU WILL HEAR SOME SAY THAT HE MADE THE DEVIL; GOD FORBID. LUCIFER **BECAME** THE DEVIL. HE WAS **NOT CREATED** THE DEVIL. GOD **BECAME** MAN (i.e. JESUS WAS NOT CREATED). HE WAS NEVER A MAN FROM ETERNITY PAST. ALL CULT SYSTEMS ARE BASED ON SALVATION BY WORKS. **RELIGION PREACHES** SALVATION BY WORKS AND GLO's ARE RELIGIOUS ORGANIZATIONS. SALVATION BY WORKS IS THE MOST SUCCESSFUL **ANTI-CHRIST DOCTRINE**, AND THE GLO'S HAVE USED IT FROM **START** TO PRESENT. **EACH BOLD PHRASE BELOW INDICATES THE STRESS ON WORKS.**

IN A BRIEF EXCERPT FROM THE HYMN OF ALPHA PHI ALPHA WE SEE THIS CONCEPT:

"**MANLY DEEDS**, SCHOLARSHIP, AND LOVE FOR ALL MANKIND **ARE THE AIMS OF OUR** DEAR **FRATERNITY.**"

Words by Brother Abram L. Simpson, Music by Brother John J. Erby
Xi Chapter

(Charles H. Wesley, The History of Alpha Phi Alpha-Development in College Life, 14th printing, 12th ed. (Chicago, Illinois, 1981)

ALPHA PHI ALPHA'S AIM IS NOT TO WIN SOULS, BUT THE BIBLE SAYS IT'S WISE TO DO SO (**PROVERBS 11:30**). SATAN USES THE "LOVE FOR ALL MANKIND" AS A SMOKESCREEN TO HIS REAL PURPOSE. STRESSING WORKS AS SUFFICIENT, NOT FAITH.

THE NATIONAL SONG OF ALPHA KAPPA ALPHA, BY J. MARJORIE JACKSON, STATES ITS ACCEPTANCE AND VIEW ON THE IMPORTANCE OF WORKS:

"**BY MERIT** AND CULTURE
WE **STRIVE** AND WE **DO**
THINGS THAT ARE WORTHWHILE"

THE MOTTO OF ZETA PHI BETA IS TO "Enhance, **Accomplish**, And **to serve**." (Zeta Phi Beta, Biographical Directory, 1976, Foreword.)

THE UNWRITTEN MOTTO OF OMEGA PSI PHI IS, "Lifting as we climb."

THE MOTTO OF ALPHA DELTA PI IS, "We live for each other."
(http://www.geocities.com/CollegePark/Union/1348/History.html)

THE MOTTO OF PHI BETA SIGMA IS "Culture for service, **service for humanity**". (Phi Beta Sigma Fraternity, Inc., THE CRESCENT: Official Organ of the Phi Beta Sigma Fraternity, Inc., SPRING 1949, p. 42.)

I DON'T SEE **THE NAME OF JESUS**, THE WORD **HOLINESS**, LED BY THE SPIRIT, WALK BY THE SPIRIT, GOD FIRST, LIVE FOR JESUS, OR **SERVE GOD ANYWHERE. NO GREEK CHRISTIANS!!!** DON'T GO AND CHANGE THAT RITUAL NOW. IT'S TOO LATE. IT'S TIME TO MAKE LIFE'S BEST DECISION: REPENT!!!

15.) **MATTHEW 4:17** Repent for the kingdom of God is at hand is **JESUS' MOTTO**

LUKE 13:3 I tell you, Nay, but, except ye repent, ye shall all likewise perish.

ACTS 17:30 And the times of this ignorance God winked at; but now **commandeth all men everywhere** to **repent:**

MATTHEW 6:33 But seek ye first the kingdom of God, and his righteousness; and all these things shall be added unto you.

ROMANS 4:25 Who was delivered for our offences, and was raised again for our justification.

I CORINTHIANS 15:17 Wherefore receive ye one another, as Christ also received us to the glory of God.

THEIR PRINCIPLES AND DOCTRINES ARE NOT CONCERNED WITH YOUR SPIRITUAL WELFARE; NEITHER CAN THEY CHANGE YOU SPIRITUALLY. IN ALL THE LITERATURE ON GLO's THAT I HAVE READ (OVER A **1000** PAGES), **NONE HINT** AT ANY SCRIPTURE WRITTEN ABOVE. THE LAST 2 SCRIPTURES ARE THE DOCTRINE AND FOUNDATION OF A TRUE CHRISTIAN'S FAITH AND CHRISTIANITY'S THEOLOGY: **THE RESURRECTION.** WITHOUT THE RESURRECTION, THERE IS NO CHRISTIANITY OR CHRISTIAN FAITH. THE RESURRECTION IS NOT THE FOUNDATIONAL DOCTRINE OF GLO's. LISTEN ALL READERS, AND ESPECIALLY CHRISTIANS. GLO's WERE, ARE, AND NEVER WILL BE FOR CHRISTIANS. THEY ARE CONCERNED WITH **1.)** THEIR OWN ACHIEVEMENTS, **2.)** WORKING FOR THEIR OWN GLORY, AND **3.)** GIVING THEIR PRAISE TO THEMSELVES. THESE ALL TYPIFY **SATANIC PRIDE, NOT RESURRECTION GLORY.** CHRISTIANS SHOULD **DISASSOCIATE** THEMSELVES FROM THE GLO AND ITS MEMBERS **NEVER** TO REJOIN, BUT ONLY TO WITNESS CHRIST TO THEM.

I CORINTHIANS 3:11 For other foundation can no man lay than that is laid, which is Jesus Christ.

JESUS IS THE RESURRECTION AND THE LIFE.

TO MY KNOWLEDGE, GLO's DO NOT RECOGNIZE IN WRITING OR IN ANY OTHER WAY, THE **DEITY OF JESUS**; YET, THEY PROCLAIM A CHRISTIAN FOUNDATION. TO PORTRAY JESUS IN ANY OTHER WAY (i.e. LESS THAN GOD) IS **BLASHPEMY**. THEREFORE, ALL GLO's DO BLASPHEME BY CLAIMING THROUGH THEM YOU CAN HAVE ETERNAL LIFE. PASTOR, MINISTER, LAYPERSON, YOU HAVE SOME EXPLAINING TO DO IF YOU SUPPORT GLO's OR BELONG TO ONE. ACCORDING TO THE SCRIPTURES, GLO's ARE WITHOUT JESUS. THEREFORE, GLO's ARE WORTHLESS, USELESS AND IN VAIN. ANY ORGANIZATION AND PERSON WITHOUT CHRIST AT THE FOUNDATION CAN'T STAND THE TEST OF THE WORD. THERE IS NO CHRISTIANITY WITHOUT CHRIST. CHRISTIANITY WITHOUT CHRIST IS JUST A godless RELIGION HEADED FOR A godless HELL. EXCEPT THE LORD BUILD A HOUSE, HE THAT LABORS, LABORS IN VAIN. ONE'S MEMBERSHIP, INTEREST IN, OR ACTIVITY WITH GLO's IS USELESS, WASTED, TIME AND ENERGY. ONCE CHRIST IS ESTABLISHED AS THE

FOUNDATION OF ANY GROUP, IT MUST PASS THE TESTS OF THE WORD OF GOD. IT MUST BE PURE, JUST, HOLY, HONEST, AND OF A GOOD REPORT. GLO's DO NOT FALL UNDER ANY SUCH CATEGORY. THIS IS WHY A CHRISTIAN SHOULD NEVER BE A MEMBER OF, OR IN AGREEMENT WITH GLO's. AN EXAMPLE IS HAVING A CONTRACT/COVENANT TO SELL MEDICAL INSTRUMENTS TO AN ABORTION DOCTOR OR AN OB/GYN. ONE USES THE INSTRUMENTS TO MURDER BABIES, THE OTHER USES THEM TO DELIVER CHILDREN. IF ONE COULD STILL BE SAVED AND PERFORM SINFUL ACTS, THEN HE IS IMPLYING THAT JESUS IS A SINNER BECAUSE OF YOUR COVENANT WITH THE LORD. JESUS INSTEAD CANCELS HIS COVENANT WITH YOU WHEN YOU DECIDE TO PRACTICE SIN. YET, AT ANY TIME YOU **TRULY REPENT**, HE RESTORES THE COVENANT (i.e. HE TAKES YOU BACK, BECAUSE YOU TOOK HIM BACK). WHEN A CHRISTIAN HAS A CHOICE BETWEEN GOOD AND EVIL, GOOD MUST BE HIS CHOICE OR IT IS SIN (**JAMES 4:17**). LET ME PUT IT THIS WAY; WOULD YOU RATHER MARRY (MAKE A COVENANT WITH) A SAVED OR UNSAVED PERSON? TO SUPPORT THE SCRIPTURES IN **I CORINTHIANS 7 AND II CORINTHIANS 6:14-18**, IT'S WRONG FOR A CHRISTIAN TO DO IT. THE

FOUNDATION UPON MARRYING AN UNSAVED PERSON WOULD BE WEAK AND TREACHEROUS. SO IT IS THE SAME WHEN ONE YOKES THEMSELF TO AN UNGODLY ORGANIZATION, FULL OF UNGODLY PEOPLE.

BY NOT PROCLAIMING THE DEITY OF JESUS AND JESUS AS THE **SOLE** FOUNDATION OF A PERSON'S LIFE, YOU MIGHT AS WELL BE A MUSLIM, JEHOVAH'S WITNESS, MORMON, OMEGA, TEKE, DELTA, OR AKA, BECAUSE THEY DO NOT EITHER. THEY CAN ALL BE GROUPED INTO ONE CATEGORY AS WELL; **SINNERS**

II CORINTHIANS 11:14 And no marvel; for Satan himself is transformed into an angel of light.
LUCIFER WORKS HARD TO MAKE **GOOD WORKS** APPEAR TO BE ENOUGH TO RECEIVE A HEAVENLY REWARD. REMEMBER THAT HE IS A LIAR AND THE FATHER OF LIES. CHRISTIANS FALL BECAUSE THEY ARE IGNORANT TO THE DEVIL'S DEVICES, BUT THE SCRIPTURES SAY THAT WE SHOULD NOT BE (**II CORINTHIANS 2:11**). PEOPLE ARE DESTROYED BECAUSE THEY LACK KNOWLEDGE OF GOD'S WORD. THIS IS THE PROBLEM WITH GLO's AND THE GREEK CHRISTIANS. THIS IS WHY THE DEVIL HAS NO PROBLEM USING THEM FOR HIS PURPOSES. MANY YOUNG ORDAINED MINISTERS ON COLLEGE CAMPUSES JOIN THESE GLO's AND BECOME THE DEVILS' FALSE APOSTLES. EVERYWHERE I

TURN, GREEK CHRISTIANS ARE PROFESSING TO BE ORDAINED MINISTERS. GOD WILL SAY TO THEM ON JUDGMENT DAY, **I NEVER KNEW YOU**.

ALL OF THESE SCRIPTURES, IN CONTEXT, CLEARLY SHOW THAT GLO's ARE SCRIPTURALLY UNACCEPTABLE. THE MEMBERS ARE DECEIVED, LIED TO, AND BRAINWASHED INTO BELIEVING THEY ARE FOUNDED UPON CHRISTIAN PRINCIPLES. I HAVE ONE QUESTION FOR GLO's. WHY NOT CLAIM THE PRINCIPLES AND DOCTRINES OF ISLAM, MORMONISM, CATHOLICISM, HINDUISM, BUDDHISM, etc.? BESIDES, ALL GLO's USE THE DOCTRINES OF THESE RELIGIONS IN SOME WAY.

Notes

CHAPTER 4
PART 3

THEOLOGICAL CONTRAST AND COMPARISON

As I have mentioned before, GLO's (Greek-lettered organizations) use the Bible **sparingly and craftily** in efforts to justify their existence. GLO's **PURPOSELY exclude or deny, suppress or hide**, and obviously **twist** the **fundamental doctrines** of **Christianity,** and deny the **DEITY of JESUS**. The fundamental doctrines being THE LIFE, DEATH, BURIAL, AND RESURRECTION OF JESUS CHRIST and all the true saints, REPENTANCE FROM DEAD WORKS, JUSTIFICATION BY FAITH, THE DOCTRINE OF ETERNAL JUDGMENT. WHY CLAIM CHRISTIAN PRINCIPLES AND A BIBLICAL FOUNDATION WHEN THEY ARE SO SUPERFICIAL AND SO IMPROPERLY MISUSED? BECAUSE THE DEVIL HATES CHRISTIANS, AND WILL DO EVERYTHING HE CAN TO DECEIVE THEM.

THIS SECTION SHOWS **WHAT GLO's REALY BELIEVE, HOW THEY ACT ON WHAT THEY BELIEVE** (i.e. how the devil uses them), AND **HOW THE WORD OF GOD COMPLETELY UNMASKS THEM.**

YOU SEE RAT POISON IS 2% POISON, AND 98% FOOD. THE RATS ARE DECEIVED, BECAUSE TO THEM IT'S FOOD. LATER MOST ARE DEAD, BUT SOME RATS DON'T CONSUME ENOUGH POISON AT ONE TIME TO DIE, AND BECOME IMMUNE TO THE POISON. THE MORE **POISON (DECEPTION)** ONE CAN CONSUME WITHOUT DYING, THE MORE IMMUNE ONE BECOMES TO THE WORD OF GOD. SOME CAN AND HAVE LITERALLY BECOME IMMUNE TO BOTH THE DECEPTION OF THE DEVIL, AND THE TRUE FOOD WHICH IS THE WORD OF GOD. THE

COMING APART AT THE SEAMS

WORD OF GOD HAS LITTLE OR NO EFFECT BECAUSE THE DECEPTION IS SO GREAT, AND THE CHRISTIAN ENDS UP ON A DOWNWARD SPIRAL TO DESTRUCTION WITHOUT EVEN KNOWING IT.

II CORINTHIANS 4:4(amp) For the god of this world has blinded the unbelievers' minds [that they should not discern the truth], preventing them from seeing the illuminating light of the Gospel of the glory of Christ (the Messiah), Who is the image and Likeness of God.

YOU END UP NOT JUST BELIEVING LIES BUT EXCHANGING THE LIES OF SATAN WITH THE KNOWN TRUTHS OF GOD.

ROMANS 1:25 Because they exchanged the truth of God for a lie and worshipped and served the creature rather than the Creator, Who is blessed forever! Amen (so be it).

THE GLO's, UNDER SATAN'S INFLUENCE, ARE **DECEPTIVE "TRUTH" GIVERS** WITH GREAT SUCCESS.

II CORINTHIANS 11:13-15(amp) For such men are false apostles [spurious, counterfeits], deceitful workmen, masquerading as apostles (special messengers) of Christ (the Messiah). And it is no wonder, for Satan himself masquerades as an angel of light. So it is not surprising if his servants also masquerade as ministers of righteousness. (But) **their end will correspond with their deeds.**

THIS IS HOW SATAN DECEIVES THROUGH GLO's. THE PUBLIC, PLEDGES, AND MEMBERS HAVE BEEN

SUCKED INTO A COMFORT ZONE OF **DISINFORMATION. GLO's SPEAK LIES THROUGH HYPOCRISY. SOME GREEK CHRISTIANS BECOME DISSATISFIED WITH THE SUNDAY ROUTINE, AND READING THE WORD BECOMES BORING.** THESE ORGANIZATIONS, WHILE GIVING US ENTERTAINMENT AND FELLOWSHIP, BOMBARD US WITH SO MUCH MIXTURE OF TRUE AND FALSE. A CHRISTIAN JUST GIVES UP TRYING TO FIGURE THE LIES FROM THE TRUTH. THE PLEDGE OR GREEK CHRISTIAN ENDS UP BEING CONFUSED AND DISINFORMED, BUT SATISFIED WITH THE HYPE AND SOCIAL ASPECTS OF THE GLO. THE CONFUSED CHRISTIAN BECOMES OVERWHELMED AND CAN'T HANDLE THE DEVIL'S SPIRITUAL ONSLAUGHT. THE SOCIAL PART IS WHAT BECOMES EASILY ACCEPTABLE. THE ONCE TRUE CHRISTIAN EVENTUALLY GIVES IN AND BECOMES A **TRUE GREEK.** WHEN A TRUE CHRISTIAN CAN BE PERSUADED TO SUBMIT TO PHYSICAL BRUTALITY, (Hazing is not loving your neighbor) OR TO SING **PRAISES** TO SIGMA GAMMA RHO/ALPHA KAPPA ALPHA/OMEGA PSI PHI; **THIS IS IDOLATRY.** FOR THE SAKE OF BROTHERHOOD AND/OR SISTERHOOD, YOUR COMMON SENSE AND SALVATION HAS BEEN ABANDONED. THIS ABANDONMENT DID NOT HAPPEN OVERNIGHT. IT WAS A PLANNED DECISION. God's Word says to **flee idolatry (I JOHN 5:21),** and to **love your neighbor as yourself (LUKE 10:27-28).** SALVATION IS NOT SELF-ABASEMENT TO PEOPLE. IT IS **SELF-HUMILITY TO GOD** RESULTING IN GODLY EXALTATION **AT THE VERY MOMENT ONE REPENTS.** PLEDGING AND/OR INTAKE IS A **PROCESS** OF "BEING" **HUMILIATED, INTIMIDATED, AND DEBASED** AT YOUR EXPENSE. HUMILITY TO GOD IS NOT HUMILIATION BY GOD. **TRUE HUMILITY DELIVERS, BUT BEING HUMILIATED IS BONDAGE. LET ME** CONTRAST PLEDGING AND INTAKE TO SLAVERY. PLEDGING IS **VOLUNTARY** ENSLAVEMENT OF ONE PHYSICALLY, MENTALLY AND SPIRITUALLY. BUT SLAVERY IS DONE BY FORCE (i.e. IT'S **INVOLUNTARY).** AFTER PLEDGING, YOU RECEIVE MANLY EXALTATION (A MEASLY TWO OR THREE GREEK LETTERS), BUT **NOTHING ETERNALLY** IN YOUR FAVOR. A SLAVE CAN GO TO HEAVEN.

MATTHEW 23:12 And whosoever shall **exalt himself** shall **be abased;** and he that shall **humble himself** shall **be exalted.**

LUKE 4:5-6 And the devil, taking him up into an high mountain, shewed unto him all the kingdoms of the world in a moment of time. And the devil said unto him, all these powers will I give thee, and the glory of them: for that is delivered unto me; and to whomever I will I give it.

EXALTATION CAN ONLY COME FROM GOD. MAN, THE DEVIL, OR ONESELF CANNOT EXALT ANYONE OR THEMSELVES.

IN CHRIST, YOU ARE A SLAVE TO RIGHTEOUSNESS AND FREE FROM SIN. IN A GLO, YOU ARE A SLAVE TO SIN, SEPARATED AND FREE FROM RIGHTEOUSNESS.

ROMANS 6:6-23 Knowing this, that our old man is crucified with him, that the body of sin might be destroyed, that henceforth we shall not serve sin. For he that is dead is freed from sin. Now if we be dead with Christ, we believe that we shall also live with him: Knowing that Christ be raised from death dieth no more; death hath no more dominion over him. For in that he died, he died unto sin once: but in that he liveth unto God. Likewise reckon ye also yourselves to be dead indeed unto sin, but alive unto God through Jesus Christ our Lord. **Let not sin** therefore **reign** in your mortal body, that ye should obey it in the lusts thereof. **Neither yield ye**

your members as instruments of unrighteousness unto sin: but **yield yourselves unto God** as those that are alive from the dead, and your members as instruments of righteousness unto God. For sin shall not have dominion over you: for ye are not under the law, but under grace. What then? shall we sin, because we are not under the law, but under grace? God forbid. **Know ye not, that to whom ye yield yourselves servants to obey, his servants ye are to whom ye obey: whether of sin unto death, or of obedience to righteousness.** But God be thanked, that ye were servants of sin, but ye have obeyed from the heart that form of doctrine which was delivered you. Being then made free from sin, ye became the servant of righteousness. I speak after the manner of men because of infirmity of your flesh: for as ye have yielded your members servants to uncleanness and to iniquity; even so now yield your members servants to righteousness unto holiness. For when ye were the **servants of sin**, ye were **free from righteousness**. What fruit had ye then in those things whereof ye are now ashamed? for the end of those things is death. But now being made **free from sin**, and **become servants to God**, ye have your fruit unto holiness, and the end everlasting life. For the wages of sin is death; But the gift of God is eternal life through Jesus Christ our Lord.

I BELIEVE THAT ONE'S ABILITY TO PERCEIVE THE TRUTH IS LOST OR GREATLY HINDERED WHEN THEY ACCEPT SPIRITUAL BONDAGE AND SIN IN THEIR LIVES AND THE LIVES OF OTHERS. FOR WHAT REASON WOULD YOU ALLOW SOMEONE TO BEAT YOU OR TO DICTATE ANTICHRIST DOCTRINE TO YOU? IT'S DONE FOR THE SAKE OF MEMBERSHIP IN THAT GROUP. ANY INDIVIDUAL'S BODY, MIND, OR SPIRIT THAT IS VOLUNTARILY SUBMITTED TO ABUSE, BUILDS A CALLOUS ON THE AREA THAT IS BEATEN REPEATEDLY. THE HEART/CONSCIENCE BUILDS A CALLOUS EVERY TIME IT HEARS THE CALL FROM JESUS AND REFUSES. SO THICK IS THE CALLOUS, THAT A LIFE THREATINING INCIDENT MAY CAUSE ONE TO BLASPHEME GOD INSTEAD OF PRAY AND CALL ON HIS HOLY NAME. A CLEAR EXAMPLE IS THE HARDENING OF PHARAOH'S HEART. EVEN AFTER THE DEATH OF HIS FIRSTBORN SON, HE PURSUED THE CHILDREN OF ISRAEL. A CALLOUS HEART IS ONE THAT REPEATEDLY DISOBEYS GOD. AS LONG AS YOU REMAIN IN OR HAVE A DESIRE TO JOIN A GLO, THE CALLOUS ON YOUR HEART WILL CONTINUE TO GROW EACH TIME YOU HEAR IT'S WRONG AND DO NOT DENOUNCE. THE POISON THAT IS DECEPTION **APPEARS** TO HAVE NO EFFECT ON YOU, **BUT** LET ME SAY THAT, "THE WAGES OF SIN IS DEATH"(**ROMANS 6:23a**). DON'T GROW COLD TO CHRIST WHO IS YOUR **ONLY** WAY TO SALVATION (**JOHN 14:6**), AND THE ONLY SOURCE OF TRUTH (**JOHN 8:32**). "BUT THE GIFT OF GOD IS ETERNAL LIFE THROUGH JESUS CHRIST OUR LORD."(**ROMANS 6:23b**.) YOUR TIME OF DECISION FACES YOU **NOW** TO BREAK THE STRONGHOLDS AND DESTROY THE YOKES. WILL IT BE JESUS AND THE UNCOMPROMISED WORD OF GOD, OR THE GLO's WHO **PERVERT** THE WORD OF GOD WITH THEIR VENOMOUS TEACHINGS? GLO's TRULY HAVE SOME MEMBERS THAT ARE A BROOD OF VIPERS (i.e. those angels of light and false apostles). THEY'RE JUST READY FOR THE NEXT CHRISTIAN TO COME ALONG AND CHALLENGE THEM. CHRISTIAN MAN OR WOMAN!! YOU NEED TO BE READY, BUT DON'T WORRY, THIS BOOK WILL PREPARE YOU, AND YOU ALREADY HAVE THE WORD OF GOD.

I WANT YOU TO READ WHAT GLO's REALLY BELIEVE

FREDERIC L. HATCHETT

(THEIR THEOLOGY)!!

IN THIS SECTION, AS WELL AS OTHER PARTS IN THE BOOK, I MAY NOT MAKE DIRECT MENTION OF A GLO, BUT THERE IS NOT ONE GLO THAT IS EXCLUDED FROM ALL OF THE POINTS TO BE MADE BELOW.

THE DOCTRINES OR TEACHINGS OF THESE GROUPS ARE JUSTIFICATON BY **WORKS,** THE LIFE, DEATH, BURIAL, RESURRECTION, <u>PRAYERS OF THE DEAD</u>, AND ASCENSION OF THEIR DEAD BROTHERS AND SISTERS INTO SOME PARADISE THAT IS USUALLY CALLED, "OMEGA CHAPTER", "HAVEN OF REST, OR SOME "HEAVENLY CHAPTER" SET ASIDE FOR THEM AND THEIR BROTHERS OR SISTERS. **WITH ALL THE INFORMATION GATHERED SO FAR, I HAVE NOT ENCOUNTERED ONE BIT THAT IMPLIES A BROTHER OR SISTER BEING SUBJECT TO JUDGMENT AND GOING TO HELL FOR NOT KNOWING JESUS.** THE BURIAL CEREMONIES IN THE RITUAL ONLY MENTION A HEAVENLY GAIN FOR ALL BROTHERS OR SISTERS. THERE IS NOT EVEN A HINT OF A SAVING FAITH **WITH CHRIST, THUS PUTTING HIS WORK ON THE CROSS TO SHAME.** THIS SAYS THAT THEIR WORKS FOR THEIR GLO's ARE GOOD ENOUGH FOR GOD'S ACCEPTANCE. **BY WHOSE STANDARDS IS A GLO WORTHY?** DEFINITELY NOT GOD'S!! **INSTEAD IT'S THEIR OWN.** PLEDGING AND BRAINWASHING ARE THE **RAT POISON (DECEPTION)** OF THESE GROUPS. THEIR FOOD IS THE BIBLE, BUT IT IS USED DECEPTIVELY AND PERVERSELY. ONE IS **FORCED** TO LEARN THEIR HUMAN WISDOM THROUGH SONGS, POEMS, AND OTHER MEN'S PHILOSOPHIES ABOUT LIFE, OR FACE OPPOSITION AND OSTRACIZATION BY THEIR OWN MEMBERS. THIS IS ONE FORM OF BONDAGE. <u>IF YOU DON'T LEARN YOU MAY GET YOUR SHIRT RIPPED, BEAT UP, PADDLED OR FEAR WEARING WHAT YOU FOOLISHLY GOT BEAT FOR IN THE FIRST PLACE. THAT'S RIGHT! IF YOU DON'T KNOW THE SECRETS, ALL THAT PARAPHRENELIA YOU EARNED AND PAID FOR IS UNSAFE TO DISPLAY. IF YOU DIDN'T PLEDGE, EXPECT TO BE TAUGHT NOTHING BY YOUR SO-CALLED BROTHERS.</u> BUT IF YOU LEARN THE KNOWLEDGE WELL, YOU MAY HAVE THE JOY OF RIPPING SOMEONE ELSE'S SHIRT! THIS IS WHY I CALLED

COMING APART AT THE SEAMS

THESE GROUPS CONTRADICTORS OF THE WORD OF GOD. THEY ARE TRUE HYPOCRITES. WHY SHOULD ONE WORRY ABOUT THEIR OWN BROTHERS OR SISTERS BEATING THEM UP OR TAKING ANYTHING FROM THEM? **THEIR EXCUSE IS, "DON'T YOUR OWN BROTHERS AND SISTERS FIGHT OR BEAT YOUR TAIL TO LEARN A LESSON."** THIS MAY OCCUR, BUT IT DOESN'T MAKE IT RIGHT. THE PARENTS ARE THE **ONLY** ONES WHO SHOULD ADMINISTER DISCIPLINE IN THE HOUSEHOLD UNLESS THEY GRANT THAT AUTHORITY TO ANOTHER. THIS IS A POOR EXCUSE FOR HAZING, PRE OR POST-INITIATION. THEY ALSO CONDONE ONE ANOTHER TO FIGHT WHEN A BROTHER IS NOT UP TO PAR ON HIS HISTORY, POEMS, OR OTHER RELEVANT KNOWLEDGE TO THE GLO. I SAW TWO GREEK BROTHERS COME CLOSE TO BLOWS, BECAUSE THE OTHER DID NOT KNOW WHO THE ACTIVE PRESIDENT OF THEIR FRATERNITY WAS AT THAT TIME. I KNEW A MAN WHO WAS TAKEN INTO THE WOODS AND GOT HIS SHIRT RIPPED FOR APPARENTLY NOT KNOWING THE ANSWER TO A QUESTION. AS IT TURNED OUT, THE MAN WAS RIGHT, VERY MAD AND STARTED LOOKING FOR HIS CHAPTER BROTHERS TO FIGHT. IT'S A SHAME, BROTHERS FIGHTING BROTHERS. WHERE'S THE UNITY THEY PROFESS? IT'S ALL A FRONT.

What GLO's do is they **1.)** Get your allegiance to their doctrinal system which **demands total obedience** in the face of any abuse (i.e. you do not tell what happens while pledging, even if you get your tooth knocked out or bones broken), **2.) Demand an oath of secrecy**, **3.)** They claim to **grant eternal life** for dedicated service, and **4.)** Require a belief in **a god or Supreme Being of your choice** before or after pledging. Even to the ones who know about hazing, all of these characteristics make GLO's very appealing. But just wait for that butt kicking and/or mental humiliation they never tell you the truth about. This hazing sometimes occurs **after** you become a brother. If your pledge process is not suitable to the Big Brothers, the abuse continues and you are not considered a "legit" brother or sister until they say so. That is why the Bible is a necessary tool for exposing these hypocrites. By their **practices and doctrines**, these groups can be classified as a **religion, but are they Christlike? NO!**

JAMES 1:26-27 If any man among you **seems** to be **religious**, and bridleth not his tongue, but deceiveth his own heart, this man's religion **is in vain. Pure religion and undefiled** before God and the Father is this, to visit the fatherless and widows in their affliction, **and to keep himself unspotted from the world.**

THE SCRIPTURE IS STATING A CLEAR FACT THAT THE THINGS A PERSON SAYS ARE CONNECTED TO THE REALITY OF WHO THEY ARE. GOSSIPING, USING PROFANITY, LYING, OR A PERSON WHO SAYS OR DOES JUST ABOUT ANYTHING, AND LIVES WITHOUT RESTRAINT HAS A VAIN, UNREAL, AND DECEPTIVE RELIGION (i.e. his religious practices are useless). WHEN JESUS RETURNS HE MUST FIND YOU WITHOUT SPOT OR WRINKLE. IF YOU ARE OF THE WORLD (**I JOHN 2:15**), LIKE GLO's, YOUR OUTCOME IS A SAD ONE. GOD WILL NOT TAKE THOSE WHO LOVE THE WORLD OUT OF THE WORLD. WHY SHOULD HE? THEY ARE NOT LOOKING FOR HIS GLORIOUS APPEARING, AND THEY DON'T WANT TO REALLY LEAVE ANYWAY. FAITH OBEYS THE WORD OF GOD. YOU CAN'T SAY IN ONE BREATH, "I LOVE GOD" AND FORNICATE, PARTY, OR HAZE SOMEONE WITH YOUR NEXT BREATH. THE "GREEK CHRISTIAN" SAYS THAT THEY DO NOT PARTICIPATE IN HAZING, BUT THEY **KNOW** IT OCCURS. **CALL NATIONALS AND REPORT IT! FAT CHANCE THOUGH!** YOU'RE TO AFRAID OF WHAT YOUR OWN SISTERS OR BROTHERS MAY DO, INSTEAD OF THE WELFARE OF ANOTHER HUMAN BEING. IN JAMES 4:17, GOD COMMANDS US TO DO GOOD, AND IF WE DO NOT, IT IS SIN TO US. IF THAT PERSON DIES, YOU ARE ACCOUNTABLE. TAKE A STAND FOR THAT WHICH YOU KNOW IS WRONG. IF YOU DON'T TAKE A STAND, YOU ARE A HYPOCRITE. **HYPOCRITES GO TO HELL.**

MATTHEW 23:13-16 But **woe unto you**, scribes and Pharisees, **hypocrites**! for

COMING APART AT THE SEAMS

ye shut up the kingdom of heaven against men: for **ye neither go in yourselves**, neither suffer ye them that are entering to go in. Woe unto you, scribes and Pharisees, **hypocrites**! for ye devour widows' houses, and for a pretence make long prayer: therefore ye shall receive greater damnation. Woe unto you, scribes and Pharisees, **hypocrites**! for ye compass sea and land to make one proselyte, and when he is made, ye make him twofold more the child of hell than yourselves. Woe unto you, ye blind guides, which say, Whosoever shall swear by the temple, it is nothing: but whosoever shall swear by the gold of the temple, he is a debtor!

GLO's ARE NOT CHRISTLIKE. GREEK CHRISTIANS!! IT'S TIME TO REPENT AND DENOUNCE. YOU MUST EVEN REPENT OF THE DESIRE FOR OR AGREEMENT WITH GLO's (Greek-lettered organizations).

They claim brotherhood / sisterhood and **eternal bonds knowing or** not knowing that these traits **exist in Christ ONLY.** GLO's DO NOT BELIEVE IN FRATERNAL OR "SORORAL" DEATH OR DISSOLUTION OF THESE BONDS AFTER DEATH. THIS IS **NOT CHRISTLIKE** CONCERNING RELATIONSHIPS AMONGST GLO's. AN EXCERPT FROM THE RITUAL OMEGA PSI PHI STATES,

"REALIZING THAT THERE IS **NO FRATERNAL DEATH.**" (OMEGA PSI PHI FRATERNITY (Incorporated 1914), THE RITUAL, 1970, p. 24.)

THIS IS ONLY TRUE WITH CHRISTIAN RELATIONSHIPS. ONLY TRUE CHRISTIANS ARE RAISED TO LIFE AND REMAIN BROTHERS AND SISTERS FOR ETERNITY.

MATTHEW 12:50 For whosoever shall **do the will of my Father** which is in heaven, the same is my brother, and sister, and mother. These words **Jesus said Himself.**

LUKE 8:21 And he answered and said unto them, My mother and my brethren are these which **hear** the word of God **and do it.**

These scriptures clearly state that only the truly saved can be brothers and sisters. Blood relationships (physical) are worthless if they are not in Christ (spiritual).

This spiritual relationship between saved people is their relationship they have with The Father THROUGH JESUS CHRIST, and the desire to do the will of the Father, **not the will of some ungodly organization.** The Bible says if man props something up it cannot have any worth, except it is JESUS. GLO's prop up **their** ideas of scholarship, fidelity, integrity, uplift, etc. **THEY DO NOT LIFT UP JESUS.** Therefore, outside of a believing relationship in Christ, no PURPOSEFUL bonds of brotherhood and sisterhood can exist. Even flesh and blood relations have no benefits unless they are saved. A flesh and blood relationship does not grant one salvation. There is no salvation in any other except Jesus.

ACTS 4:12 And there is salvation in and through no one else, for there is no other name under heaven given among men by and which we must be saved.

COMING APART AT THE SEAMS

Your brother, sister, mother, or father can't save you or each other, nor can anyone save himself or herself. The whole concept of brotherhood and sisterhood by oath or group affiliation in the Greek system is a misconception, false teaching, and false belief (**A LIE**). "Greek Christians" you are living a lie. Actually, these organizations are directly contradicting (blaspheming) the Word of God. They are defining brotherhood and sisterhood **in their own way**, not the way God established it from before the foundations of the earth. The spirit of deception, or that, which disables you from receiving revelation from God, is in operation in your life. Although the principle of brotherhood and sisterhood is plain to see in the Bible, the devil uses deception to keep people spiritually blind (i.e. one gets no revelation of what they have seen or heard.)

To claim the belief of brotherhood and sisterhood in any other name is vain, rebellious and ungodly. The people who profess to be Christians and don't leave GLO's are in rebellion against God's Word and hell-bound.

I SAMUEL 15:23 For rebellion is as the sin of witchcraft, and stubborness is as iniquity and idolatry. because thou hast rejected the word of the Lord, he hath also rejected thee from being king.

The prayers of the dead are another common theology OF GLO's.

"In the celestial chapter to which they belong, all our erstwhile brothers send forth their hosannas. Their prayers are with us." (OMEGA PSI PHI FRATERNITY (Incorporated 1914), THE RITUAL, 1970, p. 33)

I am pleased to tell you that scripture does not support this "doctrine". There is only **one** example of a dead person praying. You need at least 2 or 3 witnesses to confirm any doctrine. His prayer was not answered. It was to NO avail. It is Luke 16. Notice his location and condition. **There is no definitive scripture that says dead saints pray.**

You have already seen and will see why later that those in GLO's are not fit for the kingdom of God.

Have you ever considered asking yourselves these questions (**Christians especially**)? What does the **Bible** say about these types of organizations? What is the **origin**? Why do they do the things they do? Are you more of a person because you belong to one of these groups? Would **denouncing** them in the name of JESUS make you less of a person?? If HE is ALL you need and Jesus is, Why be a Greek, mason, etc.? As you will see, the Bible has many scriptures to support claims why Christians should not pledge. Here is one quick example. This Old Testament scripture condemns the practices of the **occult**. Look up the word in a dictionary. You will find a striking similarity between the definition, and the characteristics of GLO's. The Bible condemns the practices of the occult.

DEUTERONOMY 18:9-12 When thou art come into the land which the Lord thy God giveth thee, **thou shalt not learn to do after the abominations** of those nations. There shall not be found among you any one that maketh his son or his daughter pass through the fire, or that useth divination, or an observer of times, or an enchanter, or a witch, or a charmer, or a consulter with familiar spirits, or a wizard, or a necromancer. For all that do these things are an abomination unto the Lord: and because the Lord thy God doth drive them out from before thee.

When rituals are being performed, a deity is being called upon. If it's not the God of Abraham, Isaac, and Jacob, then it's an abomination. GLO's practice the occult. You have God's warning. Initiation rites and death rites that are practiced by GLO's are based on ancient occult practices handed down through time. It's nothing but impure hand-me-down tradition. It's of the devil, and GLO's are doing it.

As a Christian, one must consider their ways, because you never know when death will come to take you. GLO's **deceitfully** hide behind benevolence and good works fooling many into thinking that doing good is a substitute for Biblical salvation. Yet, their rituals say much to the contrary. GLO (Greek-lettered organization) death rites of passage or funeral rituals speak of some **fake heavenly location (omega chapter, ouranos, Haven of Rest, or omega omega chapter)** their dead brothers or sisters enter after death; their literature **NEVER** speaks of a relationship with CHRIST as THE NECESSITY for salvation. Much of what they say **sounds good**, but **it's not good**. For the sinner, in or out of a GLO you are condemned. GLO's craftly misuse scripture by reasoning it based on human wisdom alone; but look at what God's word says.

ISAIAH 55:8-9 For my thoughts are not your thoughts, neither are your ways my ways, saith the Lord. For as the heavens are higher than the earth, so are my ways higher than your ways, and my thoughts than your thoughts.

Not consulting God's Word is self-exaltation and the beginning of heresy. You claim to have the answer to the problem without the solution. God says come let us reason together in **ISAIAH 1:18**. Christian witnesses and uninformed readers must pay close attention to your reasoning. Purposely leaving out Jesus and God's Word at **the root** of an organization is suicidal, insane and sinful. **GLO's DO THIS!!!!!**

His ways are not the ways of GLO's, Masonic Orders, Hare Krishna, Jehovah's Witnesses or any other evil ways that have been concocted by man. Jesus will never and has never placed His blessings upon evil.

DELIBERATELY INTERPRETING SCRIPTURES ACCORDING TO HUMAN STANDARDS IS ANOTHER PLOT BY FRATERNAL ORDERS **TO** ENGRAFT OR INCLUDE CHRISTIANITY AS A DECEPTIVE SMOKE SCREEN. IT GIVES A FEEL GOOD RELIGIOUS APPEAL THAT **COMFORTS** THE **POTENTIAL MEMBERS** AND **KEEPS** THE **PRESENT MEMBERS** FROM LEAVING. UNFORTUNATELY, SOME "CHRISTIAN" FRATERNITIES AND SORORITIES ARE ENGRAFTING SIMILAR EVIL PRACTICES INTO THEIR ORGANIZATIONS. I EVEN KNOW A FRATERNITY THAT USES SCRIPTURE TO JUSTIFY PHYSICAL HAZING.

II TIMOTHY 2:3 says, Thou therefore endure hardness, as a good soldier **of Jesus Christ;**

NOT kappa, delta, omega, etc.

COMING APART AT THE SEAMS

UPON EXAMINING THE RITUAL OF OMEGA PSI PHI FRATERNITY, THEY PURPOSELY LEAVE OUT "OF JESUS CHRIST", AND IT BECOMES CLEAR THAT THEY BE GOOD SOLDIERS "OF OMEGA".

"The Neophyte Commandant shall make the following statement: "Friend, the Apostle Paul said to the young man he was training, Timothy, 'endure hardness as a good soldier'." Then it goes on to say, "Every **Son of Omega** shall be courageous." (OMEGA PSI PHI FRATERNITY (Incorporated 1914), THE RITUAL, 1970, p. 18-19.)

The real scripture, **II TIMOTHY 2:3**, reads as follows, Thou therefore endure hardness as a good soldier **of Jesus Christ**.

Why Omega Psi Phi? Why did you leave out Jesus' name? HYPOCRITES!! That's what your organization is, and always will be. Call me **(919/829-3513)** or e-mail me at (**reprebres@cs.com**) writing me a letter explaining a foundation on Christian principles. And leave out the name of JESUS, because GLO's do anyway. Please don't make yourselves look any more foolish. I will insert your letter in a book revision.

PROVERBS 30:5-6 Every word of God is pure: he is a shield unto them that put their trust in him. **Add not thou unto his words,** lest he reprove thee, and **thou be found a liar.**

MATTHEW 10:33 But whosoever shall deny me before men, him will I also deny before my Father which is in heaven.

May I remind all Omegas and those in other GLO's that Matthew 10:33 are Jesus' personal words. Read verse 32 to get a better understanding of verse 33.

THIS IS A BLATANT DENIAL OF JESUS. YET, OMEGA'S BOAST PROUDLY THAT ITS FIRST RITUAL WAS THE BIBLE, AND THAT ONE OF THE FOUNDERS WAS A BISHOP. YET, THEY HAVE DENIED THE ONE WHO DIED FOR ALL THAT ALL CAN BE SAVED. THIS SPIRIT OF DECEPTION MAKES IT EASY TO SEE HOW THEY GET THEIR PLEDGES TO BELIEVE THAT DOING STUPID THINGS WILL PREPARE THEM FOR THE FUTURE. SINCE PHYSICAL HARDSHIP IS IN THE BIBLE OR BECAUSE IT HAS BEEN A PART OF HISTORY, THE PLEDGES AND MEMBERS BELIEVE IT MUST BE OKAY. STILL, OMEGA PSI PHI NEVER FULLY REVEALS OR EXPLAINS II TIMOTHY 2:3 IN ITS CONTEXT (i.e. **IT APPLIES TO SAVED PEOPLE ONLY**). BECAUSE SOMETHING OCCURS IN THE BIBLE, DOES NOT MEAN GOD CONDONES IT. WHETHER ONE ASKS, FORCES, OR THREATENS ONE TO DO SOMETHING FOOLISH; REMEMBER THAT THEY ARE JUST AS FOOLISH TO ASK, AS YOU ARE TO DO. THEY MAKE PHYSICAL ABUSE FOR THEIR ORGANIZATIONS APPEAR TO BE RIGHTEUOS PERSECUTION. CHRISTIAN'S MUST REMEMBER; IT'S IN WHO'S NAME YOU SUFFERING FOR THAT'S IMPORTANT. WILLFULLY ALLOWING ABUSE TO BE DONE TO YOUR BODY IS DEFILING THE TEMPLE GOD. YET, SUFFERING FOR RIGHTEOUSNESS SAKE, THIS IS WELL-PLEASING TO GOD MAKING IT WORTHY OF REWARD.

I PETER 3:13-14 And who is he that will harm you, if ye be followers of that which is good? But and if ye **suffer for righteousness' sake, happy are ye**: and be not afraid of the terror, neither be troubled;

I PETER 4:12-19 Beloved, think it not strange concerning the fiery trial which is to try you, as though some strange thing happened unto you: But rejoice, inasmuch as ye are **partakers of Christ's sufferings**; that, when his glory shall be revealed, ye may be glad also with exceeding joy. **If ye be reproached for**

the name of Christ, happy are ye; for the spirit of glory and of God resteth upon you: on their part he is evil spoken of, but on your part he is glorified. But **let none** of you **suffer as a murderer**, or as a **thief**, or as an **evildoer, or** as **a busybody** in other men's matters. **Yet, if any man suffer as a Christian, let him not be ashamed**; but let him glorify God on this behalf. For the time is come that judgment must begin at the house of God: and if it first begin at us, what shall the end be of them that obey not the gospel of God? and **if the righteous scarcely be saved**, where shall the ungodly and sinner appear? Wherefore let them that suffer according to the will of God commit the keeping of their souls to him in well doing, as unto a faithful Creator.

RIGHTEOUS PERSECUTION AND SUFFERING ARE NOT TO BE BROUGHT ON BY VOLUNTEERING YOURSELF WITHOUT CAUSE (i.e. DON'T STEAL TO SUFFER PERSECUTION). RATHER SUFFER PERSECUTION BY WITNESSING CHRIST IN PUBLIC SCHOOL DURING RECESS OR LUNCH, OR WRITE A BOOK DECRYING ABORTION OR EVOLUTION. SUFFERING FOR RIGHTEUOSNESS SAKE IS THE RESULT OF WHO CHRIST IS, NOT WHO YOU ARE!!! BEING A, **"SON OF FIRE AND BRIMSTONE"**, WHICH IS AN UPPER LEVEL MEMBER OF **PHI BETA SIGMA** IS THE WRONG NAME TO SUFFER FOR. CHRISTIANS WHO ALLOW THEMSELVES TO BE HAZED IS JUST PLAIN STUPID AND RECKLESS STEWARDSHIP OVER THEIR SPIRIT'S, MIND'S, AND BODIES' WHICH ARE GOD'S. DO NOT CONFUSE EVENTS (FACTS OR OPINIONS) WITH TRUTH. TRUTH IS ETERNAL AND ABSOLUTE WHILE FACTS ARE DISCOVERED. FACTS, UNLIKE OPINIONS, ARE VERIFIABLE. A FACT IS OR **BECOMES** A RESULT OF TRUTH OR IT IS VERIFIED BY TRUTH (e.g. **ROMANS**

6:23). DANIEL, FOR **PRAYING DAILY (FACT)**, WAS PUT IN THE LION'S DEN **(FACT)**. SHADRACH, MESHACH, AND ABEDNEGO WERE THROWN INTO THE FIERY FURNACE **(FACT)** FOR **NOT BOWING DOWN TO OTHER gods (FACT)**. **THE TRUTH IS EXODUS 20:3, AND THE FACT WAS THEIR OBEDIENCE.** JESUS WAS PUT ON THE CROSS **(FACT VERIFIED BY TRUTH)** FOR "BLASPHEMY", BECAUSE HE WAS A MAN CLAIMING TO BE GOD **(TRUTH VERIFIES THE FACT)**. THE APOSTLES WENT THROUGH TRIALS BECAUSE THEY KNEW, DID AND SAID THINGS BASED ON **THE TRUTH** WHICH WAS THE REASON FOR THEIR OBEDIENCE TO GOD. **THE FACTS ARE** WHAT THEY DID AND WHAT HAPPENED TO THEM. MOSTLY IMPORTANTLY, IF THE PUBLIC, THE PLEDGES OR MEMBERS HAVE **HEARD** OR **KNOW THE TRUTH, JESUS,** AND COULD SEE INSIDE THE SECRECY AND RESEARCH IT, ATLEAST THEY COULD MAKE A QUALITY DECISION ABOUT JOINING OR DENOUNCING. THEN WITH **ALL THE FACTS (i.e. WHAT THEY HAVE READ, HEARD OR SEEN)** CAN NOW BE BASED ON **THE TRUTH** OF THE WORD OF GOD. WITH ALL THE REVELATION SO FAR, HOW COULD A PERSON STILL WANT TO BE A GREEK CHRISTIAN? THROUGH OTHERS AND MYSELF THEY CERTAINLY CAN GET THE INFORMATION THEY NEED. **I PLAN TO TELL ALL I HAVE RECEIVED FROM THE HOLY SPIRIT, EXPERIENCED, HEARD, AND SEEN, AS A SINNER AND NOW BORN-AGAIN CHRISTIAN,** ABOUT EVERY GREEK-LETTERED ORGANIZATION, **BASED ON THE BIBLE.** THIS INCLUDES THEIR SECRETS, WHICH ARE THEIR BLOODLINE. **I DO KNOW THAT IT'S USELESS TO EXPOSE THEIR SECRETS WITHOUT COMPARING THEM TO THE WORD OF GOD.** I DO NOT CONDONE EXPOSING SECRECY WITHOUT BIBLICAL EXPLANATION. TO DO THIS IS TO ACT IN PRIDE AND FROM AN EVIL MOTIVE. THOUGH IT IS TEMPTING, TRUE CHRISTIANS SHOULD NOT DO IT. APPROXIMATELY 150 YEARS AGO, MASONS WERE NOT EVEN ALLOWED TO BE MEMBERS IN THE CHURCH. SOME WERE EVEN BURNED TO DEATH, AND THIS I DO NOT CONDONE. SO MASONS HAD TO MAKE SOME EXTERNAL **(RELIGIOUS)** CHANGES TO GAIN ACCCEPTANCE OF THE CHURCHES, ALONG WITH COMPROMISE (ESPECIALLY CHURCH LEADERSHIP) OF COURSE. MEANWHILE, THEY REMAINED THE SAME INTERNALLY **(OCCULTIC)**. A GREEK CHRISTIAN OR

MASON'S COMMON RESPONSE TO THE QUESTION PERTAINING TO THE BELIEFS OF THE GROUP IS, "IT IS BASED ON THE BIBLE, AND WE ARE FOUNDED ON CHRISTIAN PRINCIPLES." THEY OFFER THIS ANSWER OF COURSE WITHOUT ANY BIBLICAL PROOF TO THE POTENTIAL MEMBER. SECRET GROUPS ALSO **WILLFULLY WITHHOLD** THIS INFORMATION AND **TEACH THEIR (NEW) MEMBERS** TO DO SO. AS I HAVE SAID BEFORE, **THEY LITERALLY COVET AND IDOLIZE THEIR SECRETS.** SO MUCH THAT A POTENTIAL PLEDGE OR ANYONE WHO IS NOT A MEMBER OR INTERESTED CANNOT MAKE A **FAIR ASSESSMENT** OF WHAT THEY ARE GETTING THEMSELVES INTO OR WHAT THEY ARE REALLY ABOUT. "IT'S A SECRET," THEY SAY. YOU WILL FIND OUT EVERYTHING ONCE YOU BECOME **"ONE OF US"**. THEY DO THIS TO AVOID CONFLICT. THEY HAVE FEAR OF LOSING MEMBERSHIP, ESPECIALLY COMPROMISED CHRISTIANS (i.e. TIMID MINISTERS, PASTORS, etc.) WHO GIVE THEM A GOOD IMAGE.

MAY I SAY TO THE TRUE CHRISTIAN, THAT ONCE YOU BECOME ONE OF THEM, YOU ARE NO LONGER ONE OF CHRIST'S. THAT IS SOMETHING TO FEAR.

II TIMOTHY 1:7 For God hath not given us the spirit of fear, but of power, love, and of a sound mind.

WHENEVER YOU ARE CHRIST'S, YOU HAVE NOTHING TO FEAR. BUT IF YOU DO NOT HAVE HIM, YOU HAVE EVERY REASON TO BE AFRAID. IF THIS IS THE CASE, YOU ARE NOT IN THE WILL OF GOD. THE TRUE CHRISTIAN MUST ALSO NOT FEAR TELLING THE TRUTH TO GREEKS.

THE GREEK'S BELIEF **SYSTEM OF EXCLUSION** ALLOWS A MEMBERSHIP FULL OF **RELATIVISM AND DIVERSITY TOWARD** ALL BELIEFS AND FORMS OF WORSHIP. A PASTOR WITH THIS FRAME OF MIND CAN LEAD SO MANY TO CONFORM OR COMPROMISE TO THEIR DISTORTED CHRISTIAN BELIEFS, ESPECIALLY A WEAK CHRISTIAN. IT'S A NECESSITY THAT WE AS TRUE

CHRISTIANS KNOW HOW TO ANSWER THE MANY QUESTIONS GREEK CHRISTIANS WILL ASK, AND FALSE STATEMENTS THEY WILL BOAST. FRATERNITY/SORORITY MEMBERS WILL SAY THINGS SUCH AS

1.) THAT'S YOUR OPINION ABOUT THAT SCRIPTURE. ASK THEM WHAT AN OPINION IS, AND THEN ASK THEM FOR CROSS REFERENCE SCRIPTURES, CONTEXT, HISTORICAL SETTING, etc. BECAUSE ONCE ONE SIN CAN BE JUSTIFIED, ALL SIN CAN BE JUSTIFIED. IF THEY DO NOT AGREE WITH THAT, IT IS TIME TO MOVE ON AND PRAY FOR THEM. AN OPINION IS A STATEMENT THAT CAN'T BE VERIFIED **WITH EVIDENCE**. A FACT IS A STATEMENT THAT CAN BE VERIFIED WITH EVIDENCE. MAKE THEM SHOW THEMSELVES APPROVED.

FACT: GLO's NEVER PRODUCE EVIDENCE FOR THEIR CLAIMS.

TRUTH: I PETER 3:15

2.) PLEDGING FORMS A BOND, BUILDS CHARACTER, AND PREPARES YOU FOR FUTURE HARDSHIPS. WHY DOES ONE HAVE TO BE BROKEN DOWN BEFORE ONE CAN BE BUILT UP? THE HOLY SPIRIT BUILDS CHARACTER AND FORMS BONDS THROUGH GODLY FELLOWSHIP WITHOUT PURPOSELY BREAKING ONE DOWN.

FACT: PLEDGING MAKES YOU NOTHING LIKE JESUS, BUT MORE LIKE THE DEVIL.

TRUTH: II CORINTHIANS 3:18 But we all, with open face beholding as in a glass the glory of the Lord, are **changed into the same image** from glory to glory, even as **by the spirit of the Lord.**

TRUTH: I JOHN 1:3 That which we have seen and heard declare we unto you that ye also may have fellowship with us: and truly **our fellowship is with the father, and with his son Jesus Christ.**

DOES ALLOWING YOURSELF TO BE BEATEN OR HUMILIATED BUILD CHARACTER, OR ALLOW FELLOWSHIP WITH THE FATHER AND THE SON? **DOES PLEDGING DEVELOP CHRISTLIKE CHARACTER IN ANY WAY?**

FACT AND ANSWER: NO

3.) THAT'S HOW YOU INTERPRET THE BIBLE. TELL ME HOW IT'S SHOULD BE INTERPRETED? **SEE #1.** THE CHRISTIAN WITNESS MUST USE SCRIPTURE TO PROVE THEM WRONG.

II PETER 1:19-21/II TIMOTHY 3:16

4.) WE MAY DRINK/PARTY BUT WE DO GOOD THINGS ALSO (THIS IS A GREEK CHRISTIAN FAVORITE!!!).

FACT: HYPOCRITES GO TO HELL.

TRUTH: MATTHEW 23:15 Woe unto you, scribes and Pharisees, **hypocrites**! for ye compass sea and land to make one proselyte, and when he is made, ye make him twofold more the child of hell **than yourselves.**

THE CHURCH IS DOING IT, OR I KNOW SOME CHRISTIANS THAT DO IT.

FACT: THEN IT IS NOT A CHURCH OF GOD, AND THAT PERSON IS NOT A TRUE CHRISTIAN.

TRUTH- I JOHN 3:9

DO THE ACTIVITIES LINE UP WITH THE <u>WORD OF GOD</u>? FACT: SALVATION IS NOT IN A CHURCH OR

THROUGH A PASTOR, BUT IN JESUS AND HIM ALONE.

TRUTH: ACTS 4:12 and there is salvation in and through no one else, for there is no other name under heaven given among men by and which we must be saved.

AN EXAMPLE IS A CHURCH OR A CHRISTIAN THAT SAYS IT'S OKAY TO GAMBLE. **THE BIBLE SAYS** THAT WE ARE NOT TO COVET. THE CHURCH IS SUBJECT TO THE WORD OF GOD.

ACTS 20:28/REVELATION CHAPTERS 2&3

6.) MY PASTOR, DEACON, MINISTER, ETC. IS/IS NOT ONE. HE OR SHE SAYS IT'S OK! (LOOK AT #5 AND REPLACE CHURCH WITH PASTOR). IF YOUR PASTOR WERE A CANNIBAL, WOULD YOU BE? ACCORDING TO THE TYPE OF STATEMENT ABOVE, THE ANSWER IS YES! WHAT THE DOES THE BIBLE SAY IS WHAT MATTERS? WITHOUT PROPER KNOWLEDGE, PEOPLE CAN ONLY GIVE BAD ADVICE.

I CORINTHIANS 11:1 Be ye followers of me, even as I also am of Christ.

EPHESIANS 5:1 Be ye therefore followers of God, as dear children.

FACT: IF YOUR CHURCH LEADERS ARE NOT FOLLOWING CHRIST, YOU SHOULD NOT FOLLOW THEM. YOU ARE COMMANDED TO FOLLOW GOD AND GODLY LEADERS (**HEBREWS 13:17**)

7.) MY DADDY/MOMMY ARE IN ONE. DO <u>YOU</u> KNOW IT'S WRONG?
WILL THEY DETERMINE YOUR ETERNAL DESTINY?? SIN IS SIN. REGARDLESS OF HOW YOU FEEL, GOD IS NO RESPECTOR OF PERSONS. MANY PEOPLE DON'T WANT TO BELIEVE THAT THEIR OWN PARENTS

COMING APART AT THE SEAMS

AND FRIENDS ARE ON THEIR WAY TO HELL, AND NEITHER WOULD I, BUT TRUTH IS TRUTH.

FACT: DADDY AMD MOMMY ARE NOT GOD. THERE BEING WRONG DOES NOT MEAN YOU HAVE TO BE.

TRUE CHRISTIANS: ALWAYS USE THE WORD OF GOD AND YOUR KNOWLEDGE ABOUT GLO's. LET THEM FIGHT AND ACCUSE GOD, NOT YOU. REMEMBER THAT THE BIBLE SAYS TO AVOID FOOLISH ARGUMENTS, BECAUSE THEY LEAD TO MORE UNGODLINESS. THIS WILL BE ONE OF THE COMMON OCCURRENCES IN WITNESSING TO SOMEONE YOU DON'T KNOW. IF YOU FIND YOURSELF IN THIS POSITION, ALWAYS MOVE THE CONVERSATION TOWARD THE WORD OF GOD. DO NOT USE OPINIONATED STATEMENTS. SPEAK WHAT YOU KNOW.

II TIMOTHY 2:23(amp) But refuse (shut your mind against, have nothing to do with) **trifling** (ill-informed, **unedifying,** stupid) controversies over **ignorant questionings,** for **you know** that **they foster strife** and **breed quarrels.**

ONE OF THE BEST WAYS TO DEAL WITH A GREEK CHRISTIAN IS TO ASK THEM QUESTIONS THAT YOU KNOW CONTRADICT THE WORD OF GOD. WHATEVER THEIR ANSWER, YOU HAVE THE WORD OF GOD TO SUPPORT YOU. SINCE THEY HARDLY READ THE WORD, THEY WILL SUCCUMB TO THE VERY FACT THAT THEY DON'T READ MUCH, IF ANY. WHATEVER THEY HAVE READ, GENERALLY ENDS UP GROSSLY MISINTERPRETED. THIS OPENS UP ROOM FOR YOU TO SHOW THEM THE WORD THAT THEY HAVE BEEN MISSING. REMEMBER YOUR JOB IS SOWING AND WATERING. GOD MUST GIVE THE INCREASE. I CAN PERSONALLY RECALL TEN SEEDS THAT I HAVE SOWN

OR WATERED THAT HAVE LED TO REPENTANCE AND DENOUNCEMENT. IT WAS A VERY BITTER FIGHT WITH ONE, BUT THE BATTLE IS NOT MINE, IT IS GOD'S. I JUST QUOTED SCRIPTURE IN HER HEARING. I WAS ABLE TO AFFECT HER UNKNOWINGLY AND WITHOUT ARGUING BACK AT HER. FAITH COMES BY HEARING, AND HEARIING BY THE WORD OF GOD (ROMANS 10:17).

WHENEVER THE TRUTH AGAINST GLO's IS REVEALED TO A GREEK CHRISTIAN, THEY WILL MISINTERPRET SCRIPTURE OR USE OPINIONS TO PROVE THEIR POINT.

II PETER 3:16-18(amp) Speaking of this as he does in all of his letters. There are some things in those [epistles of Paul] that are difficult to understand, **which the ignorant and unstable twist and misconstrue to their own utter destruction,** just as [**they distort and misinterpret**] **the rest of the Scriptures.** Let me warn you therefore, beloved, that knowing these things beforehand, you should be on your guard, lest you be carried away by the error of lawless and wicked (persons and) fall from your own (present) firm condition (your own steadfastness of mind). But grow in grace (undeserved favor, spirit strength) and recognition and knowledge and understanding of our Lord and Savior Jesus Christ (the Messiah). To Him (be) glory (honor, majesty, and splendor) both now and to the day of eternity. Amen (so be it)!

IF YOU ARE AN IDOLATER/FORNICATOR OR DO THOSE THINGS SUCH AS THESE, **WHAT SCRIPTURE IS THERE TO JUSTIFY ANY STAND YOU HAVE FOR YOUR RELATIONSHIP WITH JESUS? ABSOLUTELY**

COMING APART AT THE SEAMS

NONE! SO WHY TRY TO JUSTIFY OATHS, INTAKE PROCESSES, UNEQUAL YOKING, PARTIES, AND SONGS OF PRAISE TO YOUR ORGANIZATION? THE SCRIPTURE REVEALS THE REASONS.

JUDGES 21:25 In those days there was **no king** in Israel: every man did that which was right **in his own eyes**.

PROVERBS 14:12 There is a way which **seemeth right** to man; but the end thereof are the ways of death.

THE SCRIPTURES ILLUSTRATE GREEK CHRISTIANS AND THEIR OUTCOME. THEY ACT AS IF THEY HAVE NO AUTHORITY (**NO GOD**) AND THEREBY DO AS THEY PLEASE. PEOPLE WHO DO **DEMAND** PROOF (A SIGN) FOR WHAT THEY CLAIM TO BELIEVE **ARE FAITHLESS, TRYING TO REMEDY THEIR UNBELIEF WITHOUT FAITH, WHICH IS BELIEVING WITHOUT HAVING TO SEE.** WHEN YOU GIVE PROOF TO THE UNBELIEVER THAT DOES NOT MEAN THAT IT WILL PRODUCE THE SAVING FAITH TO BELIEVE IN CHRIST.

AS A WITNESS TO GREEK CHRISTIANS, DON'T GO THIS ROUTE VERY LONG. IF THEY DON'T WANT TO BELIEVE THEY WON'T.

THEN THEIR ARE PEOPLE WHO BELIEVE ANYTHING THEY SEE OR HEAR WITHOUT TESTING IT. THESE TYPES OF PEOPLE BELIEVE THEY ARE GOING TO HEAVEN JUST BECAUSE THEY GO TO CHURCH. THESE ARE PEOPLE WHO HAVE OR ARE ON THEIR WAY TO HAVING REPROBATE (REJECTED BY GOD) MINDS. DOES GOING TO HOLLYWOOD MAKE YOU AN ACTOR? OF COURSE NOT! THESE PEOPLE MAY HAVE COMMON SENSE AND A WHOLE LOT OF KNOWLEDGE, BUT THEY FEAR AND ARE NEVER ABLE TO KNOW THE TRUTH AND/OR ARE TOO LAZY TO SEEK THE TRUTH.

II TIMOTHY 1:7- For God hath not given us the spirit of fear, but of power, love, and of a sound mind.

II TIMOTHY 3:7- Ever learning, and **never able** to come to the knowledge of the truth.

I SEE THE <u>SPIRIT OF FEAR</u> THAT RESTS UPON THE MEMBERS OF THESE ORGANIZATIONS WHEN YOU CHALLENGE THEM WITH **THE WORD OF GOD**. IT IS A COMMON PATTERN OF BEHAVIOR FOR THEM. THEY **KNOW THE TRUTH**, BUT BECAUSE OF FEELINGS, EMOTIONS, THREATS OF PERSECUTION, AND SELF-WILL FOR PLEASURE, THEY **RESIST** THE HOLY SPIRIT AND **REFUSE** THE WORD OF GOD. THEY **WILLFULLY SUPPRESS** THE **TRUTH AND FACTS** TO JUSTIFY THEIR SIN.

ROMANS 1:18-32 For the wrath of God is revealed from heaven against all ungodliness and unrighteousness of men, who **hold the truth in unrighteousness**; Because that which may be known of God is manifest in them; for God hath showed it unto them. For the invisible things of him from the creation of the world are clearly seen, being understood by the things that are made, even his eternal power and Godhead; so that they are without excuse. Because that, **when they knew God**, they glorified him not as God, neither were thankful; but **became vain in their imaginations**, and **their foolish heart was darkened. Professing themselves to be wise they became fools**, and changed the glory of the incorruptible God into an image made like to corruptible man, and to birds, and four-footed beasts, and creeping things. Wherefore God also gave them up to uncleanness through the lusts of their own hearts, to dishonor their own bodies between themselves. **Who changed the truth of God into a lie**, and worshipped and served the creature more than the Creator, who is blessed for ever, Amen. For this cause God gave them up unto vile affections: for even their woman did change the natural use into that which is against nature: And likewise also the men, leaving the natural use of the woman,

COMING APART AT THE SEAMS

burned in their lust one toward another; men with men working that which is unseemly, and receiving in themselves that recompense of their error which was meet. And even as they did not like to retain God in their knowledge, God gave them over to a reprobate mind, to do these things which are not convenient; Being filled with all unrighteousness, **fornication**, wickedness, **covetousness**, maliciousness; full of envy, murder, debate, deceit, malignity; whisperers, Backbiters, **haters of God**, despiteful, **proud, boasters, inventors of evil things**, disobedient to parents, **Without understanding, covenant breakers**, without natural affection, implacable, unmerciful. Who **knowing** the judgment of God, that they which commit such things are worthy of death **not only do the same, but have pleasure in them that do them.**

TWO EXAMPLES OF WILLFUL JUSTIFICATION OF SIN: 1.) WILLFULLY REFUSING TO PRAY IN JESUS' NAME NOT TO OFFEND OTHERS. THIS IS NOT ONLY USELESS, BUT IT'S UNSCRIPTURAL AND DISOBEDIENT. THEREFORE, IT IS SUPRESSING AND DENYING THE TRUTH FOR MAN'S SAKE. **2.) RELIGIOUS TOLERANCE OR ECUMENICALISM. THIS IS UNSCRIPTURAL AS WELL. THIS IS WHAT HAS CAUSED THE SUGAR COATING OF THE GOSPEL. THIS IS WHY WE HAVE CHRISTIAN THIS AND CHRISTIAN THAT. CHRISTIAN IS A NOUN NOT AN ADJECTIVE.** THESE GROUPS ARE SUPPOSED TO PRODUCE INTELLIGENT PEOPLE, BUT THEY ANSWER BASED ON **RELATIVE** RATHER THAN **ABSOLUTE** THINKING. **RELATIVE THINKING IS OF THE WORLD AND SUBJECT TO CHANGE, BUT ABSOLUTE THINKING IS OF GOD AND UNGHANGING. RELATIVE THINKERS HAVE OPINIONS, BUT ABSOLUTE THINKERS HAVE CONVICTIONS.** FOR MANY REASONS, GREEK CHRISTIANS BELIEVE THE WORD OF GOD IS THEIRS TO DO WITH IT AS THEY WISH. AS A MATTER OF FACT, MANY STUDY THE BIBLE RIGHT ALONGSIDE THEIR GLO (GREEK-LETTERED ORGANIZATION) RITUAL BOOKS. ALL THEY ARE TRYING TO DO IS

JUSTIFY THE GOOD, BUT **WHAT THEY PURPOSELY END UP DOING IS IGNORING THE BAD**. THIS IS A VERY DANGEROUS ATTITUDE TO HAVE BECAUSE THEN THE ONLY TRUTH THAT EXISTS IS WHAT YOU CHOOSE TO BELIEVE, AND WHAT YOU EXPERIENCE AND NOT BASED ON WHAT GOD SAYS (**JOHN 14:6**). IN ESSENCE, THEY TRY TO CONTAIN GOD IN A BOX LIKE AN ANIMAL. WHAT YOU BELIEVE OR DO NOT BELIEVE DOES NOT CHANGE WHAT THE TRUTH IS, **JESUS CHRIST**. HAZING WITH A FRYING PAN IS OK FOR ONE PERSON, AND A WOODEN PADDLE FOR ANOTHER. WHERE DOES THE RELATIVISM END? SOMETIMES IT ENDS UP IN **THE GRAVE**. SO WHY THEN WOULD A CHRISTIAN ALLOW ANY **UNSAVED** PERSON TRY TO EXPLAIN BIBLICAL PRINCIPLES TO THEM BASED ON THEIR RELATIVE WAY OF THINKING?????? ALL THE CHRISTIAN SHOULD BE INTERESTED IN IS THE SCRIPTURE TO EXPOSE THEIR ERROR. A GREEK CHRISTIAN DOES NOT REASON ACCORDING TO THE WORD OF GOD. THEIR PRAYERS, HYMNS, AND PLEDGE SONGS **ARE IDOLATROUS, AND NOT HEARD BY GOD**. GOD IS **GRACIOUS ENOUGH** TO HEAR THE CRY OF A FOOL AND HELP HIM, BUT GOD HAS **OBLIGATED** HIMSELF TO HEAR THE BELIEVER.

JOHN 9:31 Now we know that **God heareth not sinners**: but if any man be a worshiper of God, and **doeth his will**, him he heareth.

God has heard the prayer of sinners. He heard Cornelius the Gentiles' prayer for personal and household salvation. God even hears fools and out of His goodness answers them (PSALMS 107:17-20). It is true that no sinner can heal the eyes of the blind. Verses 32-34 explain the reason for the statement. God guarantees one answer to the prayer of a sinner. Forgiveness if he repents.

I PETER 3:12 For the eyes of the Lord are over **the righteous**, and **his ears are open** unto **their** prayers: **but** the face of the Lord is against them that do evil.

THESE SONGS AND ACTIVITIES ARE OFTEN ACCOMPANIED BY SOME FORM OF SACRIFICE (HAZING) OR THE PERFORMANCE OF OTHER RITUAL ACTS SUCH AS INITIATION, BRANDING, AND MEMORIAL SERVICES. A TRUE CHRISTIAN SHOULD NOT HAVE ANY PART, **ACTIVE OR INACTIVE,** IN SUCH THINGS (**II CORINTHIANS 6:14-18**). YET, **THESE PEOPLE ARE ALWAYS YOUR BROTHERS AND/OR SISTERS UNTIL YOU DENOUNCE THE ENTIRE GLO** (i.e. THE UNCLEAN THING-**THE ORGANIZATION, NOT JUST CERTAIN INDIVIDUALS OR ACTIVITIES.**) **IN THAT WHICH IS BY NATURE EVIL, THERE IS NO GOOD THING.** GREEK CHRISTIANS BECOME SLAVES TO THE RITUALS, PRINCIPLES, AND DOCTRINES OF THEIR GROUP. THE SONGS, PARTIES, POEMS, STEP SHOWS, AND HAZING ARE JUST A SOME CHARACTERISTICS THAT ORIGINATED OUT OF ANCIENT GREEK CULTURE AND HAS INFUSED INTO OUR PRESENT DAY SECRET SOCIETIES (**GREEK AND NON-GREEK LETTERED ORGANIZATIONS**). ANOTHER INFLUENCE ON PRESENT DAY GREEK-LETTERED ORGANIZATIONS BY THE ANCIENT GREEKS WAS MAKING gods IN MAN'S IMAGE. THIS PRACTICE BROUGHT OUT ANOTHER STRIKING CHARACTERISTIC CALLED ELITISM. **ELITISM** IS WHEN A PERSON OR GROUP OF PEOPLE ENJOYS APPARENT SUPERIORITY OVER ANOTHER ON AN INTELLECTUAL, SPIRITUAL, SOCIAL, OR ECONOMICAL LEVEL. THIS IS WHERE "THE WE'RE BETTER THAN YOU ATTITUDE" COMES FROM. THIS TYPE OF MINDSET ORIGINATES IN IDOLATRY AND FESTERS WITH PRIDE. ALL THESE GROUPS CLAIM SOME FORM OF HIERARCHY OVER ANOTHER BY CLAIMING WHY THEY HAVE (i.e. SECRET KNOWLEDGE WAS "DEEPER" THAN ANOTHER'S OR WE DO MORE FOR THE COMMUNITY). THE GNOSTICS IN GREEK CULTURE WAS SUCH A GROUP. THEY TAUGHT THAT KNOWLEDGE WAS THE JEWEL TO SEEK AFTER, NOT FAITH. THIS TYPE OF THIRST AND DESIRE FOR KNOWLEDGE CAUSES PRIDE.

FREDERIC L. HATCHETT

I CORINTHIANS 8:1 Now as touching things offered unto idols, we know that we all have knowledge. Knowledge **puffeth up**, but charity edifieth.

KNOWLEDGE MUST BE ACCOMODATED WITH SELF-CONTROL.

II PETER 1:5 And beside this, giving all diligence, add to your faith virtue; and to virtue knowledge; add to knowledge, self-control.

THE PRIDE OF KNOWLEDGE IS CHARACTERISTIC IN GLO's ON AN **INDIVIDUAL** AND **COLLECTIVE** BASIS. IT HAS EVEN COME DOWN TO WHOEVER WAS FOUNDED FIRST HAS THE MOST KNOWLEDGE AND IS THEREFORE, THE GREATEST. THIS IS PROUDLY PROCLAIMED BY **Alpha Phi Alpha** IN THEIR MOTTO, "**FIRST** OF ALL, **SERVANTS** OF ALL, WE SHALL **TRANSCEND** ALL." GLO's PROFESS TO BE WISE MAKING THEM FOOLS. THEY CLAIM TO BE, "ALL THAT", BUT ARE NOT.

ROMANS 1:22 Professing themselves to be wise they became fools.

I CORINTHIANS 1:20 Where is the wise? where is scribe? where is the disputer of this world? hath not God made foolish the wisdom of this world?

THAT'S WHY YOU WILL ALWAYS HEAR THEM SAYING, "WE'RE DOING THIS AND THAT" OR "YOU DON'T UNDERSTAND, YOU HAVE TO BE IN OUR ORGANIZATION **TO UNDERSTAND**." UNDERSTAND WHAT??? FROM READING SOME RITUALS AND OTHER MATERIALS, I HAVE A GREAT UNDERSTANDING. OH! I SEE, BECAUSE I DIDN'T GO THROUGH YOUR GLO's PLEDGE PROCESS, I CAN'T UNDERSTAND. LET ME TELL YOU, THE READER, FROM EXPERIENCE THAT PLEDGE PROCESSES DIFFER SLIGHTLY. I HAVE SEEN MALE AND FEMALE, BLACK AND WHITE GREEK ORGANIZATION PLEDGE PROCESSES. THE

ONLY DIFFERENCE I NOTICED WAS SKIN COLOR AND SEX. BY MAKING THESE, "WE CAN'T KNOW" STATEMENTS, THEY HAVE ALREADY PROVEN MY EARLIER STAEMENT ABOUT TRUTH HAVING TO BE THE RESULT OF EXPERIENCE, INSTEAD OF IT BEING AN ABSOLUTE AND ETERNAL PRINCIPLE THAT CAN ONLY BE GRASPED BY FAITH. ALSO, THEY ARE INSULTING YOUR INTELLIGENCE, ESPECIALLY AS A CHILD OF GOD WHO HAS THE MIND OF CHRIST. GLO's DO THIS BY ASSUMING YOU CANNOT UNDERSTAND THEIR WAYS. AS A CHRISTIAN, DO YOU THINK YOU SHOULD BE YOKED WITH PEOPLE LIKE THIS: CALLING THEM YOUR BROTHERS AND SISTERS?? WE ARE TALKING ABOUT CREAM OF THE CROP STUDENTS, LAWYERS, AND EVEN DOCTORS, ARGUING OVER WHO STEPS THE BEST, WHO DRESSES THE BEST, OR WHO GETS THE BEST OF THE OPPOSITE SEX. EDUCATION DOES NOTHING TO THE SPIRIT. EDUCATION WITHOUT SALVATION IS WORTHLESS AND DEADLY. **ELITISM** IS WHY THEIR **SELECTIVE** PROCESS IS BIASED. IT IS BASED ON PRIDE AND LACK OF FAITH. THIS PRIDE IS THE REASON FOR THE FORMATION OF OTHER GLO's (e.g. DELTA SIGMA THETA SORORITY FORMED OUT OF ALPHA KAPPA ALPHA SORORITY. DURING THE FOUNDING YEARS, PEOPLE WERE TURNED DOWN FOR VARIOUS REASONS. IF YOU ARE NOT IN COLLEGE, THE MILITARY, OR GIVEN HONORARY STATUS, IT IS IMPOSSIBLE TO BE IN THE GREEK-LETTER FRATERNITIES OR SORORITIES. EVEN YOUR SKIN COPLEXION COULD CAUSE REJECTION OF MEMBERSHIP. ONE MEMBER CAN PREVENT ANOTHER PERSON FROM BECOMING A MEMBER FOR PETTY REASONS NOT FOUND IN THE BASIC GUIDELINES. THIS IS CALLED **BLACKBALLING.** THE PERSON DOING THE BLACKBALLING DOES NOT EVEN HAVE TO IDENTIFY HIS OR HERSELF. I'M SO GLAD NO ONE CAN KEEP ANOTHER FROM BEING SAVED. A LIAR, THIEF, MURDERER, A BAD GPA, OR ONE WITH NO COMMUNITY SERVICE CAN BE SAVED. **NO ONE** CAN BLACKBALL YOUR SALVATION. EVEN WHEN THE STANDARDS ARE MET OR EXCEEDED FOR GLO MEMBERSHIP, YOU CAN BE TURNED DOWN BECAUSE A

BROTHER FELT YOU LOOKED AT HIM FUNNY OR SPOKE TO HIS GIRLFRIEND.

RESPECTOR OF PERSONS OR PARTIALITY IS UNACCEPTABLE TO GOD.

JAMES 2:1(amp) My Brethren, pay no servile regard to people (show no prejudice, **no partiality**). Do not (attempt to) hold and practice the faith of our Lord Jesus Christ (the Lord) of glory (together with **snobbery**)!

SNOBBERY IS ELITISM THAT IS A PREVALENT CHARACTERISTIC OF GLO's.

LEVITICUS 19:15 Ye shall **do no unrighteousness in judgment**: thou shalt **not respect the person** of the poor, nor honor the person of the mighty: but **in righteousness** shalt thou **judge** thy neighbor.

I BELIEVE IN SETTING STANDARDS, BUT NOT THOSE THAT WOULD EXCLUDE A PERSON BASED ON **UNCONTROLLABLE CIRCUMSTANCES** SUCH AS RACE, SKIN COLOR, EYE COLOR, OR HANDICAP. ATLEAST **ALL MEN AND WOMEN CAN BE** SAVED **IF** THEY **WANT** TO, BUT ALL MEN WHO WANT TO BE KAPPAS CANNOT. WHY? ONE KAPPA (WHOSE COLORS ARE RED AND WHITE) DIDN'T LIKE THIS GUY'S BLUE AND SILVER TIE AT THE MEETING. THIS IS ENOUGH TO KEEP ONE FROM BECOMING A MEMBER. JESUS COMPELS **ALL** TO COME, AND THERE IS NO MAN WHO CAN REJECT OR BLACKBALL ANOTHER'S SALVATION, NOT EVEN JESUS. **THIS IS A MAJOR DIFFERENCE THAT NEEDS TO BE SEEN. MAN'S CONTROL IS LIMITED, BECAUSE HE LACKS AUTHORITY, BUT JESUS' CONTROL IS LIMITLESS BECAUSE OF HIS INFINITE AUTHORITY.** IF MAN HAD THE RIGHT TO REJECT YOUR CONFESSION OF SALVATION, ALOT MORE PEOPLE WOULD GO TO HELL, BECAUSE OF MAN'S SINFUL, UNMERCIFUL, JUDGMENTAL NATURE, AND THE INABILITY TO KNOW A MAN'S HEART WHICH WOULD NOT ENABLE HIM TO EFFECT THE HEART. THIS LACK OF KNOWLEDGE AND CONTROL

WAS SHOWN WHEN CHRISTIANITY AND GREEK OCCULTISM (i.e. MYTHOLOGY, SECRET ARTS, IDOLATRY, etc.) **CLASHED**. THE CHURCH AT CORINTH WAS A DIRECT RESULT OF THE MIX. THE MAIN PROBLEMS WERE THE ALREADY PRESENT IMMORALITIES OF THE PEOPLE IN THE CHURCH, NAMELY THE CORINTHIAN CHRISTIANS. THE PROBLEMS WERE MISUSE OF THE BODY (SEXUALLY-**I CORINTHIANS 5**), MISUSE OF SPIRITUAL GIFTS (**I CORINTHIANS 12**), AND IMPROPER ADMINISTRATION OF COMMUNION (**I CORINTHIANS 11**). All of this was caused by their **elitist** attitude AND unwillingness to root out their pride, **former ways of life** and **thinking** such as: idolatry, fornication, partying, and drunkenness. They did not want to renew their minds. They still craved the sins mentioned above, and any other vices that go along with a wealthy, diverse, religious, and lawless society. THEY WANTED **THEIR BRAND OF CHRISTIANITY,** BUT **TRUE CHRISTIANITY** OPPOSES LAWLESSNESS, IDOLATRY, AND FORNICATION. ANOTHER REASON FOR THEIR LOOSE LIVING WAS OTHER UNGODLY CULTURES THAT CAME THEIR AND WERE ACCEPTED BY THE PEOPLE. THIS IS SO TRUE WITH THE U.S.A., WHICH WAS ONCE A NATION THAT PUT THE TRUE GOD FIRST. WE HAVE LEFT THE TRUE GOD TO SERVE OTHER gods. THE GREEKS DID NOT CARE SO MUCH ABOUT WHO OR WHAT YOU WORSHIPPED AS LONG AS IT DID NOT UPSET THE NORM OR **THEIR INCOME. CHRISTIANITY DID UPSET THE NORM AND THEIR INCOME BY PUTTING THE IDOL MAKERS OUT OF BUSINESS, BURNING BOOKS OF WITCHCRAFT, AND NO LONGER PAYING OFFERINGS TO THE TEMPLES OF IDOL WORSHIP.** THIS IS WHAT THE GLO's OF TODAY DESIRE; **THEIR OWN WAY WHILE KEEPING GOD** IN HIS PLACE (i.e. RELIGIOUS; INSTEAD OF PUTTING HIM AT THE TOP AND CORE WHERE HE BELONGS. THIS WAS ATTEMPTED AT SHAW UNIVERSITY IN RALEIGH, NORTH CAROLINA. A BIBLICAL THEOLOGY AND APOLOGETICS CLASS FROM MOUNT ZION CHRISTIAN CHURCH, DURHAM, NORTH CAROLINA WAS SUPPOSED TO DO A BIBLICAL

PERSPECTIVE OF GLO's ON THEIR CAMPUS. THE HEAD OF STUDENT AFFAIRS, A MEMBER OF ALPHA PHI ALPHA HAD IT CANCELLED OUT OF FEAR. I TOLD HIM PERSONALLY ON THE PHONE THAT HE CAN'T STOP GOD FROM MOVING ON THAT CAMPUS, AND THAT IT IS FOOLISH TO TRY. AS USUAL, GOD HONORED THAT STATEMENT. ABOUT THREE MONTHS LATER AT A COLLEGE NIGHT CHURCH SERVICE, THE STUDENT BODY PRESIDENT OF SHAW, AND MEMBER OF ALPHA PHI ALPHA NOT ONLY CONFESSED HIS DENUNCIATION TO ME, HE WENT TO HIS FRATERNITY MEETING AND TOLD ALL OF HIS FORMER BROTHERS. THIS CONFESSION INCLUDED THE HEAD OF STUDENT AFFAIRS, THAT HE DENOUNCED ALPHA PHI ALPHA. PRAISE THE LORD!!!!!! GLO's FEAR THE CHRISTIAN CHALLENGE. THEY FEAR THE CHURCH THAT PREACHES THE UNCOMPROMISED TRUTH THAT SAYS THAT THERE'S NO SUCH THING AS A CHRISTIAN AKA, DST, OMEGA, PI KAPPA PHI, MASON, OR HOMOSEXUAL. SO THE **WORLDLY-MINDED** CHRISTIAN SEARCHES FOR AN OUTLET, OR A PLACE WHERE THEY CAN BE **COMFORTABLE**. THEY ARE LOOKING FOR SOMETHING THAT IS NOT AGAINST THEIR CONVICTIONS. AS WATER FLOWS TO THE PATH OF LEAST RESISTANCE, SO WILL A SINNER'S CONSCIENCE FLOW TO THE PATH OF LEAST TRUTH AND CONVICTION. THEY WILL ALSO SEARCH FOR ANY JUSTIFICATION (WORLDLY OR SPIRITUALLY) TO REMAIN **IN OBVIOUS SIN** AGAINST GOD. THESE PEOPLE WILL SEARCH FOR A CHURCH OR ANY GROUP THAT HAS A WORLDLY SPIRIT WITH A TOUCH OF CHRISTIANITY (i.e. GOD IS LOVE NOT A JUDGE TYPE BELIEF). **INSTEAD OF CHRISTIANITY DEFINING GREEK CHRISTIANS, GREEK CHRISTIANS SEEK TO DEFINE THEIR OWN CHRISTIANITY.** THE WORDS AND INTERPRETATIONS OF THE BIBLE ARE NOT TO BE ALTERED FOR ANY REASON OR ANYONE. THIS IS WHERE THE TERMS "WATERED DOWN" AND "SUGAR COATING" THE GOSPEL COMES FROM. I CALL IT "BAND-AID CHRISTIANITY" BECAUSE THE TRUTH IS COVERED UP ALLOWING DECEPTION AND HINDERING DELIVERANCE. THE TRUTH SPOKEN (UNCOMPROMISED) BY PASTORS SCRATCH THE

SURFACE OF GLO's CAUSING AN IRRITATION, BUT AFTER ANY NEGATIVE FEEDBACK FROM MAJOR GREEK CONTRIBUTORS TAKES PLACE, **THEY KEEP THEIR NEVER WAS, OR USED TO BE CONVICTION TO THEMSELVES.** HE OR SHE COMPROMISES NOT TO BE HEARD AGAIN FOR FEAR OF LOSING MEMBERSHIP AND/OR MONEY. **YOU'RE NOTHING BUT A HIRELING IF THIS IS THE CASE.** I ACCUSE FRATERNITIES AND SORORITIES OF BAND-AID CHRISTIANITY. THEY USE CHRISTIANITY AS A COVER UP TO THE IGNORANT AND UNINQUISITIVE. ONCE THIS HAPPENS THAT PERSON BECOMES BOUND NOT WANTING TO HEAR ANYTHING CHRISTIANITY HAS TO SAY ABOUT GLO's. THE APOSTLE PAUL UPSET THE NORM **OF COMPROMISE** WITH THE GOSPEL OF JESUS CHRIST WHICH IS **AGGRESSIVELY UNCOMPROMISING.** THIS SAME GOSPEL IS DEFINITELY UPSETTING THE NORM IN OUR SOCIETY. IT IS NOW HITTING **THE GLO's** AT THEIR **HEART**, WHICH **IS THEIR SECRECY.** EVERYTHING IS OK JUST AS LONG AS YOU DON'T TALK ABOUT JESUS AND HIS **MORAL ABSOLUTES (e.g. I AM THE DOOR, I AM THE WAY, I AM THE TRUTH, THE MARRIAGE BED IS UNDEFILED-HEBREWS 13:4-5, etc.).** THIS IS WHY GOD PUT **I CORINTHIANS 15:33, GALATIANS 6:7** AND **PSALMS 1:1** IN THE BIBLE. IF YOU **WILLFULLY** PUT YOURSELF IN HARMS WAY, YOU WILL BE HARMED. MEMBERS OF GLO's ARE CONTINUALLY UNDER GOD'S WRATH.

YOU SEE IF I WILLFULLY WENT BACK TO MASONRY AND OMEGA PSI PHI, I WOULD EVENTUALLY BECOME AS THEY ARE, DECEIVED, LOST, HYPOCRITICAL, BOASTFUL, PERVERSE, ETC. THIS BOOK WOULD BECOME MY GREATEST TORMENT IN HELL.

FORMING AN ORGANIZATION TO DO GOOD THINGS, BUT PROMISING TO ITS MEMBERS THINGS THAT ONLY GOD CAN DELIVER, PURPOSELY LEAVING OUT JESUS AND HAVING PRINCIPLES OF GREEK

PHILOSOPHY AND MYTHOLOGY IS NOT EVEN AN ORGANIZATION FORMED WITH GOOD INTENTIONS. THE FOUNDERS MAY HAVE BEEN SINCERE IN FORMING THEIR GLO's, AND THEY MAY NOT HAVE BEEN SINCERE; YET, ONE THING IS SURE, **THEY WERE SINCERELY WRONG.** THEY FAILED TO REALIZE THAT GOOD INTENTIONS CANNOT VIOLATE THE WILL OF GOD OR MAKE HIM ACCEPT SOMETHING, BECAUSE OF WHAT THEY BELIEVE IT TO BE. THEY DID NOT TAKE INTO ACCOUNT **THE SPIRITUAL REALITIES** THAT EVIL ORIGINS WILL GIVE WAY TO EVIL CONSEQUENCES, AND DIDN'T COUNT THE COST OF MIXING THE **COMPROMISING** GREEK CULTURE AND PHILOSOPHY WITH THE **ABSOLUTE, UNCOMPROMISING** CHRISTIAN PRINCIPLES OF THE BIBLE. IT IS LIKE OIL (SIN) AND WATER (RIGHTEOUSNESS). GLO's, BEING EVIL, HAVE NO PLACE OR ANY BUSINESS ADOPTING, CLAIMING, OR HAVING A FOUNDATION SET UPON CHRISTIAN PRINCIPLES. THE GLO's AND GREEK CHRISTIAN'S **gods ARE NOT THE LORD (I KINGS 18:21).** THOUGH SOME GOOD THINGS IN THE **NATURAL** ARE DONE, THE INDIVIDUALS ARE STILL IN DEEP **SPIRITUAL** TROUBLE. WE KNOW LIGHT AND DARK CANNOT COEXIST IN AGREEMENT. REGARDLESS OF MAN'S BEST EFFORTS, GLO's (Greek-lettered organizations) WILL NEVER BE ACCEPTABLE, BUT WILL ALWAYS BE DETESTABLE TO GOD. **YES, I AM SAYING THAT THE ONLY SOLUTION FOR GLO's AND ALL SECRET SOCIETIES IS COMPLETE ABOLISHMENT.** IF THIS WERE THE CASE, ALL CHRISTIAN MEMBERS MUST REPENT. IF YOU ARE NOT SAVED, YOU MUST CONFESS JESUS AS LORD AND SAVIOR TO BE BORN-AGAIN. UNFORTUNATELY, THIS IS NOT THE POPULAR VIEW. ALL THE CHARACTERISTICS OF THIS GREEK WAY OF LIFE HAVE BEEN EMBEDDED NOT ONLY INTO OUR SOCIETY, BUT ESPECIALLY THE GREEK FRATERNITIES AND SORORITIES. ALL YOU HAVE TO DO AT THE INITIATION IS SAY THAT YOU BELIEVE IN "GOD" OR A SUPREME BEING WHICH COULD BE BUDDHA, ALLAH, OR A COW. **YOU DO NOT HAVE TO IDENTIFY THE GOD YOU BELIEVE, AND THEY DON'T REQUIRE IT.** THE DEVIL MAY BE THEIR god OR

Supreme Being, AND THE DEVIL OR HIS DEMONS CANNOT AND ARE NOT FOUNDED UPON CHRISTIAN PRINCIPLES. GLO OR GREEK CHRISTIAN? HOW DO YOU EXPECT TO BE FOUNDED UPON CHRISTIAN PRINCIPLES? THE PRIZE OF INITIATION INTO A GLO IS NOT CHRIST. IT IS DELTA, KAPPA, ALPHA, etc. THE PROBLEM FOR CHRISTIANS IS THAT THE ORGANIZATION CONTINUES TO BE THEIR PRIZE, NOT THE PRIZE IN THE FOLLOWING SCRIPTURE.

PHILLIPIANS 3:14-15 I press toward the mark **for the prize of the high calling of God in Christ Jesus.** Let us therefore, as many as be perfect, be thus minded: and if any thing ye be otherwise minded, God shall reveal even this unto you.

THESE ORGANIZATIONS ONLY REQUIRE, FOR THE SAKE OF RITUALISTIC PURPOSES, FOR ONE TO GIVE LIP SERVICE TO YOUR GOD, BUT NOT REALLY BELIEVE BY FAITH.

MARK 7:6 He answered and said unto them, Well hath Isaiah prophesied of you hypocrites, as it is written, THIS PEOPLE HONORETH ME WITH THEIR LIPS, BUT THEIR HEART IS FAR FROM ME.

THE **DEVILS BELIEVE IN GOD** (THE TRUE GOD). THEY OBEY AND TREMBLE AT HIS NAME AND SO SHOULD MAN. THE VERY SAME SPIRITUAL FORCES THAT INFLUENCED THE GREEKS 2000 YEARS AGO AT CORINTH ARE **NO DIFFERENT** THAN THE ONES THAT INFLUENCE GLO's TODAY. THE DEMONS EVEN KNOW THAT THE IDOLS PEOPLE SERVE ARE NOT REAL gods, AND HAVE NO POWER OVER BELIEVERS.

MARK 16:17 And these attesting signs will accompany those who believe: **in My name** they will **drive out demons**; they will speak in new languages;

AS ONE CAN SEE GLO's ARE PLAGUED SPIRITUALLY. THERE IS ONLY ONE CURE, **EXTINCTION. SATAN WANTS YOU TO BE IN THESE GROUPS BECAUSE HE KNOWS THAT THEY WILL BE GREAT DECEIVERS BY PUTTING UP FALSE FRONTS THAT WILL WORK (II CORINTHIANS 11:14-15).** THIS IS ANOTHER SCRIPTURE THAT IS KEY TO THIS BOOK. THE DEVIL IS AN **ALMOST** PERFECT COUNTERFEITER. CHRISTIANS!! DON'T DROP YOUR GUARD!!!!!! SATAN WANTS YOU TO BE LOST, DECEIVED, AND ROBBED OF THE TRUTH.

JOHN 10:10a THE DEVIL COMES NOT, BUT TO STEAL, KILL, AND DESTROY.

WHAT JOHN SAID ABOUT 2000 YEARS AGO CONCERNING SATAN IS STILL TRUE TODAY. IF YOU SAY THAT THE CHURCH HAS COME TO DO OR IS DOING THESE THINGS, THEN YOU SAYING THE SAME ABOUT THE CHURCH'S FOUNDER, JESUS.

THE FOUNDERS OF GLO's MAY HAVE DESIRED THEM TO BE CHRISTIAN BASED, BUT THEY ARE IN NO WAY CHRISTIAN BASED, NOR ARE THEY CHRIST-CENTERED. GLO's BELIEVE THEY CAN SERVE GOD THEIR OWN WAY. WHAT HAPPENS WHEN PEOPLE SERVE GOD IN THEIR OWN WAY? THEY BOAST. CAN WE SERVE GOD IN OUR OWN WAY? NO! **HE IS THE AUTHOR AND FINISHER OF OUR FAITH (HEBREWS 12:2).**

THEOLOGICALLY AND SCRIPTURALLY GLO's ARE NOT CHRISTIAN PRINCIPLED.

CHRISTIANITY IS A SEPARATORY FAITH. IT'S TRULY NOT OF THIS WORLD. TAKE NOTE AS YOU EXAMINE THE FOLLOWING LIST.

The Word of God concerning GLO's (**GREEK-LETTERED ORGANIZATIONS**) is clear to the true Christian. Unfortunately, there are many true Christians who know too little about these secret societies. This chart should give you the necessary tools to expose GLO's for what they really are in God's eyes. Only God can give someone revelation. My hope and prayer is that He uses this chart to achieve His will.

I will use only one example of a GLO in each category, but finding **any** GLO in at least one category is sure. You will need a Bible as you read through the list.

Christianity vs.	Greek-lettered Organizations
1.) SALVATION BY FAITH EPHESIANS 2:8-9 Only God assures us of our salvation (**Romans 8:16**), and it's our fruits that our confession. Works salvation is nothing more than man's attempt to get to God their own way (i.e. Worthless Religion). In my experience of witnessing to Greek Christians, I often hear the good we do outweigh the bad. Analyze the statement clearly, and you see the confession of doing bad works. **Nowhere** in the Bible do we see this type of trade off of good and evil, in exchange for eternal life.	**1.) SALVATION BY WORKS GALATIANS 3:1-5** An excerpt from a ritual of a Greek sorority says, "Silent now are the voices of those Deltas whom we loved. Their **good works** will live on in our hearts and continue to influence our lives and Delta Sigma Theta. **Their immortality is assured throughout all eternity** as each generation of Deltas continues the organization's **good works**." (DELTA SIGMA THETA SORORITY, INC., GRAND CHAPTER, <u>CANDIDATE SYLLABUS</u>, 1990, p. 70.) Good works and immortality for a Greek Christian are not the same as it is for a True Christian. Since **Jesus is the only Way** to God for all people (**John 14:6**), He determines the way you go. It's by faith in Him alone. Make it clear to the one being witnessed to that **immortality cannot be achieved through good works**.

COMING APART AT THE SEAMS

| 2.) **FAITH IN GOD ALONE** **HEBREWS 6:2** This is the only way to salvation. This is the way Christians must live their lives. The just shall live by faith. (**Romans 1:17**) **Let the person know that members trust in each in times of need. Instead of trusting in God, they trust in the members of their organization.** (**Jeremiah 17:5**) | 2.) **FAITH IN MAN AND/OR GOD** THE KAPPA ALPHA PSI HISTORY BOOK STATES WHO THEIR FAITH IS IN. "Faith shall have to be manifested as unshakable **belief in Kappa Alpha Psi**, its ideals, its purpose, its possibilities, **its membership**, its programs and its forward movement." (William L. Crump, THE STORY OF KAPPA ALPHA PSI, A History Of The Beginning And Development Of A College Greek Letter Organization, 1911-1983, Third Edition, 1983, p.267) This quotation says to only have faith in man and GLO. **Where's Jesus?** |
| 3.) **HUMILITY TO GOD LEADING TO EXALTATION BY GOD (TRUE EXALTATION I PETER 5:6/ PROVERBS 29:23** YOU ARE BLESSED. ONLY GOD CAN GIVE ETERNAL LIFE, WISDOM AND LIGHT. MAN HAS EXALTED MANY FAMOUS PEOPLE, BUT IF THEY DIDN'T REPENT AND MAKE JESUS THEIR LORD AND SAVIOR BEFORE DEATH; THEY ARE IN HELL. NO | 3.) **HUMILITY TO MAN LEADING TO EXALTATION BY MAN(FALSE EXALTATION) JEREMIAH 17:5** YOU ARE CURSED The Ritual of Omega Psi Phi Fraternity states, "Seeing now, my friends (initiates), that you have been faithful in the little things, that in your state of darkness you have **placed implicit confidence in these my brothers**, that you crave further mysteries of the Omega Psi Phi Fraternity, let us together invoke the aid of the Supreme Basileus of the Universe." (OMEGA PSI PHI FRATERNITY (Incorporated 1914), THE RITUAL, 1970, p. 21.) This shows the humility |

MATTER HOW "GOOD" THEY WERE, AND NO MATTER WHAT ORGANIZATION THEY BELONGED TO, ALL WERE SINNERS. THE GLO's OF JESUS' DAY WERE THE SCRIBES, PHARISEES, AND SADDUCEES. YET, **JESUS SAID** THAT THEIR FATHER WAS THE DEVIL, THAT THEY WERE A BROOD OF VIPERS AND THAT THEY WERE HYPOCRITES. JESUS TOOK ON THE UNGODLY GROUPS OF HIS DAY, AND WITH HIS HELP I AM TAKING ON THE UNGODLY GROUPS OF MY DAY, **THE INFAMOUS GLO's.** EVEN JESUS ASKED HIS DISCIPLES, Why callest thou me good? There is none good but one, that is God: **Matthew 19:17a** JESUS WAS AWARE THAT BECAUSE OF HIS HUMANITY, WITHOUT GOD HE WOULD NOT HAVE BEEN ABLE TO BE GOOD BY HIMSELF to man. The Ritual, in part, goes on to say, "'Brothers, draw nigh without fear and assist me to stretch forth the strong arm of Omega in bringing these friends from the darkness of selfish and self-centered lives in to the light and fullness of life in Omega, whose standards are worthy of emulation.'" (OMEGA PSI PHI FRATERNITY (Incorporated 1914), THE RITUAL, 1970, p. 21.) This shows how the GLO attempts to exalt you from your ignorance to their wisdom, from your darkness to their light. **Any Christian should feel insulted and outraged to be told that their life with Christ is incomplete, and that they are selfish and in darkness.** MANY GLO's CLAIM THAT UNTIL A PERSON IS INITIATED, THEY ARE IN DARKNESS. IT IS ONLY WHEN SOMEONE IS INITIATED THAT THEY MAKE THE TRANSITION FROM DARKNESS TO LIGHT OR IGNORANCE TO WISDOM. ONLY GOD CAN GIVE THESE THINGS. ONE CANNOT RECEIVE GODLY WISDOM OR GET TO GOD BY SIMPLY JOINING A GLO. BY TRUSTING IN YOUR OWN AND/OR A GLO's RIGHTEOUSNESS, WILL NOT GIVE YOU ETERNAL LIFE (**LUKE 18:14**).

COMING APART AT THE SEAMS

ALONE.	
4.) COMMANDED TO REPENT REPENTANCE IS THE CHANGING OF ONE'S MIND TOWARD GOD. IT IS ACTUALLY A THREE STEP PROCESS FOUND IN **PSALM 51**. 1.) ADMITTING YOU ARE A SINNER. 2.) ASKING GOD'S FORGIVENESS. 3.) A WILLINGNESS TO CHANGE. **ACTS 17:30/MATTHEW 4:17/LUKE 13:3** THE SCRIPTURES HEAR ARE CLEAR. IF YOU DON'T REPENT, YOU GO TO HELL! LET ONE KNOW THAT GLO's WILL NOT COMMAND ONE TO REPENT, BECAUSE JESUS IS NOT THE HEAD OF THEIR ORGANIZATION. THEREFORE, HE WILL NOT BE SOUGHT OUT FOR REPENTANCE. INSTEAD, GREEK CHRISTIANS WILL SEEK THE PRINCIPLES OF THEIR GLO.	**4.) NO NEED FOR REPENTANCE** WHY? GLO's WILL TELL YOU THAT YOU ARE JUSTIFIED BY BEING A MEMBER AND DOING THE WORKS OF A GLO. IN ALL THE LITERATURE I HAVE READ ABOUT GLO's AND ANY OTHER SECRET SOCIETY, NONE HAVE MENTIONED TRUE REPENTANCE AND ACCEPTING JESUS CHRIST AS LORD AND SAVIOR. Delta Sigma Theta believes that their intake program can bring about change. The question that comes to mind is if it's true repentance. Their Candidate Syllabus says, "Delta, then, can use the intake program as an opportunity to help new Deltas see themselves as **worthy** and beautiful." (DELTA SIGMA THETA SORORITY, INC., GRAND CHAPTER, CANDIDATE SYLLABUS, 1990, P. 38.) One can never be worthy without being SAVED. No acknowledgment of one's sins to Jesus is mentioned here or in any other GLO to my knowledge. If so, send me all written material concerning your GLO. For the reader and especially the Christian witness, this challenge will put the Greek Christians on shaky ground, because of their secrecy (see part 13).
5.) SINNER TO SAINT ETERNAL	**5.) INITIATE TO MEMBER SINNER TO SINNER ETERNAL DEATH TO**

| DEATH TO ETERNAL LIFE (CHANGED LIFE) JOHN 1:12/I CORINTHIANS 6:11 WHEN A PERSON BECOMES A CHRISTIAN, THEY ARE NO LONGER A SINNER. THE SPIRIT OF GOD CONVERTS **(CHANGES) YOU SPIRITUALLY** FROM BEING A CHILD OF THE DEVIL, TO BEING A CHILD OF HIS. CHRISTIANS ARE NEW CREATURES (**II CORINTHIANS 5:17**). GOD OWNS YOU BY THE FACT THAT HE CREATED YOU SPIRIT, MIND AND BODY. THE TRUTH IS THAT YOU MUST SUBMIT TO HIS OWNERSHIP OR BE IN REBELLION. TO SERVE GOD ALONE OR MAKE HIM THE HEAD OF YOUR LIFE, MEANS THAT **YOU SERVE NO OTHER gods. TRUE CHRISTIANITY IS PUTTING GOD AT THE HEAD OF OUR SPIRIT, MIND AND BODY.** | ETERNAL DEATH (UNCHANGED LIFE)- THE PERSON WHO JOINS A GLO REMAINS A SINNER (i.e. THERE IS **NO SPIRITUAL CHANGE OR CONVERSION**). EVEN MORE TRAGIC IS THE FACT THAT ONE IS DRAWN DEEPER INTO SIN BY JOINING A GLO. JOINING A GLO DOES NOT CHANGE ONE'S RELATIONSHIP WITH GOD. AN OATH TO A GLO DOES NOT CONVERT A SINNER TO A SAINT. IT ACTUALLY CONVERTS YOU TO A HIGHER DISCIPLESHIP OF SATAN. THE RELIGIOUS DOCTRINES OF GLO's LEAD TO GREATER DECEPTION OF TRUTH AND DARKNESS (**ISAIAH 8:20**). THEIR DOCTRINES PROVE THAT THERE WAS NO TRUE LIGHT IN THOSE WHO FOUNDED THEM. BY VIRTUE OF THE **FACT** THAT NO GLO PUTS GOD AT THE HEAD OF THEIR BELIEFS IS CUT AND DRY PROOF THAT **THEY SERVE ANOTHER god. EVEN IF THEY WERE TO PUT IT IN WRITING, THEIR ACTIONS WOULD THEN HAVE TO PROVE WHAT THEY SAY.** Tau Kappa Epsilon on the internet states, "The mythological ideal or patron of Tau Kappa Epsilon is **Apollo,** one of the most important of Olympian divinities. The Grecian **god** of music and culture, **of light** and the ideals toward which all Tekes must constantly be striving. Typifying the finest development of manhood, the selection of Apollo is most appropriate." (TKEnet: TKE Symbols and Traditions |

	http://ww.tke.org/tkesymb.shtml#Apollo
6.) RIGHTEOUSNESS OF CHRIST GALATIANS 2:20/ROMANS 3:25-26/ISAIAH 54:17 NO MAN ALONE CAN BE MORE RIGHTEOUS THAN ANOTHER, BECAUSE ALL RIGHTEOUSNESS BELONGS TO JESUS. THE ONLY WAY TO RECEIVE HIS RIGHTEOUSNESS IS BY FAITH IN HIM (i.e. YOU MUST BE SAVED- **TITUS 3:5**). CHRISTIANS KNOW WHO THEIR MASTER IS AND WHAT HE REQUIRES. JESUS IS THE LAWMAKER AND LAW ENFORCER. HE HAS THE AUTHORITY AND POWER TO JUDGE ALL THINGS SEEN AND UNSEEN.	6.) RIGHTEOUSNESS OF OMEGA, KAPPA, DELTA, TKE, SIGMA, etc. ISAIAH 57:12 & 64:6/ROMANS 10:3-GLO's AND THEIR MEMBERS ARE VERY GUILTY OF DOING WHAT THIS SCRIPTURE SAYS. THE RIGHTEOUSNESS OF GLO's DOES NOT EXIST, BECAUSE THEY BELIEVE IT CAN COME BY WORKS. THE BIBLE SAYS THAT RIGHTEOUSNESS CAN ONLY BE RECEIVED BY FAITH (**ROMANS 3:28**). GLO's CAN'T GIVE WHAT THEY DON'T POSSESS. THEREFORE, THEY DON'T HAVE THE AUTHORITY TO JUDGE ANOTHER MEMBER, BECAUSE THEY THEMSELVES ARE NOT AND CANNOT BE RIGHTEOUS. THEY DON'T HAVE THE GOD-GIVEN AUTHORITY TO ESTABLISH RIGHTEOUSNESS. THIS IS WHY THEY LET SINNERS IN TO THEIR ORGANIZATIONS, AND WHY DRINKING, FORNICATION, ADULTERY, HAZING, PROFANITY, etc. RUNS RAMPANT THROUGHOUT THESE ORGANIZATIONS. THE FIRST STANZA OF, THE ALPHA PHI ALPHA HYMN, SHOWS THAT THEY PLACED WORKS ABOVE FAITH. "In our dear A Phi A fraternal spirit binds. All the noble, the true, and courageous **Manly deeds**, scholarship, and love for all mankind **Are the aims** of our dear fraternity." Words by Brother Abram L. Simpson, Music by Brother John J. Erby Xi Chapter (Charles H. Wesley, The History of Alpha

	Phi Alpha- Development in College Life, 14th printing, 12th ed. (Chicago, Illinois, 1981)
7.) WORSHIP THE TRUE GOD- JOHN 4:24 WE WORSHIP GOD ALONE. WE DO NOT NEED THE GLO's SYMBOLS, RITUALS, POEMS, DOCTRINES, AND SONGS. NO THANK-YOU! WE HAVE OUR OWN, AND THEY WERE GIVEN AND INSPIRED BY GOD.	7.) WORSHIP FALSE GREEK gods AND gods THEY ARE NOT EVEN AWARE OF. THEY DO ALOT OF THIS BY PRACTICING RITUALS. A RITUAL IS THE HOW ONE WORSHIPS A DEITY, WHETHER IT IS ONE TRUE GOD OR THE MANY FALSE gods. THE LATTER BEING IDOLATRY. PSALMS 96:4-5/GALATIANS 4:8 BY WORSHIPPING THEIR ORGANIZATION AND THE gods ASSOCIATED WITH THEM, THEY CANNOT WORSHIP THE GOD OF ABRAHAM, ISAAC, AND JACOB. GREEK CHRISTIANS CAN'T EVEN KEEP THE FIRST COMMANDMENT!! **THAT'S REAL PATHETIC** SEEING THAT THEY CLAIM TO BE FOUNDED ON CHRISTIAN PRINCIPLES. **DISOBEYING THE FIRST COMMANDMENT.** IOTA PHI THETA (**CENTAUR**) ALPHA KAPPA ALPHA (**ATLAS**) DELTA SIGMA THETA (**MINERVA**) TAU KAPPA EPSILON (**APOLLO**) SIGMA GAMMA RHO (**AURORA**) PHI BETA SIGMA (**PROMETHEUS**) THESE SYMBOLS ARE ALL IDOL gods or MYTHOLOGICAL OFFSPRING OF gods. MANY OTHER gods ARE A PART OF GLO's ACTIVITIES THOUGH THEY ARE NOT DIRECTLY INVOLVED IN SYMBOLISM OR NAMED IN RITUALS. **Delta Sigma Theta's Candidate Syllabus** states, "We **turned for guidance to** one of the most ancient initiation rites, **the**

COMING APART AT THE SEAMS

	Elusinian mysteries. The object of those rites was to ascend through the natural elements to a **'new life'** (being carried forward through all the elements)." (DELTA SIGMA THETA SORORITY, INC., GRAND CHAPTER, CANDIDATE SYLLABUS, 1990, p. 40.) The Elusinian mysteries are the **worship** of Demeter and Persephone, the goddesses of the harvest. Any Delta, and any other Greek Christian must simultaneously deny **EXODUS 20:13, I TIMOTHY 4:7, ISAIAH 44:6, PSALM 96:4-5,** and countless other scriptures in order to associate with any group that teaches such blasphemy and idolatry. I challenge; even dare anyone to substantiate the quote above as being scriptural.
8.) PRAYERS HEARD BY GOD I PETER 3:12a/JOHN 9:31b WE ARE ALLOWED TO ENTER INTO HIS PRESENCE BECAUSE OF HIS SHED BLOOD, AND OUR BELIEF IN HIS SHED BLOOD. **Note:** The scriptures are the same, but each is divided in two parts. One part is for the saved, and the other for	8.) PRAYERS NOT HEARD BY GOD JOHN 9:31a/I PETER 3:12b IT IS CLEAR THAT GREEK CHRISTIANS ARE AS ALL OTHER MEMBERS (i.e. SINNERS). ALL OF THOSE MANNUFACTURED PRAYERS SOLICITED BY GLO's NEVER MAKE IT THROUGH TO GOD; NEITHER DO MANY OF THEIR PERSONAL PRAYERS. I SAY TO GREEK CHRISTIANS, WHY KEEP TRYING? REPENT AND DENOUNCE INSTEAD. **NO JESUS! NO CONNECTION! See Chapter 4 Part 3 for best explanation of John 9:31**

FREDERIC L. HATCHETT

the unsaved.	
9.) GOOD ROOT, GOOD TREE, GOOD FRUIT MATTHEW 7:17-19/JOHN 15 OUR ROOT IS JESUS. NOTHING ELSE NEEDS TO BE SAID.	9.) BAD ROOT, BAD TREE, BAD FRUIT. MATTHEW 7:17-19. GLO's CLAIMS OF MANY FAMOUS AND INFLUENTIAL MEMBERS MEANS NOTHING TO GOD. THEY ARE ALL BAD FRUIT. CHAPTER 3 PART 1 OF THIS BOOK PROVES THE BAD ROOT. Page 30 of the Candidate Syllabus of Delta Sigma Theta Sorority, shows the source of their inspiration and influence. "The most direct line of descent from Greek societies to America is the Freemasons (called Masons). Historians of American fraternities and sororities trace most of our rituals, ceremonies and rites to the Masons. An examination of Masonic rituals open to scholars suggest that our Founders were also influenced by Masonic ritual, symbolism and initiation experiences." (DELTA SIGMA THETA SORORITY, INC., GRAND CHAPTER, CANDIDATE SYLLABUS, 1990, p. 30.) IT IS HISTORCALLY RELIABLE WHERE THE MASONS ACTIVITIES ARE DERIVED. IT IS ALSO HISTORICALLY PROVEN THAT THE GREEK CIVILIATION WAS FOUNDED UPON IDOLATRY. THEREFORE, THE ROOTS OF GLO's ARE BAD SEEING THAT THEY GET THEM FROM THEIR ANCIENT GREEK COUNTERPARTS. THIS IS THE BASIC ORDER OF ORIGIN FOR TODAY'S SECRET SOCIEITES: 1.) **SATAN** 2.) NIMROD- FATHER OF THE BABYLONIAN CULT SYSTEM. 3.) EGYPTIAN CULT SYSTEM 4.)

COMING APART AT THE SEAMS

	GREEK CULT SYSTEM (PREDOMINATELY POLYTHEISTIC AND gods MADE IN MAN'S IMAGE.) 5.) MASONIC ORDERS 6.) GREEK-LETTERED ORGANIZATIONS **THE ROOT IS OBVIOUSLY BAD**
10.) THE BIBLE IS THE ONLY RULE BY WHICH WE LIVE, BECAUSE IT IS **GOD'S WORD.** **II PETER 1:19-21/II TIMOTHY 3:15-16** HOLINESS, BORN AGAIN SANCTIFICATION, BAPTISM, LAYING ON OF HANDS, JUSTIFICATION, THE BLOOD OF JESUS, REDEMPTION, SALVATION, THE WORD OF GOD, THE NAME OF JESUS, etc.	10.) **THE GLO's** RULES ARE THE WAY THEIR MEMBERS ARE TOLD TO LIVE BY ACCORDING TO **THEIR RITUALS.** GREEK CHRISTIANS CAN ONLY GET CONFUSED TRYING TO LIVE A DOUBLE LIFE OF TRYING TO BE A CHRISTIAN WHEN THEY ARE IN A GLO. IT CAN'T BE DONE. **PROVERBS 3:5-6/JUDGES 21:25** THEIR PRINCIPLES OF MANHOOD, BROTHERHOOD, SISTERHOOD, WOMANHOOD, SERVICE, SCHOLARSHIP, PERSERVERANCE, AND WISDOM, ARE NO MATCH FOR WHAT YOU SEE IN THE BOX BESIDE THIS ONE. THIS IS BECAUSE GLO's DO NOT DEFINE THEM ACCORDING TO THE WORD OF GOD. ALL OF THESE CHARACTERISTICS WITHOUT CHRIST **ACCORDING TO THE TRUTH** ARE MEANINGLESS.
11.) THEOCRACY- GOD IS OMNIPOTENT, OMNISCIENT, AND OMNIPRESENT. WHEN ONE ALLOWS GOD TO RULE THEIR LIFE AND GODLY MEN RULE IN GOVERNMENT LOVE, JOY, AND PEACE WILL RULE THEIR HEARTS. WITH GOD AS THE	11.) **DEMOCRACY-** DEMOCRACY WITHOUT GOD IS HELL RUN WILD. MAN CAN DO NOTHING WITHOUT CHRIST. GLO's HAVE NO KING. SINCE ALL MEMBERS ARE SINNERS, CHAOS IS THE ONLY RESULT. IN A DEMOCRACY, EVIL RULE PRODUCES EVIL DECISIONS, DIRECTIONS, AND DESTINIES, JUST AS AN EVIL KING WOULD DO THE SAME. A GODLY DEMOCRACY IS GREAT, BECAUSE THE LEADERS AND PEOPLE FOLLOW GOD'S WAYS, JUST AS A GODLY KING WOULD DO

FREDERIC L. HATCHETT

JUDGE, JURY, KING, LAWMAKER, etc. CHRISTIANS DON'T HAVE TO WORRY ABOUT ANYTHING. **ISAIAH 33:22/PROVERBS 29:2**	ALSO. THIS IS NOT SO IN GLO'S, BECAUSE NO ONE IS TRULY FOLLOWING GOD (i.e. they are all sinners.) THEREFORE, NO PEACE CAN EVER BE ACHIEVED. There is no peace, says my God, for the wicked.(**ISAIAH 57:21**)/**PROVERBS 29:1**
12.) LIBERTY OF THE SPIRIT- WE DO NOT HAVE TO PERFORM RITUALS TO WORSHIP GOD. WE CAN WORSHIP HIM AT CHURCH, HOME, SCHOOL, OR IN THE CAR. WE HAVE NOTHING TO PROVE TO JESUS TO BE ACCEPTED, FOR HE ALREADY MADE IT CLEAR WE COULD DO NOTHING FOR OURSELVES. **II CORINTHIANS 3:17(amp) JEREMIAH 29:11**	**12.) BONDAGE TO THE FLESH-** INITIATES ARE BOUND BECAUSE THEY MUST PROVE THEIR WORTHINESS BY WHAT THEY DO IN THE FLESH (i.e. PLEDGING). GREEK CHRISTIANS ARE BOUND TO THEIR ORGANIZATIONS. THIS BONDAGE CAN BE SEEN IN THEIR DOCTRINES. FALSE WORSHIP FOUND IN THEIR RITUALS. The Sigma Gamma Rho's "Pledge". "To thee only, Sigma Gamma Rho, **I pledge my life**, my best efforts, and cooperation. **In thee** I pin **my faith, hope, and trust,** so that the order of Sigma Gamma Rho shall be a beacon of light to all womankind who are interested in every phase of education." (The Handbook of Sigma Gamma Rho Sorority, Inc., 1980, p. 9. Quoted from Elder James P. Tharrington, Jr., Should Christians Pledge Fraternities and Sororities, For His Glory Printing And Publishing, 1990, p. 23.) Things they should be confessing to Jesus are confessed to their sorority. The bondage is easy to spot. They ask for your life dedication, and that you put your trust in the organization. This is a curse.(**JEREMIAH 17:5**)

COMING APART AT THE SEAMS

	GALATIANS 4:8-9(amp) VERSE 9 IS FOR THOSE WHO GAVE THEIR LIFE TO CHRIST BEFORE THEY BECAME GREEKS, AND FOR ANY WHO DENOUNCED AND WENT BACK TO THEIR GLO. IT IS ALSO FOR ANY CHRISTIAN WHO IS IN AGREEMENT WITH GLO's. IF YOU HAVE ANY CHRISTIAN FRIENDS WHO ARE GREEKS, YOU MUST WITNESS TO THEM. IF THEY CHOOSE NOT TO REPENT AND DENOUNCE, YOU MUST BREAK FELLOWSHIP.
13.) Secrecy- Practiced neither by Jesus, nor by true Christians. **Acts 26:26/John 18:20/Matthew 10:26-28 Could you see Jesus beating people with paddles just to become a Christian? ABSURD!**	13.) **Secrecy**- A most vital and necessary characteristic of GLO's. Your ignorance about their organization is the only leg they have on which to stand. If you know their secrets, you have broken their only support system. Knowing their secrets enables you to take them down from the inside. A house divided cannot stand. Once you know their secrets, you are just as much a part of their house as them **without being unequally yoked.** In secrecy, Greek organizations have murdered, ruptured spleens, broken bones, damaged lungs and kidneys, blinded people,

	and humiliated them to the point of nervous breakdowns.
14.) THERE IS NO SUCH THING AS UNEQUAL YOKING IN TRUE CHRISTIANITY, BECAUSE NO ONE IS PRACTICING SIN. THERE IS UNITY ON ALL ESSENTIAL AREAS IN THE WORD OF GOD SUCH AS: SEX, ABORTION, THE DEITY OF JESUS, THE RESURRECTION, CREATION, THE EXISTENCE OF HEAVEN AND HELL, AND MANY OTHER ESSENTIALS.	**14.) UNEQUAL YOKING IS A SIN PRACTICED, CONDONED AND EXISTENT IN GLO's II CORINTHIANS 6:14-18** SINCE GREEK CHRISTIANS BELIEVE THEY ARE TRUE CHRISTIANS, WHY DO THEY CALL SINNERS THEIR BROTHERS AND SISTERS? WHY DO THEY HAVE CONSTANT FELLOWSHIP WITH THEM? **IS THEIR A SOLUTION FOR THEIR UNEQUAL YOKING? YES.** IT'S CALLED **REPENT AND DENOUNCE.** WHAT DOES THIS MEAN? IT MEANS, IF SOMEONE CALLS YOU AN OMEGA OR ZETA, YOU SAY TO HIM OR HER; I'M NO LONGER IN THAT ORGANIZATION, NOR DO I CONSIDER MYSELF TO BE AN OMEGA OR ZETA. I HAVE BROKEN FELLOWSHIP WITH MY ORGANIZATION, THE FRATERNITY OR SORORITY AS FAR AS MEMBERSHIP AND ACTIVITY IS CONCERNED IS **DEAD.** ANY ACKNOWLEDGMENT THAT YOU ARE A GREEK MEANS YOU ARE STILL ONE. IT DOESN'T MATTER IF YOU ARE INACTIVE, HAVEN'T PAID DUES, AND DO NOT ASSOCIATE WITH OTHER MEMBERS. YOU STILL ARE CONFESSING TO BE A GREEK. BY PRACTICING THE SIN OF UNEQUAL YOKING, GREEK CHRISTIANS PROVE THEY ARE SINNERS BY NATURE. **I JOHN 3:8 (amp)** How can you separate from one who is still your brother or sister? Your choice of who to hang with does not change the reality

	that you are still yoked **spiritually** to each and every individual in your GLO.

CHRISTIAN WITNESS!! REMEMBER THAT SUCCESS IN THE SPIRIT IS THE UNSEEN REALITY OF YOUR ACCOMPLISHMENT. NEVER BE DISCOURAGED JUST BECAUSE SOMEONE DOESN'T TAKE HOLD TO YOUR CONVICTION. (**ISAIAH 55:11**)

Notes

CHAPTER 5
THE CHURCH vs. FRATERNITIES AND SORORITIES

GREEK CHRISTIANS HAVE A KNACK FOR ATTACKING AND ACCUSING THE CHURCH AND CHRISTIANS AS EXCUSES FOR THE THINGS THEY DO. THIS CHAPTER WILL SET IT ALL STRAIGHT, AND PROVE THAT THEY ARE OFF TARGET AND EXTREMELY HYPOCRITICAL IN GIVING SUCH CRITICISM. **IF** GREEK CHRISTIANS WERE REALLY CHRISTIANS, THEN THEY WOULD BE GUILTY OF TWO THINGS. 1.) IN ATTACKING THE CHURCH, THEY ATTACK THEMSELVES, AND 2.) IN ATTACKING CHRISTIANS, THEY ARE ATTACKING THEIR BROTHERS AND SISTERS. HOW FOOLISH THIS WOULD BE, **IF** IT WERE TRUE.

COMING APART AT THE SEAMS

The church is **UNIQUE** by definition. The word for church comes from "ekklesia" which means, "separate from the world" or "called out ONES". THIS MEANS THAT ALL TRUE CHRISTIANS MAKE UP THE TRUE CHURCH. THIS PROVES POINT #1 IN THE INTRODUCTION OF THIS CHAPTER.

ACTS 7:38 This is he, that was **in the church** in the wilderness with the angel which spake to him in the Mount Sinai and with our fathers: who received the lively oracles to give unto us:

It is used of the Jews in this specific scripture, "as the people who were called out of the rest of the world to have a special national relationship to God." Since **the individual Christian is himself a church** and a part of the body of Christ (THE UNIVERSAL CHURCH) of which Christ is the Head, he must leave anything sinful behind. THIS PROVES POINT #2 OF THE ABOVE INTRODUCTION TO THIS CHAPTER THAT GREEK CHRISTIANS ATTACK THEIR OWN BROTHERS.

II TIMOTHY 2:22 Flee also youthful lusts: but follow righteousness, faith, charity, peace, with them that call on the Lord out of a **pure** heart.

Once saved, **a person** must be willing to CHANGE. A church building (the local church) has no need of repentance and is not separate from the world. "It is a local, visible, temporal manifestation of the **universal church or body of believers**." People do need to repent and are COMMANDED to be SPIRITUALLY separate from the world (**I JOHN 2:15**) because saved individuals, (the ekklesia's), will at one time be taken out of this physical world to heaven as a universal body of believers. This ends the presence of the church on earth for a season. Jesus will accept you as you are and will even come to you. It is then that you must follow Him.

MATTHEW 11:28-30 Come unto me, all ye that labor and are heavy laden, and I will give you rest. Take my yoke upon you, and learn of me; for I am meek and lowly in heart: and ye shall find rest unto your souls. For my yoke is easy, and my burden is light.

REVELATION 3:20 Behold, I stand at the door, and knock: if any man hear my voice, and open the door, **I will come into him**, and sup with him, and he with me.

After you accept Him, you must submit to the Holy Spirit to change you and shape you up.

ROMANS 12:1-2 I beseech you therefore, brethren, by the mercies of God, that ye present your bodies a living sacrifice, holy, acceptable which is your reasonable service. And be not conformed to this world: but be ye transformed by the renewing of your mind, that ye may prove what is that good, and acceptable, and perfect, will of God.

We as Christians now have a **heavenly citizenship**.

PHILIPPIANS 3:20(amp) But **we are citizens** of the state (commonwealth, homeland) which is **in heaven**, and from it also we earnestly and patiently await [the coming of] the Lord Jesus Christ (the Messiah) [as] savior,

We are now **ambassadors** to heaven. Soul winning is a command, not an option. It is a required ministry.

II CORINTHIANS 5:17-20 Therefore if any man be in Christ, he is a new creature: old things are passed away: behold, all things are become new. And all things are of God, who has reconciled us to himself by Jesus Christ, and hath given to us **the ministry of reconciliation**; To wit, that God was in Christ, reconciling the world unto himself, not imputing their trespasses unto them; and hath committed unto us the word of reconciliation. Now then **we are ambassadors for Christ**, as though God did beseech you by us: we pray you in Christ's stead, be ye reconciled to God.

We are the kings and priests of the heavenly King and High Priest. We represent all of those who have gone on to be with the Lord. The church is a body of believers, not a building made with hands, but we are the temple of God (**I CORINTHIANS 3:16 and 6:16**). Each believer will be judged individually, not collectively, for the deeds they perform.

ROMANS 2:6 Who will render to every man according to his deeds:

The believer will also be judged for their thoughts, words and intentions. When Jesus sent the letters to the seven churches in Revelation, He was talking to the whole church (i.e. the body of believers, but to each person in the church as well). Just because some people in a church you attend may be dealing drugs doesn't mean you are going to hell for their sin, but if they claim to be Christians it is a sin for true Christians not to judge them and expose them likewise. My righteousness in Christ will not get him to heaven either. **In the case of all sin**, Jesus has already passed judgment on them. But **when sin is known by any individual** in that church, judgment of that sin must take place privately first. **Knowingly and willingly** joining oneself to something (**GLO's**) or someone evil (**a sinner or "confessing" Christian who is practicing sin**) makes you a part of it **regardless of your reason to join**. Although Jesus sat with the publicans (sinners), He did not become one or act like one to show them the way. Read the scripture carefully: It says they came to sit with Him, not Him to them. It does not say that He fellowshipped with them.

MATTHEW 9:10-13 And it came to pass, as Jesus sat at meat in the house, behold, many publicans and sinners came and **sat down with him and his disciples**. And when the Pharisees saw it, they said unto his disciples, Why eateth your Master with publicans and sinners? But when Jesus heard that, he said unto them, They that be whole need not a physician, but they that are sick. But go ye and learn what that meaneth, I will have mercy, and not sacrifice: for **I am not come to call the righteous, but sinners to repentance.**

A Christian does not have to join Alpha Phi Alpha, AKA, Pi Kappa Alpha, or any GLO to be a light to them or to call them to repentance. For those who have a desire to join a GLO, they have what is called an **inordinate** affection. These are bad desires that the Bible says to kill, deaden, and deprive of power of which some were and some are bound.

COLOSSIANS 3:5-7 Mortify therefore your members which are upon the earth; fornication, uncleanness, **inordinate affection**, evil concupiscence, and covetousness, which is idolatry: For which things sake the wrath of God cometh on the children of disobedience: In the which ye also walked some time, when ye lived in them.

The desire to join a GLO on the surface may **seem** righteous, but the real motives will eventually be revealed. In this case, as a Christian, you have joined the world and separated yourself from the True Church (**I JOHN 2:15**); and yes, for the simple fact of joining a GLO, a "Christian" once on fire for God will go to HELL. Does it **seem** harsh and outlandish?

Yes! Yet, Jesus said in **JOHN 6:47-69** (especially verses 60, & 66-68), "lest you eat My flesh and Drink my blood, you shall have no part with me". **I want you to read about the response of the people to this declaration, and then look at Peter's response.** One of the churches in Revelation had no faults, but in it were liars. God said he would expose them, and prayerfully they would repent. This doesn't mean every individual in that church would go to heaven, if the rapture came. Judgment is upon you as an individual in this life. It does not make a difference what the Christians and the church is doing, but it matters what the Bible says you are supposed to do. The church is a place where Christians grow in the Word, and sinners hear the Word to be convicted of sin. All of John 15, especially the first six verses, tells the meaning of the church, **the body of believers**, and how it works. Yet, one can see how we are dealt with as individuals. If a person(s) wants to start a Christian business club, it must be Christ-Centered and its foundation must be in Christ.

I CORINTHIANS 3:11 For other foundation can no man lay than that is laid, which is Jesus Christ.

The first standard would be purity (i.e. No sinners allowed AS MEMBERS- a little leaven leaveneth the whole lump). The maintenance of purity is accomplished by having all unrepentant members expelled.

I CORINTHIANS 5:5-7 To deliver such a one unto Satan for the destruction of the flesh, that the spirit may be saved in the day of the Lord Jesus. Your glorying is not good. Know ye not that a little leaven leaveneth the whole lump? **Purge** out therefore the old leaven, that ye may be a new lump, as ye are unleavened. For even Christ our passover is sacrificed for us.

GALATIANS 5:13(amp) For you, brethren, were [indeed] called to freedom; only [do not let your] freedom be an incentive to your flesh and an opportunity or excuse [for selfishness], but through love you should serve one another.

The Greek-Lettered Organizations are founded upon ancient philosophical belief systems that are in no way Biblically based or Christ-centered. This is clearly seen in the language and emphasis of their written, oral, and ceremonial rituals. **They all point to their organizations, not Jesus.** The Word of God is the basis of judgment for **all** things. Remember every church is not a church of God.

ACTS 20:28(amp) Take heed therefore unto yourselves, and to all the flock, over the which **the Holy Ghost hath made you overseers**, to feed **the church of God**, which he hath purchased with his own blood.

Just as the word of God gives clear instructions on how the church should operate, so do individuals have the same standard: **the Word of God.** Hitler is going to be judged by the same standard as Billy Graham: **the Word of God. GLO's do not meet up to the standards set by the Word of God. Why,** because Jesus is not the center focus of their ceremonies, songs, poems, etc. Instead of Jesus being lifted up, the organization is exalted. The key to any successful organization, including the Church or any Christian organization, is to **command** complete purity and holiness in thought, word, and action of its members. Unlike the GLO's, masons or eastern stars, leaven (**sin**) plagues these groups because they do not command purity and holiness based on the Bible. The leaders of these groups claim they cannot command Biblical holiness and maintain its membership. So there you have it, the amount of membership is more important than their eternal life. This is the main reason for including the benefit of

COMING APART AT THE SEAMS

eternal life for being a good Delta, Alpha, Omega, etc. The truth remains that their members are sinners. They are sinners by never having been saved, or they have been saved and refuse to accept the truth about their organizations; and like members of the body, if **one member is** sick, the whole body suffers. For example, if some members love to haze, they can cause sickness of the whole GLO. They do this by spreading their opinions to other members. As soon as someone gets hurt, the whole body (the GLO) gets the blame, instead of the individuals alone. This type of spiritual sickness has lead to physical deaths. Spiritual death (**sin**) is already present in the entire GLO (**ROMANS 6:23**). There is no good in a GLO. **Spiritual sickness (leaven, sin)** will also plague those churches whose leaders refuse to deal with or get rid of GLO members who refuse to repent and remove the leaven from their lives. Knowing from scripture that a little leaven, leaveneth the whole lump, just imagine what a whole bunch of leaven could do. One must realize two things; **1.)** Just because a church or churches are doing it or **2.)** A Christian or some Christians are doing it does not mean it is right for other Christians to participate. Whenever a Greek Christian attacks the church, remind them that the church is under the authority of Jesus. People are to look to Jesus for truth not a man or a church that is not abiding by the Word of God.

I JOHN 2:27(amp) But as for you, the anointing (the sacred appointment, the unction) which you received from him abides [permanently] in you; [so] then you have no need that anyone should instruct you. But just as his anointing teaches you concerning everything and is true and is no falsehood, so you must abide in (live in, never depart from) him [being rooted in him, knit to him], just as [his anointing] has taught you [to do].

FREDERIC L. HATCHETT

The relationship of Christ to the church is UNIQUE and very important. **IT IS ETERNAL because its Founder is ETERNAL.** No other organization in the world can make that claim, but they can and must proclaim Christ as their center and foundation to be acceptable to God.

The **ORIGIN** of the church was prophesied by Jesus to Peter in,

MATTHEW 16:13-18(amp) Now when Jesus went into the region of Caesarea Philippi, he asked his disciples, who do people say that the son of man is? And they answered him, some say John the Baptist; others say Elijah; and others say Jeremiah or one of the prophets. He said to them, But who do you [yourselves] say that I am? Simon Peter replied, You are the Christ, the son of the living God. Then Jesus answered him, Blessed (happy, fortunate, and to be envied) are you, Simon Bar-Jonah. For flesh and blood [men] have not revealed this to you, but my father who is in heaven. And I tell you, you are Peter [Greek, Petros a large piece of rock] and **on this rock** [Greek, petra a huge rock like Gibraltar] **I will build my church, and the gates of Hades** (the power of the infernal region) **shall not overpower it** [or be strong to its detriment or hold out against it].

The confession of Christ, Who is revealed to us by the Father, is realized in the spiritual reality of being saved (i.e. A SPIRITUAL CONFESSION YIELDS A SPIRITUAL CONVERSION **WHETHER TO SALVATION OR DAMNATION**). The fulfillment of this scripture or beginning of the church age we live in today is the **Day of Pentecost (Acts 2)**.

"The ultimate purpose of the church is to bring honor and glory to its head, Jesus Christ. It does this as it fulfills its two purposes related to God's program for the world. The one purpose of the church, as it

COMING APART AT THE SEAMS

relates to the world, is evangelism. Another purpose of the church, as it relates to the world, is edification. According to **Ephesians 4:12** the saints need to be edified (built up) for two goals: 'For the perfecting of the saints' and 'for the work of the ministry.'" ("From the King James Version New Open Bible, copyright 1990, Thomas Nelson, Inc. Publishers. Used by permission. All rights reserved.")

Evangelism is for GROWTH and Edification for SPIRITUAL MATURATION TO PERFORM **(DO)** THE WORK OF GOD. **The RELATIONSHIP OF THE CHURCH TO CHRIST** is vital, because it is UNIQUE to all other organizations.

Secular and non-religious organizations do not claim Christian principles, and therefore we should not expect them to uphold those things. The relationship was **initiated (the origin/root)** by Christ who loved the church and gave Himself for it. This love and relationship is shown in SEVEN ways.

a.) "' The shepherd and the sheep' emphasizes both the warm leadership and protection of Christ and the helplessness and dependency of believers. (**JOHN 10:1-18**)." ("From the King James Version New Open Bible, copyright 1990, Thomas Nelson, Inc. Publishers. Used by permission. All rights reserved.")

MANY MEMBERS ARE LED TO BELIEVE AND RELY ON THEIR GLO FOR HELP WHENEVER THEY NEED IT. UNFORTUNATELY, THIS IS RARELY THE CASE. GLO's OFFER NO TRUE PROTECTION OR INFALLIBLE LEADERSHIP. MEMBERS OF GLO's AND A GLO ITSELF DEPEND ON EACH OTHER. JESUS IS SELF-SUFFICIENT AND ALL SUFFICIENT AT THE SAME TIME. WHO WOULD YOU RATHER BE UNDER? YOU CAN'T HAVE BOTH!

b.) "'The vine and the branches' points out the necessity for Christians to depend upon Christ's sustaining strength for growth (**JOHN 15:1-8**)." ("From the King James Version New Open

FREDERIC L. HATCHETT

Bible, copyright 1990, Thomas Nelson, Inc. Publishers. Used by permission. All rights reserved.")

John 15:1-8 I am the **true vine**, and my father is the husbandman. Every branch in me that beareth not fruit he taketh away: and every branch that beareth fruit, he purgeth it, that it may bring forth more fruit. Now ye are clean through the word which I have spoken unto you. Abide in me, and I in you. As the branch can not bear fruit of itself, except it abide in the vine; no more can ye, except ye abide in me. I am the vine, ye are the branches: He that abideth in me, and I in him, the same bringeth forth much fruit: for **without me ye can do nothing. If a man abide not in me, he is cast forth as a branch, and is withered; and men gather them, and cast them into the fire, and they are burned.** If ye abide in me, and my words abide in you, ye shall ask what ye will, and it shall be done unto you. Herein is my father glorified, that ye bear much fruit; so shall ye be my disciples.

THERE CAN BE SEPARATION FROM THE TRUE VINE UNAWARES TO YOURSELF AND OTHERS. THIS IS THE REASON WHY WE SHOULD EXAMINE OURSELVES AND CONFESS OUR SINS DAILY. UNEQUAL YOKING IS CONDEMNED. THIS MEANS THAT SEPARATING ONLY FROM THOSE SINNING SISTERS OR BROTHERS IS NOT ENOUGH IN RELATION TO THE GLO, BECAUSE AN INDIVIDUAL **BY HIMSELF** DOES NOT HAVE THE POWER TO SEVER A SPIRITUAL BOND, WHICH COMES BY THE SWEARING OF AN OATH. THEREFORE, **THERE IS NO SEPARATION WITHOUT DENUNCIATION** FOR ANYONE IN A GLO). IF YOU'RE A "Christian" KAPPA, **YOUR DECISION** TO SEPARATE FROM A FORNICATING KAPPA, DOES NOT CHANGE THE FACT THAT HE IS STILL YOUR BROTHER (i.e. HE IS STILL A KAPPA AND SO ARE YOU). YOU ARE STILL BROTHERS, AND BECAUSE YOU CONFESS CHRIST, YOU ARE STILL UNEQUALLY YOKED BY REMAINING A MEMBER. IT IS DIFFERENT WITH CHRISTIANS. YOU KNOW A BROTHER OR SISTER IN CHRIST, AND THAT IS PRACTICING SIN, BUT YOU DO

NOT KNOW IT. FIRST, THE PERSON IS ALREADY SEPARATED FROM CHRIST **FOR PRACTICING SIN (I JOHN 3:9)**. SECOND, IF YOU KNOW THIS PERSON IS IN SIN AND REFUSES TO REPENT OF SIN, YOU MUST SEPARATE PHYSICALLY AND SPIRITUALLY BY CUTTING OFF **ALL FELLOWSHIP**. CHRIST HAS ALREADY CANCELLED HIS SPIRITUAL BOND TO ALL CHRISTIANS BY **HIS OWN POWER**. A GLO OR ITS MEMBERS **DO NOT HAVE THE POWER** TO CANCEL A SPIRITUAL YOKE **ALONE**. THEREFORE, **UNLESS COMPLETE DENUNCIATION** TAKES PLACE, YOU ARE THEIR GLO SIBLING FOR LIFE, AND BECAUSE OF THIS **YOU WILL ALWAYS BE UNEQUALLY YOKED.** SO AS LONG AS YOU REMAIN A GREEK CHRISTIAN, YOU ARE BREAKING THE COMMANDMENT OF GOD FOUND IN II CORINTHIANS 6:14-18. HOW CAN ANYONE CALL HIMSELF OR HERSELF A CHRISTIAN BY DOING SUCH A THING? WELL CALLING YOURSELF A CHRISTIAN AND BEING ONE IS TWO VERY DIFFERENT THINGS.

    c.) "'Christ as the high priest' and 'the church as a kingdom of priests' stresses the joyful worship, fellowship, and service which the church can render to God through Christ (**HEBREWS 5:1-10/7:1&8:6/I PETER 2:5-9/REVELATION 1:6**)." ("From the King James Version New Open Bible, copyright 1990, Thomas Nelson, Inc. Publishers. Used by permission. All rights reserved.")

    A GLO CANNOT RENDER SERVICE TO GOD THROUGH CHRIST, AND NEITHER CAN ITS MEMBERS. GLO's ARE COMMUNITY AND SELF-SERVICE ORGANIZATIONS, NOT SERVERS OF GOD. ALL GLO's CLAIM THAT SERVICE IS THEIR AIM, YET YOU NEVER HEAR "GREEK CHRISTIANS" ADMIT THEY ARE SERVING TWO MASTERS. A SERVICE BASED ORGANIZATOINS MUST HAVE SERVANTS WHO ARE SERVING THE GLO IN SOME WAY. IN NO WAY CAN GLO's AND GREEK CHRISTIANS STRESS WORSHIP, FELLOWSHIP, AND SERVICE TO GOD THROUGH

CHRIST, BECAUSE THEY HAVE NO RELATIONSHIP WITH CHRIST. GLO's DO NOT RECOGNIZE JESUS AS THEIR LORD. THEIR DOCTRINE OF **RELIGIOUS TOLERANCE,** WHICH ALLOWS THOSE OF ANY RELIGION TO JOIN, SHOWS THEIR LACK OF REVERENCE FOR JESUS AND GOD'S WORD. IT ALSO SHOWS THAT GLO's DON'T MIND FELLOWSHIPPING WITH OCCULTISTS, MORMONS, OR MUSLLIMS TO NAME A FEW. **NO CHRISTIAN FOUNDATION CAN BE ESTABLISHED ON RELIGIOUS TOLERANCE (ECUMENICALISM).**

d.) "'The Cornerstone and the building stones' accenting the foundational value of Christ to everything the church is and does, as well as Christ's value to the unity of believers. Love is to be the mortar which solidly holds the living stones together (**I CORINTHIANS 3:9&13:1-13/EPHESIANS 2:19-22/I PETER 2:5).**" ("From the King James Version New Open Bible, copyright 1990, Thomas Nelson, Inc. Publishers. Used by permission. All rights reserved.")

I DO NOT SEE WHERE GLO's OR THEIR MEMBERSHIP FIT IN AS THE BUILDING STONES!!! **IDOLATRY** IS NOT BASED ON FAITH, **GLO's OFFER NO HOPE FOR ETERNAL LIFE, HAZING** IS NOT BUILT ON LOVE AND **SECRECY** IS NOT BASED ON HONESTY.

e.) "'The **Head** and the many-membered **body'** is frequently used in Scripture to illustrate several tremendous truths: the church is a vibrant organism, **not merely an organization;** it **draws** its **vitality and direction from Christ,** the head; and each believer has a unique and necessary place in its growth (**I CORINTHIANS 12:12-13&27/EPHESIANS 4:4).**" ("From the King James Version New Open Bible, copyright 1990, Thomas Nelson, Inc. Publishers. Used by permission. All rights reserved.")

NO GLO FITS THIS DESCRIPTION EITHER. THEY DRAW THEIR STRENGTH AND VITALITY FROM THEIR DOCTRINES, SYMBOLS, HYMNS, POEMS, etc. INSTEAD

COMING APART AT THE SEAMS

OF RELYING ON THE HEADSHIP OF CHRIST, THEY WOULD RATHER RIDE ON THE REPUTATION OF **FAMOUS MEMBERS AND THEIR GOOD WORKS.**

    f.) "'The last Adam and new creation' presents Christ as the initiator of a new creation of believers as Adam was of the old creation (**I CORINTHIANS 15:22,45/II CORINTHIANS 5:17**)." ("From the King James Version New Open Bible, copyright 1990, Thomas Nelson, Inc. Publishers. Used by permission. All rights reserved.")

AMBASSADORSHIP IS THE INITIAL FOCUS OF THE NEW CREATION IN CHRIST. SINCE GLO's DO NOT PRACTICE AMBASSADORSHIP (SOUL-WINNING), WHERE WILL THE GLO AND GREEK CHRISTIAN FIT IN WITH THE NEW CREATION? NOWHERE!!

    g.) "'The Bridegroom and the bride' beautifully emphasizes the intimate fellowship and co-ownership existing between Christ and the church (**EPHESIANS 5:25-33/REVELATION 19:7-8&21:9**)." ("From the King James Version New Open Bible, copyright 1990, Thomas Nelson, Inc. Publishers. Used by permission. All rights reserved.")

GLO's IN NO WAY CAN CLAIM THESE TYPES OF RELATIONSHIPS WITH THE CHURCH (i.e. THEY CANNOT BE FOUNDED UPON CHRISTIAN PRINCIPLES). CHRIST SHARES THIS, "INTIMATE FELLOWSHIP", WITH NO ONE OTHER THAN **TRUE CHRISTIANS.** THIS CO-OWNERSHIP MAKES A MURDER IN THE NAME OF CHRISTIANITY A FALSE STATEMENT, BECAUSE CHRIST IS NOT A MURDERER. THE CHURCH/ **HIS CHURCH** IS STILL UNSPOTTED IN GOD'S SIGHT, BECAUSE THAT PERSON'S SALVATION AND TRUE CONNECTION TO THE CHURCH WAS CUT-OFF BEFORE ANY ACT WAS EVER CARRIED OUT. SIN BEGINS IN THE HEART, NOT WHEN IT IS COMMITTED. SINCE A CHRISTIAN CANNOT DELIBERATELY PRACTICE SIN, JESUS' CHURCH IS ALWAYS PURE. REMEMBER THAT HE IS THE TRUE VINE, AND ANY BRANCH THAT IS ATTACHED TO HIM IS TRULY SAVED. THOSE BRANCHES THAT DO NOT PRODUCE FRUIT ARE CUT OFF, WITHER, AND GATHERED TO BE BURNED.

CHRISTIANITY/CHURCH WAS NOT DETERMINED, AND IS NOT CONTROLLED BY INDIVIDUALS as it is with GLO's. GLO's DO NOT SEEK THE HOLY GHOST FOR GUIDANCE, NOR DO THEY RECOGNIZE HIM AS GOD. ONE'S **PERSONAL** RELATIONSHIP WITH CHRIST BY CONFESSION AND **PRACTICE** IS WHAT CHRISTIANITY TRULY IS AND NOTHING ELSE.

SPIRITUALLY, GLO's (MEMBERS INCLUDED) ARE LUKEWARM, AND FIT TO SPEWED OUT OF CHRIST'S MOUTH. THEY HAVE ZEAL TO DO GOOD, BUT NOT ACCORDING TO RIGHTEOUSNESS AND OBEDIENCE. THEY GO TO CHURCH, BUT DO NOT WITNESS JESUS. THEY HAVE BIBLE STUDIES, BUT THERE IS NO DISCERNMENT. THEY HAVE THE FORM OF GODLINESS, BUT DENY THE TRUE POWER OF GOD BY THEIR DEEDS. YET, CHRIST, IN **REVELATION 3:20** IS SO GREATLY CONCERNED FOR YOU, HE COMES TO YOU AND CALLS YOU TO REPENTANCE AND VICTORY THAT YOU MAY SIT WITH HIM ON THE THRONE. ALL YOU NEED TO DO IS ANSWER, AND THEN OBEY.

REVELATIONS 3:15-20 I know thy works, that thou art neither cold nor hot: I would thou wert cold or hot. So then because thou art lukewarm, and neither cold or hot: I will spew thee out of my mouth. Because thou sayest, I am rich, and increased with goods, and have need of nothing; and knowest not that thou art wretched, and miserable, and poor, and blind, and naked: I counsel thee to buy of me gold tried in the fire, that thou mayest be rich; and white raiment, that thou mayest be clothed, and that the shame of thy nakedness do not appear; and anoint thine eyes with eye salve, that thou mayest see. As many as I love, I rebuke and chasten: be zealous therefore, and repent. Behold, I stand at the door, and knock: if any man hear my voice, and open the door, I will come in to him, and will sup with him, and he with me.

PLEASE!!! READ THIS SCRIPTURE CAREFULLY, BECAUSE WORKS AND PROSPERITY IS ONE OF THE

COMING APART AT THE SEAMS

BIGGEST EXCUSES MADE BY BOTH CHRISTIAN AND NON-CHRISTIAN MEMBERS OF GLO's TO JUSTIFY THEMSELVES, THEIR ORGANIZATION, AND THEIR SOUL SALVATION BEFORE GOD. **I BELIEVE THIS SCRIPTURE, READ WITH AN OPEN HEART AND MIND, WILL LEAD MANY GREEK CHRISTIANS TO SEE THEIR ORGANIZATIONS AS USELESS, UNGODLY, AND TOTALLY UNWISE FOR THEM TO BE MEMBERS OF SUCH ORGANIZATIONS.** FOR THIS SCRIPTURE SHOWS THE **RELIGIOUS ATTITUDE** BY MAN IN HIS ATTEMPT TO GAIN GOD'S FAVOR BY HIS OWN EFFORTS WHICH WAS CAIN'S MISTAKE BY TRYING TO OFFER TO GOD THE FRUIT OF THE GROUND WHICH GOD REJECTED, FOR HE HAD CURSED THE GROUND. THIS IS THE EMBODIMENT OF GLO's AND EVEN CHURCH DENOMINATIONS THAT ARE TEACHING THIS FALSE DOCTRINE OF SALVATION BY WORKS. THE CHURCH IS NOT HUMAN IN ORIGIN NOR WAS IT BUILT UPON THE WORK OF MAN, AND IT'S CERTAINLY NOT UNDER MAN'S CONTROL.

MATTHEW 15:16-18 And Jesus said, Are ye also yet without understanding? Do not ye yet understand, that whatsoever entereth in at the mouth goeth into the belly, and is cast out into the draught? But those things which proceed out of the mouth come forth from the heart; and they defile the man.

THEREFORE, HUMAN ERROR CANNOT BE ATTRIBUTED TO CHRIST OR HIS CHURCH. THE CHURCH AND MANKIND WAS BOUGHT WITH THE PRICE OF JESUS' BLOOD. THIS IS THE SAME BLOOD THAT TOOK AWAY THE SINS OF THE WORLD.

HEBREWS 9:22 And almost all things by the law purged with blood; and without shedding of blood is no remission.

WE MESSED UP, FOR HE IS UNABLE TO ERR.

PSALM 18:30 As for God, his way is **perfect**: the word of the Lord is tried: he is a buckler to all those that trust in him.

WE MUST REPENT.

LUKE 13:3 I tell you, Nay: but, except you repent, ye shall all likewise perish.

JESUS HAS NO NEED TO, NOR MUST HE REPENT.

NUMBERS 23:19 God is not a man, that he should lie; neither the son of man, that he should repent: hath he said, and shall he not do it? or hath he spoken, and shall he not make it good?

THE BIBLE CLEARLY STATES THAT GOD'S WAY IS PERFECT AND THAT IT WILL NOT FAIL. THIS MEANS THE CHURCH IS PERFECT, BECAUSE OF THE ROOT. THE ROOT IS PERFECT AND HIS NAME IS **JESUS**. THE ROOTS OF GLO's ARE NOT JESUS, THE WORD OF GOD, CHRISTIANITY, OR TRUTH. THE ROOT OF GREEK-LETTERED GROUPS IS "THE LIE", SATAN, THE DEVIL, THE DECEIVER, THE SERPENT AND THE FATHER OF ALL LIES. GOD MAY BE **A PART** OF THEIR TEACHINGS, **BUT NOT THE FOUNDATION**, AND WITHOUT HIM AS THE FOUNDATION EVERYTHING IS SURE TO FALL. JESUS DOES NOT CHANGE OR ALTER THE TRUTH BECAUSE OF OUR "SEEMINGLY" GOOD INTENTIONS. YOU MUST UNDERSTAND THIS POINT FROM A SPIRITUAL PERSPECTIVE. CHRISTIANS COMPARE THEIR ACTIONS WITH THE WORD OF GOD WHICH SAYS, SIN IS SIN; BUT GLO's COMPARE THEMSELVES BASED ON WHAT **THEIR OWN PRINCIPLES AND TRADITIONS** THAT THEY SET IN PLACE, NOT UNDERSTANDING THAT **THESE PRINCIPLES ARE NOT DOCTRINES OF THE BIBLE.** THEIR PRINCIPLES AND TRADITIONS **ARE NOT ABLE** TO LEAD ONE TO SALVATION, OR TAKE AWAY THE **SINFUL NATURE** OF A MAN. SINCE ETERNAL LIFE IN HEAVEN WITH CHRIST IS TRULY WHAT ALL MEN WANT, GLO's KEEP THEM FROM ACHIEVING THIS DESIRE.

MARK 7:1-16 Then came together unto him the Pharisees, and certain of the scribes, which came from Jerusalem. And when they saw some of his disciples eat bread with defiled, that is to say, with unwashen, hands, they found fault.

COMING APART AT THE SEAMS

For the Pharisees, and all the Jews, except they wash their hands oft, eat not, holding the tradition of the elders. And when they come from the market, except they wash, they eat not, And many other things there be, which they hath received to hold, as the washing of cups, and pots, brasen vessels, and of tables. Then the Pharisees and scribes asked him, why walk not thy disciples according to the tradition of the elders, but eat bread with unwashen hands? He answered and said unto them, Well hath Esaias prophesied of ye hypocrites, as it is written, THIS PEOPLE HONOURETH ME WITH THEIR LIPS, BUT THEIR HEART IS FAR FROM ME. HOWBEIT **IN VAIN THEY DO WORSHIP ME, TEACHING FOR DOCTRINES THE COMMANDMENTS OF MEN.** For **laying aside the commandment of God, ye hold the tradition of men**, as the washing of pots and cups: and many other such like things ye do. And he said unto them, Full well reject the commandment of God, that ye may keep your own tradition. For Moses said, HONOUR THY FATHER AND THY MOTHER; AND, WHOSO CURSETH FATHER OR MOTHER, LET HIM DIE THE DEATH: But ye say, If a man shall say to his father or mother, It is Corban, that is too say, a gift, by whatsoever thou mightest be profited by me; he shall be free. And ye suffer him no more to do ought for his father or his mother; **Making the word of God of none effect through your tradition**, which ye have delivered: and **many such like these do ye**. And when he had called all the people unto him, he said unto them, Hearken unto me every one of you, and understand: There is nothing from without a man, that entering into him can defile him: but the things which come out of him, those are they that defile the man. If any have ears to hear, let him hear.

    THEREFORE, GLO's ARE LEAVING MEN AND WOMEN IN A STATE MOST MISERABLE, A SINNER **TOTALLY SEPARATED FROM GOD**. WHILE THE BIBLE SAYS,
    JOHN 3:3 Except a man be born again, **he cannot** see the kingdom of God.

WHEN ONE IS BORN-AGAIN, THE HOLY SPIRIT CHANGES THE OLD SINFUL NATURE TO A NEW REGENERATED SPIRITUAL NATURE THAT IS ABLE TO KEEP ONE FROM **SERVING** SIN.

ROMANS 6:16 Know ye not, that to whom ye yield yourselves servants to obey, his servants ye are to whom ye obey; whether of sin unto death, or of obedience unto righteousness.

IF ONE IS TRULY BORN AGAIN, THEY TRULY **KNOW** THEY MUST COMPLETELY SEPARATE FROM GREEK-LETTERED ORGANIZATIONS. THIS WILL ALLOW A PERSON TO REAP THE FULL BENEFITS OF PARTICIPATING IN THE LOCAL CHURCH **UNHINDERED** BY THEIR SO-CALLED "RELIGIOUS" ORGANIZATIONS. THE PROBLEM WITH ALL GLO's IS THAT THEY PUT ON **A FORM** OF GODLINESS. THEY TRY TO CLAIM RIGHTEOUSNESS WITHOUT **THE SUPPLIER OF RIGHTEOUSNESS**.

ISAIAH 54:17 No weapon that is formed against thee shall prosper; and every tongue that shall rise against thee in judgment thou shalt condemn. This is the heritage of the servants of the Lord, and **their righteousness is of me**, saith the Lord.

"Seven benefits of participation in a local church are immediately apparent in **ACTS 2:42-47**.

    1.) INSTRUCTION
    2.) FELLOWSHIP
    3.) OBSERVANCE OF ORDINANCES
    4.) CORPORATE PRAYER
    5.) EFFECTIVE OUTREACH
    6.) COMMON CAUSE
    7.) MUTUAL ASSISTANCE

In addition to these, four other benefits of participation in the local church are clear:

COMING APART AT THE SEAMS

8.) WORSHIP (**ACTS 20:7**)
9.) DISCIPLINE (**MATTHEW 18:15-17**),
10.) PASTORAL OVERSIGHT (**I PETER 5:1-3**).
11.) OBEDIENCE TO GOD'S COMMAND (**HEBREWS 10:25**).

PARTICIPATION IN THE LOCAL CHURCH IS NOT OPTIONAL FOR BELIEVERS. IT IS COMMANDED AND IT YIELDS ETERNAL BENEFITS." ("From the King James Version New Open Bible, copyright 1990, Thomas Nelson, Inc. Publishers. Used by permission. All rights reserved.")

AS A GREEK CHRISTIAN, YOU ARE PART OF A SCAM THAT DOES NOT YIELD ETERNAL BENEFITS AND WILL ULTIMATELY DESTROY YOUR SOUL (**MATTHEW 10:26**). **WHY?** REBELLION VIA **UNBELIEF** (i.e. **YOU KNOW GLO's ARE UNGODLY, BUT REFUSE TO DENOUNCE**). EVEN SOME GLO HISTORY BOOKS I HAVE READ, SPEAK OF ANTI-SECRET ORGANIZATION PERSECUTION THAT OCCURRED PRIOR TO THEIR FOUNDING. MEN AND WOMEN WHO FOUNDED THESE ORGANIZATIONS HAD KNOWLEDGE OF THE TRUTH ABOUT SECRET GROUPS, **BUT CHOSE TO REJECT IT. THEY KNEW WHERE THE CHURCH STOOD.** YOU KNOW YOUR FRATERNITY OR SORORITY DOES NOT OFFER AND CANNOT OFFER WHAT YOU NEED FOR ETERNAL LIFE, BUT YOU STILL REMAIN A MEMBER, AND FOR WHAT? ETERNAL DAMNATION! YOU WANT TO JOIN TO BE A LIGHT FOR JESUS, BUT YOU YOURSELF ARE IN DARKNESS.

MATTHEW 6:23 But if thine eye be evil, thy whole body shall be full of darkness. If therefore **the light** that is **in thee be darkness**, how great (terrible) is that darkness.

ANYTHING MEN DO THAT THEY CONSIDER TO BE GODLY MUST BE FOUNDED IN CHRIST AND HIS PRINCIPLES. THE CHRISTIANS THAT FIND THEMSELVES IN SIN IN CAN ONLY BE ACCEPTED BACK INTO THE CHURCH (THE BODY OF BELIEVERS) BY REPENTING. BY DOING THIS, HE IS MADE RIGHT WITH **CHRIST FIRST WHICH PUTS HIM BACK INTO THE CHURCH (THE BODY**

OF CHRIST/BELIEVERS). THE ROOT OF THE CHURCH (ALL BELIVERS) IS JESUS WHO MAKES AND KEEPS ONE IN RIGHT STANDING WITH GOD, **NOT THE LOCAL CHURCH ITSELF.** THE CHURCH **AS AN INSTRUMENT** IS GOD'S APPROVED PLACE FOR TRUE CHRISTIANS (SEPARATE FROM THE WORLD-**EKKLESIA**) WHERE WE ARE COMMANDED TO GO (**HEBREWS 10:25-26/ACTS 2:41-42**) TO LEARN, WORSHIP, FELLOWSHIP, BREAK BREAD, AND GIVE HIM PRAISE AND THANKS. ASIDE FROM IT BEING A COMMAND, ALL CHRISTIANS SHOULD WANT TO DO ALL OF THE ABOVE ANYWAY. BUT **WHERE** DO MEMBERS OF THESE GROUPS NEED TO GO TO BE MADE RIGHT? THE SAME PLACE SINNERS MUST GO TO BE MADE RIGHT? IF IT IS NOT TO CHRIST **ALONE**, THEN TO HELL THEY GO!! THEIR ORGANIZATIONS CAN OFFER THEIR OWN FORGIVENESS AND SYMPATHY FOR A WORNGDOING, BUT NOT TRUE REPENTANCE THAT YIELDS RIGHTEOUSNESS, SALVATION, ETERNAL LIFE, AND FREEDOM FROM PRACTICING SIN. YET, THEY MAKE SUCH CLAIMS BY PROMOTING "CHRISTIAN" PRINCIPLES AND GOOD WORKS TO COVER THEIR UNGODLY AND VAIN BELIEFS, DEEDS, SECRETS AND PRINCIPLES WITHOUT ESTEEMING HIGHLY GOD'S SALVATION BY GRACE THROUGH FAITH (**EPHESIANS 2:8-9**). A CHRISTIAN OR SINNER IS SUBTLY AND CRAFTILY CONVINCED WITH WORDS LIKE **WORKS AND CHRISTIAN FOUNDATION** TO BELIEVE THAT GREEK-LETTERED ORGANIZATIONS HAVE THE SAME REWARDS AND BENEFITS OF BIBLICAL SALVATION REGARDLESS OF SOME SINFUL THINGS THEY PRACTICE AND PROMOTE. LOOK AT WHAT HAPPENED WITH CAIN AND ABEL. ABEL (REPRESENTING **THE TRUE BELIEVER**) WORSHIPPED GOD OBEDIENTLY WITH A BLOOD SACRIFICE. CAIN (**REPRESENTING UNBELIEVERS- i.e. GLO's AND THEIR MEMBERS**) **ATTEMPTED** TO WORSHIP GOD WITH A SACRIFICE FROM THE FRUIT OF THE GROUND WHICH HAD BEEN CURSED. INSTEAD OF OBEYING GOD WITH A BLOOD SACRIFICE, HE CHOSE TO DISOBEY. THEY **BOTH PERFORMED THE WORK OF GIVING A SACRIFICE**, BUT ONLY ONE WAS ACCEPTABLE TO GOD, WHILE THE OTHER WAS NOT.

EPHESIANS 2:10 For we are his workmanship, created in Christ Jesus

unto good works, which God hath before ordained that **we should walk in them.**

YOUR RELATIONSHIP WITH GOD DETERMINES HIS RESPONSE TOWARDS YOU. NO RELATIONSHIP-NO RESPONSE/ RIGHT RELATIONSHIP-BLESSED RESPONSE. THESE ORGANIZATIONS ASK FOR GOD'S BLESSINGS AND FAVOR BY OFFERING CURSED WORKS COMING FROM CURSED ORGANIZATIONS. **GOD CANNOT BLESS THAT WHICH HE HAS CURSED, NOR CAN HE CURSE THAT WHICH HE HAS BLESSED.** THE WAY OF CAIN LEADS TO MORE UNGODLINESS SUCH AS SACRIFICIAL WORSHIP (CHILDREN INCLUDED) AND OTHER ALTERNATIVE FORMS OF WORSHIP LIKE POLYTHEISM. THERE ARE INDIVIDUALS WHO BELIEVE GOD WILL ACCEPT WHATEVER THEY DO REGARDLESS OF **HIS** EXPRESSED WRITTEN HATRED OF SUCH THINGS ALREADY FOUND IN HIS WORD. THIS IS WHAT HAPPENED TO CAIN. THE RESULT OF HIS ONE ACT OF DISOBEDIENCE IS WHAT LEAD TO MORE DISOBEDIENCE. BECAUSE HE REFUSED TO REPENT, HE BECAME **THE FIRST MAN TO COMMIT MURDER** IN HUMAN HISTORY. **POLYTHEISTIC PEOPLE** (ESPECIALLY THE GREEKS/BABYLONIANS) BELIEVED SOME gods HAD TO BE PLEASED BY **HUMAN SACRIFICE- II KINGS 16:3, SEX-** FOR THE FERTILITY gods (**BAAL WORSHIP**), **PERVERSE FESTIVALS** (SUCH AS THE MARDI GRAS), **CUTTING, TATTOOING, OR BRANDING OF THE FLESH. EVEN THE JEWS HAD CONFORMED THEMSELVES TO SUCH PRACTICES, AND NOW PEOPLE EVERYWHERE HAVE FOLLOWED.**

LEVITICUS 19:28(amp) You shall not make any cuttings in your flesh for the dead nor print or tattoo any marks upon you; I am the Lord.

BURNING OF THE SKIN (BRANDING) IS A COMMON PRACTICE IN GLO's. EVEN IF THIS SCRIPTURE DID NOT APPLY, I CORINTHIANS 3:16 & 6:19 DO APPLY. THOUGH IT IS MOSTLY VOLUNTARY, IT IS **KNOWN** TO OCCUR **INVOLUNTARY (i.e. individuals are branded against their own will.)** THE SPIRIT OF PRIDE AND STUPIDITY IS ONE OF THE CAUSES FOR ONE TO BURN A GLO's INSIGNIA ON THEIR SKIN. DO ANY OF YOU REALLY BELIEVE THAT A PASTOR WOULD WANT TO

FREDERIC L. HATCHETT

BRAND SOMEONE WITH THE CHURCH INSIGNIA? I TRULY HOPE NOT.

Notes

CHAPTER 6

BEWARE OF FALSE PROPHETS AND TEACHERS

This chapter will show the **similarities** between the false prophets and teachers of the Bible and GLO's of today. The following three scriptures describe their motives, lifestyles, and teachings.

II PETER 2:1-2,20(amp) But also [in those days] there arose false prophets among the people, just as there will be false teachers among yourselves, who will subtily and stealthily introduce heretical doctrines (destructive heresies), even denying and disowning the master who bought them, bringing upon themselves swift destruction. And many will follow their immoral ways and lascivious doings; because of them the true Way will be maligned and defamed. For if, after they escaped the pollutions of the world through [the full, personal] knowledge of our Lord and savior Jesus Christ, they **again become entangled** in them and are overcome, their last condition is worse [for them] than the first.

INCLUDED IN THE LARGE CROWD OF FALSE PROPHETS AND TEACHERS OF TODAY ARE GLO's. FROM THE PASTORS, BISHOPS, AND MINISTERS DOWN TO THE BABY CHRISTIANS, THEY TO DENY AND DISOWN JESUS BY TEACHING AND DOING THINGS THAT ARE CONTRARY TO GOD'S WORD. ATTACKING THE CHURCH, PRACTICING UNGODLY RITUALS, HAZING, **SALVATION BY WORKS**, GIVING GLORY TO THEIR ORGANIZATIONS THROUGH SONGS AND POEMS, AND BEING A RESPECT OF PERSONS. THE TRUE CHRISTIAN THAT BECOMES A GREEK CHRISTIAN REFUSES TO **LEAVE** THE POLLUTIONS OF THE WORLD THAT EXIST IN GLO's, AND BECOME ENTANGLED IN THEM AGAIN. WITH OVER ONE MILLION GREEKS, THAT ARE SUPPOSED TO BE UNIFIED, YOU WOULD THINK THAT THE OUTCRY AGAINST HAZING WOULD BE MUCH MORE WIDESPREAD. YET, THE OUTCRY IS NOTHING BUT A LOW WHISPER, BECAUSE **THE MAJORITY STILL AGREES WITH THE PRACTICE AS LONG AS NO ONE GETS HURT OR CAUGHT**. STILL, HAZING IS **RUINING LIVES**. THE BIBLE SAYS THAT MANY WILL FOLLOW THESE TYPE OF PEOPLE, AND ONE MILLION IS MANY. GREEK CHRISTIANS ARE ON THEIR WAY TO IMMINENT DESTRUCTION. UNLESS THEY REPENT AND DENOUNCE, THEIR FATE WILL BE WORSE THAN IT WAS WHEN **THEY FIRST BELIEVED**.

MATTHEW 7:15-16(amp) Beware of false prophets among you,

who come to you as sheep, but inwardly they are devouring wolves. You will fully recognize them by their fruits. Do people pick grapes of thorns, or figs of thistles?
READ VERSES 17-29 ALSO.

IN COMPARING THESE FALSE PROPHETS WITH GREEK CHRISTIANS, THEY CAN LOOK LIKE SHEEP, BUT THEY CAN'T ACT LIKE SHEEP. A GREEK CHRISTIAN'S FRUITS (WORKS) WILL NOT MATCH THE LIVES THEY CLAIM TO LIVE. THIS IS WHY JESUS SAID THAT HE NEVER KNEW THEM. **JESUS FULLY RECOGNIZED THEM BY THEIR FRUITS, AND SO CAN TRUE CHRISTIANS.** YOUR FRUITS DETERMINE WHO YOU ARE, AND THEY WERE **FALSE** PROPHETS, NOT REAL ONES. SOME BAD FRUITS THAT I KNOW TO LOOK FOR IN THE GREEK CHRISTIANS ARE **PRIDE**, TOTALITARIANISM, **COMPROMISE, TWISTING AND MISINTERPRETATION OF SCRIPTURE.** THIS IS ALL DUE TO THE **LACK OF STUDYING GOD'S WORD, EXCUSING IMMORAL BEHAVIOR** OF **THEMSELVES OR OTHERS, CONTRADICTION** OF GOD'S WORD, AND **LACK OF CONVICTION** ON CONTROVERSIAL SUBJECTS **THOUGH THEY ARE CLEAR IN SCRIPTURE.** THERE ARE CERTAIN THINGS IN SCRIPTURE THAT ALL CHRISTIANS

MUST BE IN UNITY. THESE ARE CALLED, "THE ESSENTIALS." THEN THERE ARE THOSE "NON-ESSENTIALS" WHERE LIBERTY IS GRANTED.

ALL GREEK CHRISTIANS PAST, PRESENT, AND FUTURE: **NO MATTER HOW GREAT THE WORKS**, JESUS WILL SAY TO THEM (**VERSE 23**), "I never knew you; depart from Me, you who act wickedly [disregarding my commands]." WHY? BECAUSE GREEK CHRISTIANS BREAK MANY OF GOD'S COMMANDS. ALL CHAPTERS TO THIS POINT SPEAKS OF THOSE COMMANDS GREEK CHRISTIANS BREAK.

I GUARANTEE THAT THESE BAD FRUITS I MENTIONED WILL SHOW UP. **BEWARE** OF GREEK CHURCH LEADERS WHO DON'T HAVE CONVICTIONS ABOUT THINGS THAT ARE CLEARLY EXPLAINED IN SCRIPTURE. TO THE CHRISTIAN WITNESSS: DO NOT BE AFRAID OF ANY CHURCH LEADER IN A GLO. CONFRONT THEM IN LOVE AND WITH THE TRUTH. "**BE STRONG AND OF GOOD COURAGE.**" (**JOSHUA 1:6**)

JUDE 4(amp) For certain men have crept in stealthily [gaining entrance **secretly** by a side door]. Their doom was predicted long ago, **ungodly** (impious, profane) persons who **pervert the grace** (the spiritual blessing and favor) of **our** God into lawlessness and wantonness and immorality, and disown and deny **our** sole Master and Lord, Jesus Christ (the Messiah, the Anointed One).

IN ORDER FOR GLO's TO GAIN ACCEPTANCE BY THE CHURCH, THEY FIRST HAD TO CREEP IN UNAWARES (secretly). THEY WANTED TO GAIN A FOOTHOLD BEFORE BEING EXPOSED. EACH OF THESE SCRIPTURES SPEAKS OF SECRECY IN SOME WAY. SECRECY IS THE GLUE THAT HOLDS GLO's, FALSE PROPHETS AND FALSE TEACHERS TOGETHER. **SECRECY HAS BEEN THE STORY OF THEIR LIFE. WITHOUT SECRECY GLO's WOULD BE NOTHING.** NO ONE WOULD JOIN THEM, BECAUSE THEY WOULD SEE THEM FOR WHAT THEY ARE, A CLUB OF MEN AND WOMEN WITH NO TRUE COMMON BOND. A BUNCH OF WHOREMONGERS, DRUNKARDS, AND PARTY PEOPLE RUN WILD. **WHAT CHURCH MEMBERS OUGHT TO DEMAND OF THEIR GREEK PASTORS IS FULL DISCLOSURE OF THEIR GLO SECRETS. THEY SHOULD ALSO TRY TO GET THE GLO RITUAL AND REVEAL IT TO THEIR PASTOR AND THE MEMBERS OF THE CHURCH.**

WELL WHAT DO FALSE TEACHERS AND PROPHETS OF THE BIBLE HAVE TO DO WITH GLO's TODAY? THE RESEMBLANCE WILL SURPRISE YOU.

1.) THEY CREPT INTO THE CHURCHES UNAWARES.
GLO's HISTORY PROVES THIS. THE VERY FIRST ONES KNEW THEY HAD TO HAVE A FIRM

RELATIONSHIP WITH THE CHURCH BEFORE THEY COULD BE ACCEPTED ON A LARGER SCALE. THEY HAD TO KEEP A LID ON SIN OR SUCCUMB TO REJECTION, AS DID THE MASONS AT ONE TIME. FINANCIALLY, MEMBERSHIP IS THE WAY THEY SURVIVE. IF YOU CUT OFF THEIR FINANCES, THEIR SO-CALLED GREAT BONDS OF BROTHERHOOD AND SISTERHOOD WOULD DISINTIGRATE LIKE SMOKE IN THE AIR.

2.) THEY CREPT IN DECEITFULLY DISGUISING THEMSELVES AS CHRISTIANS (SHEEP).

THERE'S A BIG DIFFERENCE BETWEEN ACTING LIKE A CHRISTIAN, AND BEING ONE. THE FORMER SUFFERS NOTHING, THE LATTER SUFFERS PERSECUTION ON EVERY SIDE. THE LORD KNOWS HIS OWN.

3.) THEY TEACH HERESIES WHICH CAUSE DIVISIONS IN THE CHURCH. A HERETIC IS ONE WHO **PURPOSELY CHOOSES** TO BELIEVE AND HAVE OPINIONS THAT DIFFER FROM THE WORD OF GOD. A HERESY IS THE SUBSTANCE OF THE OPINION. A HERESY THAT GLO's PROMOTE IS SALVATION BY WORKS. OTHER HERETICAL TEACHINGS ARE NO BODILY RESURRECTION, REQUIREMENT OF PHYSICAL CIRCUMCISION, AND EVOLUTION.

GLO's AND GREEK CHRISTIANS PURPOSELY TEACH AND PROMOTE THINGS CONTRARY TO GOD'S WORD (**CHAPTERS 1-5 GIVE EXAMPLES**). THIS ATTITUDE IS WHAT HAS LEAD TO THE FORMATION OF SO MANY DENOMINATIONS OF THE CHURCH, AND LOOK AT ALL THE GLO's THAT EXIST TODAY. MY POINT IS THIS: I HAVE NOT HEARD, NOR DO I KNOW OF ANY

NON-DENOMINATIONAL OR FULL GOSPEL PASTORS OR BISHOPS THAT BELONG TO A GREEK-LETTERED ORGANIZATION (GLO). IF THERE ARE ANY, **I ASK THEM TO TAKE A STAND AGAINST THIS BOOK, BUT BE WILLING TO DO IT FACE-TO-FACE PREFERABLY IN A FORUM STYLE SETTING.**

4.) THEY FOSTER REBELLION AGAINST CHURCH LEADERSHIP.

WHEN A GREEK CHRISTIAN KNOWS THEIR PASTOR PREACHES AGAINST GLO's, AND TRIES TO CONVINCE YOU OTHERWISE, THEY ARE SOWING REBELLION INTO YOUR HEART. WHO IS MORE IMPORTANT TO YOU? A LOST SINNER, OR YOUR GOD-GIVEN LEADER?

5.) THEY CARE ABOUT SOUL DESTROYING, NOT SOUL WINNING.

THIS STATEMENT IS SPECIFIC TO ALL READERS. GREEK PASTORS/MINISTERS/BISHOPS/ELDERS CANNOT BE INTERESTED IN YOUR SOULS, IF THEY DON'T CARE FOR THEIR OWN. THE PURPOSE OF THIS BOOK IS TO HELP THE READER SEE THAT MEN OF GOD IN GLO's ARE JUST AS LOST AS THE NEXT SINNER. INSTEAD OF LOOKING AT THEIR TITLES, ONE NEEDS TO COMPARE THEIR FRUITS TO GOD'S WORD. IF THEY ARE BEARING BAD FRUIT, THEY CAN'T CARE ABOUT SOULS. IT'S NOT A SINNER'S NATURE TO CARE ABOUT THE **SPIRITUAL** WELFARE OF ANOTHER.

IF THESE FIVE REASONS MEAN NOTHING TO YOU, READ THAT SCRIPTURE AGAIN. NOTICE HOW JUDE SEPARATES THE FALSE FROM THE

REAL BY USING THE WORD, **"OUR"**. HE IS MAKING A POINT OF **RELIGIOUS INTOLERANCE** (a very GOOD fruit). TRUE CHRISTIAN; DO NOT PUT UP WITH THE ACCEPTANCE OF OTHER RELIGIONS FOR ANY REASON. GREEK CHRISTIANS! YOU KNOW THAT YOUR GROUPS ARE TOLERANT TO OTHER RELIGIONS WITH THEIR NON-SECTARIAN PRAYERS. WHY DON'T THEY SIMPLY SAY, "NO PRAYERS WILL BE DONE IN THE NAME OF JESUS". GREEK PASTORS KNOW IT ALSO; ALL GREEK CHRISTIANS ARE UNEQUALLY YOKED WITH UNBELIEVERS. IF GLO's ARE TOLERANT TO RELIGION, SO ARE ALL GREEKS, CHRISTIAN OR NOT. THE WORD OF GOD REBUKES YOU.

IF YOUR PASTOR DOES PREACH AGAINST GLO's, YOU ARE SUPPOSED TO OBEY HIS WORD AS A WORD FROM GOD. IF HE IS A TRUE PASTOR AND NOT A HIRELING, YOU SHOULD TRUST THAT WHAT HE PREACHES COMES DIRECTLY FROM THE HOLY SPIRIT. IF YOU HAVE NO CONNECTION WITH YOUR PASTOR, THEN YOU DON'T HAVE A CONNECTION WITH CHRIST. IT WAS GOD THAT GAVE US PASTORS AFTER **HIS** OWN HEART, AND HE COMMANDS YOU TO OBEY YOUR PASTOR (**HEBREWS 13:17**).

FALSE PROPHETS AND TEACHERS ARE **CARNALLY MINDED (i.e. THEY CARE NOTHING ABOUT SPIRITUAL THINGS OR THE LOST SOULS OF MEN AND WOMEN)** AND HAVE NO PROBLEM COMPROMISING THE WORD OF GOD AND SOULS ALONG WITH IT. I HAVE SAID THIS IN CHAPTER 4, AND I WILL SAY IT AGAIN.

ANY ORGANIZATION THAT CLAIMS TO BE FOUNDED UPON CHRISTIAN PRINCIPLES **MUST HAVE SPECIFIC STANDARDS**. THE **FIRST** STANDARD MUST BE THAT **ALL MEMBERS ARE BORN AGAIN**. IF THIS STANDARD IS NOT UPHELD, NO OTHER STANDARDS ARE ABLE TO BE UPHELD.

I CORINTHIANS 5:6-7 Your glorying is not good. Know ye not that a little leaven leaveneth the whole lump? Purge out therefore the old leaven, that ye may be a new lump, as ye are unleavened. For even Christ our passover is sacrificed for us.

NO GLO HAS THIS PRINCIPLE AT ALL; THEREFORE, NO GLO WAS EVER FOUNDED UPON CHRISTIAN PRINCIPLES. CHRISTIAN!! BY JOINING A GLO, **YOU ARE BRINGING SIN INTO YOUR OWN HOUSE (YOUR BODY)**, WHICH IS THE TEMPLE OF THE HOLY GHOST. THE BIBLE SAYS,

"IF YOU DEFILE THE TEMPLE, HIM WILL GOD DESTROY." THIS MEANS THAT

WHEN GREEK CHRISTIANS LURE TRUE CHRISTIANS TO THEIR ORGANIZATIONS WITH FALSE TEACHINGS, THEY ARE DEFILING THAT PERSONS TEMPLE. GOD WILL DESTROY THE GREEK CHRISTIAN FOR DOING SO.

I CORINTHIANS 3:16-17 Know ye not that ye are the temple of God, and that the Spirit of God dwelleth in you? If any man defile the temple of God, him shall God destroy; for the temple of God is holy, which temple ye are.

ANY CHRISTIAN IN A GLO BETTER GET OUT BEFORE DEATH OR THE RAPTURE. I HAVE KNOWN SOME TO DIE NOT DENOUNCING THEIR ALLEGIANCE TO THEIR GLO. I OFTEN THINK OF WHAT THEY ARE GOING THROUGH, AND IT MAKES ME ALL THE MORE BOLDER TO SPEAK OUT AGAINST GREEK-LETTERED ORGANIZATIONS AND ANY GROUP LIKE THEM. **DEATH TO ME IS LIFE, SO WHY FEAR. I HAVE EVERYTHING TO GAIN, AND ABSOLUTELY NOTHING TO LOSE.**

THIS STATEMENT HERE IS MORE THAN ENOUGH TO LET A **TRUE CHRISTIAN** WHO IS HAVING ANY SECOND THOUGHTS TO STOP WONDERING ABOUT **JOINING A GLO**, AND FOR A **GREEK CHRISTIAN** WHO IS HAVING SECOND THOUGHTS ABOUT **STAYING IN A GLO** TO STOP WONDERING.

MY EXPERIENCE WITH THESE FALSE PROPHETS (**BAD SHEEP WITH BAD FRUIT**) IS COMMON. HOW DID JESUS SAY THE JEWS SHOULD HAVE KNOWN THEM? IF NOT BY HIS WORDS, THEN CERTAINLY KNOWN BY HIS DEEDS. HOW THEN SHOULD WE KNOW A GLO? BY THEIR DEEDS, NATURE, FRUIT, AND MOST IMPORTANTLY THEIR **ORIGIN**. THIS NATURE WILL BE MANIFESTED IN THE MEMBERS. I SEE THEM GO AGAINST THEIR PASTOR'S COMMAND, **FULL OF PRIDE, REBELLION, AND UNBELIEF.** A PASTOR'S ONLY RECOURSE IS TO EVENTUALLY BOOT THEM OUT OF THE CHURCH BEFORE SERIOUS PROBLEMS OCCUR. I HAVE KNOWN IT TO HAPPEN. UNFORTUNATELY, MANY GREEK CHRISTIANS BELIEVE DENOUNCING IS BASED ON SELF-REVELATION AND SELF-CONVICTION. YET, NEITHER OF THESE ARE SELF-ENDOWED CHARACTERISTICS OF MAN. REVELATION OF TRUTH COMES FROM GOD ALONE THROUGH HIMSELF OR HIS AGENTS, AND THE CONVICTION COMES FROM THE HOLY SPIRIT. IT'S A MATTER OF BELIEF OR UNBELIEF ONCE REVELATION HAS OCCURRED OR YOU HAVE HEARD THE TRUTH. IT'S A MATTER OF OBEDIENCE OR DISOBEDIENCE ONCE CONVICTION HAS ENTERED THE MIND.

ONCE THE TRUTH HAS BEEN GIVEN, IGNORANCE NO LONGER EXISTS. YOU EITHER BELIEVE, OR DO NOT BELIEVE. ONCE YOU SAY, "I SHOULD DENOUNCE," AND YOU DON'T, YOU HAVE DISOBEYED GOD. IF YOU DO, THEN YOU OBEYED. IF YOU ARE UNSURE ABOUT GLO's, YOU BETTER RESEARCH. I MUST SAY THIS THOUGH, IF YOU FIND THEM TO BE GODLY, SOMEONE IS LYING TO YOU OR YOU'RE LYING TO YOURSELF. ARE GLO'S CENTERED IN

FREDERIC L. HATCHETT

CHRISTIANITY, JUDAISM, ISLAM, HINDUISM, BUDDHISM, etc.? NO!! THEY USE BITS AND PIECES OF THESE RELIGIONS. THEREFORE, THEY CAN NEVER BE <u>CHRIST-CENTERED</u>.

IN CONCLUSION, GLO's ARE **DESTRUCTIVE HERESIES** THAT WERE SUBTLY AND STEALTHILY INTRODUCED TO THE CHURCH UNDER THE GUISE OF SECRECY AND GOOD WORKS **THAT DID AND STILL DO DENY CHRIST**. THE WORST OF THE FALSE TEACHERS IN GLO's ARE THE CLERGY WHO MASQUERADE THEIR CALLING FOR FINANCIAL, POLITICAL, AND PERSONAL GAIN, OR ANY OTHER DESIRE THEY WANT TO FULFILL. MANY OF THESE FALSE TEACHERS IN GLO's ARE MAKING "THE **WAY" (JESUS/CHRISTIANITY)** RECEIVE A BAD NAME. THEY DISREGARD WHAT THE BIBLE SAYS FOR THEIR OWN PERSONAL INTERESTS. THEY HAVE NO PROBLEM BLASPHEMING THE WORD OF GOD, OR PUTTING CHRIST ON MAN'S LEVEL. FOR THESE TEACHERS TO HAVE KNOWN THE WAY AND TURN FROM IT WILL BE GREATLY TORMENTED. THESE GREEK PASTORS, EVANGELISTS, TEACHERS, PROPHETS, APOSTLES, AND OTHER CHURCH LEADERS MAKE MANY PROMISES OF FREEDOM TO DO THIS OR THAT, YET THEY THEMSELVES ARE IN BONDAGE TO THAT VERY THING THEY LURED YOU INTO. A GLO IS NOTHING BUT A SATANIC TRAP, ESPECIALLY TO THOSE WHO ARE NOT FULFILLED IN CHRIST (i.e. THEY HAVE NOT MADE CHRIST THEIR ALL IN ALL). THEY TELL THE PEOPLE WHAT THEY WANT TO HEAR, CONSTANTLY STROKING THEM, WHILE ALSO BAITING THEM FOR THEIR MONEY AND ANY OTHER GAIN. FALSE TEACHERS ARE EASILY RECOGNIZED BY THE FACT THAT THEY DO NOT FOLLOW GOD'S COMMANDMENTS.

YET AND STILL, THE DESIRE TO JOIN OR REMAIN IN A GLO IS SO STRONG, SOME (EVEN CHRISTIANS) WILL NOT ABIDE IN THE DOCTRINE OF CHRIST. FOR FALSE PROPHETS, TEACHERS, AND ANY **THAT LEARN THE TRUTH** ABOUT GLO's, **LEVITICUS 4:23** COMMANDS YOU TO REPENT AND TELL THE TRUTH FROM THEN ON.

LEVITICUS 4:23 Or **if his sin**, wherein he hath sinned, **come to his knowledge**; he shall bring his offering, a kid of the goats, a male without blemish:

HIS OFFERING IS HIS ACKNOWLEDGMENT AND REPENTANCE OF SIN. HE SHOWED HIS REPENTANCE BY HIS ACTION OF OFFERING A SACRFICE. THIS IS WHY DENOUNCING **AND LEAVING** THE GLO ARE BOTH NECESSARY. TOTAL SEPARATION PROVES YOUR REPENTANCE IS REAL. **GREEK CHRISTIANS WHO ARE CHURCH LEADERS HAVE A PROFOUND INFLUENCE ON GLO MEMBERSHIP AND THEIR CONGREGATIONS.** WEAK CHRISTIANS ARE EASY PREY, ESPECIALLY WHEN THEY HEAR THAT PASTOR SUCH-AND-SUCH IS IN THIS SORORITY, OR PROPHET SO-AND-SO IS IN THAT FRATERNITY.

I HAVE A WARNING FROM THE WORD OF GOD TO ALL GREEK CHRISTIANS IN THE CLERGY. IT'S **MATTHEW 7:21-23**. YOUR TITLE IS NOTHING WITHOUT OBEDIENCE TO GOD. THERE ARE MANY SCRIPTURES, OLD AND NEW TESTAMENT, THAT WARN SPIRITUAL LEADERS ABOUT REBELLION AND DISOBEDIENCE TO GOD. TAKE HEED GREEK PASTORS AND OTHER GREEK

FREDERIC L. HATCHETT

CHURCH LEADERS; YOU HAVE A RESPONSIBILITY TO YOUR SHEEP. **ARE YOU A HIRELING, OR A PASTOR? CHRISTIANS: DON'T LOOK TO MAN FOR YOUR ANSWERS.** (I JOHN 2:27)

Notes

CHAPTER 7

THE SPIRIT OF PREJUDICE

WHEN ONE LOOKS AT PREJUDICE FROM THE COLOR/RACE ASPECT, THEY DEFINE IT AS A PRE-JUDGMENT OF A PERSON BASED ON THEIR RACE OR COLOR OF SKIN (i.e. BLACKS DON'T TAKE BATHS, ALL WHITE PEOPLE ARE AFRAID OF BLACKS, ALL CHINESE PEOPLE KNOW MARTIAL ARTS, etc.). THE WORLD IS FULL OF EXAMPLES, AND SO IS THE BIBLE.

IF IT WERE NOT FOR THE LAW, I DO NOT BELIEVE GLO's WOULD BE INTEGRATED TO THE SMALL DEGREE THEY ARE NOW. I HAVE SEEN, HEARD, AND EXPERIENCED THE PREJUDICED ON BOTH SIDES OF RACES. GLO's, LET'S NOT GO INTO DENIAL; THE SPIRIT OF PREJUDICE NOT ONLY STILL EXISTS IN GLO's, **IT FLOURISHES**.

ACTS 17:24-30 God that made the world and all things therein, seeing that he is Lord of heaven and earth, dwelleth not in temples made with hands; neither is worshipped with men's hands, as though he needed any thing, seeing **he**

FREDERIC L. HATCHETT

giveth to all life, and breath, and all things; And hath made of **one blood all nations of men** for to dwell on all the face of the earth, and hath determined the times before appointed, and the bounds of their habitation; that they should seek the Lord, if haply they might find him, though he be not far from us: for in him we live, and move and have our being; as certain of your own poets have said, For we are his offspring. Forasmuch then as we are the offspring of God, we ought not to think that the Godhead is like unto gold, silver, or stone, graven by art and man's device. And the times of this ignorance God winked at; but now **commandeth all men everywhere** to **repent:**

WHEN ONE READS THIS SCRIPTURE, IT IS CLEAR TO SEE THAT WE ARE ALL ONE CREATION, ONE BLOOD, ONE COLOR (MANY SHADES), ON ONE EARTH, WITH THE SAME COMMAND TO ALL: REPENT. REPENTANCE IS WHAT CAUSES A DIVISION OF THE ONLY TWO **TRUE RACES**, THE **SAVED** AND THE **UNSAVED**. THIS SERIOUS PROBLEM WITH THE **SPIRIT OF PREJUDICE EXISTS IN ALMOST IN ALL SECRET SOCIETIES, THE CHURCH, AND IS A REFLECTION OF THE WORLD WE LIVE IN TODAY.** THE INTENT OF THE FOUNDERS OF BOTH WHITE AND BLACK GLO's WAS TO BE ONE COLOR ONLY (i.e. COMPLETELY SEGREGATED). PREJUDICE HAS CAUSED GREAT LOSSES IN THE CHURCH WHERE GREAT GAINS COULD HAVE BEEN MADE. IF THE TRUTH BE KNOWN, PREJUDICE ONLY HOLDS WEIGHT IN THE HANDS OF THE ONE WITH

COMING APART AT THE SEAMS

POWER. PREJUDICE IS A SPIRIT AND THEREFORE, HAS NO **COLOR** BARRIERS. A PERFECT EXAMPLE OF **INTRA**-RACIAL PREJUDICE AND PROOF THAT IT IS SPIRITUAL IS SHOWN THROUGH THE PRACTICE OF HAZING. THE DEVIL USES DECEPTION ON THE BIG BROTHERS, BIG SISTERS, AND THE INITIATES (ONES TRYING TO BECOME MEMBERS.) THEY ARE CONSTANTLY TELLING YOU THAT YOU MUST HUMBLE YOURSELF TO THEM. THEY HAVE THE **POWER** BY POSSESSING WHAT YOU WANT, MEMBERSHIP IN THEIR GLO. PEOPLE OF **LIKE-RACE AND COLOR** BEATING AND HUMILIATING EACH OTHER ARE CLEAR EVIDENCE OF **INTRA**-RACIAL PREJUDICE. THIS IS SELF-EXALTATION OF THEMSELVES AND PRIDE IN THEMSELVES OVER PEOPLE OF THEIR OWN RACE/COLOR. THE BIBLE HAS MANY EXAMPLES OF THIS **INTRA**-RACIAL PREJUDICE. ALL THROUGHOUT THE GOSPELS THERE ARE THE PHARISEES AND SADDUCEES (BOTH JEWISH SECTS), PLOTTING AND SCHEMING TO KILL JESUS (A JEW HIMSELF). IN THE BOOK OF ACTS, THE SAME JEWS ARE CONSTANTLY FEUDING WITH THE APOSTLES, SOME WHO ARE JEWS, OVER THE TEACHINGS OF JESUS (A JEW). **INTER**-RACIAL PREJUDICE CLEARLY EXISTS IN BIBLICAL AND PRESENT DAY TIMES. IN **GALATIANS 2:11-12,** PAUL HAD TO

REBUKE PETER FOR NOT WANTING TO BE SEEN BY JEWS **WITH THE GENTILES**. INVOLUNTARY SLAVERY (EGYPTIAN ENSLAVEMENT OF THE JEWS AND WHITE ENSLAVEMENT OF THE BLACKS) IS CLEAR EVIDENCE OF **INTER**-RACIAL PREJUDICE IN ITS MOST FAMILIAR FORM. **INTER**-RACIAL PREJUDICE HAS BEEN SEEN IN GLO's SINCE THEIR MODERN BEGINNINGS. READER; DO NOT BE FOOLED BY THE RHETORIC; THE WHITE GLO'S WANTED TO BE WHITE, AND THE BLACK GLO's WANTED TO BE BLACK. ONLY THE LAW HAS CAUSED INTEGRATION. **IT WAS NOT WILL OR DESIRE**. ALL PREJUDICE, IN EVERY FORM, WILL BE DEALT WITH BY A HOLY GOD. THE DESCRIPTION OF HEAVEN IS CLEAR PROOF THAT PREJUDICE IS NOT TOLERATED BY JESUS.

REVELATION 5:9 And they sung a new song, saying, Thou art worthy to take the book, and to open the sins thereof: for thou wast slain, and hast redeemed us to God by the blood out of **every kindred, and tongue, and people, and nation;**

PETER HAS SOMETHING TO SAY ABOUT BEING PREJUDICE IN,

ACTS 10:34-36&47 Then Peter opened his mouth, and said, Of a truth I perceive that **God is no respector of persons**: But in every nation he that feareth him, and worketh righteousness, is accepted with him. The word which God sent unto the children of Israel, preaching peace by Jesus Christ: (he is Lord of all:) Can any man forbid water, that these should be baptized, which has received the Holy Ghost as well as we?

GOD CONFIRMS THE TRUTH WHEN THE GENTILES RECEIVED THE HOLY GHOST. HERE ARE A FEW EXAMPLES OF THOSE WHO HAVE PRACTICED PREJUDICED. SAUL HAD HIS KINGSHIP REMOVED FOR HIS DISOBEDIENCE WHICH RESULTED IN HIS BEING PREJUDICE AGAINST DAVID (**INTRA**-RACIAL), AND HITLER'S PREJUDICE AGAINST THE JEWS (**INTER**-RACIAL) RESULTED IN UNEXPECTED DEFEAT BY A LESSER FOE. IN THE SUDAN, THEY ARE SELLING THEIR OWN RACE INTO SLAVERY (**INTRA**-RACIAL). OUR ENSLAVEMENT OF 400 YEARS AGO WAS A MUTUAL AGREEMENT BETWEEN AFRICANS, WHO SOLD US, AND WHITES WHO BOUGHT US (**BOTH INTRA&INTER-RACIAL PREJUDICE AT THE SAME TIME**). NOW ALL THE RACES ARE CRYING ABOUT PREJUDICE, AFFIRMATIVE ACTION, 40 ACRES AND A MULE AND QUOTAS. ALL THE JEWS WANTED IN EGYPT WAS THREE DAYS TO GO AND FAST AND PRAY <u>TO THEIR GOD</u>, WHILE PRESENT DAY

SOCIETY RUNS <u>TO MAN</u> TO SOLVE OUR PROBLEMS. ALL PEOPLE WHO WERE SUBJECTED TO INVOLUNTARY SLAVERY HAD LEGITIMATE REASONS TO ASK FOR RETRIBUTION, BUT YOU FOOLS IN GLO's ALLOW YOURSELVES TO BE BEATEN AND/OR HUMILIATED BY YOUR OWN RACE OR ANOTHER RACE FOR GREEK LETTERS. YOU DESERVE NO RETRIBUTION FOR YOUR STUPIDITY. AFTER ALL THE EXAMPLES OF SLAVERY, WHICH WE SHOULD ALL HATE, **WHY WOULD YOU PUT YOURSELF IN SLAVERY/BONDAGE (PHYSICAL AND/OR SPIRITUAL) BY PLEDGING?** IF YOU SUFFER ANYTHING BY PLEDGING, BLAME THE DEVIL NOT RACE, WHETHER IT BE YOUR OWN OR ANOTHER. **THINK OF HOW FOOLISH IT IS TO HATE SOMEONE FOR THEIR RACE, FOR A SITUATION THEY HAD NO CONTROL OVER (i.e. THEIR SKIN COLOR AND/OR RACE).** GREEK-LETTERED ORGANIZATIONS (GLO's), WHETHER BLACK AND WHITE ARE PREJUDICE AGAINST THEIR OWN RACES AND OTHER RACES WHICH CAN BE SEEN THROUGH THE PROCESS OF HAZING AND DISPARITY OF MEMBERSHIP. HAZING IS ALWAYS SPIRITUAL FIRST, THEN MENTAL, AND PHYSICAL. THE RESULT OR FINAL PRODUCT OF HAZING WILL NEVER BE A HOLY MAN OF GOD. GOD CALLS US TO REPENTANCE, NOT HUMILIATION,

PADDLES, OR INSULTS. GOD CALLS, PREPARES, AND SENDS PEOPLE TO DO HIS WILL, NOT SOME ORGANIZATION LIKE A GLO. PLEDGING ITSELF IS A CLEAR EXAMPLE OF **SELF-ENSLAVEMENT** AND **SELF-STUPIDITY**. THOSE WHO DO THE HAZING ARE JUST AS FOOLISH AS THE ONES TAKING IT. OH YE! BEFORE YOU START WITH THAT WE DON'T HAZE ANYMORE, WE DON'T PLEDGE RHETORIC: MANY INCIDENCES OF HAZING HAVE OCCURRED AFTER THE INTAKE PROCESS WAS IMPLEMENTED IN 1990. SINCE THEN THERE HAVE BEEN SEVERAL DEATHS, BEATINGS WITH A HAMMER, INJURIES RESULTING IN THE NEED FOR KIDNEY DIALYSIS, AND A $375,000 LAWSUIT SETTLEMENT. I DON'T CARE WHAT GLO's PUT ON PAPER, OR WHAT LAWS ARE PUT ON THE BOOKS, HAZING WILL NOT ONLY GET WORSE, **HAZING WILL NEVER STOP!!!!!**

IF YOU ARE, OR BELIEVE YOU ARE A CHRISTIAN, THEIR IS NO JUSTIFICATION FOR YOU WANTING TO JOIN OR REMAIN IN A GLO. I AM NOT SAYING THAT EVERYONE IN A GLO IS PREJUDICED, BUT I AM SAYING THAT EVERY MEMBER IN A GLO IS UNDER THE INFLUENCE OF THE SPIRIT OF PREJUDICE. IF SO, ALL WHO CLAIM TO BE SAVED ARE UNEQUALLY YOKED WITH

THE DEVIL. AT THIS POINT YOU ARE NO LONGER IGNORANT, BUT IN **KNOWLEDGABLE UNBELIEF,** AND TO DO SOMETHING WITHOUT FAITH (OR BELIEVING) IS SIN.

I TIMOTHY 1:12-17 And I thank Christ Jesus our Lord, who hath enabled me, for that he counted me faithful, putting me into the ministry; Who was before a blasphemer, and a persecutor, and injurious: but **I obtained mercy, because I did it ignorantly in unbelief.** And the grace of our Lord was exceeding abundantly with faith and love which is in Christ Jesus. This is a faithful saying, and worthy of all acceptation, that Christ Jesus came into the world to save sinners, of whom I am chief. Howbeit for this cause I obtained mercy, that in me first Jesus Christ shall shew forth all long-suffering, **for a pattern to them which should hereafter believe on him to life everlasting.** Now unto the king eternal, immortal, invisible, the only wise God, be honour and glory for ever and ever. Amen.

PAUL CHANGED BECAUSE HE HAD RECEIVED AND BELIEVED JESUS. HE DID NOT CONTINUE TO BE A BLASPHEMER OR PERSECUTOR. YOU SHOULD NOT CONTINUE TO BE A MEMBER OF A GLO. ENOUGH HAS BEEN GIVEN TO YOU FOR YOU TO MAKE THE CHOICE TO DENOUNCE ALL DESIRES FOR ALL GLO's.

TO ACT ON THAT WHICH IS NOT IN AGREEMENT WITH YOUR CONVICTION IS SIN: **ROMANS 14:23**). THIS MEANS TO ALL "GREEK CHRISTIANS" AND THOSE CHRISTIANS THAT HAVE ANY UNCERTAINTY OR DOUBT (UNEASY CONSCIENCE) ABOUT GLO's ARE NOW

LEFT STANDING CONDEMNED BEFORE GOD. A DOUBLE-MINDED MAN IS UNSTABLE IN **ALL** HIS WAYS. YOU MUST MAKE UP YOUR MIND.

CONCLUSION

PREJUDICE DISQUALIFIES ANYONE FROM THE KINGDOM OF GOD. WE KNOW THAT GLO's PRACTICE THIS SIN. THEREFORE, ANY "CHRISTIAN" BELONGING TO OR INTERESTED IN GLO's WILL BE IDENTIFIED WITH PREJUDICE. IF IT IS NOT BY ACTION, THEN IT WILL BE BY **ASSOCIATION** (i.e. **UNEQUALLY YOKED**). JESUS AND THE DEVIL ARE NOT RESPECTOR OF PERSONS. THE ONLY DIFFERENCE IS THAT THE DEVIL USES THIS CONCEPT AGAINST US BY RELEASING THE SPIRIT OF PREJUDICE TO HATE EACH OTHER, BUT GOD ENCOURAGES US TO BE LIKE HIM, AND TO LOVE ALL REGARDLESS OF RACE/COLOR. BILLIONS HAVE DIED AND MILLIONS ARE DYING OF BOTH INTRA AND INTER-RACIAL PREJUDICES.

Notes

CHAPTER 8

THE TRUE ROLE OF FRATERNITIES AND SORORITIES IN THE BLACK COMMUNITY

Culture is basically the characteristics and features of a particular people. Dialect, language, race, geographic location, religious beliefs, etc. are all a part of cultures.

WHAT ARE BLACK GREEK-LETTERED ORGANIZATIONS WORTH TO THEIR COMMUNITIES AND THEIR CULTURE?

1.) GLO's are false witnesses.
They do this by gaining favor through acts of kindness. Some of the works they do are not bad. Those works should be continued **with the exception** that you get saved and denounce your GLO and do the works for God. Not to EARN His favor, but because of your relationship with Jesus. Even "Greek Christians" know those scholarships, voter registration drives, and after school tutorials

are done in the name and glory of their GLO, and not in the name of Jesus. Say what you want to say, and do what you want to do; it's not to the glory of God, and you can't make God accept it, which is what GLO's try to do. **TITUS 1:15-16(amp)** says that unbeliever's are unfit and worthless for good works. You are separating yourself from the rest of your brothers and sisters who are doing it for the GLO. This means you are not in agreement with them.

AMOS 3:3 How can two <u>walk together</u> accept they be agreed?

The only way Greek Christians can walk together in agreement with your Greek "brothers and sisters" is to compromise the Gospel of Jesus Christ.

2.) Hazing by GLO's proves **cultural and community irrelevancy** and **pure hypocrisy**.

BLACK GLO'S ARE <u>ONE</u> OF THE BIGGEST SELLOUTS OF THE BLACK COMMUNITY.

How can hazing justify cultural significance and a positive role in the community? In a country that has made inroads toward equality, members in **BLACK GLO's** are still enslaving people of their own race and/or color. They do this by beating, humiliating, deceiving, embarrassing, frustrating, injuring, dehumanizing, and sometimes killing their brothers and sisters by race, and supposed to be up and coming Greek <u>brothers or sisters</u>. Tell me what kind of cultural or community activities a dead person can participate in except his or her own funeral. The GLO's role in the black community is an unworthy and cheap substitute for the church. A GLO's role may be political, social, or economical, but it can never be spiritual according to the Word of God, **because they offer nothing that leads to eternal life**. Can they do everything the church does? NO! Read chapter 5. What has any GLO done that the church has not already accomplished? Nothing! Whenever they do projects, they hold their banner high. People may thank God and the GLO for it, but can the doer, the Greek Christian receive anything from God? **No!** The praises of man are what they are looking for (men-pleasers), and the praises of man are what they will receive. Anyone who is a member of a GLO got there in an ungodly manner. **Their sinful entrance is no different than their sinful membership.** All the good works done in the name of a GLO are of no value to the one doing it, but when the saved does the will of God, God rewards them. When the church removes its hand from the community, it will die, and no GLO can revive or save it. When the church starts making the decision to take the community, outside forces have to bow. I blame the church for not taking control, and allowing other ungodly organizations to come in and run things, giving people a false hope.

There's no hope in GLO's. A true Christian's hope is Jesus. I blame Christians and churches that know the truth about GLO's, but do nothing. Sissies! When churches divide on Biblical Truths, it causes confusion, which is of the Devil. On the issue of GLO's, the church as a body and Christians as individuals need to **unify around**

the Word of God. Instead, the Greek Christians are rebellious and refuse to repent (i.e. they know the truth, but are in unbelief). Then there are those stingy church members who can help the cause, but refuse to share what they know (i.e. they still keep the secrets after denouncing, or don't share important facts that one needs to know to defend the faith). This proves they are still in bondage to the GLO. If not, they would freely give all of their materials to one who is active in informing others about their own **apparent "conviction"**. Another serious problem with Christians is the evangelism concerning GLO's. **Christ should always be witnessed first** and then membership of the GLO second. The PULPIT needs to condemn GLO's, and so do the individual Christians who know it's wrong. We have the Word of God to stand on; they have foolishness, philosophy, mythology and many other useless defenses. Instead many just sit back and watch their brothers and sisters make a hellish decision with nothing to say. This book says more than enough to state your claim. State it, and let the Holy Ghost do the rest.

In conclusion, all the handbooks of GLO's that I have read, except Iota Phi Theta, state they are founded upon Christian principles. Therefore, they must have at least one standard. All members have to be saved. Since none, including Iota Phi Theta, make this requirement they can't be founded on Christian principles. **If any organization is not SPIRITUALLY relevant, they can't be CULTURALLY relevant.** This applies to all GLO's. No GLO has the doctrine that leads to eternal life, that accepts the deity of Christ, or professes the following scripture,

MATTHEW 6:33 But seek ye first the kingdom of God, and his righteousness; and all these things shall be added unto you.

So what is the true role and relevance of Black GLO's in their community and on their culture? Lies, deceit, and spiritual destruction.

Notes

CHAPTER 9

TESTIMONIES

MINISTER Janice R. Davis

I WAS INTRODUCED TO GREEK-LETTERED ORGANIZATIONS BY THREE FAMILY MEMBERS WHO WERE ALREADY INVOLVED IN THEM BEFORE I WAS BORN. I WAS ATTRACTED TO GREEK-LETTERED ORGANIZATIONS BECAUSE I BELIEVED THAT IT EXEMPLIED TRUE UNITY AND FELLOWSHIP BETWEEN SISTERS. I WAS ALSO ATTRACTED TO THEM BECAUSE, I WANTED TO BE IDENTIFIED WITH WHAT I THOUGHT WAS A STRONG INFLUENTIAL CONNECTION OF INTELLIGENT WOMEN, THEIR IDEALS, GOALS, AND OUTWARD PARAPHERNALIA. I DECIDED TO JOIN BECAUSE I WANTED TO A JOIN A SPECIFIC GLO AND THE TIES THAT I HAD WITH MY FAMILY MEMBERS WHO WERE ALREADY A PART OF THE SAME GLO. I REALLY CONNECTED AS A CHILD. I DENOUNCED MY GLO BECAUSE I READ IN THE BIBLE IN **LUKE 10:27-28**, "And he answering said, thou shalt love the Lord thy God with all thy heart, and with all thy soul, and with all thy strength, and with all thy mind, and thy neighbour as thyself." I KNEW THAT MY GLO (Greek-lettered organization) REQUIRED ME TO GIVE THIS KIND OF REVERENCE TO IT AND I ALSO KNEW THAT IF I WAS A MEMBER I WOULD BE

WALKING CONTRARY TO GOD'S WORD. IT IS AN ABOMINATION AND I WOULD BE OFFERING UP WORSHIP TO SOMETHING OTHER THAN JEHOVAH GOD. I WAS SAVED BEFORE I DENOUNCED THE GLO. AFTER I CAME INTO THE KNOWLEDGE OF GOD'S HOLY SCRIPTURES, I BEGAN TO LIVE WHAT I STUDIED. I KNEW THAT DENOUNCING WAS THE RIGHT THING TO DO. I FOUND OUT THAT GLO'S WERE SINFUL BY CONTINUING TO READ THE BIBLE, AND AS I SOUGHT THE SCRIPTURES, THE WORD OF GOD REVEALED WHAT THINGS WERE SINFUL, SUCH AS THE WORKS OF FLESH IN **GALATIANS 5:19-21** AND **REVELATION 21:8**. THESE WERE SOME OF THE SCRIPTURES THAT I STUDIED. I WAS TREATED VERY GOOD BY MY BROTHERS AND SISTERS. I HAD KNOWN MANY OF THEM SINCE MY CHILDHOOD. THOSE WHO WERE NON-GREEK TREATED ME FAIRLY WELL. I FELT VERY POSITIVE ABOUT MY DECISION TO DENOUNCE AND WAS STRONGLY CONVICTED TO IMMEDIATELY DENOUNCE IT. I STILL HAVE THE SAME CONVICTION THAT I HAD ELEVEN YEARS AGO. THE ENEMY TRIED TO BRING A SENSE OF SECRECY DUE TO THE FACT THAT I HAD FAMILY MEMBERS WHO WERE STILL A PART OF THE GLO. HOWEVER I STOOD FIRM AND DECLARED MY SEPARATION.

"Wherefore come out from among them and be ye separate, saith the Lord, and touch not the unclean thing; and I will receive you, and will be a father unto you, and ye shall be my sons and daughters, saith the Lord Almighty." (**II CORINTHIANS 6:17-18**)

FREDERIC L. HATCHETT

I WAS A COLLEGE FRESHMAN WHEN I SAW THE INHUMANE EFFECTS OF WHAT HAZING WILL DO TO A PERSON'S LIFE, EMOTIONS ETC. MY ROOMATE HAD A FRIEND THAT WANTED TO PLEDGE A FRATERNITY. WHILE PLEDGING, HE WAS BRUTALLY HAZED. HE WAS HIT IN THE HEAD WITH A SHOVEL AND WAS HOSPITALIZED. AFTER HIS RELEASE, MY ROOMMATE AND I SAW HIS HEAD. IT WAS HORRIBLE AND VERY GROTESQUE. THE FLESH ON THE TOP OF HIS HEAD WAS HEALING INTO A THICK WAVE, IF YOU CAN IMAGINE A WAVE OF FLESH. THIS SAME YOUNG MAN ALSO REVEALED THAT HE WAS HUNG FROM A TREE WITH A NEUSE. HE WAS TOLD THAT HE WAS ASSURED THAT HE WOULD NOT CHOKE OR DIE BECAUSE THEY KNEW EXACTLY WHERE TO PLACE THE NEUSE. ANOTHER INCIDENT INVOLVED A COLLEGE FRESHMAN THAT LIVED ON MY DORM HALL. SHE HAD GONE WITH HER ROOMMATE TO A FRATERNITY PARTY. WHILE AT THE PARTY, SHE WAS DRUGGED AND RAPED. THIS WAS CALLED, "RUNNING A TRAIN," BECAUSE IT CONSISTED OF A NUMBER OF MALES THAT RAPED A VICTIM. HER ROOMMATE AND HER BOYFRIEND, WHO WAS A MEMBER OF THE FRATERNITY, DELIVERED HER BACK TO THE DORM, DAZED AND CRYING. HER GARMENTS HAD BEEN TORN. THE VICTIM HAD TO LEAVE COLLEGE BECAUSE OF THE MENTAL AND EMOTIONAL TRAUMA THAT SHE EXPERIENCED. ANYONE INTERESTED IN PLEDGING A GLO SHOULD KNOW FIRST THAT YOU CANNOT BE A CHRISTIAN AND BE INVOLVED WITH THE WORKS OF DARKNESS.

II CORINTHIANS 6:14 SAYS, "Be ye not unequally yoked together with unbelievers: for what fellowship hath righteousness with unrighteousness? And what communion hath light with darkness."

SATAN COMES AS AN ANGEL OF LIGHT AND IS A DECEIVER, THE MANY WORKS THAT A GLO IS INVOLVED IN SUCH AS EDUCATIONAL AND COMMUNITY PROGRAMS EARN NO FAVOR WITH GOD (**EPHESIANS 2:8-9 TITUS 3:5**). GOOD WORKS ARE PURE AND UNDEFILED BEFORE GOD, AND KEEPING YOURSELF UNSPOTTED FROM THE WORLD. THIS IS PURE RELIGION. (**JAMES 1:27**)

Fred Hatchett

IS MY LIFE IN DANGER? YES. FOR WRITING THIS BOOK, YES. ANY REGRETS? ABSOLUTELY NONE! I LOVE THE LORD, EVEN UNTO DEATH. FOR I KNOW THAT I WILL NOT TRULY DIE, BUT BE RAISED TO LIFE EVERLASTING. THIS BOOK IS NOT FOR ME, BUT FOR THOSE WHO BELIEVE AS I DO, AND FOR THOSE WHO DO NOT KNOW THE TRUTH THAT THEY PERHAPS WILL DENOUNCE AND REPENT.

WHEN GOD CALLED ME OUT OF MY GLO, I HAD NO IDEA THIS BOOK WOULD BE THE ONE OF THE RESULTS. THIS BOOK IS ONLY THE BEGINNING IN THE RECONCILING OF LOST SOULS IN GLO'S TO GOD THROUGH JESUS CHRIST. **IN MY FIVE YEARS AS A MEMBER OF OMEGA PSI PHI FRATERNITY, AND TWO YEARS AS A 32° MASON, AND SIX YEARS AS A CHRISTIAN, I CANNOT BE TOLD THAT I DON'T KNOW WHAT I'M TALKING ABOUT CONCERNING ANYONE'S GLO.** I KNOW ONE THING ALL TOO

WELL, AND THAT IS GLO's HAVE DONE WHAT CHRISTIANITY CAN NEVER DO, AND THAT IS THEY HAVE RUINED MANY LIVES. **WHEN ONE PERSON DIES OR IS INJURED IN A HAZING INCIDENT, MANY ARE EFFECTED BESIDE THAT INDIVIDUAL.** LET ME MAKE ONE THING VERY, VERY CLEAR!! HAZING DEATHS AND INJURIES ARE **NOT ACCIDENTAL.** THEY ARE **INTENTIONAL, BRUTAL, AND PRE**-DETERMINED IN THE HAZER'S MIND. THE DEMONIC METHODS OF HAZING ARE CONCOCTED IN THE MIND AND PUT INTO ACTION ON THE PLEDGES BODY. CHRISTIAN MAN OR WOMAN! PLEASE MEDITATE ON THIS NEXT STATEMENT. **IF JESUS REQUIRES NOTHING UNGODLY IN SUBMISSION FROM YOU, WHY SHOULD YOU ALLOW PEOPLE TO REQUIRE UNGODLY SUBMISSION?** I WILL TELL YOU WHY. IT'S BECAUSE **THEY HAVE NOTHING CHRISTLIKE TO OFFER YOU.** GLO's **CAN'T** OFFER JOY, PEACE, OR LOVE BECAUSE THEY **DON'T** POSSESS IT. THEY **CAN'T** PRAY FOR YOU, BECAUSE THEY HAVE **NO RELATIONSHIP WITH JESUS.** THEY **CAN'T BE CHRIST'S WITNESS,** BECAUSE THEY **DON'T KNOW HIM. THEY HAVE NOTHING TO OFFER THAT LEADS ONE TO ETERNAL LIFE.** THEY CAN OFFER CONNECTIONS, PARTIES, A RITUAL, A HISTORY BOOK, AND **HAZING TIPS.** SO WHAT GOOD WERE THEY TO ME? NONE!!! WHAT THE DEVIL INTENDED FOR MY BAD, GOD CAME AND TURNED IT INTO GOOD. THE WRITING OF THIS BOOK IS THAT "GOOD."

MY REASON FOR JOINING WAS TO HELP THE COMMUNITY THROUGH AN ESTABLISHED ORGANIZATION. IT BEING FOUNDED ON CHRISTIAN PRINCIPLES HAD NOTHING TO DO WITH IT: I WAS A SINNER. I FULFILLED MY REASON TO JOIN ONLY TO SEE IT CRUSHED BY

COMING APART AT THE SEAMS

ELITISM AND **JEALOUSY**. MANY IDEAS MYSELF AND OTHERS OFFERED WERE BEAT DOWN BEFORE THE MEMBERSHIP HEARD IT. **WHY? BECAUSE WE WERE TOO YOUNG IN THE "FRAT" TO KNOW ANYTHING.**

AS I BEGAN TO READ THE BIBLE, I BEGAN TO REALIZE THAT GLO's HAD ONLY **A FORM OF GODLINESS**. SHORTLY AFTER AN INITIATION WHERE ONE OF MY FRIENDS GOT TURNED DOWN, **I CAME TO HATE THE POLITICS OF THE FRATERNITY,** BUT REMAINED, BECAUSE OF MY FRIENDSHIPS. **TWO MONTHS LATER, I GAVE MY LIFE TO JESUS.** I DID NOT KNOW AT THIS TIME THAT GLO's WERE UNGODLY ORGANIZATIONS. AS I READ THE BIBLE MORE, **THE REALITY OF MY MEMBERSHIP IN A GLO AND FELLOWSHIP WITH SINNERS** CAME TO LIGHT AT A STEPSHOW PRACTICE. I TOLD THE GUYS THAT WE SHOULDN'T **USE PROFANITY AND DO ACTS OF VULGARITY.** GUYS WHO **WERE** MY FRIENDS TURNED ON ME. **I CHALLENGED THEM WITH HOLINESS, AND THEY RESPONDED WITH PROFANITY AND DISRESPECT. THIS WAS THE BEGINNING OF THE END OF MY MEMBERSHIP.** AS I CONTINUED READING THE BIBLE, I STARTED NOTICING THE MORAL DEGRADATION OF THOSE I CALLED MY BROTHERS. ADULTERY, FORNICATION, PROFANITY, DRUNKENESS AND EVEN HOMOSEXUALITY HAD MADE ITS WAY INTO THIS FRATERNITY. THEY EVEN INITIATED A MUSLIM. OMEGA PSI PHI CLAIMED TO BE FOUNDED UPON CHRISTIAN PRINCIPLES. HOW DARE THEY ALLOW A MUSLIM TO SWEAR AN OATH TO A GOD THEY DON'T BELIEVE IN? I MAY HAVE BEEN YOUNG IN THE "FRAT", BUT THEY KNEW THEN WHO I WAS AND THAT (JESUS) WAS MORE IMPORTANT TO ME THAN OMEGA PSI PHI. BUT ONE THING I REALIZE

NOW IS THAT GOD TO OMEGA IS JUST A GENERIC TERM WITHOUT SIGNIFICANT MEANING. THE HEAD OF A CERTAIN PROGRAM SPONSORED BY OMEGA PSI PHI DIDN'T EVEN WANT ME TO PRAY **IN JESUS' NAME** AT A FUNCTION, BECAUSE IT MIGHT OFFEND SOMEONE. LATER I REALIZED THAT MY MEMBERSHIP WITH THEM WAS **AN UNEQUAL YOKE** AND CAUSING ME TO BE **A PRACTICING SINNER, I REPENTED AND GAVE MY LIFE BACK TO CHRIST, BUT HAD NOT DENOUNCED.** ONE WEEK LATER, THE HOLY GHOST SAID, **"GET OUT OF THE FRATERNITY NOW."** I REALIZED THEN THAT MY HEART WAS STILL IN IT. WITH NO HESITATION, I GATHERED ALL BUT ONE PIECE OF MY PARAPHRENALIA AND THREW IT IN THE GARBAGE. I DID NOT WANT TO PART WITH MY PADDLE. MAKING EVERY EXCUSE TO GOD WHY I SHOULD KEEP IT FAILED. ONCE I SNAPPED IT INTO PIECES, **MY BONDAGE TO THE FRATERNITY WAS OVER. MY DENUNCIATON WAS COMPLETE (i.e. I WAS, BUT I AM NO LONGER AN OMEGA). MY DENUNCIATION IS 4 YEARS AND COUNTING. SINCE 1995, I HAVE NEVER ONCE DESIRED TO GO BACK. MY REASONS FOR JOINING WERE NOT ENOUGH TO KEEP ME FROM LEAVING.** I FOUND THAT JESUS (ALONE) GAVE ME MUCH MORE THAN THEY EVER COULD. HE GAVE ME ETERNAL LIFE, PEACE, JOY, LOVE, TRUTH, AND EVERY OTHER GOOD AND PERFECT GIFT.

Notes

CHAPTER 10
PART 1

WORDS OF ADVICE

YOU WILL NEED THE WORD OF GOD AS YOU READ THIS CHAPTER.

A.) EVERYTHING WE 1.) SAY (OUR WORDS), 2.) THINK (OUR THOUGHTS), 3.) INTEND TO DO (OUR INTENTIONS OR MOTIVES), AND 4.) DO (OUR ACTIONS) HAVE TEMPORAL AND ETERNAL REWARDS AND CONSEQUENCES. EITHER THESE FOUR ARE PURE OR IMPURE, RIGHT OR WRONG, GODLY OR UNGODLY. ONE MAY SAY, "HOW CAN YOU BE SURE THAT YOU'RE SAVED?" YOU ARE KNOWN BY YOUR FRUITS. WHENEVER ONE DECIDES TO ENGAGE IN ANY ACTIVITY MENTIONED IN PART **A** (1-4), CONSIDER IT WISELY, FOR IT MAY BE THE LAST DECISION YOU EVER MAKE (EZEKIEL 33). THE BIBLE SAYS NOT ONLY TO EXAMINE YOURSELF (II CORINTHIANS 13:5), BUT TO PROVE ALL THINGS (I THESSALONIANS 5:21), TEST THE SPIRITS (I JOHN 4:1), EXAMINE EVERY THOUGHT (II CORINTHIANS 10:4-5), AND THAT YOU ARE ACCOUNTABLE FOR EVERYTHING YOU SAY (MATTHEW 12:36-

37). AS A CONFESSING CHRISTIAN, YOU CANNOT TAKE LIGHTLY YOUR MEMBERSHIP, INTEREST IN, OR AGREEMENT WITH GREEK-LETTERED ORGANIZATIONS. IF YOU HAVE READ THIS BOOK, DO NOT DO WHAT MANY OTHERS WILL; HARDEN THEIR HEARTS (HEBREWS 3:8). WHILE READING, IF YOUR CONSCIENCE ALERTED YOU THAT SOMETHING WAS WRONG, I WOULD LISTEN TO IT; GOD GAVE IT TO YOU. IF YOU ARE THAT ONE WHO HAS BEEN WAVERING DUE TO LACK OF EVIDENCE, YOU HAVE SEEN IT AND THERE IS MORE. ARE YOU WAVERING BECAUSE OF PEER PRESSURE? THINK OF GOD'S WRATH. ACCEPT THE TRIALS AND PERSECUTIONS OF LIVING FOR GOD (MATTHEW 5:11-12), AND DENOUNCE YOUR GLO.

B.) I PERSONALLY SPEAK FROM EXPERIENCE THAT THESE ARE THINGS THAT I HAVE HAD TO DEAL WITH AFTER DENOUNCING. THE FIRST ATTACK WAS DIRECTLY FROM THE DEVIL IN A DREAM. THE HUMAN ATTACKS USED BY THE DEVIL WERE 1.) ALIENATION, 2.) THREATS, 3.) INSULTS, 4.) MY REASONS HAD NO BIBLICAL SUPPORT AND 5.) YOU'RE ONE FOR LIFE. READER, PLEASE PAY CLOSE ATTENETION! IT WAS NOT ONLY THE REVELATION THAT CAUSED ME TO DENOUNCE. IT WAS THE HOLY SPIRIT WHO CONVICTED ME. I REALIZED THAT JESUS WAS NOT AND COULD NOT BE AT THE CENTER OF MY LIFE AS A GREEK CHRISTIAN. I KNEW FOR SOME TIME THAT I WAS UNEQUALLY YOKED WITH UNBELIEVERS AND COMITTING IDOLATRY (REVELATION 21:8). IT WAS MY OBEDIENCE TO THE CONVICTING POWER OF THE HOLY

SPIRIT THAT LED TO MY DENUNCIATION. THE FRUIT OF MY CONVICTION WAS GETTING RID OF MY BELONGINGS.

C.) WHENEVER YOU QUESTION GLO's OR ASK SOMEONE ELSES OPINION ABOUT THEM, YOUR CONSCIENCE (GIVEN TO YOU BY GOD) HAS ALREADY LET YOU KNOW THAT SOMETHING IS WRONG. IF YOU KNOW YOU HAVE EVEN A SLIGHT INTEREST, DO NOT SEEK JUSTIFICATION FROM A MEMBER OF ANY GLO, THAT'S NOT HARD. YOUR ASKING A MEMBER IS ACTUALLY JUST TRYING TO FIND SOMEONE TO AGREE WITH WHAT YOU REALLY WANT TO DO. YOU SHOULD GO TO A CHRISTIAN WHO YOU KNOW IS AGAINST IT, AND LISTEN TO WHY THEY BELIEVE WHAT THEY BELIEVE. DO THE THINGS I SAY TO DO IN THIS BOOK, AND YOU WILL SEE THE TRUTH FOR YOURSELF. PLEASE DO NOT ASK AN UNSAVED PERSON FOR ADVICE OR HANG AROUND THEM. THIS INCLUDES YOUR PASTOR AND OTHER CHURCH LEADERS THAT ARE GREEK; PSALM 1:1 COMMANDS AGAINST IT, II CORINTHIANS 6:14-18 CONDEMNS IT, AND I CORINTHIANS 15:33 TELLS YOU WHAT WILL HAPPEN IF STAY AROUND THEM. DON'T ASK A MEMBER WHO CLAIMS TO BE SAVED, BECAUSE 1.) THEY ARE NOT SAVED. 2.) THEY MAY HAVE ALREADY FOUND A CLEVER WAY TO JUSTIFY THAT BEING BOTH A CHRISTIAN AND A GREEK IS ALL-RIGHT WITH GOD. 3.) THEIR BROTHERHOOD/SISTERHOOD WITH SINNERS MAKES THEM GUILTY BY ASSOCIATION. 4.) ANY GREEK CHRISTIAN WHO IS CONVICTED TO STAY IN A GLO WILL NOT RESPOND WELL TO THE CHRISTIAN WITNESS. 5.) GREEK

CHRISTIANS WHO KNOW THE WORD OF GOD WELL ARE DANGEROUS, BECAUSE THEY KNOW HOW TO MAKE THE TRUTH SEEM LIKE A LIE, AND A LIE SEEM LIKE THE TRUTH. 6.) THEY CANNOT WORSHIP GOD, BECAUSE THEY HAVE NO RELATIONSHIP WITH CHRIST. WHY? BECAUSE THEY DO NOT LOVE GOD WITH ALL THEIR HEART, SOUL, STRENGTH, AND MIND. I GIVE AN **EXTREME** WARNING TO SEPARATE FROM THEM AND OBSERVE THEM BASED ON THE WORD OF GOD. IF YOU JUSTIFY GLO's WITH THE BIBLE AT THIS POINT, WRITE ME! I WANT TO KNOW YOUR REASONING WITH THE SCRIPTURES.

D.) REMEMBER THIS ALL OF YOU CHURCH AND CHRISTIAN ATTACKERS! CHRISTIANITY CANNOT DESTROY ONE'S LIFE, BUT IT IS POSSIBLE FOR YOU TO GIVE UP AND LOSE YOUR SALVATION. THOSE OF YOU WHO ARE ALWAYS ATTACKING CHURCHES AND CHRISTIANS AS DOING THE THINGS YOU ALL DO IN GLO'S; THEY ARE NOT WHO YOU ARE SUPPOSED TO LOOK TO FOR SALVATION, ETERNAL LIFE, AND TRUTH. ALL YOU ARE DOING IS MAKING EXCUSES BY COMPARING YOURSELF TO OTHER SINNERS. THE BIBLE SAYS TO **EXAMINE YOURSELF** TO SEE IF YOU ARE IN THE FAITH, BUT INSTEAD YOU WANT TO **EXAMINE EVERYONE ELSE, BUT YOURSELF.** I ALREADY EXAMINED MYSELF IN THIS AREA AND FOUND OUT I WAS GUILTY. NO TRUE CHURCH OR TRUE CHRISTIAN CAN PRACTICE HAZING (PHYSICALLY OR MENTALLY), STEALING, FORNICATION, THE USE OF PROFANITY, AND MURDER. THEY WILL NOT CONDONE ABORTION,

DRINK LIQUOR (GET DRUNK) OR PRACTICE IDOLATRY. SO WHATEVER CHURCH OR CHRISTIAN YOU COMPARE YOURSELF OR YOUR GLO TO THAT JUSTIFIES SUCH SIN IS NOT A TRUE CHURCH OR TRUE CHRISTIAN.

E.) THE LATEST PLOY OF GLO's IS THE USE OF STATISTICS TO MAKE THEIR ORGANIZATIONS LOOK GOOD. TRUE CHRISTIANS! DO NOT BE FOOLED BY THESE MATHEMATICALLY DECEPTIVE NUMBERS. GLO's MAKE UP SUCH A SMALL PERCENTAGE OF A SCHOOL'S POPULATION THAT THEIR OVERALL CONTRIBUTION TO THE WHOLE POPULATION IS NEGLIBLE. THEY CLAIM BETTER GRADES THAN NON-GREEKS, WITHOUT TELLING PEOPLE THE MINIMUM GRADE POINT AVERAGE NECESSARY TO JOIN. THEY ALREADY HAVE A HEAD START.

Notes

CHAPTER 10
PART 2

DENOUNCING YOUR GREEK-LETTERED ORGANIZATION

THIS PART IS SIMPLE ONCE YOUR MIND IS MADE UP. YOU ARE AT THE POINT THAT YOU KNOW GLO'S ARE UNGODLY, AND HAVE NO PLACE IN A TRUE BELIEVER'S LIFE. NOW, THE CHOICE IS YOURS. I KNOW YOU HAVE HEARD "ONCE ONE ALWAYS ONE", BUT THE WORD OF GOD SAYS DIFFERENT. IT SAYS I JOHN 1:9, LUKE 13:3, JAMES 4:17, PHILIPPIANS 3:13-15, AND II

CHRONICLES 7:14. ALL YOU HAVE TO DO IS BELIEVE THE WORD OF GOD, AND NOT WHAT PEOPLE HAVE BEEN SAYING. WHILE YOU ARE MAKING YOUR DECISION CONSIDER THESE WORDS:

1.) CULT
2.) OCCULT
3.) ELITISM
4.) IDOLATRY
5.) HAZING
6.) UNEQUALLY YOKED
7.) DEATH
8.) MAIMED
9.) RITUALS
10.) SECRECY
11.) PREJUDICE
12.) DRUNKENESS
13.) ETERNAL DEATH

(HELL)
14.) FORBIDDEN OATHS

NOW CONSIDER THESE:

1.) GOD THE FATHER
2.) JESUS CHRIST
3.) THE HOLY SPIRIT
4.) ETERNAL LIFE
5.) SALVATION
6.) HEALTH
7.) WEALTH
8.) LOVE
9.) JOY
10.) PEACE
11.) SOBER
12.) FAITH
13.) HOPE
14.) RELATIONSHIP WITH GOD
15.) WORSHIP & PRAISE

IF YOU HAD TO CHOOSE BETWEEN THE TWO LISTS, WHICH ONE WOULD YOU CHOOSE? OF COURSE!!

NEXT I WOULD LIKE TO SHOW YOU THE FOUR TYPES OF PEOPLE THAT WILL DENOUNCE, AND WHAT THEY MUST DO.

I.) YOU ARE SAVED AND DECICED TO JOIN, OR YOU ARE ALREADY A MEMBER AND YOU GET SAVED.

a.) YOU MUST **FIRST** REPENT AND DENOUNCE BY CONFESSING THAT:
1.) JESUS IS NOW YOUR **ONLY** LORD, MASTER, AND SAVIOR (ROMANS 10:9-10/I JOHN 1:9
2.) THAT YOU NO LONGER PROFESS ANY LOVE FOR YOUR FORMER GLO

OR ANY OTHER GLO's (JAMES 1:8, JAMES 4:8)

3.) THAT YOU LOVE EACH AND EVERY MEMBER (MATTHEW 5:44), AND THAT YOU WILL WITNESS TO THEM (I CORINTHIANS 5:17-21), BUT IF THEY CONFESS CHRIST, AND REFUSE TO REPENT AND DENOUNCE YOU WILL SEPARATE FROM THEM (I CORINTHIANS 5:11-13). REMIND YOURSELF AND THOSE WHO DENY CHRIST THAT THEY ARE NO LONGER YOUR BROTHERS OR SISTERS IN THE GREEK WAY OR IN THE LORD (II CORINTHIANS 6:14-18).

4.) ONCE YOU HAVE REPENTED AND DENOUNCED, ASK GOD FOR GREATER REVELATION ABOUT YOUR CONVICTION AND SHARE IT WITH OTHERS TO RESTORE THEIR SPIRITUAL LIVES (EPHESIANS 5:11).

WHEN YOU FIRST GET SAVED, YOU ARE **CLEANSED** FROM ALL SIN. MANY DO NOT DENOUNCE, BECAUSE THEY HAVE BEEN BRAINWASHED BY THE GLO THAT THEY ARE FOUNDED

UPON CHRISTIAN PRINCIPLES, AND THAT THEY ARE A GREEK FOR LIFE. WHEN THE HOLY SPIRIT SPEAKS TO YOU, YOU MUST DENOUNCE AND NEVER GO BACK OR ACCEPT THE EXISTENCE OF GLO's AS A POSITIVE THING. THE FIGHT IS ON AND YOU MUST EXERT YOUR WILL AGAINST THE WILL OF GREEK CHRISTIANS AND SATAN, SO THAT THE YOKE OF SIN WHICH WAS DESTROYED WILL STAY DESTROYED (i.e. <u>YOU</u> MUST WALK AFTER THE SPIRIT, AND NOT AFTER THE FLESH). ONE WHO IS ALREADY A MEMBER OF A GLO AND GETS SAVED IS DELIVERED FROM THE YOKE OF THE GLO AT THAT MOMENT, BUT IF NO REVELATION IS RECEIVED ABOUT GLO's, A PERSON WILL HAVE NO REASON TO WALK IN THAT DELIVERANCE AND WILL NOT DENOUNCE THE GLO. IN THIS CASE, THE SINFUL YOKE OF THE GLO HAS NOT BEEN REVEALED TO THE PERSON. ONCE YOU LEARN THE TRUTH ABOUT GLO's AND THEIR SINFULNESS, IT IS THEN UP TO YOU TO OBEY YOUR CONVICTION

THAT JESUS HAS ALREADY DESTROYED THE YOKE (LEVITICUS 4:23). THIS IS WHAT BRINGS ABOUT REPENTANCE AND DENUNCIATION. THIS WAS THE REASON HE WAS SENT INTO THE WORLD (I JOHN 3:8- TO DESTROY THE WORKS OF THE DEVIL). THE REASON SO MANY TRUE CHRISTIANS ARE BECOMING "GREEK CHRISTIANS," AND SO MANY UNSAVED MEMBERS GET SAVED AND REMAIN "GREEK CHRISTIANS" IS BECAUSE THEY CHOOSE NOT TO OBEY THE TRUTH. THEY DO NOT WANT TO HAVE THE YOKE OF BEING OR DESIRING TO BE IN A GLO DESTROYED, WHILE OTHERS DON'T KNOW THE TRUTH AND JOIN OUT OF IGNORANCE; EITHER WAY, THE YOKES THAT DRAW THEM TO GLO's, MUST BE REVEALED AND DESTROYED TO FREE THEM. MANY, ONCE THEY GET SAVED, BELIEVE THAT THEIR SALVATION CAN BE DONE THEIR OWN WAY. UNFORTUNATELY, INSTEAD OF CHOOSING FREEDOM (JOHN 8:32), THEY CHOOSE BONDAGE (GALATIANS 4:9). JUST BECAUSE SOMEONE IS

DELIVERED FROM PRISON DOES NOT MEAN THAT THEY ARE DELIVERED FROM THE BONDAGE OF CRIMINAL LIFE. IF SO, WHY ARE THERE SO MANY REPEAT OFFENDERS? THEY DO NOT WANT TO LIVE ACCORDING TO THEIR DELIVERANCE. IT IS THE SAME WITH SIN. UNTIL YOU BELIEVE THAT YOU ARE DELIVERED, THE REALITY OF YOUR FREEDOM WILL NOT BE REAL TO YOU. THEREFORE, YOU WILL FIND YOURSELF GOING BACK TO A PARTICULAR SIN. THIS IS WHY THE BIBLE SAYS THAT WE MUST RENEW OUR MINDS.

II.) SAVED BUT INTERESTED IN A GLO. ALTHOUGH YOU NEVER JOINED, THE DESIRE MUST GO.

YOU NEED TO DO A SELF-CHECK
II CORINTHIANS 13:5

1.) BECOME SERIOUSLY DISINTERESTED.

II CORINTHIANS 10:3-5/JAMES 4:7.

2.) ATLEAST PUT OFF PLEDGING TO SEEK THE TRUTH. OBSERVE AND ASK QUESTIONS.
   a.) IF THEIR ORGANIZATIONS ARE SO GREAT, WHY THE SECRECY? (READ CHAPTER 2)
   b.) WHAT'S UP WITH THE PARTIES, HAZING, STEP SHOWS, AND UNGODLY SEMINARS.
   c.) OBSERVE ALL ACTIONS (GROUP AND INDIVIDUAL). IF YOU SEE ANY PRACTICES THAT ARE NOT OF GOD, THIS SHOULD BE YOUR SIGNAL TO NEVER JOIN. BELIEVE ME THERE ARE PLENTY.
   d.) IF YOU FEEL YOU HAVE TO GO TO AN INTEREST MEETING, AT LEAST GO INFORMED AND ARMED WITH THE TRUTH AND THE FACTS.

III.) UNSAVED MEMBER OF A GLO

1.) YOU REALIZE GLO'S ARE DEMONIC AND WANT OUT, BUT YOU DON'T WANT TO GET SAVED.

   a.) GOOD MOVE TO DENOUNCE, BUT REMEMBER THAT YOU ARE STILL NOT SAVED AND THAT'S IS REAL BAD. THE DEVIL WILL RETURN TO STRENGHTEN YOUR DESIRE TO GO BACK TO YOUR BROTHERS OR SISTERS. THE DEVIL WILL USE HYPOCRISY, LIES, FALSE AFFECTION, ABANDONMENT, OR ANY OTHER MEANS TO GET YOU BACK IN "THE FOLD" OF YOUR GLO.

   b.) YOU WANT TO BE SAVED. GIVE YOUR LIFE TO JESUS FIRST. IF SO, ALL SIN IS FORGIVEN AND THE GLO BOND OR YOKE IS DESTROYED, BUT YOU MUST HAVE THE WILL TO KEEP THE YOKE DESTROYED BY YOUR NEW SAVIOR AND LORD. I STILL STRONGLY SUGGEST THAT YOU **VERBALLY** DENOUNCE

YOUR GLO ALONG WITH YOUR CONFESSION OF SALVATION.

PROVERBS 18:21 Life and death is in the power of the tongue: and they that love it shall eat the fruit thereof.

IV.) UNSAVED AND INTERESTED IN A GLO

    a.) AFTER READING THIS FAR, YOU OUGHT TO BE SAVED AND KILLED THE INTEREST, BUT I UNDERSTAND THE STRONG DESIRE TO JOIN.

    b.) ASK THE MEMBERS SOME QUESTIONS THAT HIT HOME. TELL THEM YOU WANT TO KNOW EVERYTHING (secrets, rituals, history, poems, etc.) BEFORE YOU MAKE YOUR DECISION. REMEMBER THAT BY BEING UNSAVED, YOU MAY NOT SEE THE TRUTH. FIND SOMEONE YOU KNOW THAT DISAGREES WITH GLO's AND CARES FOR YOUR SOUL. THEY CAN GIVE

YOU THINGS TO LOOK AND LISTEN FOR. CONFIRMATION IS A STRONG TESTIMONY, AND IT MAY BE WHAT CAUSES YOU TO RECONSIDER.

REMEMBER THAT WHETHER YOU ARE SAVED OR UNSAVED, <u>GLO'S</u> ARE NOT OF GOD. SINNERS WILL DO WHAT THEY DO, AND THAT'S PRACTICE SIN. YET, THEY DO HAVE A CONSCIENCE, AND THEY MAY SEE THE EVILS OF GLO's. THOSE WHO ARE SAVED MUST DO WHAT THE WORD SAYS, AND THAT IS TO BE YE SEPARATE, TOUCH NOT THE UNCLEAN THING, BE NOT PARTAKERS WITH THEM (GLO's), HAVE NO FELLOWSHIP WITH THEM AND COME OUT FROM AMONG THEM.

EPHESIANS 5:1-12 Be ye therefore **followers of God** as dear children: And walk in love, as Christ hath loved us, and hath given himself for us an offering and a sacrifice to God for a sweet smelling savour. But fornication, and all uncleanness, or covetousness, let it not be once named among you, as becometh saints; Neither filthiness, nor foolish talking, nor jesting, which are not convenient: but rather giving of thanks. For this ye know, that no whoremonger, nor unclean person, nor covetous man, who is an idolater, hath any inheritance in the kingdom of Christ and of God. **Let no man deceive you with vain words**: for because of these things cometh the wrath of God upon the children of disobedience. **Be not** ye therefore **partakers with them.** For ye were **sometimes** in darkness, but **now** are ye light in the Lord: walk as children of light: (For **the fruit of the Spirit is in all goodness and righteousness and truth;**) **Proving what is acceptable of unto the Lord.** And **have no fellowship** with the unfruitful works of darkness, but rather **reprove them.** For it is a shame even to speak of those things which are done of them **in secret.**

HOW DO I LEAD OTHERS IN PRAYER AND DENUNCIATION? I DO HAVE CERTAIN THINGS FOR THAT PERSON TO REPEAT, BUT OTHER THAN THAT, I AM LED BY THE SPIRIT.

Notes

CHAPTER 10
PART 3

WITNESSING

I.) PREPARATION

   a.) FIRST ONE MUST PRAY, FAST, AND HAVE BASIC KNOWLEDGE (SPECIFIC IF POSSIBLE) OF WHY GLO's ARE DEMONIC. IF YOU KNOW THE GLO YOU ARE DEALING WITH, IT IS BEST TO RESEARCH IT.

   b.) BE COMPASSIONATE- YOU KNOW AND HAVE THE TRUTH. REMEMBER YOU ARE ATTACKING THEIR god. A GREEK CHRISTIAN'S GLO IS VERY PRECIOUS TO THEM.

   c.) SEE WHERE THEY ARE IN CHRIST. MANY BELIEVE THAT THEY ARE SAVED. ESTABLISH A GOOD RELATIONSHIP WITH THAT PERSON (IF POSSIBLE). INVITE THEM TO CHURCH. YOU DON'T HAVE TO GO FOR THE JUGULAR RIGHT AWAY.

   d.) THE BEST WAY THE HOLY SPIRIT HAS SHOWN ME TO INITIATE A

CONVERSATION ABOUT GLO's IS AS FOLLOWS: "I 'HAD' A FRIEND THAT USED TO BE IN A GLO, BUT THEY DENOUNCED IT, OR I 'WAS' IN A GLO." THE PAST TENSE WILL EAT THEM ALIVE. THIS AROUSES SERIOUS CURIOSITY AND QUESTIONS. THIS TYPE OF STATEMENT GETS YOUR FOOT IN THE DOOR FOR DISCUSSION.

e.) SOME ALREADY KNOW ABOUT THE CHRISTIAN WITNESS, AND HAVE TRIED TO BECOME "WITNESS PROOF". YOU HAVE THE MIND OF CHRIST: YOU SHOULD KNOW WHEN TO QUIT WITNESSING (i.e. WHEN THEY ACT STUBBORN).

MATTHEW 7:6(amp) Do not give that which is holy (the sacred thing) to the dogs, and do not throw your pearls before hogs, lest they trample upon them with their feet and turn and tear you in pieces.

When the conversation moves away from **Jesus** and denouncing, ask them if they would be interested in some scriptures to read. If not, it's time for you to move on.

IF YOU KNOW A PERSON(S) IS NOT IN A GLO BUT INTERESTED, LET THEM KNOW THE TRUTH. TELL THEM WHAT TO LOOK FOR.

II.) INFORMATION YOU NEED

NOTE: MOST WILL BE PROVIDED IN THIS BOOK.

1.) **ORIGIN AND PROGRESSION OF SECRET SOCIETIES-** FROM ANCIENT TO MODERN.

2.) **ALL THE SIMILARITIES OF ANCIENT AND MODERN SECRET SOCIETIES.**

3.) **ANY GLO LITERATURE-** RITUALS, HANDBOOKS, HISTORY BOOKS, SONGS, POEMS, MEANINGS OF SYMBOLS, etc.

III.) ROLE PLAY

1.) ROLE-PLAY IS DONE BEST WITH A FORMER MEMBER. BE PREPARED FOR **RELIGIOUS** FEEDBACK. IT IS NOT BASED ON THE WORD OF GOD. IT IS BASED ON HUMAN PHILOSOPHY MIXED WITH GOD'S WORD. IT ALL SOUNDS

GOOD, BUT YOU MUST BE ABLE TO SIFT THROUGH THE MANURE.

2.) IN A ROLE-PLAY WHERE THE PERSON DOES NOT REALLY CARE, FLOOD THEM WITH SCRIPTURAL REASONS WHY GLO'S ARE UNGODLY. THE WORD OF GOD IS THE BEST WEAPON YOU HAVE. USE IT AS MUCH AS POSSIBLE. COVET THE BEST GIFTS WHEN WITNESSING TO GREEK CHRISTIANS. ASK GOD FOR WORD OF WISDOM, WORD OF KNOWLEDGE, AND DISCERNMENT OF SPIRITS.

3.) THE PERSON IN THE GLO SHOULD ACT OUT DIFFERENT TEMPERMENTS. THIS WILL HELP THE ONE WITNESSING BECOME USED TO HOW THEY REALLY ACT.

IV.) THE BASICS TO KNOW AS A WITNESS

1.) ORIGIN OF SECRET SOCIETIES

2.) ABOUT SECRECY

3.) HAZING/INTAKE/PLEDGING- ALL THE SAME

4.) OATHS-THE UNIVERSAL LINK TO ALL MEMBERS.

5.) UNEQUAL YOKING- OTHER'S FRUITS (SINS) BECOME YOURS TOO.

6.) IF AND WHEN APPROPRIATE, LET THEM KNOW THAT YOU HAVE READ THEIR RITUAL, HISTORY, SONGS, POEMS, OR THAT YOU TALKED TO AN EX-MEMBER OF THEIR GLO. REFER THEM TO A PERSON WHO HAS DENOUNCED THE GLO THEY BELONG TO, IF POSSIBLE.

7.) GET THEM TO ADMIT CERTAIN FACTS ABOUT THEIR GLO BY ASKING QUESTIONS

   a.) DOES YOUR OATH MAKE ALL PRESENT AND/OR PAST MEMBERS YOUR BROTHERS OR SISTERS? IF YES, USE II CORINTHIANS 6:14-18/AMOS 3:3. IF NO, ASK THEM THE PURPOSE FOR JOINING.

   b.) QUESTION THEM ABOUT SECRET ASPECTS THAT YOU KNOW ABOUT. IT GIVES YOU THE CHANCE TO SEE IF THEY (ESPECIALLY A "GREEK CHRISTIAN") WILL LIE TO PROTECT THEIR GLO. IF THEY LIE, LET THEM KNOW THEY LIED

AND NEED TO DENOUNCE AND REPENT, NOT JUST FOR LYING, BUT FOR PUTTING THEIR GLO's SECRETS BEFORE GOD'S COMMANDS.

8.) ASK THEM QUESTIONS ABOUT TRUTH. ANY TRUTHS FROM THE WORD OF GOD THEY AGREE WITH THAT CONFLICT WITH GLO's NEED TO BE POINTED OUT TO THEM. WHAT I AM ACTUALLY SAYING IS, BAIT THEM WITH TRUTHS THAT YOU KNOW ARE IN CONFLICT WITH GLO's, AND ANY THEY AGREE WITH USE AS PROOF OF A GLO's UNGODLINESS. EXAMPLE: RITUAL IS WORSHIP AND WORSHIP REQUIRES A GOD. ASK THEM WHICH GOD DO YOUR RITUALS WORSHIP? AND THEN MAKE THEM PROVE IT.

9.)   VERY,   VERY IMPORTANT!

THE FOLLOWING SCRIPTURES ARE CALLED, "THE GLO INESCAPABLES". THESE ARE SCRIPTURES AND THEIR RESPECTIVE CATEGORIES TO USE THAT THE GREEK CHRISTIAN CANNOT ESCAPE, TALK THEIR WAY OUT, PHILOSOPHY OR REASON WITH EXCEPT THEY WRITE A DIFFERENT BIBLE. AS A WITNESS TO

GREEK CHRISTIANS, THESE ARE THE LAST BUT DEFINITELY NOT LEAST OF THE "INESCAPABLES."

   a.) UNEQUAL YOKING- AMOS 3:3/II CORINTHIANS 6:14-18/ HEBREWS 7:26

   b.) UNHOLY FELLOWSHIP- EPHESIANS 5:1-7

   c.) SWEARING & OATHS- MATTHEW 5:33-37

   d.) SECRECY- JOHN 18:20/ACTS 26:26

   e.) SERVING MORE THAN GOD ALONE (i.e. TWO MASTERS)- MATTHEW 6:24/JOSHUA 24:15

   f.) UNHOLY WORSHIP BASED ON GLO's PERFORMANCE OF RITUALS- MATTHEW 4:10/JOHN 4:23

A-F are covered sufficiently enough by God's Word, this book and their actions.

10.) MAKE YOURSELF FAMILIAR WITH THESE COMMON PHRASES AND EXCUSES USED BY MEMBERS OF GLO's WHO HAVE BEEN CONFRONTED BY CHRISTIANS OR

ARE RELIGIOUS. LISTEN TO THEM WHEN YOU TALK TO ONE.

1.) WE DO GOOD THINGS. SO DO INMATES. JUST DOING IS NOT WHAT COUNTS. WHAT IS THE MOTIVE BEHIND THE DEED? WHO GETS THE GLORY? WHO ARE YOU DOING IT FOR? THEREFORE, FOUR CONDITIONS MUST BE MET:

    A.) YOU MUST BE SAVED AND PURE (i.e. NO UNCONFESSED SIN IN YOUR LIFE).
A GREEK CHRISTIAN FORFEITS THIS PRIVILEGE BY BEING IN A GLO.

    B.) THE MOTIVE MUST BE PURE.

    C.) THE DEED MUST BE PURE.

    D.) GOD MUST GET ALL THE GLORY (NOT JUST FROM THE INDIVIDUAL, BUT THE PROJECT ITSELF. IF THE PROJECT IS NOT BEING DONE IN THE NAME OF JESUS, AN INDIVIDUAL CAN'T CLAIM THAT HE'S DOING IT FOR JESUS.

I CORINTHIANS 3:10-15 According to the grace of God which is given unto me, as a wise master builder, I have laid the foundation, and another buildeth thereon. But let every man **take heed how he buildeth thereupon.** For other foundation can no man lay than that is laid, which is Jesus Christ. Now if any man build upon his foundation gold, silver, precious stone, wood, hay, stubble; Every man's work shall be manifest: for the day shall declare it, because it shall be revealed by a fire; and the fire shall try every man's work of what sort it is. If any man's work abide which he hath built thereupon, he shall receive a reward. If any man's work shall be burned, he shall suffer loss: but he himself shall be saved; yet so as by fire.

2.) HOW DO YOU KNOW ABOUT WHAT WE DO, YOU'RE NOT A PART OF OUR GROUP? YOUR FRUIT SHOWS ME.

MATTHEW 7:17-19 Even so every good tree bringeth forth good fruit; but a corrupt tree bringeth forth evil fruit. And a good tree cannot bring forth evil fruit, neither can a corrupt tree bring forth good fruit. Every tree that bringeth not forth good fruit is hewn down, and cast into the fire.

3.) JESUS SAT WITH THE SINNERS. WHY CAN'T I BE IN THE FRAT? **HEY YOU? YE YOU! GREEK CHRISTIAN!!!** STOP QUOTING **MATTHEW 9:11** ONLY. **READ VERSES 12 AND 13 ALSO.** DID JESUS BECOME A PUBLICAN? **NO!** DID HE BECOME A SINNER? **IMPOSSIBLE!!** HE WAS NOT **YOKED** TO THEM, NOR WAS HE IN CONSTANT, **HABITUAL** FELLOWSHIP WITH THEM EITHER. HE WAS THERE TO CALL SINNERS UNTO REPENTANCE.

TO THE PERSON THAT WITNESSES TO A GREEK CHRISTIAN: THIS IS ONE OF THEIR FAVORITE SCRIPTURES. LET IT BE YOUR PLEASURE TO SHOW THEM THE OTHER TWO VERSES, AND THE FACT THAT THEY ASKED HIM TO COME AND SIT WITH THEM. JESUS WAS NOT **YOKED** WITH THEM.

II CORINTHIANS 6:14-18 Be ye not unequally yoked together with unbelievers: for what fellowship has righteousness with unrighteousness? and what communion hath light with darkness? And what concord hath Christ with Belial? Or what part hath he that believeth with an infidel? And what agreement hath the temple of God with idols? for ye are the temple of the living God; as god hath said, I will dwell in them; and I will be their God, and they shall be my people. Wherefore come out from among them and be ye separate, saith the Lord, and touch not the unclean thing; and I will receive you, I will be a Father unto you, and ye shall be my sons and daughters, saith the Lord Almighty.

Hebrews 7:26 For such an high priest became us, who is holy, harmless, undefiled, **separate from sinners** and made higher than the heavens;

4.) WE'RE ALL HUMAN AND GOING TO CONTINUE PRACTICING SIN. JESUS' EXAMPLE OF A SINLESS LIFE PUTS THIS EXCUSE TO SHAME.

MY RESPONSE TO THAT IS, WHY MAKE THE SACRIFICE HE DID FOR A BUNCH OF FUTURE LOSERS?

II CORINTHIANS 5:21 For he hath made him to be sin for us, who knew no sin; that we might be made the righteousness of God through him.

HEBREWS 5:8 But God shows and clearly proves his [own] love for us by the fact that while we were still sinners, Christ [the messiah, the anointed one] died for us.

I JOHN 3:6(amp) No one who abides in Him [who lives and remains in communion with and obedience to Him-**deliberately, knowingly, and habitually] commits (practices) sin. No one who [habitually] sins** has either seen or known Him [recognized, perceived, or understood Him, or **has had an experiential acquaintance with him].**

THE SCRIPTURE ABOVE PROVES THAT STATEMENT #4 IS NOT ONLY A PATHETIC LIE, BUT THAT GOD IS ABLE TO KEEP YOU FROM PRACTICING SIN. ANY GREEK

CHRISTIAN THAT MAKES THIS STATEMENT PROVES THE TRUTH OF I JOHN 3:6 (i.e. **they never knew God.**)

5.) THAT'S YOUR OPINION. I HAVE MY BELIEF, AND YOU HAVE YOURS.

THE ONLY OPINION REASONABLE IS GOD'S OPINION, ALTHOUGH I WOULD NOT CALL IT AN OPINION.

II CORINTHIANS 10:3-5 For though we walk in the flesh, we do not war after the flesh: (For the weapons of our warfare are not carnal, but mighty through God to the pulling down of strongholds;) Casting down imaginations, and every high thing that exalteth itself against the knowledge of God, and bringing into captivity **every thought** to the obedience **of Christ;**

ISAIAH 55:8-9 For my thoughts are not your thoughts, neither are your ways my ways, saith the Lord. For as the heavens are higher than the earth, so are my ways higher than your ways, and my thoughts above your thoughts.

IF SCRIPTURE CANNOT BACK UP YOUR "OPINION", **IT'S A LIE.**

6.) THAT'S HOW YOU INTERPRET THE BIBLE. NO! THE BIBLE INTERPRETS ITSELF AND THE HOLY SPIRIT GIVES US THE INTERPRETATION.

II PETER 1:19-21 We have also a more sure word of prophecy; whereunto ye do well that ye take heed, as unto a light that shineth in a dark place, until the day dawn, and the day star arise in your hearts: Knowing the first, that no prophecy of the scripture is of any private interpretation. For the prophecy came not in the old time by the will of man: but holy men of God spake as they were moved by the Holy Ghost.

I JOHN 2:27(amp) But as for you, the anointing (the sacred appointment, the unction) which you received from him abides [permanently] in you; [so] then you have no need that anyone should instruct you. But just as his anointing teaches you concerning everything and is true and is no falsehood, so you must abide in (live in, never depart from) him [being rooted in him, knit to him], just as [his anointing] has taught you [to do].

A GREEK CHRISTIAN IS NOT ABIDING IN CHRIST. THEREFORE, **THEY NEED INSTRUCTION FROM A TRUE CHRISTIAN**. THEN, HOPEFULLY THEY WILL SEE AND ACCEPT THE TRUTH AND REPENT.

II TIMOTHY 2:24-25 And the servant of the Lord must not strive; but be gentle unto all men, apt to teach, patient, In meekness instructing **those who oppose themselves**; if God **peradventure** will give them repentance to the acknowledging of the truth.

7.) THE OATH, PARTIES, STEPPING, HAZING, ETC. MEANS NOTHING TO ME, JUST THE GOOD BROTHERS AND SISTERS, THE GOOD THINGS THEY DO, AND THE BENEFITS THEY HAVE TO OFFER. THEN YOU ARE TRULY IN A GLO. **YOU CANNOT BE A PART OF THE WHOLE WITHOUT BEING CONNECTED TO ALL THE OTHER PARTS.** (I CORINTHIANS 12)

ACTUALLY, GREEK CHRISTIANS ARE LUKEWARM BECAUSE THEY ARE NOT COMPLETELY INVOLVED IN ANYTHING: THE CHURCH OR YOUR GLO.

REVELATION 3:15-16 I know thy works, that thou art neither cold nor hot: I would thou wert cold or hot. So then because thou art lukewarm, and neither cold nor hot, I will spew thee out of my mouth.

AS LONG AS YOU CLAIM MEMBERSHIP, AND YOU KNOW THESE DEEDS ARE OCCURRING, YOU MAY NOT ACTIVELY OR MENTALLY BE PERFORMING THE ACT, BUT

YOU ARE SPIRITUALLY INVOLVED **BY YOUR OWN CONFESSION** (SAYING YOU ARE A BROTHER OR SISTER) **AND OWN WILL** (REFUSING TO DENOUNCE COMPLETELY). THEREFORE, YOU ARE IN SIN. TO BE IN SPIRITUAL AGREEMENT, MEANS COMPLETE AGREEMENT REGARDLESS OF PHYSICAL SEPARATION.

AMOS 3:3 Can two walk together, except they be agreed?

HOW CAN TWO SAY THEY ARE ALPHA'S AND NOT BE BROTHERS? GREEK CHRISTIANS CAN'T CLAIM SEPARATION FROM EVIL MEMBERS JUST BECAUSE THEY DECIDE TO.

8.) THE CHURCH IS DOING IT. THE ACTIONS OF THE CHURCH, ANGELS, SINNERS, AND CHRISTIANS ARE SUBJECT TO THE AUTHORITY OF CHRIST.

ROMANS 7:4 Wherefore, my brethren, ye also are become dead to the law by the body of Christ; that ye should be married to another, even to him who is raised from the dead, that **we should bring forth fruit unto God.**

READ CHAPTER 5 FOR DISCUSSION OF #8.

9.) WE DON'T BOW DOWN TO OUR GROUP AND WORSHIP IT.

THE POSITION OF ONE'S BODY IS NOT WHAT DETERMINES WORSHIP. THE RITUAL CEREMONIES ARE JUST FORMALITIES OF WORSHIP THAT SUBSTITUTE SOMETHING OR SOMEONE FOR CHRIST AS THE OBJECT OF WORSHIP.

I CORINTHIANS 1:11-13 For it hath been declared unto me of you, my brethren, by them which are of the house of Chloe, that there are contentions among you. Now this I say, that every one of you saith, I am of Paul; and I of Apollos; and I of Cephas; and I of Christ. Is Christ divided? was Paul crucified for you? or were ye baptized in the name of Paul?

COLOSSIANS 2:8,16-19 Beware lest any man spoil you through philosophy and vain deceit, after the tradition of men, after the rudiments of the world, and not after Christ. Let no man therefore judge you in meat, or in drink, or in respect of any holyday, or of the new moon, or of the sabbath days: Which are a shadow of things to come; but the body is of Christ. Let no man beguile you of your reward in a voluntary humility and worshipping of angels, intruding into those things which he hath not seen, vainly puffed up by his fleshly mind, And not holding the Head, from which all the body by joints and bands having nourishment ministered, and knit together, increaseth with the increase of God.

IDOLATRY AT THE ROOT IS THE WORSHIP OF DEMONS.

10.) WE PRAY TO GOD, GO TO CHURCH, READ THE BIBLE, HELP THE POOR. BUT YOU HAVE AND SERVE OTHER gods. YOU PARTY, YOU CALL SINNERS YOUR BROTHERS AND SISTERS. YET, SOME OF YOU CLAIM TO BE ONLY A COMMUNITY SERVICE ORGANIZATION, A BUSINESS ORGANIZATION WITH NO RELIGIOUS AFFILIATIONS. IF SO, THEN WHY DO YOU HAVE RITUALS, PRAYER, PRIDE IN MEMBERS WHO ARE IN THE CLERGY??? THEN THERE ARE THOSE WHO CLAIM A FOUNDATION ON CHRISTIAN PRINCIPLES. YOU ARE EITHER LIARS, HYPOCRITES, OR BOTH!!!!!!!!!

II CORINTHIANS 6:14-18 Be ye not unequally yoked together with unbelievers: for what fellowship has righteousness with unrighteousness? And what communion hath light with darkness? And what concord hath Christ with Belial? Or what part hath he that believeth with an infidel? And what agreement hath the temple of God with idols? for ye are the temple of the living God; as god hath said, I will dwell in them; and I will be their God, and they shall be my people. Wherefore come out from among them and be ye separate, saith the Lord, and touch not the unclean thing; and I will receive you, I will be a Father unto you, and ye shall be my sons and daughters, saith the Lord Almighty.

THERE ARE MANY ORGANIZATIONS THAT ARE STRICTLY BUSINESSES. THEY DO NOT HAVE RITUALS, COVENANTS, AND BROTHERHOOD/SISTERHOOD AFFILIATIONS. JC PENNEY, RAY KROC (McDonalds), DR. NAISMITH (PREACHER/INVENTOR OF BASKETBALL), AND OTHERS DID IT WITHOUT THESE RELIGIOUS REQUIREMENTS. HOW COME GLO'S CAN'T DO IT? BECAUSE THEY ARE OBVIOUSLY MORE THAN JUST A BUSINESS/COMMUNITY SERVICE ORGANIZATION, THEY ARE ALSO RELIGIOUS BY NATURE.

11.) OUR GOOD OUTWEIGHS THE BAD.

II TIMOTHY 2:19 Nevertheless the foundation of God standeth sure, having this seal, The Lord knoweth them that are his. And, **Let every one** that nameth the name of Christ **depart from iniquity**.

YOU ARE EITHER FOR GOD OR FOR THE DEVIL. IT CAN NEVER BE BOTH.

12.) PLEDGING BUILDS A BOND.

NO! IT PROVES THE INDIVIDUALS IN GLO'S HATE GOD.

I JOHN 4:20-21 If any man say, I love God, and hateth his brother, **he is a liar:** for he that loveth not his brother whom he hath seen, how can he love God whom he hath not seen? And this commandment we have from Him, That he loveth God love his brother also.

13.) WE PAY DUES

THIS MONEY IS GIVEN TO DEMON-LED AND INSPIRED GLO's, BUT GOD SAYS TO BE A WISE STEWARD WITH THE MONEY HE GIVES YOU. WHAT ABOUT TITHES AND OFFERINGS? DO ALL GREEKS DO THIS?

14.) I CAN SERVE AND LOVE GOD AND BE IN THE FRAT.

NO YOU CAN'T!!!

MATTHEW 4:10 Then saith Jesus unto him, Get thee hence, Satan: for it is written, Thou shalt worship the Lord thy God, and **him only shalt thou serve.**

JAMES 4:4(amp) You [are like] unfaithful wives [having **illicit love affairs with the world** and breaking your marriage vow to God! Do you not know that **being the world's friend is being God's enemy?** So whoever chooses to be a friend of the world takes his stand in being an enemy of God.

GLO's ARE OF THE WORLD. THE LOVE FOR THEM IS EXPRESSED IN WORD, SONG, DEED, AND ASSOCIATION.

ROMANS 6:16 Know ye not, that to whom ye yield yourselves servants to obey, his servants ye are to whom ye obey; whether of sin unto death, or of obedience unto righteousness.

MATTHEW 6:24 No man can serve two masters; for either he will hate the one, and love the other; or else he will hold to the one, and despise the other. Ye cannot serve God and mammon.

15.) I'M NOT ACTIVE ANYMORE. I DON'T GO TO MEETINGS ANYMORE.

THEN WHY ARE YOU STILL CLAIMING TO BE IN THE GLO? TOTAL DENUNCIATION BY WORD AND DEED IS NECESSARY, BECAUSE THE WORDS OF YOUR MOUTH HAVE THE POWER TO DESTROY YOUR GLO RELATIONSHIP YOU STARTED WITH THE WORDS OF YOUR MOUTH.

PROVERBS 18:21 Death and life are in the power of the tongue: and they that love it shall eat the fruit thereof.

16.) I IGNORE THE BAD AND KEEP THE GOOD.

THEN YOU NEED TO IGNORE YOUR GLO COMPLETELY.

AMOS 3:3 Can two walk together, except they be agreed?

17.) THE CHURCH HAS HYPOCRITES. LOOK AT JIM BAKKER! YES, WE KNOW THERE ARE, FOR CHRIST, PAUL, AND JOHN WARNED US THAT THERE WOULD BE.

LUKE 12:1-2 In the mean time, when there were gathered together an innumerable multitude of people, insomuch that they trode one upon another, he began to say unto his disciples first of all, Beware ye of the leaven of the Pharisees, which is hypocrisy. For there is nothing covered, that shall not be revealed; neither hid, that shall not be known.

I CORINTHIANS 11:19 For **there must be also heresies** among you, that they **which are approved** may be made manifest among you.

I JOHN 2:18-19 Little children, it is the last time: and as ye have heard that antichrist shall come, even now are there many antichrists; whereby we know that it is the last time. They went out from us, but they were not of us: for if they had been of us, **they would no doubt have continued with us:** but they went out, **that they might be made manifest that they were not all of us.**

18.) WE HELP THE CHURCH.

WHAT ABOUT YOURSELVES? HELPING THE CHURCH DOES NOT EARN SALVATION. ANY CLAIM THAT WORKS EARNS OR HELPS YOUR SALVATION IS HERESY.

GALATIANS 1:8-9 But though we, or an angel from heaven, preach any other gospel unto you than that which we have preached unto you, let him be accursed. As we said before, so say I now again, if any man preach any other gospel unto you than that ye have received, let him be accursed.

EPHESIANS 2:8-9 It is by grace ye are saved through faith, and that not of yourselves: It is the gift of God: Not of works, lest any man should BOAST.

19.) THERE ARE MINISTERS, PASTORS, DEACONS, ETC., IN GLO's.

SIN IS SIN. ALL INDIVIDUALS WILL GIVE AN ACCOUNT TO GOD FOR THEIR ACTIONS.

REVALATION 20:11-15 And I saw a great white throne, and him that sat on it, from whose face the earth and the heaven fled away; and there was found no place for them. And I saw the dead, **small and great**, stand before God; and the book was opened: and another book was opened, which is the book of life: and the dead were judged out of those things which were written in the books, according to their works. And the sea gave up the dead which were in it; and death and hell delivered up the dead which were in them: and they were judged **every man** according to their works. And death and hell were cast into the lake of fire. And **whosoever** was **not found** in the book of life was cast into the lake of fire.

20.) JESUS KNOWS MY HEART

JEREMIAH 17:9 The heart is desperately wicked, and deceitful above all things, who can know it?

HE ACCEPTS ME AS I AM. TRUE!!!

MATTHEW 11:28 Come unto me **all** that labor and are heavy laden, and I will give you rest.

THIS IS PRIOR TO SALVATION. AFTER SALVATION, HE HAS ACCEPTED YOU AS YOU WERE, BUT NOW HE COMMANDS THAT YOU BE AS HE IS.

I JOHN 2:3-6 And hereby we do know that we know him, if we keep his commandments. He that saith, I know him, and keepeth not his commandments, is a liar, and the truth is not in him. But whoso keepeth his word, in him verily is the love of God perfected: hereby know we that we are in him. He that saith he abideth in him ought himself also so to walk, even as he walked.

HE ASKS YOU TO COME AS YOU ARE (MESSED UP), AND THEN DO WHAT HE COMMANDS SO HE CAN MAKE YOU WHO YOU OUGHT TO BE IN HIM.

MATTHEW 11:28-30 Come unto me all that labor and are heavy laden, and I will give you rest. **Take my yoke upon you**, and **learn of me**; for I am meek and lowly in heart: and ye shall find rest unto your souls. For my yoke is easy, and my burden is light.

HE HAS CALLED ALL BELIEVERS TO HOLINESS.

I PETER 1:15-16 But as he which has called you is holy, so be ye holy in all manner of conversation; Because it is written, Be ye holy; for I am holy.

21.) YOU DON'T KNOW ME. HOW CAN YOU JUDGE ME? THE BIBLE SPEAKS ON JUDGMENT OF OTHERS.

TITUS 3:10-11 A man that is an heretic after the first and second admonition reject; Knowing that he that is such is subverted, and sinneth, be condemned of himself.

MATTHEW 18:15-17 Moreover if thy brother shall trespass against thee, go and tell him his fault between thee and him alone; if he shall hear thee, thou hast gained thy brother. But if he will not hear thee, then take with thee one or two more, that in the mouth of two or three witnesses every word may be established. And if he shall neglect to hear them, tell it unto the church: but if he neglect to hear the church, let him be unto thee as an heathen man and a publican.

ROMANS 16:17-18 Now I beseech you, brethren, mark them which cause divisions and offences contrary to the doctrine which ye have learned; and avoid them. For they that are such serve not our Lord Jesus Christ, but their own belly; and by good words and fair speeches deceive the hearts of the simple.

GALATIANS 6:1 Brethren, if a man be overtaken in a fault, ye which are spiritual, **restore** such an one in the spirit of meekness; considering thyself, lest thou be tempted.

I TIMOTHY 1:19-20 Holding faith, and a good conscience; which some having put away concerning faith have made shipwreck: Of whom is Hymaneus and Alexander; whom I have delivered unto Satan, that they may learn not to blaspheme.

I Corinthians 5:5 To deliver such an one unto Satan for the destruction of the flesh, that the spirit may be saved in the day of the Lord Jesus Christ,

I Corinthians 5:9-13 I wrote unto you in an epistle not to company with fornicators: Yet not altogether with the fornicators of this world, or with the covetous, or extortioners, or with idolaters; for then must ye needs go out of the world. But now I have written unto you not to keep company, if any man that is called a brother be a fornicator, or covetous, or an idolater, or a railer, or a drunkard, or an extortioner, with such an one not to eat. For what have I to do judge them also that are without? **do not ye judge them that are within?** But them that are without God judgeth. Therefore put away from among yourselves that wicked person.

JUDGE NOT, LEST YE BE JUDGED (APPLIES TO ONE WHO IS COMMITTING THE SAME SIN, AND STILL TRIES TO JUDGE ANOTHER. JUDGMENT IN HYPOCRISY IS THE KEY TO UNDERSTANDING THIS SCRIPTURE.

MATTHEW 7:1-5 JUDGE NOT, that ye be not judged. For with what judgment ye judge, ye shall be judged: and with what measure ye mete, it shall be measured to you again. And why beholdest thou the mote which is in thy brother's eye, but considerest not the beam that is in thine own eye? Or how wilt thou say to thy brother, Let me pull out the mote out of thine eye; and, behold, a beam is in thine own eye? **Thou hypocrite**, first cast out the beam out of thine own eye; and then shalt thou see clearly to cast out the mote out of thy brother's eye.

SCRIPTURE CLEARLY SUPPORTS THE RIGHT AND AUTHORITY TO JUDGE ANOTHER CHRISTIAN FOR THE

SOLE PURPOSE OF RESTORING THEM. TO THOSE THAT WITNESS TO GREEK CHRISTIANS; REMEMBER, IT'S THE WORD OF GOD THAT JUDGES. TAKE NO PERSONAL RESPONSIBILTY FOR BEING THE JUDGE. TRUE CHRISTIANS JUDGE BASED ON THE WORD OF GOD. TO JUDGE ANY OTHER WAY IS WRONG.

THERE ARE PLENTY OF SCRIPTURES TO SUPPORT THE PURPOSE, RIGHT AND AUTHORITY FOR ONE TRUE CHRISTIAN TO JUDGE ANOTHER WHO PROFESSES TO BE A CHRISTIAN. I, JUDGING BY THE WORD OF GOD, AM COMPLETELY SURE THAT GREEK CHRISTIANS MUST DENOUNCE, DENY, AND REPENT FOR THEIR INVOLVEMENT IN A GLO. AFTER SPEAKING THE TRUTH, THE ONLY THING YOU CAN DO FOR THEM IS BE A **LIVING** EXAMPLE OF WHAT IT IS TO BE A CHRISTIAN, BUT HOW CAN A FORNICATOR, IDOLATER OR LIAR BE A LIVING EXAMPLE OF JESUS CHRIST? THEY CAN'T. ALL THEY PROVE IS THAT THERE IS SIN. SINNERS NEED NO JUDGEMENT FROM CHRISTIANS, BECAUSE THEY HAVE NO NEED TO BE JUDGED BY ANY MAN. GOD IS THEIR JUDGE. WITNESS THEM TO CHRIST. THEY NEED TO BE SAVED FIRST.

I CORINTHIANS 2:15-16 But he that is spirit **judgeth all things**, yet **he himself is judged by no man**. For who hath known the mind of the Lord, that he may instruct him? But we have the mind of Christ.

Go to these websites and check out what some Christians **believe**, **say**, and **do**. It will even astonish a sinner. On one of the sites, the owner, a sinner had to tell some confessing Christians to stop using profanity, suspending them for a couple of days. The websites are: www.stepshow.com and www.greekchat.com

22.) I'M IN IT FOR THE CONNECTIONS

SOME SAY THEY JOIN ONLY FOR THE CONNECTIONS. WHY ARE THEY AT THE PARTIES, MEETINGS, FELLOWSHIPS, AND CALLING THE MEMBERS BROTHERS OR SISTERS? ALL THEY WOULD REALLY HAVE TO DO IS

REMAIN FINANCIAL BY PAYING THEIR DUES TO BE CONSIDERED LEGITIMATE. IF THE INDIVIDUAL WANTS THE CONNECTION, **THEY HAVE TO CONFESS AND PROVE THEIR MEMBERSHIP.** FOR THE CHRISTIAN, IF JESUS IS YOUR CONNECTION, WHAT OR WHO ELSE DO YOU NEED? GREEK CHRISTIANS ARE GUILTY OF TRUSTING IN MAN TO BE SUCCESSFUL, OR FOR THE OPPORTUNITY TO GET AHEAD. THE BIBLE SAYS YOU ARE CURSED.

JEREMIAH 17:5(amp) Thus says the Lord: Cursed [**with great evil**] is the strong man who trusts in and relies on frail man, making weak [human] flesh his arm, and whose mind and heart turn aside from the Lord.

23.) WHAT DENOMINATION ARE YOU?

LET THEM KNOW YOU ARE **A CHRISTIAN**, AND THAT THE JESUS DOES NOT RECOGNIZE DENOMINATIONS. THIS IS A DECOY USED BY THE DEVIL TO GET YOU OFF TRACK. WATCH FOR ALL OF HIS DECOYS. TRUE CHRISTIANS ARE NOT IGNORANT OF HIS DEVICES.

24.) THESE ORGANIZATIONS HAVE BEEN AROUND FOR OVER 200 YEARS. WE MUST BE DOING SOMETHING RIGHT.

MANY RELIGIONS HAVE BEEN AROUND FOR MUCH LONGER, BUT PEOPLE IGNORE THE FACT THAT MANY OF THESE PEOPLE ARE GOING TO HELL. LOOK AT THE MURDER AND TERROR THAT ISLAM HAS BROUGHT THE WORLD. YET, THEY ARE THE FASTEST GROWING RELIGION. YET, THEY ARE VERY WRONG. SUCCESS WITHOUT JESUS CHRIST IS EMPTY.

ON TOP OF ALL THIS, ASK THEM TO EXPLAIN WHAT THEY WOULD SAY TO GOD, IF THEY HAD TO GIVE GOD FIVE GOOD REASONS WHY HE SHOULD LET THEM INTO HIS KINGDOM. THEIR GLO IS SURE TO COME UP. MAKE SURE EVERY ANSWER IS BIBLICAL. ASK THEM WHY THEY THINK GOD MAY NOT LET THEM GO TO

HEAVEN. LISTEN VERY CLOSELY TO THEIR RESPONSE FOR **CONTRADICTION** AND **DOUBT**.

 ALWAYS KEEP IN MIND THAT GOD GIVES THE INCREASE. YOUR ONLY RESPONSIBILITY IS TO PLANT AND WATER SEEDS. EVERYONE YOU WITNESS TO IS NOT GOING TO RECEIVE WHAT YOU PRESENT TO THEM. YOU NEED NOT WORRY. GOD WILL HAVE HIS WAY. HIS WORD NEVER RETURNS VOID, AND IT DOES ACCOMPLISH THAT WHICH HE SENT IT FORTH TO DO. A GREEK CHRISTIAN SHOULD NEVER FEEL COMFORTABLE AROUND YOU CONCERNING HIS MEMBERSHIP IN A GLO. CHRISTIANS ARE SUPPOSED TO JUDGE CHRISTIANS. GREEK CHRISTIANS MUST BE JUDGED NOW, IN HOPES THAT ALL WILL DENOUNCE. THIS PROBLEM OF ACCEPTING GREEKS HAS CREEPED ITS WAY INTO CHRISTIAN MINISTRIES. THEY TRY TO BIBLICALLY COEXIST WITH THE GREEKS, AND BIBLICALLY THIS CANNOT BE DONE. I READ AN ARTICLE ABOUT CAMPUS CRUSADE FOR CHRIST'S, **"GREEKLIFE"**, AND HOW GREEK CHRISTIANS SUFFER PERSECUTION FOR BEING IN A GLO. THEY HAD THE NERVE TO SAY THEY WERE SUFFERING FOR BEING A CHRISTIAN. NO! YOU ARE SUFFERING AS EVILDOERS. THIS IS ANOTHER TYPICAL **SELLOUT TO SATAN MINISTRY** WHO WOULD RATHER WALK IN DISHONESTY THAN IN TRUTH. ANOTHER MINISTRY SOLD OUT TO THE DEVIL IS FOUND ON THE CAMPUS OF SHAW UNIVERSITY IN RALEIGH, N.C. IT IS CALLED G.U.T.S. (GREEKS UNITED TO SERVE). IT IS HEADED UP BY TWO GREEK CHRISTIANS. ONE IS AN "ORDAINED MINISTER", HAROLD TIMBERLAKE

OF ALPHA PHI ALPHA FRATERNITY, AND THE OTHER, ANGELA KING, BELONGS TO ZETA PHI BETA SORORITY. HOW CAN AN "ORDAINED MINISTER" SERVE TWO GODS? SATAN SEDUCED HIM. LET ME TELL YOU STRAIGHT, **YOU CANNOT BELONG TO A GLO AND BE A TRUE CHRISTIAN AT THE SAME TIME.** THEY ARE JUST TWO OF MANY THAT CHOOSE TO COMPROMISE THE GOSPEL OF JESUS CHRIST AND LEAD OTHERS ALSO.

IF CHURCHES WILL ACCEPT GREEK ORGANIZATIONS, WHY DON'T YOU THINK A CAMPUS MINISTRY WILL ACCEPT IT?

ECUMENICALISM OR RELIGIOUS TOLERANCE HAS ENTERED INTO THE GREEK SYSTEM. ECUMENICALISM IS NOTHING MORE THAN A, "CAN'T WE ALL JUST GET ALONG BELIEF," WHILE AT THE SAME TIME **TRUE CHRISTIANS ARE THE ONLY ONES EXPECTED TO DENY BIBLICAL TRUTH.** THE DEVIL IS A FOOL!!!!!!!!!!!

Notes

CHAPTER 10
PART 4

CONCLUSION

PARTS 1, 2, & 3 OF MY PURPOSE HAVE BEEN FULFILLED. ALL I AM WAITING FOR ARE THE MULTIPLE INCREASES INTO OR BACK INTO THE KINGDOM. PLEASE e-mail (reprebres@cs.com) OR CALL YOUR DENUNCIATONS @ 919/829-3513. MY WEBSITE IS www.geocities.com/glos_havebeenexposed

SALVATION OF THE SOUL WILL EVENTUALLY CAUSE PERSONAL STRIFE WITH OTHERS AND WITHIN YOUR MIND. TAKE CHRIST AND HIS WORD TO YOUR NEXT CHAPTER MEETING. TELL YOUR "BROTHERS AND SISTERS", "NO MORE STEPPING, DRINKING, FORNICATING, PARTYING", etc. YOU WILL SEE THEIR REACTION. IT WON'T BE BROTHERLY OR SISTERLY.

Here is the catch to this whole book. Once one has read or heard this information, they are **responsible** for that information and can no longer cry ignorance to God in the Final Judgment. I, knowing the truth, could no longer cry ignorance. If you decide to live for Jesus, live for Jesus. If so, one must throw away all symbols (paraphernalia) such as shirts, rings, license plates, watches, etc. The only things you **may** want to keep (don't keep them if you feel uncomfortable) are the ritual, songs and poems, and history book for witnessing tools for your members of your former GLO. Some people have to see it with their own eyes. Remember you must compare everything to the Word of God. The bottom line is you should not in any way attract another member, publicly, by wearing or displaying paraphernalia or by starting a conversation that doesn't show your apparent conviction of denouncing. Approach them. Go to them. The Lord has used me to convince my line brother, a Pastor, and four of my friends to denounce their fraternities and sororities as well as keep others from joining. If you do not want to keep your materials, **please send them to me**. I will use it for pamphlets, tapes, and anything to win souls for the Kingdom of God and the expressed purpose of bringing these organizations to complete ruins. PLUS, THE BOOK BURNING THAT I MENTIONED IN THE BEGINNING WILL COME TO PASS. IT WILL BE TELEVISED IN THE MIGHTY **NAME OF JESUS**.

A person who is in any secret society before they get saved must realize that there is no excuse, need, or **biblical support** for them to stay in the group after they get saved. They must realize that they are babes in Christ and need only read the Bible, pray, and find a church that teaches the Bible as the infallible word of God. Misinterpretation or twisting of the scriptures **for one's own desires** is very dangerous.

II PETER 3:16-18(amp) Speaking of this as he does in all of his letters. There are some things in those [epistles of Paul] that are difficult to understand, which the ignorant and unstable twist and misconstrue to their own utter destruction, just as [they distort and misinterpret] the rest of the scriptures. 17 Let me warn you therefore, beloved, that knowing these things beforehand, you should be on your guard, lest you be carried away by the error of lawless and wicked [persons and] fall from your own [present] firm condition [your own steadfastness or mind]. 18 But grow in grace (undeserved favor, spiritual strength) and recognition and knowledge and understanding of our Lord and Saviour Jesus Christ (The Messiah). To him [be] glory (honor, majesty, and splendor) both now until the day of eternity. Amen (so be it)!

THE BIBLE EXPLAIN'S ITSELF JUST FINE WITHOUT YOUR HELP. THIS IS WHY YOU SEE NO DISAGREEMENT IN SCRIPTURE (**IT'S GOD'S WORD**).

I compel **any saved man or woman** to take a real look at their organization and to come out of them and tell others. Is the **foundation** it claims to be built on, actually the one it is standing on??? **Read I Corinthians 3:10-11. Acts 17:11** encourages one to search the Word of God to see if what people say are true according to God's Word. **TO PROVE ALL THINGS BY THE WORD OF GOD IS A TRUE AND FAITHFUL SAYING (PSALM 119:9, 11, 15, 17, 42, 89, 97-101, 105, 140, 160, 163, AND HEBREWS 4:12).** As a Christian witness, the Word of God must be your example to search out the truth about these organizations and witness to others about their ungodliness. There are excellent books and other literature that expose these groups for what they really represent (i.e. the OCCULT/CULT). Now put your **PRIDE** aside and read this book again without a prejudice point of view, that some of you may have or got while reading. Remember! I was on the GLO side for almost five years, and I am still on the saved side. I know many that were in other GLO'S tell me the truth about theirs. This book is not a bunch of hear say. It is documented proof. Whether I quote it or not, you can assuredly believe I have some form of written proof in my possession. I also used observation, common sense, and the TRUTH of the Word of God and found GLO's **GUILTY AS CHARGED**. Jesus is the Savior of the world, but is He your Lord. If he is your Lord, you must do what the Master of your eternal life says. HIS Word has rendered these groups useless, dark, saltless, and of no use for His purpose. ANY CHRISTIAN WHO IS A MEMBER OF OR CONDONES THE EXISTENCE OF GLO's HAS LOST THEIR CONVICTION OF WHO GOD IS AND THE

BOOK HE GAVE TO US. IF YOU BELIEVE THAT THE BIBLE IS THE WORD OF GOD, YOU CANNOT HAVE A HEART TOWARD GLO's. For every excuse or action taken to rectify their agenda, does not really matter. If the root is evil, and it is, so is the organization, and the people who cleave to it, PERIOD! This I have clearly proven based on the Word of God. **MATTHEW 7:15-20** states clearly how to determine the good from the bad. Read it aloud!! If you know in your heart that you are in sin and do not belong in these groups, Jesus says in,

MATTHEW 11:28-30 Come unto Me, all ye that labor and are heavy laden, and I will give you rest. Take My yoke upon you and learn of Me; and ye shall find rest unto your souls. For My yoke is easy, and My burden is light.

The scripture does **not imply coming to anyone or anything else. Not to** kappa, omega, alpha, sigma, delta, aka, sigma gamma rho, groove, swing, zeta, denomination, or any other secret order. No hazing, intake, or branding necessary: Just the repentance of your sins to God and a promise to change from your old ways. If you decide to get saved and/or repent for being a part of these groups and decide denounce the GLO, want to send your rituals, or have any questions please call me 919/829-3513, e-mail me at **reprebres@cs.com** or check out my website a **www.geocities.com/glos_havebeenexposed**, and leave a way for me to get in touch with you. You can call me too. My number is also on the copyright page.

LET JESUS BE GLORIFIED!!!!!!!!!

I LOVE YOU ALL IN THE LORD,

Minister Fred Hatchett

Notes

CHAPTER 10
PART 5

INVITATION

Jesus Saves!!!
REPENT!!!

If you want to be saved, admit that you are a sinner, ask God to forgive you, and most of all be willing to change. After you do this, read **ROMANS 10:9-10** and say "I" and state your name everywhere it calls for you to do so. Example: I, **your name**, confess with my mouth the Lord Jesus and I, **your name**, believe in thine heart that God hath raised Him from the dead. Then read **PHILIPPIANS 3:14-15** and **Don't look back!!!!!!!!!!!**

MATTHEW 11:28-30 Come unto me, all ye that labor and are heavy laden, and I will give you rest. Take my yoke upon you, and learn of me; for I am meek and lowly in heart: and ye shall find rest unto your souls. For my yoke is easy, and my burden is light.

REVELATION 3:19-20 As many as I love, I rebuke and chasten: **be zealous** therefore, **and repent**. Behold, I stand at the door and knock; if **any man** hear my voice, and open the door, I will come in to him, and will sup with him, and he with me.

ACTS 17:30 And the times of this ignorance God winked at; but now **commandeth all men** everywhere **to repent:**

I TIMOTHY 2:4 Who will have **all men to be saved**, and come to knowledge of the truth.

II PETER 3:9 The Lord is not slack concerning his promise, as some men count slackness; but is longsuffering to us-ward, not willing that any should perish, but that **all should come to repentance.**

GOD LOVES YOU AND HE WANTS YOU COMPLETELY (SPIRIT, SOUL, AND BODY). DENOUNCE YOUR GLO OR ANY DESIRE FOR ONE AND BECOME HIS TOTALLY.

Then go to **II CORINTHIANS 5:17-20** to see who you are now and what you have been called to do for **the Lord, which is a witness to others for Christ.**

WHO WANTS TO LEAVE RIGHT NOW?
IF YOU STAND WITH GOD, HE WILL STAND WITH YOU.
IF YOU STAND WITH ME, I WILL STAND WITH YOU.
I TOOK THE STAND!!! AND WILL KEEP STANDING.
IT'S TIME FOR YOU TO TAKE YOUR STAND, AND NOT TURN BACK.
WHATCHYA GONNA DO??? YOU WERE ONCE IN IGNORANCE, BUT NOW YOU HAVE THE REVELATION????? WILL YOU BELIEVE AND REPENT OR REMAIN IN UNBELIEF WHICH IS SIN?

Notes

CHAPTER 10
PART 6

THE CHALLENGE

Can any GLO, by producing **all** of their information (secret included) prove that they are founded upon Christian Principles. If so, prove it by sending me a copy of all rituals, history books, handbooks, constitution and by-laws, and any other pertinent information.

I want to say something to the Church sponsored and Christian GLO's. Why do you need a fraternity or sorority, when you already belong to one? It's called The Body of Christ? There is only one organization that I know of that I would not speak against, except as a matter of preference. The Church for some reason seems to need the world's help and ideas to promote the Gospel. All I say to these organizations is be careful. You cause confusion when you are Greek, yet claim to be different and opposed to the traditional GLO's. The social fellowships, Groove Phi Groove(GΦG) and Swing Phi Swing(SΦS) attempted to break away from GLO's and failed miserably (i.e. they are no different that GLO's). Are "Christian" GLO's willing to expose other GLO's, when they are themselves one? Could I go around wearing one of their shirts without repercussions or harassment? What would they say to me? I mean; I'm a Christian. That should automatically make me a part of their GLO. I mean; why the Greek letters in the first place? Why be like the world and/or of the world? Why the jackets and shirts with the letters? Aren't you representing Jesus? As far as honor societies go, no covenant or ungodly ritual, NO PROBLEM!!!!!!!! You were chosen on the basis of going above what was expected academically. You are being honored. The only thing I question, not condemn, is why Greek letters?

FINAL COMMENTS

Many will refute the information in this book, but I guarantee if you ask to see their ritual or other sources, they won't allow you to. Now if these groups are so much about doing good, **it seems that the best place to start is with them revealing the truth and being honest.**

IN EXAMINING THE MANY RITUALS I HAVE IN MY POSSESSION, ONE THING IS FOR SURE, A COMMON ORIGIN. WHITE AND BLACK GLO's HAVE SO MANY SIMILAR TERMS AND PHRASES: MANY OF WHICH ARE MASONIC. THIS IS WHY I NEED YOUR HELP. SEND ME THE RITUALS AND I WILL EXPOSE THEM.

Since the initial completion of this book, The Holy Spirit has revealed other things to me. Some are in here, and others I will reveal in the pulpit, seminars, Bible Colleges on the internet, and to others in any way I am able to.

THESE ARE JUST SOME REMINDERS FOR YOU, MY BROTHERS AND SISTERS WHO KNOW THAT GLO'S ARE UNGODLY: I CAN'T WAIT TO HEAR THE VICTORY REPORTS FROM YOU ALL.

QUOTES AND SCRIPTURES IN BOLD ARE FOR EMPHASIS ONLY.

Notes

GLOSSARY

AKA's- Individuals belonging to Alpha Kappa Alpha Sorority.

Alphas- Individuals belonging to Alpha Phi Alpha Fraternity.

Chapter- A local representation of a national fraternity or sorority.

Deltas- Individuals belonging to Delta Sigma Theta Sorority (DST).

GLO- Greek-lettered organization.

GLO's- Greek-lettered organizations

Greek Christian- One who confesses Jesus Christ as their Lord and savior and belongs to a GLO, **BUT are not TRUE Christians based on their membership in GLO.**

Initiate- A person who is pledging a GLO.

Intra-racial- Occurring within the same race.

Inter-racial- Occurring between two or more different races.

Omegas- Individuals belonging to Omega Psi Phi Fraternity.

Sigmas- Individuals belonging to Phi Beta Sigma Fraternity.

Soror- What members of the same sorority call each other.

Tekes- Individuals belonging to Tau Kappa Epsilon Fraternity.

Zetas- Individuals belonging to Zeta Phi Beta Sorority.

Notes

INDEX

Adjuration, 222, 231
Alpha Delta Pi, 198, 199, 205
Alpha Kappa Alpha, 24, 25, 193, 202, 225, 229, 262, 458
Alpha Phi Alpha, 37, 178, 196, 197, 204, 205, 210, 214, 285, 322, 337, 350, 458
Apollo, xx, 37, 259, 262, 335
Atlas, 262
Aurora, 200, 262
Babylonian, Egyptian, and Greek Cults and Culture, 11
Black Greek-Lettered Organization and Their Community, Chapter 8, 392
Blackballing, 323
Brainwashing, 28, 134, 135, 298
Branding, 69, 123, 124, 215, 321, 367, 451
Brotherhood, 9
Challenge, 454
Christ-Centered, 351
Christian Principles, 454
Christlike, 8, 31, 300
Church, 23, 29, 40, 58, 350, 352, 454
Conclusion, 34, 140, 380, 391, 397
Cult, 19, 36, 37
Dance Routines, 67

Dead Works, 11, 12, 292
Delphi, 2
Delta Sigma Theta, 30, 37, 186, 194, 205, 207, 223, 239, 242, 260, 262, 267, 332, 335, 338, 340, 458
Denouncing Greek-Lettered Organizations, 410
Diversity, 68, 86, 311
Dogs, 146, 151
Eleusinian Mysteries, 61
Excuses, 239
Gods, xiii, 31, 37, 42, 65, 69, 75, 95, 97, 143, 155, 234, 258, 329, 367, 447
Great Beyond, 2
Greek Christians, 13, 19, 29, 32, 34, 38, 39, 42, 46, 47, 48, 58, 160, 167, 169, 180, 191, 204, 207, 226, 229, 237, 303, 332, 335, 392, 393, 396
Greek Church Leadership, 372
Greeklife, 446
Greeks United To Serve, 446
Haven of Rest, 181, 305
Hazing, 123, 183, 202, 203, 294, 393

Hireling, 327, 376, 382
Idolatry, 58, 173, 242, 257, 263
Idols, 40, 51, 90, 94, 112, 127, 152, 204, 236, 258, 275, 329, 431, 437
Inescapables, 428
Initiate, 458
Initiation, 122, 305
Intake Process, 136, 256, 389
Invitation, 452
Iota Phi Theta, 37, 257, 262, 397
Judging, 156, 444
Kappa Alpha Psi, xx, xxi, 45, 181, 195, 201, 202, 209, 214, 242, 243, 255, 333
Masonic Order, xix, 53, 274, 284, 306
Minerva, xix, 6, 37, 52, 74, 133, 194, 239, 242, 262, 267
Mythology, 42, 64, 65, 66, 120, 142
Nimrod, 62
Oaths, 41, 57, 84, 117, 125, 220, 221, 222, 223, 225, 230, 231, 232, 233, 240, 317, 412, 427, 429
Occult, 14
Omega Psi Phi, 34, 74, 91, 123, 130, 163, 205, 214, 224, 225, 226, 227, 228, 239, 251, 260, 261, 267, 307, 333, 458
Origin of Greek-Lettered Organizations, 50

Phi Beta Sigma, 189, 214, 262, 278, 285, 458
Pledging, 187
Polytheism, 61, 284, 367
Prejudice, 172, 383, 384, 385, 386, 411
Principles, 8, 11, 39, 53, 63, 67, 79, 80, 116, 119, 124, 142, 162, 197, 198, 204, 207, 224, 235, 278, 287, 291, 320, 327, 362
Promises, 232
Religion, 65, 66, 120, 332
Religious Tolerance, 68, 169, 274, 319, 358, 447
Rhomania, 147
Rituals, 13, 22, 46, 61, 66, 75, 80, 82, 86, 120, 137, 143, 147, 152, 167, 179, 187, 220, 228, 253, 258, 261, 305, 321, 338, 352, 370, 411, 420, 425, 428, 436, 451
Secrecy, 14, 19, 28, 44, 343
Secret Society, 1, 216, 245, 335, 449
Service, 1, 6, 8, 13, 31, 40, 73, 74, 101, 128, 143, 154, 158, 162, 176, 182, 185, 187, 200, 226, 264, 276, 285, 299, 323, 329, 341, 348, 357, 436

Sigma Gamma Rho, 123, 186, 200, 201, 262, 342
Sphinx, 37, 209, 210
Stepping, 70, 124, 219, 434, 448
Swearing, 221, 232, 356, 429
Symbolism, 256
Tau Kappa Epsilon, xx, 37, 186, 259, 262, 335, 458
Thurgood Marshall, 178
Tradition, 13, 45, 60, 85, 140, 305, 363, 436
Witnessing, xvi, 7, 35, 78, 84, 112, 118, 138, 175, 309, 315, 332, 423, 448
Words of Advice, 405
Zeta Phi Beta, 278, 285, 459

ENDNOTES

[1] VINE, UNGER, WHITE, VINE'S COMPLETE EXPOSITORY DICTIONARY OF OLD AND NEW TESTAMENT WORDS, p. 555. "Used by permission of Thomas Nelson, Inc."
[2] Ibid, p. 13
[3] Ibid, p. 438
[4] Ibid, p. 13
[5] Ibid, p. 253
[6] Ibid, p. 613
[7] Ibid, p. 491

ABOUT THE AUTHOR

Minister Fred Hatchett was born May 1, 1966 in New York, N.Y. He is the husband of Jarrette Hatchett, and father of three sons, Terrod, Lamar, and Terrance.

Fred was born again on December 24, 1993. Minister Hatchett has Bachelor Degrees in Zoology and Chemistry from North Carolina State University. He also has a Bachelor Degree in Theology from Hosanna Bible College at Mount Zion Christian Church in Durham, North Carolina. Minister Hatchett is also a member and licensed minister at Mount Zion Christian Church. His Pastor is Apostle Donald Q. Fozard Sr. Minister Hatchett is a former five-year member of Omega Psi Phi Fraternity, Inc., and former 32° Mason. He denounced the Masonic Order approximately one year after initiation. After denouncing Omega Psi Phi in April 1995, Fred received the Baptism of the Holy Ghost with the evidence of speaking in other tongues later that year. Minister Hatchett has spoken at several college campuses witnessing the truth to Christians about Greek-lettered organizations.